"Let the Church Sing!"

"Let the Church Sing!"

Music and Worship in a
Black Mississippi Community

Thérèse Smith

Ⓡ University of Rochester Press

The publication of *"Let the Church Sing!"* was made possible, in part, through support from the Howard Hanson Institute for American Music at the Eastman School of Music of the University of Rochester.

First published 2004
by the University of Rochester Press

The University of Rochester Press
668 Mt. Hope Avenue, Rochester, NY 14620, USA
Boydell & Brewer, Ltd.
P.O. Box 9, Woodbridge, Suffolk IP12 3DF, UK
www.urpress.com

ISBN: 1–58046–157–3

Library of Congress Cataloging-in-Publication Data

Smith, Thérèse, 1959–
    Let the church sing! : music and worship in a black Mississippi community / Thérèse Smith.
        p. cm.
    Includes bibliographical references and index.
    ISBN 1–58046–157–3 (hardcover : alk. paper)
    1. Gospel music—Mississippi—History and criticism.   2. African American Baptists—Mississippi—Music—History and criticism.   I. Title.
ML3187.S55 2004
286′.1762–dc22   2004008953

British Library Cataloging-in-Publication Data
A catalogue record for this title is available from the British Library

Printed in the United States of America
This publication is printed on acid-free paper

To

Mum and Dad, Mary T. and the late Billie Smith

Dirk

Ben and Sarah

Contents

List of Figures   viii
List of Music Examples   ix
Compact Disc Contents   xi
A Note on the Transcriptions   xii
Preface   xv

1. Introduction   1
2. Identity   27
   "You could tell me all day what it means to you
   to be an Irish . . ."
3. Concepts of Time   59
   "Total good aspect comes from the Lord"
4. Tradition   85
   "Have you ever seen Jackson State marchin' band?"
5. Moving in the Spirit   113
   "If it ain't no shoutin', no Spirit in it"
6. Prayer   141
   "Prayer will change your condition"
7. Sermon   169
   "Now Lord, You know more than I know"
Conclusion   206

Appendix 1. Outline of a Black Baptist Service   210
Appendix 2. Transcribed Prayers   213
   Abbeville, Miss., August 29, 1982. A Deacon
   Abbeville, Miss., September 5, 1982. A Pastor
   Lexington, Ky., August 25, 1985. A Deacon
   Abbeville, Miss., August 29, 1982. Rev. Kenneth Bonner
Appendix 3. Transcribed Sermons   222
   Clear Creek M.B.C., October 19, 1986.
   Rev. Grady McKinney
   Clear Creek M.B.C., January 19, 1986.
   Rev. Grady McKinney
   Clear Creek M.B.C., November 16, 1986.
   Rev. Grady McKinney

Notes   243
Bibliography   259

Index   287

Figures

1. Northern Mississippi   14
2. Soil erosion   15
3. Kudzu vine   16
4. Kudzu vine   16
5. "Ole Miss" fraternities and sororities   17
6. Poor Black dwellings   18
7. Clear Creek Missionary Baptist Church   20
8. Graveyard and cotton fields behind Clear Creek Missionary Baptist Church   21
9. The Sanctuary, Clear Creek M.B.C.   22
10. "Colourstruck"   28
11. The Baptismal pool, Main St. Baptist church in Lexington, Ky.   53
12. The Baptismal pool itself, Main St. Baptist church in Lexington, Ky.   54
13. The Baptismal pool for Clear Creek Missionary Baptist church   55
14. Cotton boll   88
15. Deacon leading prayer   146
16. Rev. Grady McKinney preaching   156
17. Rev. Ben Baker preaching   159

Music Examples

2.1. Typical "devil's music" (blues) chord progression,
as performed by Herbert Bonner. 37

2.2. Typical gospel chord progression, as performed
by Herbert Bonner. 38

2.3. "Up where we belong"/"Lord lift us up,"
performed as a gospel song by the Clear Creek singers. 41

2.4. "Take me to the water," the hymn that
accompanies Baptism, as performed by the Clear Creek
M.B.C. congregation. 56

2.5. "Wade in the water," "compounded" by the
Main Street Baptist Church congregation. 57

3.1. Dr. Watts hymn, "I love the Lord," lined out by
Deacon Lee Earl Robinson and elaborated by the Clear
Creek M.B.C. congregation. (See CD track 1.) 65

3.2. "You oughta take some time out." Gospel piece
performed by the Clear Creek Youth Choir. 72

4.1. "Sinner please don't let this harvest pass."
Spiritual, performed solo, in slow, unmetered style. 92

4.2. "Sinner please don't let this harvest pass."
Spiritual, performed in gospel choral style. 95

5.1. "Shouting," in relation to sermon excerpt,
November 15, 1987: "Gabriel is comin' out that mornin',"
Rev. Grady McKinney, Clear Creek M.B.C. (See CD track 2.) 135

6.1. Juxtaposition of upper and lower thirds of the
triad within two halves of a single phrase: "Not because
Father, that we did all you told us to do." 147

6.2. Prayer excerpt, August 29, 1982, Rev. Kenneth
Bonner, 82nd Annual Session of the Tallahatchie-Oxford
Missionary Baptist District Association and Auxiliaries,
Abbeville, Miss. 152

6.3. Stock melodic and rhythmic formulae. 153

6.4. Prayer excerpt, October 18, 1987, Rev. Grady
McKinney, Clear Creek M.B.C. (See CD track 3.) 158

6.5. Relatively elaborate congregational response,
Main Street Baptist Church. 159

6.6. Prayer excerpt, January 13, 1986, Rev. Benjamin
     Baker, Main Street Baptist Church. (See CD track 4.)   165
6.7. Characteristic congregational responses.   166

7.1. Sermon excerpt, November 16, 1986: "I don't
     claim to be a great philosopher," Rev. Grady McKinney,
     Clear Creek M.B.C. (See CD track 9.)   197

Appendix 2. Prayer, August 29, 1982, Rev. Kenneth Bonner,
     82nd Annual Session of the Tallahatchie-Oxford Missionary
     Baptist District Association and Auxiliaries, Abbeville, Miss.   217

Compact Disc Contents

Track:

1. Dr. Watts hymn, "I love the Lord," lined out by Deacon Lee Earl Robinson and elaborated by the Clear Creek M.B.C. congregation, January 19, 1986. (See example 3.1.)
2. "Shouting," in relation to sermon excerpt, "Gabriel is comin' out that mornin'," Rev. Grady McKinney, Clear Creek M.B.C., November 15, 1987. (See example 5.1.)
3. Prayer, Rev. Grady McKinney, October 18, 1987. (See example 6.4.)
4. Prayer, Rev. Benjamin Baker, Main Street Baptist Church, January 13, 1986. (See example 6.6.)
5. Sermon excerpt, "He died," Rev. Grady McKinney, Clear Creek M.B.C., November 1, 1987. (See p. 184.)
6. "Amazing Grace," in slow, unmetered style, Clear Creek M.B.C. congregation, January 19, 1986. (See p. 184.)
7. Sermon excerpt, "Satan was one of God's angels," Rev. Grady McKinney, Clear Creek M.B.C., January 19, 1986. (See p. 189.)
8. Sermon excerpt, "Harvest," Rev. Grady McKinney, Clear Creek M.B.C., leading into congregational hymn, "When all God's children," October 19, 1986. (See p. 191.)
9. Sermon excerpt, "I don't claim to be a great philosopher," Rev. Grady McKinney, Clear Creek M.B.C., leading into lined hymn, "That awful day," November 16, 1986. (See example 7.1.)

All of these recordings are reproduced with permission.

A Note on the Transcriptions

The musical transcriptions that appear throughout the text are based on my field recordings, many of which are reproduced on the compact disc accompanying this book, and are intended to illuminate the musical analyses. The transcriptions are descriptive; I have striven to transcribe the particular example (rather than a representative or archetypal template) but, while incorporating detail, I have also tried to avoid over-cluttering the transcriptions. I have tried to keep them legible for the "average" music reader. Because of this emphasis on legibility, I have generally grouped notes according to musical beats or pulses, even where the music is sung, rather than stem them separately for each syllable of text. There is, however, one important exception to this. It is a well-established fact that African American performance of music typically exploits a subdivision of the basic rhythmic pulse into both duple and triple sub-beats, into twos and threes, exploiting what is often referred as horizontal hemiola. In examples transcribed in compound time, therefore (see example 3.2), I have, where appropriate, grouped the notes alternately into quarter-note beats, rather than tie a series of eighth notes. (European readers will note that I have generally adopted American designations for note durations—this being an American-based study—thus, crochet = quarter note; minim = half note; semibreve = whole note; quaver = eighth note; semiquaver = sixteenth note, etc.)

Recordings have been transcribed at pitch and, where pertinent, approximate metronome markings have been indicated. Where the musical example is not metered, or where the speed of the rendition is not particularly germane (where an average or moderate speed would serve to illustrate the example), metronome markings have been omitted. If, on the other hand, the metronome markings are pertinent, but not strictly adhered to, I have modified them with some indication such as "freely" or "~". Some standard ethnomusicological modifications have been made to Western staff notation (which, while ideally suited to the repertoire for which it was developed, is not so well suited to other traditions), and these are generally keyed at the bottom of each example. The exact pitch (as to octave) referred to in the musical analysis is usually clear from the musical example, but where there might be room for misinterpretation, I have designated specific pitches thus: lower case letters designate pitches from middle C to the B, third line, treble clef; c^1 designates the octave above that, i.e., from C, third space, treble clef; upper case letters designate the pitches in the octave below middle C, i.e., from C second space bass clef.

Some inevitable compromises have, of course, had to be made, particularly in the transcriptions of the chanted musical examples. Where the
choice was between rendering rhythmic designations that were exact but
so detailed as to be illegible, or not indicating any rhythmic durations at
all, for example, I have chosen to tread a middle ground and give some
detailed indications of duration. The reader should bear in mind, however,
that these should not be strictly interpreted, but interpreted somewhat
freely, in consultation with the accompanying recordings. Despite their
attendant problems, I hope that these transcriptions will add a layer of
musical meaning that has been lacking in many other studies.

Preface

Driving down the road from Memphis, Tennessee, into northern Mississippi, I listen to the limousine driver as he talks about his rattlesnakes. As he relates how he feeds and breeds them, and drains the poison from them, and notes the fluctuating but high returns on rattle poison, I watch the countryside change and revel in the exotic landscape. Gradually the kudzu vine creeps out to engulf everything, silently covering and strangling all that comes in its path. Levelling man's work, it indiscriminately swallows trees and telegraph poles, grass and asphalt. Nothing but the swamps halts its deadly progress. Ironically, these pools of death teeming with life, which strip trees and leave them naked and rotting in water, seem to be the only forces which can effectively challenge the fatal vitality of the kudzu.

The limousine driver is now elaborating on the various species of rattlesnakes and the relative potency of their poisons. "A baby rattler's bite is the most deadly of all," he says, pausing for effect. Realising that some response is expected, I express my surprise; "Really?" "Oh yes," he says, "the fang holes are so small, you see, and so close together, that it is almost impossible to draw the poison out again." I think of the potions, incenses, and books of voodoo spells I had purchased in Memphis on a previous trip and now sequestered in my luggage in the trunk, and marvel, as always, at the exoticism and spirituality of the world into which I am being transported. I open the window for a breath of fresh air, forgetting how oppressive the heat outside is. Only our small air-conditioned bubble contradicts the nature of this place as we roll on down the highway to Oxford. On a lazy summer's afternoon, almost nothing stirs.

I lived, studied, and taught in the United States for a period of ten years between 1981 and 1991. I moved there (funded by the Fulbright Commission, whose support I gratefully acknowledge) to study African American religious music, and this remained my main focus throughout the years of my stay. Periods of study at Brown University in Providence, Rhode Island (first for the degree of M.A. and then Ph.D., and which generally fell within the academic calendar) allowed for somewhat limited, but almost continuous fieldwork over the years of my residence in the United States: participation at weekend services and activities at local churches in Providence, some attendance at choir rehearsals during the week, and participation also with on-campus choirs and race relations organisations. This ongoing fieldwork in the North was balanced with more intensive periods of fieldwork in the South (with from a number of weeks at a stretch to up to four months devoted exclusively to fieldwork) in two primary geographic areas: Lexington, Kentucky, and Springhill/Oxford, Mississippi. This field-work was made possible through the generosity of several foundations—the Charlotte Newcombe Foundation, the Institute for Intercultural Studies, the Francis E. Harnish scholarship (Brown University) and, through the Center for the Study of Southern Culture (CSSC) at the University of Mississippi, the National Endowment for the Arts and the Mississippi Arts Commission, who supported the making of a documentary LP, *Moving in the Spirit*—all of whose support I gratefully acknowledge here. As I had to prove to the Immigration and Naturalization Services each year my ability to support myself for the following twelve months before my visa would be issued, this research was made possible only through their generous support, and that of Brown University.

Numerous scholars and friends offered no less valuable support, and these I would also like to acknowledge here. At Brown University, for my training in ethnomusicology and for the curiosity he encouraged in me through his openness and receptivity, I owe a special debt to the late Jim Koetting. Jeff Titon stepped into the void left by Jim, and to him and the other members of the Music Department, in addition to scholars in other parts of the university, especially Bill Beeman and Bruce Rosenberg, I remain indebted. Katherine Hagedorn, Ferd Jones, Lisa Lawson, Karen Linn, Patty Repar, Allen Renear, Debby Sherman, and especially Kate Powers, have both buoyed me up and kept solid ground beneath my feet. On the many occasions when I began to doubt it myself, Kate Powers believed unflaggingly that this project would come to fruition and offered practical assistance, firm friendship, and intellectual and spiritual encouragement. To Dirk Köhler, who graciously accepted and supported a project that had already absorbed a large part of my life before he entered it, and to Ben and Sarah for the levity and joyful sense of perspective that childhood offers, I owe a resounding debt of gratitude. And I would like to thank my parents, Mary T. and the late Billie Smith, whose loving support encouraged what must have initially seemed an improbable and risky undertaking. *Go raibh míle maith acu uile.*

For exceptional kindness to a young researcher in Mississippi, the late Sister Thea Bowman, Frank Childrey, Everline Dunne, Bill Ferris, Vaughn and Sandy Grisham, Winthrop Jordan, Lee and Julie Potts, Charles Wilson Reagan, Suzanne and Warren Steel, the John Whites, and Harold Wilson, amongst others, a warm thank you. I owe a special debt of gratitude, of course, to the three church communities where I conducted my research—Clear Creek Missionary Baptist Church, Miss., Congdon Street Baptist Church, Providence, R.I., and Main Street Baptist Church, Lexington, Ky.—in addition to the myriad of other churches that I visited from time to time. At the University of Rochester Press, I would especially like to thank Ralph Locke, who supported this manuscript from the outset; Timothy Madigan, Editorial Director of the Press; Sue Smith, Production Manager, for her expert guidance and encouragement; and Louise Goldberg, copyeditor extraordinaire, whose endeavours have been above and beyond. Finally, I would like to acknowledge a publication grant from University College Dublin, Dublin 4, Ireland, which has partially funded publication of this book as have the Irish Research Council for the Humanities and Social Sciences and the Howard Hanson Institute for American Music at the Eastman School of Music of the University of Rochester.

In all, I spent approximately three months conducting fieldwork in Kentucky and twelve months in Mississippi, spread over a number of years, primarily between 1982 and 1988. As the church in Lexington, Ky., records and broadcasts its services, I was able to supplement my field time there with many other months of recordings of services, which the church sent to me at my request. There were also, of course, periodic trips home to Ireland and trips to various other parts of the United States.

In the context in which I was immersing myself, I began to perceive two great divides in the American psyche: that between black and white, which I found to be pervasive, and the less critical or prominent, but nonetheless important division between North and South.[1] None of the graduate students with whom I initially became acquainted at Brown University had ever visited the Deep South, nor had they any interest in doing so; and very few had ever dated interracially, nor would they contemplate such a relationship. I also became acutely aware of the vast disparity between the relative poverty of small black communities in Mississippi and the prevailing affluence of the student body at a well-endowed Ivy League university. All of these experiences have helped shape this work.

When it came to writing this book, I elected to focus the study on one small black community in Mississippi, that of Clear Creek Missionary Baptist Church. I selected Clear Creek because it is both typical and exceptional. It became, therefore, the community where I conducted my most exhaustive fieldwork: spending my most protracted periods in the field there, interviewing church officials and other church members ranging in age from pre-teen to approaching one hundred years of age, participating in virtually all church-related activities, from Bible study to picnics and homecoming celebrations, eventually even joining the church delegation when they were invited to visit other churches. Once we got to know each other a little, the church members welcomed me with exceptional kindness, providing rides when I was car-less, patiently answering my endless questions; one member even installed a radio in the car I eventually managed to purchase so that the long drive alone from Mississippi back to Providence (a distance of some 1,290 miles) would be less tedious. There were also, of course, less happy occasions: an interview that became so intense and personal that the member later requested that I delete the whole tape, a disagreement that almost brought my research to an abrupt halt. But my abiding memory of Clear Creek is of a warm welcome for a single white woman in a racially divided State.[2]

Methodology in the field varied according to location. In Rhode Island my time was necessarily dominated by the demands of a very rigorous graduate programme, yet my reason for coming to the United States had been to study African American religious music and as, in a sense, "the field" was all around me, I spent as much time as I could with one local church (Congdon Street Baptist Church), visiting others from time to time for comparative perspective. In Mississippi, I was fortunate to be able to supplement my fieldwork with background study at the University of Mississippi, at the Blues Archive, the University library, and the Center for the Study of Southern Culture (CSSC), particularly through the good graces of then-director of the Center, Bill Ferris. This allowed me to gain a historical and general perspective on the region, and also to compare my findings with audio and video documentary evidence stored at the CSSC. Because connections existed between some members of the Clear Creek community and the black student body at the university, it was natural for me to attend choir rehearsals and other black-organised events at the university. On some Sundays I attended other local black churches for comparative perspective, or travelled with the Clear Creek delegation to churches farther afield. And I tuned in regularly to the membership's favourite radio show *Highway to Heaven*, which was broadcast out of Holly Springs, Marshall county, and where I became acquainted with the favourite Gospel songs of the day; and the recorded sermons of the Rev. J. M. Gates (whose sermons represent one quarter of the seven hundred sermons issued on race records[3] between 1925 and 1941), R. M. Massey, and Al Greene; as well as more contemporary recordings such as those by Tommy Ellison, and "The Bishop," the Rev. Leo Daniels, and the Rev. Willie Morganfield, among others.

In Kentucky, partly because the church (Main Street Baptist Church) was much larger and more affluent, with many more projects in hand and various groups meeting every night of the week, my fieldwork concentrated on that single church. I visited other churches generally only on special occasions, often along with the church delegation. Because the church was downtown, the membership was not drawn from a single community but from a wide variety of backgrounds and experiences, as well as from various locales: the membership in essence re-created the community each time they came together.

I first became acquainted with the Clear Creek community at the 82nd annual convention of the Tallahatchie-Oxford Missionary Baptist District Association at the Project Center outside Oxford, in August 1982. The TOMB, as members call it, is an association of some twenty Missionary Baptist churches in the area. It brings together the many small communities into a larger, more powerful body and organises special events and fifth Sunday services, while still respecting the autonomy of each church. The following is an account of its formation as related in the booklet produced for the dedication of the new building in May 1986.

A few years removed from the dark days of slavery, a new fellowship was formed by the emancipated freed laymen and preachers who had sprung up from among the fellow slaves with fire in their hearts. [. . .] Out of this fellowship and Association we formed, namely the TALLAHATCHIE OXFORD MISSIONARY BAPTIST ASSOCIATION. It was so named because several churches were located near the tributary to the Tallahatchie River and many churches were located in Oxford. [. . .] After purchasing approximately 80 acres on January 4, 1905 the Association's main desire was to build a school to train pastors, deacons and laymen in Christian Education. During the early 1900s the Association convened annually at local churches of the district to make reports of Church activities and to transact business of the Association.

In 1939, 2.9 acres of land was sold to the State Highway Department, Jackson MS. This project was known as State Project no. 6-1051-A. In 1944 the first building was built on the property. This was a small wood-framed building which graced the grounds until January 1986, when it was replaced by the current structure. (History of the Tallahatchie-Oxford Missionary Baptist District Association, Inc., May 10, 1986: 4.)

At the 82nd convention many important functions were performed by members of Clear Creek Missionary Baptist Church (M.B.C.), and it was clear that they were held in high regard by the larger community. The Clear Creek membership, and one family in particular, i.e., the Bonners, were used to people expressing more than passing interest in their music; they had on several occasions, for example, performed for the scholars who convene each summer in Oxford for the William Faulkner Symposium offered by the CSSC at the University of Mississippi. My purpose, nonetheless, seemed odd to them, as previous interest had been mostly for entertainment and enjoyment. But the fact that I was interested in the music's religious foundation and the role both have in their lives later gave me easier access to and greater credibility in the community.

My first evening in church was to suggest my sometimes stumbling relationship with the church and the kindness with which I was always treated. I had arrived in Oxford that evening and had spent several hours trying to get a taxi from the university out to the church, with no success. Finally, in despair, I called a friend's parents, with whom I had spent a week on a previous visit, and asked if they might drive me out to the church. My friend's mother was nervous about driving at night out to a "Negro area," so despite my protestations, she awoke her husband, who was in bed with the 'flu, to go with her; he would not have allowed her to go on her own. In this fashion, and much indebted to them, I arrived at the church.

I was late, and it was clear that the Youth Meeting was in session. As there was scaffolding about the front doors, I went around to the side and entered through the wing. What I had not realised was that entrance through these doors led directly onto the altar. I was also unaware that the choir rehearsal was embedded in the context of Youth Meeting, which has its own Devotion and Prayer Service. (Before long I was to appreciate that this is the typical pattern for rehearsals. Music is invariably embedded in a prayerful context. The work that goes into rehearsal is offered to God in the same fashion as hymns are during the service.) Laden with recording equipment, I arrived upon the altar in the midst of prayer. I must have presented a strange spectacle. Confused myself, I had difficulty recognising anyone. I asked someone where Sheila Bonner was, and he pointed her out to me down at the back of the church. I went down and introduced myself, and she told me to sit down beside her. It took me a few minutes to get my bearings: there was scaffolding all about the inside of the church also, as the sanctuary was being refurbished. I had understood this to be a rehearsal, yet here was the choral director sitting at the back of the church while several older women, whom I did not recognise, addressed the young people in the choir stalls. At this stage the church clerk, Mrs. Eulastine Thompson, came down and introduced herself, and requested my name and purpose. This was difficult, as my first name (Thérèse) is unusual in the United States, certainly so in Mississippi, and my purpose no less so. I explained as best I could while we whispered quietly at the back of the church, lest we disturb prayers at the front. Still, my presence was distracting and gave rise to considerable speculation. I was later to discover that there had been speculation, over the first four months or so of my visit, that I was with either the F.B.I. or the C.I.A., as no plausible explanation seemed to account for the presence of a single white woman in this community.

Gradually, things settled down, and after a while it came time for rehearsal. It was, of course, necessary for me to stand to introduce myself and state my purpose, which I did. Discretion being the better part of valour, and feeling horribly conspicuous, I decided to abandon my recording equipment for this first session and settled down to listen. Herbert Bonner took his position at the piano, and Sheila hers in front of the choir, and the rehearsal was under way. As I watched and listened, and gradually perceived the interdependence of music and worship, identity, Spirit, and belief, I wished to learn more about the intersection of these spheres and the church's articulation of this complex whole.

My primary interest, then, is in music as an expression of the worldview of a single contemporary community, for I believe that music functions to create a community, temporary or otherwise, John Blacking's famous humanly organized sound creating "soundly organized humanity" (1973). This interest is, in this study, grounded in an African American Baptist community because the beauty and strength of African American music initially attracted me (as it still does) and because, as I began to explore this music in community, I found those same characteristics in many other aspects of the lives of the members of Clear Creek M.B.C.

This book, while it attempts to integrate material from several different fields (African American Studies, Anthropology, Musicology and Music Theory, Philosophy, Psychology, Religion, Sociology and others), is firmly based in my own discipline, Ethnomusicology, which has considerably enriched my comprehension of life. The idea of a community study is by no means new, and many scholars who have studied individual communities have tried to show the unique qualities of particular communities. While I think that the Clear Creek M.B.C. community has a unique identity, my interest lies in the way the Clear Creek community wrestles with change and other problems with which all communities wrestle—the organisation of time, identity, expressive culture, sound, how the world is made and our relationship to it.

An in-depth study based in fieldwork is, I believe, the best if not the only way to approach such nebulous but extremely important issues, and it is herein, in the thoughts of members, that the strength of this study lies. I did not go to Mississippi with only certain hypotheses to test: I went to observe and above all to listen. Talking with the members, trying to grasp how they perceive and intend their actions—"the picture they have of the way things in sheer actuality are, their most comprehensive ideas of order" (Clifford Geertz, 1973: 89)—yet keeping in mind the usual discrepancy between thought and action (what people say they do and what they actually do), my vision of what was happening in church shifted considerably.

This study is not a closed one: it is an introduction.

1

Introduction

This book is an examination of facets of worldview and their articulation in expressive culture through religious ritual, music specifically. The primary focus of the book is one small black community in rural Mississippi. In order to understand and present effectively that community's intersection of the existential, social, and aesthetic spheres, I have structured study around issues such as identity, time, belief-system, and tradition, rather than basing it on traditional concepts such as genre. From my perspective as an outsider, through participation-observation in community events and conversations with small groups and individuals, I have tried to understand and here present the community's worldview, a worldview that posits clear oppositions and seeks to mediate effectively between them.

The Clear Creek Missionary Baptist Church (M.B.C.) community shares in common with other African American Baptist communities basic aspects of belief and worship practice. An explosion in scholarship in this area in the past fifteen years or so renders superfluous detailed examination of those generalities here. The interested reader is referred to full-length studies such as C. Eric Lincoln and Lawrence H. Mamiya's *The Black Church in the African American Experience* (1990), Walter Pitt's *Old Ship of Zion* (1993), Mechal Sobel's *Trabelin' On: The Slave Journey to an Afro-Baptist Faith* (1988). Other, shorter articles, which are less detailed, but offer up-to-date, factual information, include the following: Larry G. Murphy's "Baptists, African American," in the *Encyclopaedia of African American Religions* (1993: 64–66), Clarence G. Newsome's "A synoptic survey of the history of African American Baptists," in the *Directory of African American Religious Bodies* (1995: 20–31), Eric J. Ohlmann's "Baptists and Evangelicals," in *The Variety of American Evangelicalism* (1991: 148–60). Each of these studies in its own particular way offers invaluable background on the history, beliefs, and worship practice of the African American Baptist church. Few recent studies, however, offer any detailed contemporary ethnographic data based on long-term fieldwork with one particular community. What is unique in the present study is the in-depth treatment of the intersection of belief system, expressive culture, and worldview of a single, more-or-less self-contained African American Baptist community in the Deep South. Jeff Titon's

Powerhouse for God: Speech, Chant, and Song in the Appalachian Baptist Church (1988) accomplishes much the same thing for a somewhat similar white community in the Blue Ridge mountains, but with a more historical bent than the present study.

In 1994 James P. Wind and James J. Lewis, in a two-volume study, *American Congregations*, brought together small and fascinating studies by individual scholars of a variety of American congregations. In the introduction to the first volume, Wind and Lewis argued convincingly that the strength and foundation of American religion lies in its congregations, to a degree arguably unique in the Western hemisphere, and called for more community-based studies.

> The local congregation preceded that most American of religious institutions, the denomination. Indeed, congregations preceded most other permanent institutions in America. This is not to say that America is distinctively religious. But it is to say that American religion has been, and by and large remains, distinctively congregational (1994: 1:1).

The twelve chapter-length studies included in the first volume range across a wide variety of denominations and ethnic groups, but are necessarily limited by constraints of time and space. In contrast to these brief portraits, few in-depth, community-based studies have emerged. (Obvious exceptions are Beverly Patterson's *The Sound of the Dove: Singing in Appalachian Primitive Baptist Churches* (1995), and that of Titon cited above.) Kip Lornell and Anne K. Rasmussen's *Musics of Multicultural America: A Study of Twelve Musical Communities* (1997), offers a parallel to Wind and Lewis's study, but for music as opposed to religion, and generally in the popular music sphere.

Recent studies of African American religion on the other hand have continued, by and large, to have a historical bent: see, for example, Hans Baer and Merrill Singer's comprehensive *African-American Religion in the Twentieth Century: Varieties of Protest and Accommodation* (1992), which not only provides an overview of the topic during the twentieth century, but (in the words of the authors) "attempts to recognize the diversity of forms that African-American religion takes" (ibid.: xii); as well as the excellent collections edited by Timothy E. Fulop and Albert J. Raboteau, *African-American Religion: Interpretive Essays in History and Culture* (1997), and by Paul E. Johnson, *African-American Christianity: Essays in History* (1994). Even ground-breaking studies focusing on the role of African American women, such as Evelyn Brooks Higginbotham's *Righteous Discontent: The Women's Movement in the Black Baptist Church, 1880–1920* (1993), or the collection edited by Judith Weisenfeld and Richard Newman *This Far by Faith: Readings in African-American Women's Religious Biography* (1996), have continued down this historical path. This emphasis on historical studies has generally also persisted when the studies are community-based: see, for example, Ingrid Overacker's *The African American Church Community in Rochester, New York, 1900–1940* (1998). Studies of African American religious music, on the other hand, have tended to concentrate on an individual genre, sometimes in historical perspective: see, for example, the following book-length studies (numerous articles on similar topics may be found in the bibliography): Ray Allen, *Singing in the Spirit: African-American Sacred Quartets in New York City* (1991); Don Cusic, *The Sound of Light: A History of Gospel Music* (1990); Gerald Davis, *I Got the Word in Me and I Can Sing It, You Know: A Study of the Performed African-American Sermon* (1985); Michael Harris, *The Rise of Gospel Blues: The Music of Thomas Andrew Dorsey in the Urban Church* (1992), Kip Lornell, *Happy in the Service of the Lord: Afro-American Gospel Quartets in Memphis* (1988), Bernice Johnson Reagon, ed., *We'll Understand It Better By and By: Pioneering African American Gospel Composers* (1993), to mention but a few.

The scholarship cited above has contributed enormously to an understanding of African American religion in general and African American religious music in particular. But I have chosen an in-depth community-based study because I believe that this has additional riches to offer. Thus this study is based in a single community, but also seeks to offer comparative analyses from other communities, and to analyse how typical, yet exceptional the Clear Creek M.B.C. community is. Additionally, it considers this community in its more universal aspects of worldview.

The threads of music, feeling, religion, Holy Spirit, and improvisation are woven for the members of the Clear Creek M.B.C. community into an intricate pattern. While the primary focus of this study is music, since the music cannot exist apart from these other forces, analysis must take all of them into account. The viewpoints of members of the community are, I believe, essential to a relevant and adequate understanding of any aspect of culture.

> The only way in which we can become sure of the existence of other people is by the act of respect, prior to all phenomenological reflection. In fact, even a phenomenology of sympathy [. . .] presupposes an ethic of respect; otherwise it becomes a "deceptive" or "vain" phenomenology (H. Spiegelberg, 1965: 572, citing Paul Ricoeur).

We listen to those whom we respect. So that the reader may, to some extent at least, converse with the community members, I have included a considerable amount of recorded speech. My rationale for this is twofold: to firmly ground my interpretation and analysis in the community and bring them as close as possible to that of the community and, secondly, to encourage the reader to choose a personal vantage point and view from the window that I hope to open. Ethnomusicology has long recognised that we limit our understanding when we interact with everything on our own terms and turf; we stretch our minds when we move outside our frame of reference.

The philosophical stance that I have adopted in relation to this work is phenomenology. Paul Ricoeur describes phenomenological procedure as "going to the things themselves, respecting all the very complex aspects of consciousness, and not playing simply with the small number of concepts forged by Aristotelian analysis" (1951: 26). Within this general framework Ricoeur recognises three levels of investigation: descriptive analysis, transcendental constitution, and ontological phenomenology (Spiegelberg, 1965: 573–75). The main function of descriptive analysis is to spell out (*épeler*) the phenomena, i.e., "to spread out their aspects, particularly their intentional meanings and the act-content structure of the conscious phenomena" (ibid.: 573). (Clifford Geertz, borrowing from Gilbert Ryle, popularised this approach as "thick description" [1973: 1–30, esp. 6–10].) Ricoeur suggests that what is required is a deepening of the descriptive attitude in the sense of "participation in being," which takes account of our incarnation in the world. For Ricoeur, existential description results not from distanced objective observation, but from plunging into the experience. In this book, this is the level of description formulated through participant-observation in fieldwork.

Transcendental constitution strives to determine the constitution (delivery) of the phenomena in consciousness—in this book, in the members' collective consciousness. Phenomena such as conversion, inspiration by the Holy Spirit, and the call to preach lend themselves to this level of investigation. I have tried to go beyond description of such phenomena and to include (through informants' explication of such experiences) the group's metaphysical understanding of them, and a broader existential and psychological account of them.

The third level, ontological phenomenology, is essentially the highest level of organisation of the material—the choice of chapter topics and the structure of the chapters. My intent is to show how the members of Clear Creek articulate central facets of worldview from an existential framework of diametrically opposed poles. The framework of distinct opposites referred to above, is not unique to the Clear Creek M.B.C. community: it can be argued that it is a fundamental characteristic of the human condition. If, as Paul Tillich defines it, life is "the actualization of potential being" (1963: 3:137), then all the functions of life are dependent upon the polarities of being (the essential [created goodness] and the existential [estrangement]), and grounded in the most basic polarity, self-world. "All the ambiguities of life are rooted in the separation and interplay of essential and existential elements of being" (ibid.: 3:32). Man suffers this ambiguity because he is at once separate—"as a free-thinking being capable of meaning in language" (David Inman, 1968: 235)—and a part of: he has a world to which he is related. Tillich believes that it is this self-world relationship that is emphasised in the spiritual dimension (which he believes unique to man) and that from it result the creative functions of life: morality, culture, and religion.

Religion can be characterised as the search for authentic life: but religion itself is also ambiguous because its expressions, rooted in the material world, are ambiguous. Frederic Bartlett calls this search for unambiguous life "the inescapable search for the all-inclusive [. . .] either by ruling a lot out, or by ruling everything in" (1950: 33). He also adds to this basic characteristic of religion, essential creation of community. "Always, no matter what the time or the circumstance, there is, as I see it, inherent in the substantiation of religious belief, the effort to form a community" (ibid.: 33). This effort, of course, further reinforces ambiguity: a community or group is defined by exclusion as well as inclusion. This is a basic ambiguity of actualized justice (Inman, 1968: 264). The ontological predicament is that life is always ambiguous. I perceive the Clear Creek M.B.C. community as realising that ambiguity on more levels and in more facets of their lives than other communities. I think that they also go beyond ambiguity to clear opposition.

If, as Tillich states, "religion as ultimate concern is the meaning-giving substance of culture, and culture is the totality of forms in which the basic concern of religion expresses itself" (1963: 3:42), it is not possible to understand one without the other. Critically, the point of juncture or overlap of both, should be one of the richest sources (if not the richest source) of meaning. This is precisely what Clifford Geertz asserts:

Sacred symbols function to synthesise a people's ethos—the tone, character, and quality of their life, its moral and aesthetic style and mood—and their world view—the picture they have of the way things in their sheer actuality are, their most comprehensive ideas of order. In religious belief and practice a group's ethos is rendered reasonable by being shown to represent a way of life ideally adapted to the actual state of affairs the world view describes, while the world view is rendered emotionally convincing by being presented as an image of an actual state of affairs peculiarly well-arranged to accommodate such a way of life. This confrontation and mutual confirmation has two fundamental effects. On the one hand, it objectivizes moral and aesthetic preferences by depicting them as the imposed conditions of life implicit in a world with a particular structure, as mere common sense given the unalterable shape of reality. On the other, it supports these received beliefs about the world's body by invoking deeply felt moral and aesthetic sentiments as experiential evidence for their truth. Religious symbols formulate a basic congruence between a particular style of life and a specific (if, most often, implicit) metaphysics, and in so doing sustain each with the borrowed authority of the other (1973: 89–90).

Religion in essence serves to situate the self, the world, and the relations between them. It incorporates life's ambiguity and moves toward a resolution of that ambiguity. Religious ritual "actually creates or re-creates, the categories through which men perceive reality—the axioms underlying the structure of society and the laws of the natural and moral orders" (Victor Turner, 1968: 7).

I am interested in religion not primarily in its institutional forms or denominations, but in the form sketched above, i.e., as a system that serves to situate self, world, and the relationship between them. My interest, in other words, is the realm of the spiritual and its intersection with the material. For that reason this book is not an attempt to provide proofs or explanations: the reader will not find an argument of the traditional logical kind. My "argument" is instead one of interpretation, and it informs the whole manuscript. Exploration is intrinsically more intriguing and ultimately more educational to me than delimitation. I have, however, spent considerable time (above) sketching my philosophical stance because I believe, with Ricoeur, that no matter how hard we strive to be objective (and ethnomusicology strives valiantly to overcome ethnocentrism), we can never escape the subjectivity of our own minds and senses.

> All objectifying knowledge about our position in society, in a social class, in a cultural tradition and in history is preceded by a relation of belonging upon which we can never entirely reflect. [. . .] If the critique of ideology can partially free itself from its initial anchorage in pre-understanding, if it can thus organise itself in knowledge and enter into the movement of what Jean Ladrière characterises as the passage to theory, nevertheless this knowledge cannot become total. [. . .] All knowledge is supported by an interest, and the critical theory of ideology is itself supported by an interest in emancipation, that is, in unrestricted communication. [. . .] The critique of ideology, supported by a specific interest, never breaks its links to the basis of belonging. To forget this primordial tie is to enter into the illusion of a critical theory elevated to the rank of absolute knowledge. [. . .] Knowledge is always in the process of tearing itself away from ideology, but ideology always remains the grid, the code of interpretation, in virtue of which we are not unattached intellectuals but remain supported by what Hegel called the "ethical substance," *Sittlichkeit* (1981: 243–45).

My focus is on the expression of religion through ritual, and most especially religious expression that becomes musical performance. But this musical performance cannot be understood in isolation: it must be considered in context, underpinned by the religious beliefs and worldview that generate it and give it meaning. As Chris Waterman has remarked "adequate accounts of musical continuity and change must deal [. . .] with *relationships among patterns of musical sound and performance behavior, cultural symbolism and value, social transaction and ideology, and the material forces that encourage or constrain particular forms of expression*" (1991: 50) [my italics]. For if it is a truism that religion is a fundamental part of Southern identity, music is at the heart of African American religious expression.

When I first moved to the United States in 1981 to begin detailed study of African American religious music (having completed undergraduate studies in Music, both the oral tradition of Irish "trad," and the more conventional Western repertoire—B.A. and B.Mus.—at University College Dublin), two aspects of my "American" studies struck me as particularly surprising. Firstly, I was surprised (and sometimes frustrated) at the number of otherwise excellent studies dedicated to various aspects of African American music, religious or otherwise, that included little or no detailed reference to musical sound, recorded or transcribed. One consequence of this approach was that, inevitably, there was little comprehensive musical discussion or analysis in these studies. Initial, almost revolutionary, studies in this area tended to be historical (Eileen Southern's 1971 *The Music of Black Americans*, a sterling example), biographical (Tony Heilbut's 1971 *The Gospel Sound*), or broadly educational in bent (René-Dominique de Lerma's 1970 *Black Music in Our Culture*, or his 1973 *Reflections on Afro-American Music*, are representative examples). Occasional, exceptional studies redressed this balance somewhat (Jacqueline Djedje's 1978 *American Black Spiritual and Gospel Songs from Georgia*, for example, or some Ph.D. dissertations such as Horace Boyer's 1973 "An Analysis of Black Church Music with Examples Drawn from Services in Rochester, New York"), but the literature remained overwhelmingly lacking in examination of anything but the briefest discrete musical examples (see, for example, Horace Boyer [1979, 1983]; Mellonee Burnim [1985]; Portia Maultsby [1975, 1976]; William Tallmadge [1968, 1981]; or Pearl Williams-Jones [1975]).

With the emergence of detailed, book-length studies, generally focusing on one particular musical genre, the above emphasis nonetheless remained; a surprising dearth of discrete musical examples persisted. Thus, Ray Allen's wonderful study of African American sacred quartets in New York City, *Singing in the Spirit* (1991), itself in part a response to Kip Lornell's call for detailed research on community quartets (1988: 129), and despite centring on a body of music that is not commercially available (the music of the quartets expertly discussed by Lornell generally is), makes no attempt to supply us with musical sound in any form. Allen defends this decision as follows: "[I]n dealing with sound structure I chose to speak in the more general language of style, and whenever possible to use in-group terminology" (1991: 12).

Similarly, Gerald Davis's 1985 study of the oral African American sermon, *I Got the Word in Me and I Can Sing It, You Know*, following in the lineage of Bruce Rosenberg's landmark *The Art of the American Folk Preacher* (1970), provides superb analyses of the structure and performance characteristics of the African-American sermon, in addition to considering "factors of aesthetics, history, ethnophilosophy, and cosmology" (1985: 1). According to Davis, "[F]or the African-American preacher the structuring of his words into useful rhythmic phrases is his most compelling concern" (ibid.: 53), and he provides us with many illuminating textual transcriptions of sermon segments, but one cannot help but lament his neglect of the preacher's musical chant that gives these "rhythmic phrases" wings in performance. Jon Michael Spencer's several publications (1987, 1990, and 1993) stand apart in many ways, and include musical transcriptions or renditions. But it is difficult to decipher what Spencer intends with his musical representations: in *Sacred Symphony: The Chanted Sermon of the Black Preacher* (1987), for example, the musical transcriptions are so brief, and so out of context, that it is difficult to attribute any significant meaning to them. That Spencer refers to his sermon excerpts as "spirituals"—"songs that spontaneously evolve during contemporary black preaching and prayer are also spirituals" (ibid.: xiii)—does little to elucidate the matter.

Don Cusic's *The Sound of Light: A History of Gospel Music* (1990) is impressively historical in its sweep, considering both the history of Christianity in America and that of Gospel music within that tradition. Cusic also supplies us with biographical details and analyses of some of the most influential figures in the history of gospel music in America, and numerous transcriptions of song lyrics. Yet, despite asserting in his introduction that music "is important because it too is spiritual and can reach out and communicate spiritual truth or spiritual experience" (ibid.: iii), music as sound does not feature in any central way in this study.

Paul Oliver's *Songsters and Saints* (1984), masterfully expanding on the single-genre study, and examining as it does "Vocal traditions on Race records," treats a corpus of music that was commercially released.[1] This comprehensive and wide-ranging study provides us with numerous illustrations, photographs, advertisements, and transcriptions of song and sermon text excerpts, but only an occasional reproduction of a commercial vocal score (which would not, in any case, have been closely followed in performance). But Oliver's descriptions of details of music sound are compelling, and the recordings discussed are more or less available to the dedicated seeker. Recent years have also, of course, seen the issue of some compelling collections of community-based recordings with detailed liner notes: the Smithsonian/Folkways *Wade in the water* series, compiled by Bernice Johnson Reagon, particularly volume 2, *African American Congregational Singing* (SF40073, 1994), and volume 4, *African American Community Gospel* (SF 40075, 1994) come immediately to mind.

Most recently, Guthrie Ramsey's lively and illuminating *Race Music: Black Cultures from Bebop to Hip-Hop* (2003), paints a bold canvas for "race music" (referring to Oliver's overview of race records, above), spanning the genres of blues, gospel, rhythm-and-blues, soul, and hip-hop. While Ramsey's analyses are insightful—most notably his analysis of Karen Clark-Sheard's rendition of the gospel song "I won't complain" (see pp. 203–10)—and his writing and argument compelling, the absence of any musical transcriptions detracts from the usefulness of his comments. Overall, however, the discussion in this book is disjointed because examples are eclectically drawn from the author's experience and, unless one happens to have the recordings to hand, one is left with no option but to take on trust the conclusions that he draws. As Ramsey himself explains, he does not intend his work as a "comprehensive, strictly chronological study of African American popular music. Rather, it is a meditation on the interpretation and criticism of various aspects of its history. I attempt to forward a poetics of this music [and herein lies the book's strongest achievement] that explains some of the circumstances and consequences of its power and its relevance for specific historically situated listeners" (xi). Outside of this "poetics of music," no attempt is made to give the musical illustrations (or, arguably, icons) chosen a common ground or context. This might ultimately not have been possible to achieve satisfactorily across all the genres discussed; but the study would have benefited from a more concrete attempt to locate or ground the selections in some tangible common parameter or dimension.

This privileging of discoursing about music would not, of course, be considered unusual in historical musicology (where, it should be stressed, discussion has traditionally centred around an agreed historical canon), but it is unusual in ethnomusicology. Grounded as it was in non-literate traditions of music, ethnomusicology has privileged music sound. African American music has been predominantly an oral tradition, and performance has, therefore, been central to its realisation. My initial surprise (and sometimes frustration) stemmed from the disjuncture between these two realities. Arriving in a sense "in the field" as I commenced both academic studies and fieldwork in Providence, Rhode Island, I found myself surrounded by compelling musical sound that bore little relation either to the scholarly writings that I was studying, or to the musical texts that were occasionally utilised (hymnals, for example, were used primarily as a guide to the words of songs).

The second aspect of my initial studies that surprised me was the emphasis on "African-ness" that was foregrounded in African American studies of all stripes. Coming from a European context, I had some familiarity with African music, some West African music particularly, and I might have chosen that as a readily accepted and relatively accessible field of specialisation. And I was pursuing study of West African music at Brown University (under the direction of the late James Koetting—who had conducted fieldwork in Ghana, and taught at the University there—and the late Freeman Donkor—former lead drummer and dancer with the Ghanaian Dance Ensemble). By electing some aspect of African music as my area of study, I would have been following in the wake of some of Europe's most respected ethnomusicologists, and West Africa, moreover, is more readily accessible from Ireland than is Mississippi. But it was not the sound of West African music that particularly attracted me, in any of its many guises, but the quintessentially American sound of African American music.

As a young student, however, and a non-American, I was somewhat naive in my very limited understanding of not only the political, but also the cultural legacies in the United States of the Civil Rights and Black Power movements, and of the Black Arts Project. It was inevitable that I would be bemused by the iconic status of works such as LeRoi Jones' (Imiri Baraka) 1963 *Blues People*. Nonetheless, I was unprepared for the pervasive (but at the time, entirely necessary) emphasis on African retentions: see, for example, Richard Bastide *African Civilizations in the New World* (1971); Lazarus Ekwueme "African-music retentions in the New World" (1974); Olly Wilson "The significance of the relationship between Afro-American music and West African music" (1974); and Portia Maultsby "West African influences and retentions in U.S. Black Music: A sociocultural study" (1985). This is, naturally, a thread that has continued across the spectrum of African American studies, whether or not it is made explicit in individual titles: see, for example, Joseph E. Holloway, ed. *Africanisms in American Culture* (1990); Portia Maultsby "Africanisms in African-American Music" (1990); Joseph E. Holloway and Winifred K. Vass, eds. *The African Heritage of American English* (1993); Mozella G. Mitchell, *New Africa in America: The Blending of African American Religious and Social Traditions among Black People in Meridian, Mississippi and Surrounding Counties* (1994), to mention but a few. Mitchell outlines this perspective in her introduction:

> My interpretive framework is Afro-centric, unapologetically. My tendency is to see the residual African customs and traditions beneath the overlay of Western religious character among the people of the study. For instance, one of the informants interviewed, Gertrude Darden, in her description of the environment of the area kept referring to the 'common life,' the natural flow of things, as what she treasured the most, living in harmony with nature, following the lay of the land.

Immediately upon hearing this, I see the image of Africa, the African personality and philosophical stance (ibid.: 6).

At the beginning of my studies, this type of interpretation or projection seemed to me extravagant. But it continues, at various levels of intensity, of course, to be a *leitmotif* of African American studies.

All of the above scholarship has influenced my own scholarly development and the genesis of this book. To the two major issues sketched above, I have responded in what I myself find, in retrospect, surprisingly predictable ways. Because of my prevailing interest in and love of musical sound, I have tried to include in this community study various representations of the musical sound that is at the heart of the study. Thus, for each of the concepts identified and discussed, I have provided representative examples of musical sound, which I also analyse in some detail in the text. On the other hand, I have chosen not to explore in detail issues of African retentions in the musical and cultural expression of this community. Not that I consider such issues unimportant but, as I have indicated, they have been analysed by a broad range of scholars across a wide range of disciplines in African American studies. The interested reader is referred to the Bibliography for numerous examples of such studies in addition to those mentioned above.

Since I first embarked upon this study in the 1980s, both this work and the scholarship with which it is informed have gone through many manifestations. It may be that in looking back at the twenty years or so that precede what one views as a major piece of one's own work, one always feels that there has been an explosion in relevant scholarship. But it does seem to me indisputable that the past two decades have seen an extraordinary expansion in studies on identity, the South, religion, gender and equality, race and, as one reader remarked, "cultural studies of all stripes." Ranging across a variety of disciplines, many of these developments have influenced my thinking. Some of these key studies are discussed in the text, others are not (but may be listed in the bibliography, which, nonetheless, has been considerably cut or "selected" in the interests of space). One of the dangers of trying to integrate such a variety or scholarship is, of course, that scholars in most disciplines will find works that might have been included and that have been omitted. In choosing to pursue the interdisciplinary approach that is at the heart of ethnomusicology, I have left myself open to the charge that I know less and less about more and more: it is a choice that I would still make. As Bruno Nettl has asserted:

What has characterized ethnomusicology most throughout its history is a fascination with, and a desire to absorb and understand, the world's cultural diversity. Of equal importance is the fact that a group of abiding ideological and epistemological issues have been with us from the beginning, attacked at various times and places from different viewpoints, but still with us. [. . .] And most characteristic, [. . .] ethnomusicology is a field whose fundamental nature results from its association with several disciplines which have nourished it (1991: xv).

This, I still feel, is one of ethnomusicology's greatest strengths.

In addition to ethnomusicological studies mentioned above, other ethnomusicologists (from all areas of specialisations) who have influenced my thinking are too numerous to mention here, but are, I hope, well represented both throughout the text and in the bibliography. There are, however, a few recent publications that are particularly pertinent: *Enchanting Powers: Music in the World's Religions*, edited by Lawrence E. Sullivan (1997), I found thought-provoking and evocative in its examination of religious music and its role cross-culturally. Similarly, the broad range of articles in Gregory F. Barz and Timothy J. Cooley, eds., *Shadows in the Field: New Perspectives for Fieldwork in Ethnomusicology* (1997), and in Martin Stokes' edited collection, *Ethnicity, Identity, and Music: The Musical Construction of Place* (1994) for concepts of identity and place. I have, on the other hand, elected not to follow the trend towards self-reflexivity currently coming to the forefront of the field: see, for example the studies by Michelle Kisliuk (1998) or Carol Ann Miller (1999).

Finally, in addition to the scholarship referred to above, two bodies of literature have influenced my approach in this study. The first (to which Bill Ferris at the Center for the Study of Southern Culture at the University of Mississippi, first introduced me), is Southern Studies. Reading in this field, at the time of my fieldwork, and particularly thereafter, as that field has burgeoned and as I have tried to interpret my studies effectively, has helped me to understand the Clear Creek community and its context not simply as a particular black community in Mississippi at a specific point in time, but also as sharing many aspects of their lives and worldview with other similar communities throughout the rural South. Amongst the most thoughtful (and thought-provoking) studies in this area have been those by John Boles, *Black Southerners, 1619–1869* (1983); Boles and Evelyn Thomas Nolen, eds., *Interpreting Southern History: Historiographical Essays in Honor of Sanford W. Higginbotham* (1987); W. Fitzhugh Brundage, ed., *Where These Memories Grow: History, Memory, and Southern Identity* (2000); James Cobb, *The Most Southern Place on Earth: The Mississippi Delta and the Roots of Regional Identity* (1992); Morton Sosna, *In Search of the Silent South: Southern Liberals and the Race Issue* (1997); Joel Williamson, *The Crucible of Race: Black/White Relations in the American South since Emancipation* (1986); and the collection edited by Walter Fraser, R. Frank Saunders, Jr., and John L. Wakelyn, *The Web of Southern Social Relations: Women, Family and*

Education (1985). But this is not to discount other excellent studies by James Anderson (1988), Erskine Caldwell (1995), James Grossman (1989), Cynthia Neverdon-Morton (1989), Pete Daniel (1986), and others. And then, of course, there is the *Encyclopedia of Southern Culture*, co-edited by Charles Reagan Wilson and William Ferris (1989), to which a myriad of scholars have contributed.

Equally influential on my thinking has been the field of Southern religion, of which Clear Creek is similarly (but not exclusively) representative: many scholars in fact assert that religion and Southern identity are so inextricably interwoven as to be inseparable. In the words of one of the most prominent scholars in this field "Can one think of a culture more influenced by religion than the South? It seems to be more "there" there than most other places. To examine the life of that society demands giving attention to that dimension of its life" (Samuel S. Hill, Jr., 2001: 5). Outstanding in this field are the monographs, articles, and collections edited by Samuel S. Hill, Jr.: see, for example, his *Southern Churches in Crisis* (1966), *The South and the North in American Religion* (1980), and *One Name but Several Faces: Variety in Popular Christian Denominations in Southern History* (1996); in addition to the following edited collections: *Religion and the Solid South* (1972), *Encyclopaedia of Religion in the South* (1984), and *Varieties of Southern Religious Experience* (1988).

Because of the symbiotic relationship between Southern identity and Southern religion, several of the scholars mentioned in the first category have also been very influential in the second, most notably John Boles: see, for example, his edited volume, *Masters and Slaves in the House of the Lord: Race and Religion in the American South, 1740–1870* (1988), and his edited collection, *Autobiographical Reflections on Southern Religious History* (2001). But so too have been Martin Marty (1981, and ed., 1997), Donald Mathews (1977, 1984, 2001) and, with a special interest in religion in Mississippi, Randy Sparks (1994, 2001), and Charles Reagan Wilson (1995, and ed., 1985, 1998).

To all of these scholars I owe an intellectual debt: to some also a personal debt of gratitude for thoughtfulness and friendship shown. Their writings have contributed to the strengths of this book: its weaknesses are mine alone.

The Clear Creek Missionary Baptist Church

And so to the community that is at the heart of this book. The Clear Creek M.B.C. community's geographic situation in Lafayette country in northern Mississippi, a region which is itself in many ways a study in contrasts, sets the stage for the everyday dramas that unfold there. Northern Mississippi is wooded and hilly and, as its soil is poor in

Figure 1. Northern Mississippi is wooded and hilly.

comparison with the rich flatlands of the Mississippi delta, large, powerful plantation families did not generally emerge here (see figure 1). Soil erosion is a serious problem in this area, and importation of the kudzu vine a disastrous attempt to alleviate it, since it indiscriminately swallows trees and man-made structures (see figures 2, 3, and 4). Since farm holdings were typically small, the number of slaves remained so also. Slavery seems to have been less harsh here than in other areas of the state and, therefore, less destructive of the black community. On the other hand, the smaller concentrations of slaves also precluded the formation of the large cohesive black communities posited in other areas of the plantation South, as, for example, detailed by Frances Berry and John

Figure 2. Soil erosion is a serious problem in this area.

Blassingame (1982), Herbert Gutman (1977), or George P. Rawick (1972). Although the social gulf between the white and black populations was therefore smaller, it seems likely that what differences there were were deemed more important and were clung to more tenaciously. The less material superiority the white man had over the black, the less he could afford token gestures of generosity. Native Americans survived in this area well into the nineteenth century: treaties with the Choctaw and Chickasaw tribes were signed in 1830–1832.[2] All these factors combined made of northern Mississippi a region that is unusual in the plantation South.

Figure 3. Importation of the kudzu vine was a disastrous attempt to alleviate soil erosion, since the kudzu vine indiscriminately swallows trees.

Figure 4. The kudzu vine also engulfs manmade structures.

Figure 5. The extravagant wealth of some of "Ole Miss's" fraternities and sororities (decorated for Homecoming).

Oxford, the capital of Lafayette county, is a small town. It is the home of the University of Mississippi, which attracts students from all over the South, some from northern states, and many from Asia, South Africa, Europe, and the Philippines. The university is well endowed; and the extravagant wealth of some of the fraternities and sororities on campus stands in gross contrast to the extreme poverty of some of the local people (see figure 5). A predominantly white school, which still touts the strength of the Confederacy in its mascot, Colonel Reb., and in the Confederate flag at football games and other celebrations, it now has a small but active black student body. (The issue of nomenclature in regard to the black community in America has been the subject of much philosophical and emotive debate. I have chosen the title "black" rather than "African American" in referring to this community, not lightly but in response to their own wishes, as they do not consider African American an accurate reflection of their ancestry.[3] However, it is important to bear in mind that, as Joseph Holloway remarks, the issue of "naming" has been a crucial one for this community: "the name controversy is central to understanding black culture in America because its history reveals much about ideological and cultural developments in black life" 1990: xviii). A disproportionate number of service jobs on campus are staffed by black people—groundsmen, cafeteria personnel, cooks for the fraternities and sororities, cleaners. Many of the athletes are black.[4]

Oxford itself is a typical small Southern town. At its centre stands the square, with the Lafayette County courthouse filling the centre plot. Around the square are various stores—Sneeds, an old-fashioned hardware store which still sells nails by weight and all unlikely manner of odds and ends; Elliotts, where brides-to-be register their china patterns; Promises, a religious book store; Square Books, one of the few stores to have retained the traditional second floor balcony, where one can have iced tea and pumpkin pie while browsing through a selected book. Just off the square is Jitney Jungle, a favourite local supermarket. On any given day a line of elderly men can be seen sitting in a row along the wall outside the county jail passing time. Black and white mix along the wall and in Jitney Jungle,[5] but on the whole, at least outside working hours, the two communities remain separate. Black people are rarely seen in white residential areas, except on their way to or from work (many white families employ a black woman who comes to clean at regular intervals), or when someone in the area is having a yard sale. Few of the white people with whom I spoke had ever visited any of the satellite black communities on the outskirts of Oxford. There is, however, a mix of black and white to some extent in one of the newer (ca. 1980?) apartment developments.

If one heads west out of Oxford and past the university campus towards Highway 6, one of the first sights one comes upon is a group of several huts in a row. Their condition and the surrounding mud defy any other description. The inhabitants are black, and the dwellings are a distressing sight, strongly reminiscent of sharecroppers' huts of the nineteenth century (see figure 6). Further out the highway small roads

Figure 6. If one heads west out of Oxford and past the university campus towards Highway 6, one of the first sights one comes upon is a group of several huts in a row.

head off on either side, many of them beginning in asphalt but turning into deeply rutted dirt roads almost as soon as one tops the rise away from the highway. Hidden away here, in trailers and houses of varying shapes and sizes, are many small black communities. A strange car causes much comment as it passes down one of these roads, for there are always those who notice such passings and note that the car is not that of any of the inhabitants. In this respect, in contrast to the anonymity of Northern cities and even some Southern ones, these communities resemble country villages in Ireland, my native home, for there are always sufficient people who pass the day at home at some window or leaning across the wall addressing a neighbour, that all who pass along the road traversing the community are noticed.

Most of the members of Clear Creek M.B.C. comprise one of these black satellite communities; in fact, while the community is now split in two by the highway, both portions retain the same postal address of Springhill. To describe the Clear Creek church membership as a family is a very accurate description for, of the 180 or so members, almost all are kin or have become so by marriage. Many grew up in this same area—moving around minimally as their families sought to make a living share-cropping or operating small, independently owned farms. They grew up and went to school together; the adults remember legally mandated deseg-regation of their schools during their years there. Many spent some time in larger cities further north; some settled there permanently, while others returned to build their lives in Mississippi.

Few members of Clear Creek M.B.C. operate farms any longer; the day of the small farmer is fast waning even here, and most people com-mute to Oxford or to some other town to work, as the children also commute to schools in the now centralised school system. The occupa-tions of the adults are various: some are factory workers, others office or bank personnel; others work in the stores or on the university cam-pus. Almost every family has a car of some description, as there is no local public transport. Oxford boasts only two taxi cabs. Members of the community have made several attempts to encourage self-sufficiency through initiatives such as opening small stores, but none of these has been successful, perhaps because the convenience of being able to buy locally has never quite been able to substitute for the wide range of choices and very often lower prices offered by larger stores and super-markets in town.

Church members find here not only their religious but also their social community. They meet and occasionally go out together, and their children play together. It is generally accepted that the church for the African American community becomes the social focus of its mem-bers' lives. This fact is characteristic of this community. Each family has an intimate knowledge of the others. Although this may at times seem oppressive, especially to young people who perceive that the previous generation is reluctant to relinquish their image of the former as children, it also makes for a very supportive and strong community. While the children may have white friends in the desegregated schools that they attend, none that I spoke to had ever had a white friend come over to visit, nor had any gone to a white friend's house. Again, while white and black communities coexist, only rarely is there any social inter-course between the two. The arrival of a white person such as myself in one of these communities is the occasion of considerable comment and speculation.

Black members broke with the parent Clear Creek Southern Baptist Church (which was organized August 12, 1836, by settlers from Virginia and the Carolinas) in 1877 and established Clear Creek Missionary Baptist Church. Immediately afterwards, lacking any church building, they met in a bush arbor (an improvised structure of poles roofed with tree branches). During this time the white Baptists of the parent church helped the new group to erect a church building, reportedly completed by 1880. The present building, erected in 1969, is the third that the church has

Figure 7. The Clear Creek Missionary Baptist Church building is constructed of brick and wood, with a white-fasciaed roof atop of which stands a white cross.

occupied, one of the previous buildings having been destroyed by fire. Partly as a result of this, current church records are kept in a strongbox down at the bank.

The site that the church now occupies, while on the same landholding as the others, is new because of the rerouting of the roads during the Sardis Dam and the Corps Engineers' Project in the 1940s (interview with Sam Jones, November 23, 1986). The church is set up on a small hill and can be readily seen from the highway. One approaches the church up a small incline, with cotton fields on either side. A clearing has been dug out among the trees and the church building rests upon the knoll built up with the excavated earth. The lower, cleared space, covered with gravel, serves as a parking lot. A white-painted wooden sign outside gives the name of the church and pastor and the times of services. The building is constructed of brick and wood, with a white-fasciaed roof atop of which stands a white cross (see figures 7 and 8).

Entering through the front doors of the church one arrives in a small porch. A second pair of doors leads into the sanctuary, panelled in dark wood, with red carpeting, curtains and seat covers (see figure 9). Directly in front, some twenty benches forward, is the offertory/communion table. Behind this, on a platform raised about two and a half feet, are the podium, seats for officiating ministers, and behind these again, choir stalls. A piano

Figure 8. The church graveyard is on a slope behind the church; cotton fields can be seen below in the distance.

Figure 9. The church interior is all panelled in wood, with red carpeting, curtains, and seat covers. Sunlight floods through the half-open curtains.

stands to the left of the choir stalls. Doors lead off the platform, on the left to a classroom, on the right to a wing (added in 1978) which contains several other classrooms and function rooms, the pastor's study, and a kitchen for the preparation of special meals such as the Harvest Day dinner.

The pastor of the church, Rev. Grady McKinney, is a native of Batesville, in Panola county, which is adjacent to Lafayette county. Elected as pastor to the church in 1972, he is also pastor of three other churches. Because of this fact the Clear Creek M.B.C. holds service only every first and third Sunday: at 6 p.m. on first Sundays and 11 a.m, and 6 p.m. on third Sundays. Such "staggering" of church services is a common feature in rural areas; indeed, the twenty churches in the Tallahatchie-Oxford Missionary Baptist Association share only twelve pastors amongst them.[6] Despite many members' desire for weekly church services, they are reluctant to lose Rev. McKinney, which they must if they decide on weekly services. Sunday school meets at 9.30 a.m. every Sunday, and some of the members proceed from there, on second and fourth Sundays, to service at Second Baptist Church in Oxford. Rev. Leroy Wadlington, who grew up as a member of Clear Creek, is pastor there. Rev. Wadlington has served as Associate/Black Chaplain to the University of Mississippi for several years. When the Rev. M. T. Moore split from Second Baptist in 1985 and formed Third Baptist, Rev. Wadlington was elected pastor at the former.

Clear Creek M.B.C. has a current membership of about 180 individuals, although not all of them can be considered full-fledged members, as children under twelve have not yet converted or become Christians. Conversion is a critical event in the members' lives, as it is for most evangelicals.[7] Until an individual comes forth and acknowledges Jesus Christ as his personal saviour, he is not saved. Children usually reach this understanding at about age twelve, and are baptised shortly thereafter. Mrs. Mary Penamon, at 106, is the oldest member of the church family. Because of declining health she has not been able to attend church regularly in the past few years, but she is visited regularly by church members, especially Mrs. Eulastine Thompson. Of those in regular attendance at services, Mr. Charles Campbell at 99, is the oldest. But the church also has a large young population—about thirty children between the ages of 5 and 16 attend Youth Meeting—and it seems that the youngest member of the church family is often a tiny infant. Usually about 120 people attend Sunday morning worship service. About half that number return to the Communion service at 6 p.m. on third Sundays.

Black Baptist churches, which denominationally place great emphasis on religious freedom (even in relation to denominational affiliation[8]), vary in the amount of authority with which they invest their pastors.[9] Some churches remain quite independent both from any national association of churches and from the preacher whom they select to serve as their pastor, while others revolve around a particularly strong pastor whose identity becomes intertwined with that of the church. At Clear Creek M.B.C. authority resides first with the Deacon Board, then with the Mothers of the Church, and finally with the church membership. A pastor must be appointed by the membership and he can, likewise, be dismissed by them. Given that the Clear Creek M.B.C. members spend far more time without their pastor than with him, membership authority within the church is very strong and the members see themselves as a community that certainly values, but is also independent of their pastor. This seems to be both a Baptist and an African American phenomenon.[10] In all black Baptist churches that I have visited the Music Ministry is one of the most important of church structures, and it is difficult to imagine worship without music. At Clear Creek M.B.C. certain families seem to be gifted with musical talent, and it is believed that the Pattons and their direct descendants are particularly gifted. Musical performance in Baptist churches usually rests with two important individuals (or sometimes with one person who fulfils both functions): the pianist and the choir director.

At Clear Creek M.B.C., families who can boast a keyboard player are likely to have considerable influence on the music the church performs, as the role of accompanist is critical. Good singers are also appreciated, although the judgment that someone is a "good singer" may have little to do with the intrinsic quality of the voice, but centres rather on the singer's ability to express the feeling and meaning of the song and to help the listeners to experience them. A strong voice with considerable volume is, nonetheless, much appreciated (or as Paul Oliver has put it, "if 'everything that hath breath' should praise the Lord, every ounce of breath is also used to do so"[11]), as is vocal agility.

Music is vital in the services of African American Baptist churches. It does not simply adorn the service; it seems rather to be its life breath. There are few moments in the service when music—either congregational or choral singing, or instrumental music of some sort—is not being performed; in fact, especially in southern churches, the whole service may be underpinned by a coherent tonal system. Much of the "impromptu" music within a service— chanted prayers, lined hymns, or impromptu hymns, for example—is spontaneously introduced by a member of the congregation, one of the deacons, or a minister. Even when it may follow a relatively extended period devoid of any music, its tonal centre is not arbitrary, but is generally closely related to the preceding music. The extent to which this is true varies, of course, from church to church. I have found it to be quite consistent in Baptist churches in northeast Mississippi, and especially at Clear Creek M.B.C. Because of the prevalence of chanting in these churches (and sometimes sustained humming by the congregation beneath the spoken language of the service), the tonal centre is reinforced very frequently, the spaces between any two musical items being short. This, of course, increases the chances of maintaining the tonal centre. In my recording of the 82nd Annual Convention of the Tallahatchie-Oxford Missionary Baptist Association service in Mississippi (August 29, 1982), pitch relations are as follows:

Introductory Remarks—spoken (no music).

Opening hymn, called up in D minor (key of a song being rehearsed before the service).

Scripture reading (no music).

First prayer, speech to chant; exploits the tonic-dominant relationship (D–A) and finally settles in A minor (D minor being uncomfortably high for the deacon).

Lined hymn—A minor; deacon sings sharp, finishing closer to B-flat minor.

Scripture reading—humming continues underneath.

Prayer—speech moves into chant, B-flat minor.

Hymn, begins in B-flat minor, accompanist on joining in moves the tonality to B minor (an easier key to play in).

Throughout the service there is an underlying coherence to the key relationships (largely based on tonic-dominant or major-relative minor relationships) of all the music, which is abandoned only when the accompanist either raises a piece a semi-tone to play it in an easier key, or introduces a "foreign" tonal centre with the introduction of a choral selection. This "foreign" key then becomes the new tonal centre. Such a coherent system reflects not pure coincidence but a musical framework that remains constant during the service.

The use of music within the African American church tradition points to an implied ideology: God is best approached through music: music is the most effective way to establish direct contact with the deity. This view is evident in a "typical" service, wherein music permeates every approach to the deity. Those sections not accompanied by music are generally either messages from God (as is the case with the Scripture readings) or else formalized framing texts, such as the Call to Worship and Covenant. Prayer—be it led by the pastor or one of the deacons or private and internalised prayer—is usually accompanied by music of some sort. Witnesses and testimonies emerge most often from a musical context, frequently during the course of the invitation hymn. Vocal interjections that appeal directly to the deity ("Lift me Jesus," for example), as opposed to those that express agreement or appreciation ("Well," "That's all right," "Amen") occur most usually within a musical context. I have never witnessed "falling out," "holy dance," or "possession" outside a musical context. Jeff Titon describes the function of music thus:

The music is literally moving: it activates the Holy Spirit, which sends some people into shouts of ecstasy, swoons, shakes, holy dance, and trance. If they get so carried away that they are in danger of fainting or injuring themselves, they are restrained by their neighbors until members of the nurses' guild can reach them and administer aid. In this setting, music is a very powerful activity and the church is prepared for its effects (Titon, 1984: 114).

The instances of "impromptu" music in the service further reinforce the belief that music is used to establish a special kind of contact with God. Any especially moving religious moment is reinforced by song; the pastor may call up an impromptu hymn, or another song in which the congregation and accompanist immediately join.

The Clear Creek M.B.C. community is exceptionally gifted musically and uses a wide variety of musical genres and styles. The congregation moves easily into song, and both prayer and sermon (the highlight of the service) frequently develop into chant and even more elaborate melodic song. Rev. McKinney, the church's pastor, preaches, at his best, in a style that is exceptionally beautiful aesthetically, both poetically and musically, as well as powerful in religious terms. Thus, while this community's worship is typical in many ways of that of any number of similar congregations, their articulation in expressive culture of the intersection of the existential, social, and aesthetic spheres is particularly compelling.

2

Identity

"You could tell me all day what it means to you to be an Irish . . ."

It is a generally accepted psychological premise (Cobb, 1992; Hall and Lindzey, 1957; Jackson, 1984; Marsell, 1985; Moberly, 1985) that a large part of our identity is built, paradoxically, on who we are not.[1]

> The activities which are objectified to represent the self never occur in isolation. [. . .] [T]hey are interactions between subject and world; and in objectifying these interactions, the subject objectifies not only himself or herself, but other people as well. Moreover, objectifications of other people are not simply additions to or embellishments of the self. Rather, they are essential to the very nature of the self, for they provide the system of meaning in terms of which the self is defined (Jackson, 1984: 190).

Or, as Mikhail Bakhtin put it, "we get our selves from others" (quoted in Rice, 2003: 157). An infant's first strivings towards individuality are prompted by the discovery that his mother is not himself, that she has an identity apart from him, that she is separate. This process of separation, which continues throughout our lives, is that which enables us to become ourselves, separate, autonomous, and independent, to whatever degree. It is also, of course, what gives rise to the existential *angst* that I discussed in the introduction. Even when people band together in groups, the group's identity and cohesiveness are strengthened when posited in opposition to something outside itself. Alternately, the group may further subdivide into smaller groups that build their integrity on opposition to each other. A large group of children will inevitably split into smaller groups, even into "best friend" twos, and the smaller groups will be strengthened by their opposition one to another—"We can do x, but you can't." Three is a difficult number, be it with children, or with adult lovers. We are most comfortable with clear oppositions; everything is clearer in contrast to its opposite. It does not even matter if things are not radically different, so long as we can, on some level, perceive them to be opposed. This is all we need to form the basis of our dichotomy.

One of the strongest of the many clear oppositions functioning in North American society today is that of colour. Colour is one of the most fundamental things registered about another person, more fundamental perhaps than gender.[2] And it is permanent. The poor may become rich, the ugly may be made beautiful, but one cannot dramatically alter the skin colour and physical features that announce racial heritage. (Obvious exceptions to this are the experience of the author of the novel *Black Like Me* and the experiences of those African Americans who are "bright" enough to pass as white.) Long after legally mandated desegregation, there is de facto social segregation. Leaving aside the very occasional phenomenon of "passing," it seems clear that colour is a label that is clear, unambiguous, and almost infinitely dependable. And it is used and functional on both sides of the colour line, black and white. Several young black children with whom I came in contact in Mississippi stared at me fixedly, despite the remonstrations of their parents who considered their behaviour impolite. When the children persisted in this behaviour their parents described them as "colourstruck," the colour equivalent of dumbstruck, as they had never before been so close to a white person (see figure 10).

This chapter focuses on identity: the question of group identity, of individual identity within the group, and the relationship of identity to worldview. The members of Clear Creek M.B.C. create their identity through a

Figure 10. "Colourstruck." A young member of the Clear Creek Missionary Baptist Church.

series of oppositions: black-white, saint-sinner, Christian-not yet professed, saint-backslider.[3] These oppositions set the group's boundaries, the group's relationship to other groups, and the relationship of individuals to the group. The members articulate the primary opposition of saint-sinner through the texts they use, spoken and sung, and also through the musical sound itself.

"Upstairs Believers" and Heart Religion

Clear Creek M.B.C. is a black church. It has no white members and very few white visitors. When I questioned the members about this fact, they told me that one white man many years ago used to come to the church and even wanted to become a member, but the membership voted against it. The concept of a white person wanting to join their church was so unimaginable to them that they questioned his motives.

> Now we used to have a, a white man used to come to our church regular. He wanted to join but didn't nobody know how to take him in. Didn't know what to say about him. He was sort of considered as sort of "upstairs believer." If he wanted to come in the church, wasn't supposed to turn him off; he knows he get in there for some call. He never did get in the church. Lots of folks thought he just wasn't right for wantin' to join there. He has a church of his race, right beside that one (Mr. Charles Campbell, interview, November 20, 1986).

The overall decision was that he was operating only on the level of "head religion," and the members felt that they could not be comfortable with a white member in their church. Moreover, the finality of racial lines in Mississippi is graphically drawn in Mr. Campbell's final assessment: "he has a church of his race, right beside that one," black and white exist side by side, but separate. Mr. Campbell's appraisal of "white religion" as "head religion" ("upstairs believer") was curiously echoed (in reverse) by one of the most prominent scholars of Southern religion, Samuel S. Hill, Jr., in 1996. "The Christianity of the black church bespeaks heart religion. It is inherently communal. It coordinates; it is not given to drawing up a list of essential doctrines, ranked by priority. That is to say, its theology has about it systematic coordination" (39).

The white Clear Creek Southern Baptist Church from which the black members split, is about fifty yards up the road from the black one, but there is little interaction between the two churches. Despite their proximity, I have never seen any communication between the membership of the two churches. Mississippi was, in fact, the last state to report a black church affiliate with the white Southern Baptists, and did so only in 1984 (Knight,

1993: 174). While it is true that Mississippi has been slow to desegregate, (only in the Fall of 1987 was interracial marriage legalised in the state constitution, and only by a slight margin), the division along colour lines holds for all of the areas in which I have conducted fieldwork. As James Washington has pointed out *"with the single exception* of the integrated Free Mission Society, no organic ties existed between black and white Baptist national organizations during Reconstruction or thereafter—until the predominantly white American Baptist churches and the black Progressive National Baptist Convention became 'associated organizations' in 1970" (1986: 83). While this racial separation may be most prevalent in Baptist congregations, as Pentecostal and Catholic congregations seem to be more integrated, it persists as a central concern for scholars of American religion.

> It is this problematic encounter of black and white [. . . that] is the story of a persisting and seemingly intractable gap. [. . .] The gap between the races—a gap involving both the interpretation of the American experience and the degree of empowerment within it— remains one of the foundational realities of our national religious life [. . .] one of the crucial, central themes in the religious history of the United States (David W. Wills, in Fulop and Raboteau, 1997: 15–20).

It is, moreover, significant that it was only on October 19, 1994, that the white Pentecostal Fellowship of North America publicly repented of past racial divisions and voted to disband in order to form a new multi-racial Pentecostal organization—the Pentecostal Churches of North America— with African American Pentecostals.[4] Every Baptist church that I visited in Mississippi, up and down the state, was either black or white: likewise in Kentucky and the Northeast. This separation along racial lines has its roots in the postemancipation South, which was characterised by:

> an almost complete separation of black and white Christians along racial lines. In 1876, the editor of the Raleigh Biblical Recorder gave expression to the general white Protestant sentiment. Permanent church partnerships between blacks and whites were as inconceivable as influencing "fire and gunpowder to occupy the same canister in peace." Black Christians in the post-Reconstruction South developed their own institutions, separate and apart from the white power structure (Sernett, 1991: 141).

And, as Randy Sparks has remarked, both religion and racial division have continued to shape Mississippi. "Understanding how religion has shaped Mississippi's culture and society is a complex undertaking, one made more challenging by the dramatic changes over time, by the state's particular class divisions, and, most significantly, by the race factor, which has played such a crucial role in shaping Mississippi culture" (2001: ix). Where one finds occasional white members in black churches in Mississippi in particular, their separateness is maintained by much of the congregation.[5]

This sort of colour demarcation is quite to be expected, for a number of reasons. Integration is a relatively new phenomenon, only approaching forty years of age, and even less in Mississippi where, as Charles Bolton has pointed out, "a genuine attempt to integrate Mississippi's public schools did not occur until 1970. [. . .] White resistance to school desegregation proved both deep-seated and sustained, relenting only under a steady stream of legal action by black parents and federal intervention" (2000: 781). Religion, on the other hand, is one of the oldest and most powerful meaning structures in society, especially in the black community, and it is always one of the slowest aspects of society to change. Moreover, most especially amongst Protestant denominations, religion provided the first formal institutions through which black people could congregate freely and exert considerable control over certain aspects of their lives. The black church grew, therefore, to where it is today probably the single, most influential institution in the black community, as assessed by both major and minor scholars of black religion: "For Blacks in America (or African Americans) the legacy of institutional strength, more than any other institution (i.e., the body politic, business, economic or social structures) was, and still is, the Black Church" (Leonard L. Bethel, in Leonard L. Bethel and Frederick A. Johnson, eds., 1998: introduction, no page numbers given). Or, as Baer and Singer remark, "despite limits on their freedom, independent Black churches constituted the one institution where Black people were able to act as a community, especially in the South" (1992: 14–15). Moreover, as Randy Sparks has argued, "genuine biracial worship has [. . .] seldom been a goal of either black or white Baptists. When the Cooperative Ministries Program began in 1975, both black and white ministers emphasized that biracial worship was not one of their aims" (2001: 266). To emphasise his point, Sparks quotes from an article published in the *Good News* in December 1975. "[W]hite Baptist ministers don't want blacks flocking to their churches. The pastors say black culture and flavor would be lost in the dominant white congregations. And Southern Baptists say they no longer have the ministers and personnel to staff black churches" (1975: 1).

"Shun Evil Companions"

There is, of course, more than one black community and, as scholars have recently begun to emphasize, more than one black church.[6] For the members of Clear Creek M.B.C., and in varying degrees for other black churches, there is within the black community a critical division between saints and sinners, the saved and the damned, the born-again and those who have yet to be reborn. For black Baptists in general, this opposition quite literally represents the division between heaven and hell. The second verse of a favourite Baptist hymn, "Yield not to temptation," clearly states this opposition: "Shun evil companions." The members of Clear Creek M.B.C. take this admonishment quite seriously. Their world is readily split into saints and sinners, and while they may work "out in the world" (i.e., amongst sinners), and feel constrained to try to bring those lost souls to Jesus, they are as unlikely to socialise with sinners as with white people.

The church community in effect meets all the social needs of its members, from playmates to babysitters, adult companions and spouses, a fact that is characteristic of evangelical Protestantism especially in the South (Wilson, 1995: 73). It is usually in regard to marriage that the community expands somewhat to include other church communities. At Clear Creek M.B.C. members either bring their spouses to church at Clear Creek, or they continue to attend Clear Creek while the spouses remain at their home church(es). Unless members move a considerable distance away, it is unusual for them to change their church affiliation. George Price, a deacon at Clear Creek, travels almost ten miles with his family every Sunday in order to attend Clear Creek M.B.C. Similarly, students who attend college in Jackson, one hundred and eighty miles away, attend other churches during the semester but do not move their membership from Clear Creek. While community boundaries are stretched in instances of marriage where members move a considerable distance away, they are not broken. As far as I could ascertain, none of the members had married a sinner. This, of course, may be equally because of the fact that there is virtually no social intercourse with sinners, because of allegiance to the church code. This type of community integrity is also true of many white fundamentalist churches. A worldview that posits a dichotomy between saints and sinners, saved and damned, fosters dependence upon the chosen community because of its uncompromising judgment of all others as lost. In Fredrik Barth's terms, it is a very clear and unambiguous "significant difference" or "boundary signal" (Barth, 1969: 14).

Both in theory and in practise, however, the boundary between saints and sinners is not as inflexible as one might expect. It is helpful, in this respect, to supplement Barth's concept of boundary (1969) with that suggested already in 1957 by psychologists Hall and Lindzey. They described boundaries as "dynamically established, permeable membranes," rather than sharply demarcated lines. As with other areas of their lives, church members can and do embrace what appears to be a contradictory position if the occasion warrants. While the deacons embraced Christ's teaching to Nicodemus that "Except a man be born of water and of the Spirit, he cannot enter the kingdom of God" (John 3:5), some deacons and other members were open to the possibility that for other people in other places, there might be another way to find God. (The boundary's integrity is, of course, also maintained here by distancing the challenge.) They allowed that I too might reach heaven, although I have not been born again; and also that their young children, who have not yet become Christians, would not be condemned to hell should they die before reaching the age of reason and experiencing conversion. The response I received when I challenged this kind of reasoning was almost invariably that "God is merciful."

Not all church members, of course, agree with such views, but this ability to adapt to current circumstances gives the church community great strength. Their acceptance of me, for example, moved after several years to a point where they invited me to stand up with them as part of the Clear Creek M.B.C. delegation on occasions when we visited other churches.

This issue of identity, in-group versus out-group, us versus them, is played out in music. Black church musicians in general are quite clear in their opinion of what is appropriate for church and what is not. In music the traditional dichotomy between "good music" (church music) and "devil's music" (blues initially, and now other "popular" styles) is maintained, although it is not always stated so baldly. Gospel music, because of its close musical and sometimes textual affiliation with popular musical forms, its use of an expanded number of instruments, and the creation of celebrities such as James Cleveland and Andrae Crouch, along with its considerable financial revenue, has to some degree straddled the gap between sacred and profane, religious and secular (although there are also gospel singers who refuse to enter the commercial world of gospel). This in turn has reflected back into the church communities and has quite often produced a split within the church between gospel and tradition, young and old.

"Merry Airs" and Hymns

Recognition of the opposition between sacred and secular music is not, of course, new: that opposition has in fact plagued the discussion of black religious music since the advent of slaves to America. Disquiet voiced by white preachers concerning the profane nature of "hymns" sung by slaves "after hours" at antebellum revivals, distrust at both the secular bent of their improvised lyrics and the dance-like quality of their melodies, and horror at "pagan" rituals such as the ring shout (which was all but annihilated, and survives in only a few instances, for example, on the Georgia sea islands), were all central concerns for missionaries seeking to Christianise the slaves.[7] In fact, as Portia Maultsby has remarked, "as early as 1665 and as late as 1899, missionaries, travellers, slaveholders, and slaves themselves commented about the African origin of dances, instruments, and songs associated with slaves." Missionaries often complained about such practices, which they described as "heathenish and savage manners" (1985: 30). Maultsby continues:

> As late as 1859 and 1863, missionaries and other whites reported their "shocked reactions" to Blacks' services. [. . .] In the absence of whites, Blacks freely interpreted songs taught to them by missionaries and made them conform to their own musical aesthetics. [. . .] descriptions reveal that slaves occasionally borrowed melodic ideas and textual themes from Protestant musical traditions. [But], they reinterpreted the songs by changing melodies and rhythms, replacing original texts with new ones that combined English words and phrases with those of African origin. They added refrain lines and choruses and wove shouts, moans, groans, and cries into the melody. They substituted faster tempos for the original ones and incorporated complex foot-stamping, hand-clapping, and bodily movements (1985: 32–33).

Similarly, Oral Moses (1988) quotes John Fanning Watson, who in 1819 admonished Methodists against facile borrowing from "illiterate blacks."

> We have too, a growing evil, in the practice of singing in our places of public and society worship, merry airs, adapted from old songs, to hymns of our composing, often miserable as poetry, and senseless as matter, and most frequently composed and first sung by the illiterate blacks of the society" John Fanning Watson *Methodist Error; or, Friendly Christian Advice, to Those Methodists Who Indulge in Extravagant Religious Emotions and Bodily Exercise by a Wesleyan Methodist* (Trenton, N.J.: D. and E. Fenton. Reprint. Cincinnati: Philips and Speer, 1819), 15–16 (quoted in Moses, 1988: 52).

This overwhelming concern with the secular flavour of the slaves' sacred activities emanated from and gave expression to the colonists' and missionaries' dichotomy between the sacred and the secular, which was the Reformed Protestant inheritance of the New World. It was a dichotomy that was not, however, culturally typical of a sub-Saharan, West African heritage (the area, both geographic and cultural, from which the greatest number of slaves was imported into North America), where an altogether more holistic understanding of the spiritual and secular prevailed.

While fundamentalist Protestant traditions (black and white) seek to differentiate clearly between the sacred and the profane, the reality of the African American heritage is necessarily more complex. Sacred and profane continue to jostle shoulders in African American culture, not least because there has never been an entirely satisfactory separation (or indeed reconciliation) of the two in that tradition, most particularly in the musical sphere.

If distinguishing clearly between sacred and secular is philosophically important, indeed critical, to African American fundamentalist Christians in particular, the reality of blurred boundaries and frequent interchanges between the sacred and profane remain at the heart of African American music making. So it is, for example, that with the advent of the first commercial recordings in the 1920s, some of the most successful African American sacred quartets also recorded secular jazz numbers.[8] And this type of crossover or duality continued throughout the twentieth century. Thus, in any discussion of African American music, two traditions are often present, both philosophically and musically. The saved may be invested in a clear opposition of their music (emanating from and iconic of their lifestyle) to "devil's music," but that opposition is not consistently played out either socially or in musical sound.

Many if not most medium-sized churches have a separate choir or gospel chorus that sings gospel. Such groups are generally comprised of the youth and young adults of the church, while the more traditional repertoire of spirituals, hymns, and anthems is maintained by the older choir. This has been the case in the three churches in which I have conducted in-depth studies. At Congdon Street Baptist Church in Providence, Rhode Island, the gospel choir is the largest choir and is composed of the youth and young adults of the church. This choir sings mostly gospel, and also some hymns, but I have never heard them sing the four-part Soprano, Alto, Tenor, Bass (SATB) "art song" arrangements of spirituals composed by the Johnson brothers and Nathaniel Dett, among others. Spirituals seem to be the exclusive province of the Adult Choir. Similarly at Main Street Baptist Church in Lexington, Kentucky—a large church that boasts several choirs—gospel is sung by the youth and the young adult "Voices of Evangelism."

At Clear Creek M.B.C. the division is not quite so apparent, partly because the congregation is small, partly because the choir director has made efforts to have both choirs (youth and adult) sing all kinds of music. Each choir has, nonetheless, preference for a particular type of music: the youth, gospel; and the adult, more traditional genres such as hymns and spirituals. While there have also been efforts to bring the choirs together, neither group altogether enjoys the music of the other. Deacon Leroy Thompson expressed the problem thus: "The youth enjoy the more classical and today's kind of rock spirituals, rock gospel kind of thing. And the seniors really don't like the rock gospel. The youth enjoy it, they get into it. That has caused some division, but that doesn't necessarily have to be a problem. The only thing we need to do is get together and decide" (interview, November 22, 1987). Young people often find the Adult Choir's songs "draggy and boring," as the adults find the Youth Choir's songs "too loud and flashy, and without feeling." Therefore, it is generally among the younger members of the church that the distinction between "good music" and "devil's music" is most often perceived to be blurred.

Especially in rural Mississippi (and there is not too much of Mississippi that is not rural), the two sub-cultures of Delta blues (sometimes called Southern blues, folk blues, or country blues: see Frank Tirro, 1993: 56) and fundamentalist Christianity have remained relatively intact and opposed. It is an opposition that is critical to the identity of the Clear Creek M.B.C. membership. Preachers still warn about the evils of the sinner's life: moonshine, women, and "devil's music." And the Delta blues tradition is still strong. By and large audiences for the two traditions are different; not many church folk who go to church on Sunday morning attend a blues session on Friday or Saturday night, and such behaviour would be strongly condemned in church.

> I have known some people that used to sing in the choir was stayin' out all Saturday night and go to church and sing in the choir. Ain't no way in the world my daughter goin' stay out all Saturday night getting down and go church sing Sunday. No way! . . . Because that kind of life will hurt the church in the long run. Peoples get tired of looking at you sitting up there and they know what kind of life you living and know what you doing all through the week. And then maybe Sunday you up there trying to preach and they know that you out there running 'round all the best looking ladies in the community, and you up there telling them about Jesus. Folk get tired of that stuff! And you up there singin' in the choir and you done lived any kind of life and you up there wiggling Sunday morning, that's turning folks off (Reverend Grady McKinney, pastor, interview, November 17, 1987).

Efforts are being made, however, to bring blues and gospel closer. At the annual Northeast Mississippi Blues and Gospel Folk Festival at Rust College in Holly Springs, Mississippi, blues sets alternate with gospel sets throughout the day. As the genres alternate, however, so do the Masters of Ceremonies. As an alternative approach, the 1986 King Biscuit Blues Festival in Helena, Arkansas, had both gospel and blues running simultaneously. Yet the platforms for each were at the far ends of the street that encompassed the festival, the two genres effectively separated from each other by the crafts and food stalls. While some distance between the two platforms was necessary in order to separate the sounds, more than that was at stake. There was a core audience for each platform and they did not interchange; people might leave the music and travel the length of the food and craft stalls, but they would return to the platform with which they identified, blues or gospel, rarely pausing to listen to the other music. It would appear, therefore, that these festivals have little effect on behaviour at the community level.

Perhaps because of the closeness of rural communities in Mississippi, perhaps also because the two traditions have remained healthy but opposed, the congregation of Clear Creek M.B.C. insists upon an identity diametrically opposed to that of blues culture.[9] Nowhere is this fact more strikingly illustrated than in the members' use of music. The musicians in the church, while occasionally ceding the close musical relations between gospel, jazz, and rhythm and blues, for example, go on to stress the differences they consider critical. The church choir director and pianist, Herbert Bonner, maintains that there are certain chord progressions specific to "devil's music," which arouse the wrong feelings in listeners and performers alike. Below is my transcription of an example he played to illustrate this point (see example 2.1). Herbert sketches the classic blues progression here (I, IV-I, V-I),[10] but it is considerably elaborated with chromatic chords. Typically he adds minor sevenths, ninths, and elevenths above the root position triads (see A-flat-major chord, m. 5). He enriches the harmonic vocabulary by also using chromatic passing chords (see m. 9), often to fill the gap between two positions of a triad.

Example 2.1. Typical "devil's music," (blues) chord progression, as performed by Herbert Bonner.

In order to highlight the salient characteristics of this "devil's music," below is my transcription of what Herbert played as a typical gospel progression (I-vi-ii-V-I). It should be noted that this example is in gospel chorus style, rather than gospel solo style, and so does not show elements of personalization and improvisation, so endemic to gospel solo style (see example 2.2). The gospel progression is less chromatic (only one accidental is added, the minor seventh above the tonic) and much clearer in its harmonic structure. In the blues progression, on the other hand, Herbert makes free use of chromatic alterations, typically crushing the third (G flat/G natural), to give a "blue" note, as well as adding chromatic chords as mentioned above. Because of his use of ninths and elevenths, he also creates tone clusters that increase dissonance. At measure 8, the "devil in music," the tritone (F–B♮), is clearly outlined in the bass: the B natural, is especially prominent because it forms a false relation with the B flat in the preceding chord.

Where movement in the gospel progression is largely in parallel thirds and sixths, in a smooth and unambiguous 12/8, movement in the blues progression is more idiosyncratic. While generally in parallel motion to

Example 2.2. Typical gospel chord progression, as performed by Herbert Bonner.

facilitate movement about the keyboard, a clear first inversion triad above the bass is rare. The right hand carries the weight of "melody" and harmony, the left hand serves a percussive function and outlines the basic chord progression. If the harmony is to be rich, movement must be largely parallel given the restriction of range to the stretch of a single hand. Herbert almost invariably adds a "dissonant" seventh. This creates harmonic tension which is infrequently resolved. Meter in the blues progression is confounded both by alternation of beat subdivision into twos and into threes, and by accentuation of weak beats and weak portions of beats.

The density of the blues piece is also erratic (see m. 4, eight sixteenth-notes, followed by mm. 5 and 6, which have almost no movement). The gospel piece has a fairly constant density that is illustrative of compound meter: there are no off-beat accentuations or ties from weak to strong. The meter is further reinforced by the progressive logic of the harmonic structure: propulsion from beat to beat and from chord to chord is almost inevitable given the harmonic vocabulary.

The "bad" essence of the "devil's music" is, I think, that it is disruptive. Where the gospel music is integrative, consonant, flowing in meter, and clear in harmonic structure, the blues progression is none of these. As performed by Herbert Bonner, it is dissonant, unpredictable, and non-centred. Apart from a clear, percussive bass (which is at times itself unpredictable, see mm. 7 and 8), it has little in common with Herbert's gospel progression. In addition to other unsettling characteristics, voices are dropped and added almost at random (see mm. 2 and 5). The "good" essence of the gospel piece is, I think, that it is cohesive. Absolutely logical in its thrust, it is consistent melodically, harmonically, and metrically, and constant in the number of voices (usually three, sometimes four, in the right hand).[11]

The structuring of sound in each piece can be seen as a reflection of the structuring of society. It is essential, of course, to remember that what we have here is almost a caricature of the two genres by the musical director of Clear Creek M.B.C. What Herbert is trying to illustrate here is that there are certain chord progressions specific to "devil's music," which arouse the wrong feelings in listeners and performers alike. In order to illustrate his point, he has created simplified versions of each genre, versions which, nonetheless, delineate what he perceives (and therefore relays to the community, at least in the case of gospel), as the identifying characteristics of each genre. In this context then, the gospel piece reflects a concern with order, predictability, cohesion, and integration. The progression's cycle can be repeated many times for several verses with some variation to retain interest. The voices and phrases comprise a whole that is more than the sum of its parts. It is an expression of community, such as is characteristic of Clear Creek. The blues piece is anarchic and individualistic. Parts protrude rather than coalesce. On a subsequent cycle of the progression, Herbert changed it dramatically so that it was difficult to hear that the same very general structure underpinned it. Differences were more important than similarities. The blues piece is an expression of individuality such as is characteristic of blues culture.

I do not mean to imply with this discussion, however, that blues and gospel are mutually exclusive genres. As indicated above, while a concern for the separation between sacred and secular has long been central to a discussion of African American music, parallels between the genres and interchanges amongst them have also been the norm. Gospel typically employs all the pitch inflections of the blues scale and, indeed, the classic twelve-bar blues form.[12] What is important in this discussion is the philosophical importance of the perceived opposition between the two genres.

In a somewhat contradictory fashion to the juxtaposition of sacred and secular cited above, however, the members of Clear Creek M.B.C. perform the popular theme song from the movie "An Officer and a Gentleman," i.e., "Up Where We Belong," as a gospel song.[13] It is likely that this idea originated with the Jackson Southernaires (one of the most successful of the many black gospel quartets in Mississippi) who released it on their album "Made in Mississippi,"[14] as this is the style of music to which the members habitually listen and one of the groups that the singers most admire.[15] The singers believe that by changing the words from "Love lift us up" to "Lord lift us up" the feeling, character, and intent of the song have been changed. This "turnaround," facilitated by the fact that the melody, rhythm, and harmony of the song are not so distinctive or rigid that they are distinctly blues or pop, made the song acceptable for performance in church. It is instructive to note the musical changes that have been effected in the transformation of this song into a gospel piece, and to compare it with the gospel progression above. The original popular song, in D major, is set for a male/female duet, in call-and-response during the verse and harmonising together for the chorus. The opening (as recorded by Joe Cocker and Jennifer Warnes in 1982 for the movie soundtrack) sounds wistful and vulnerable rather than "soulful" as indicated at the beginning of the score. The tone becomes assertive at the build-up towards the chorus: synthesizer, drums, and other instruments are gradually added to the piano accompaniment starting at "The road" (m. 9), and the second and fourth beats of each measure are clearly accented.

At Clear Creek M.B.C. the song is sung in a much higher key—A-flat major as opposed to the original D major—and voiced in typical Soprano, Alto, Tenor (SAT) close harmonies of predominantly parallel sixths and thirds (see example 2.3). The tempo is also slowed considerably (from $\downarrow$ = 69, indicated on the original score, to $\downarrow$ = 60, which is the tempo used by the Jackson Southernaires on their recording). This slowing of tempo is an important characteristic of black performance style and will recur frequently throughout this discussion.[16] At Clear Creek M.B.C. in particular,

Example 2.3. "Up where we belong"/"Lord lift us up," performed as a gospel song by the Clear Creek singers.

Example 2.3, cont.

the members equate slowness and feeling. They contrast white performance of "Amazing Grace" which is relatively fast, regular, and
unadorned, with their very slow, elaborate and free performance of it in
Dr. Watts style, as an indication that white style is without feeling as well
as boring.[17]

The melody (of "Love lift us up") is not only varied, but is also highly
embellished, considerably more so than in the Jackson Southernaires' version, so that, although it is at the same tempo as the latter, many more
musical notes are fitted into each beat. The embellishment is typical of
gospel solo style (and of black soul singing; musical ties between sacred and
secular are, in fact, strong[18]): it is very fast, generally conjunct, and the range
of the melody is considerably extended. As sung at Clear Creek M.B.C.,

by a female trio, all of whom are gospel soloists, it is a beautiful example of gospel solo style. The melody moves between the first and second sopranos: the first soprano has it for most of the verse, (although at "There are mountains in our way," the second soprano takes the melody, but only for that line), the second soprano for the chorus, first soprano singing a descant. Another distinctive change is that the melody, and supportive vocal lines, are consistently syncopated, but in such a fashion as to give the feeling of a free-flowing melody, i.e., the syncopation of the melody gives it a feeling closer to the timelessness of the Dr. Watts lined hymns, rather than offsetting the meter in an accented fashion.

The chorus, which is far more regular rhythmically than the verse, is reminiscent of gospel chorus style: quite straight and relatively unadorned. There are, in effect, two juxtapositions of style in this new rendition, juxtapositions that are of primary importance and that will recur throughout this book. The first is that of gospel solo as opposed to gospel chorus style. The verse, although sung here in three-part harmony, is in solo style, embellished and free-flowing: the chorus, although for the same voices, is in gospel chorus style. This alternation of styles substitutes for alternation of voices in the original popular song, which latter is retained by the Jackson Southernaires. The call-and-response of the original, which is stylistically consistent with black performance style, is abandoned by the Clear Creek singers, as they do not adopt the small but essential textual modifications that the Jackson Southernaires made to the song. The latter made the song an address to the Lord by changing the opening line of the original, i.e., "You don't know what tomorrow brings" to "You alone know what tomorrow brings." Additionally, other smaller textual modifications such as changing "From the world we know, up where the clear winds blow" to "And from the world we'll go to where the clear winds blow" make the Jackson Southernaires' version more overtly religious.

The second juxtaposition of style, related to the first, is on the level of time. The verse portion of the song is so free-flowing in the Clear Creek rendition that the effect is of timelessness rather than of syncopated rhythm. The chorus, however, is clear in its articulation of meter, so that off-beat rhythms, where they occur, sound syncopated rather than timeless. These two ways of structuring time (free and regulated) are, I believe, crucial, and will be discussed further. Suffice it to say here that not only are both discrete and coexistent, but their juxtaposition within a song is not at all unusual in this community. Acceptance of these two opposed ways of ordering sound is characteristic of the flexibility of the community's worldview.

As might be expected from such an example of musical crossover, not all members of Clear Creek M.B.C. believe that it is necessary to avoid "devil's music" altogether. Some believe that it is not music that is evil, but rather its use and the behaviour that it promotes: it is the intimate connection between blues progressions and blues culture that makes those progressions evil. The symbiosis of sound and cultural context in this instance, rather than the sounds themselves, makes blues music devil's music. As ethnomusicologists continually assert, music sound cannot be adequately understood apart from its cultural and social context. It is the identification of one with the other that creates meaning. Gregory (Greg) Thompson (a young gospel pianist at Clear Creek M.B.C), feels that he can play blues music without adopting the negative qualities it may evoke.

> I'm too deeply rooted into my beliefs and I'm too deeply rooted into the Baptist tradition, and I'll serve God, and I know that if I do sing this music (blues), I'm singing the music and the music is not me. I'm a part of gospel music. I'm not a part of blues or jazz. I'm just singing that . . . I feel as long as I know where I'm going and have my thoughts in the right perspective, there's nothing wrong with me singing jazz music or blues music (Greg Thompson, interview, November 25, 1987).

Greg's open attitude is a reflection of his home background, for his father, Leroy Thompson, a deacon of the church, also emphasizes his security in his faith and his openness to different kinds of music:

> I have that music [blues] in my home. My thing is, it can be separated. I believe you can have something and it not be a part of you. I'm not afraid of my faith is what I guess I'm saying. There are people who won't talk to a Jehovah's Witness, or people who won't talk to a Muslim because "I don't want to listen to what he has." But I'm not afraid to because I feel I'm strong in what I believe in. I can listen to Aretha Franklin, I can listen to Patti LaBelle, but it doesn't have to become a part of me (interview, November 22, 1987).

This attitude parallels the members' view that they can go out into the world and mingle with sinners in order to convert them, and yet retain their sanctity. And as Charles Wilson eloquently remarks, "[T]he dynamic imperative of Southern Evangelicalism is converting the lost" (1995: 183). There is a difference between associating with sinners and coming around to their way of thinking; but a strong sense of identity and otherness is essential to accomplish this end.

> Christ Himself found Himself dealing mostly with sinners and Repub . . . ah, Publicans. "He that is whole need not a physician. I came not to call the righteous but sinners to repentance." So, if you mingle with the sinners and let your life-light be shone upon them and not theirs' upon you, then you may be able to win some of them over to Christ. But if you are not deeply rooted in the Scriptures and have not

been well cultivated, then you should not (Lee Earl Robinson, interview, November 17, 1986).

Mingling with the "other" is only safe as long as their category as "other" is firmly established and maintained. Because children generally do not have those categories firmly established, and because they have not generally been converted themselves before the age of twelve, it is not considered safe for them to put themselves in that position.

The Clear Creek M.B.C. is not, of course, an isolated community: in many ways it is characteristic of hundreds of such small, familial churches throughout the rural South. Nor is it unusual in this borrowing from the secular musical world. Despite the strong philosophical differences that fundamental Christians stress between the sacred and secular spheres, musically there are, in fact, strong affinities between them. To quote from Portia Maultsby once again, "[G]ospel music embraces many traditions and styles that extend from spirituals, hymns, and blues to contemporary jazz, pop, soul, disco and funk. [. . .] Perhaps the greatest secular influence on gospel has been various instrumental styles. Former blues and jazz musicians were among the first to become instrumentalists for gospel singers" (1985: 41–42).[19] Or, as Guthrie Ramsey succinctly points out:

Hybridity has clearly shaped the religious realm. Thomas Dorsey's mix of blues and gospel in the 1920s and 1930s; Rosetta Tharpe's blend of jazz and gospel during the 1940s; Edwin Hawkin's and Andre Crouch's pop-gospel of the late 1960s; and the Winanses' smooth-soul gospel of the 1980s were all seen as hybrid—and quite controversial—expressions in their day. Few social or musical boundaries have been considered too contentious to cross in black religious music's quest for expressive resources. This tendency for hybridity links gospel to the larger world of black diasporic religious practices to which it belongs (2003: 191).

The huge popularity of black music in the 1960s saw some of the most promising young gospel talents leave the church to seek fame and fortune as secular pop singers. As Don Cusic remarks "Sam Cooke, Aretha Franklin, Lou Rawls, Wilson Pickett, and Dionne Warwick departed from the ranks of the faithful and went on to shape the burgeoning soul music movement. The gradual secularisation of black urban populations during this period, coupled with the growing numbers of young white listeners who avidly embraced black styles, created a huge pool of consumers who demanded black pop music but showed little interest in gospel" (1990: 7). Gradually also modernists who remained "within the fold" (Andrae Crouch is one who comes immediately to mind) began to adopt the innovations of the popular world. Yet because of the enduring tension between the sacred and secular spheres, artists were (and are still) generally "forced" to choose one affiliation or the other, and successful borrowings from the secular into the sacred, while not altogether unusual, are nonetheless not commonplace.[20]

Saints versus Sinners

The psalm that is the Call to Worship on most Sundays at Clear Creek M.B.C., reinforces the opposition between the sacred and the secular, between saints and sinners.

> Blessed is the man that walketh not in the counsel of the ungodly, nor standeth in the way of sinners, nor sitteth in the seat of the scornful.
>
> But his delight is in the law of the Lord, and in His law doth he meditate day and night.
>
> And he shall be like a tree planted by the rivers of water, that bringeth forth his fruit in his season; his leaf also shall not wither; and whatsoever he doeth shall prosper.
>
> The ungodly are not so; but are like the chaff which the wind driveth away.
>
> Therefore the ungodly shall not stand in the judgement, nor sinners in the congregation of the righteous.
>
> For the Lord knoweth the way of the righteous: but the way of the ungodly shall perish (Psalms 1:1–6).

While the opening lines of this passage seem to warn against contact with the sinner, members believe that what is being condemned is not contact with sinners but going over to their ways—walking in their counsel, standing in the way of sinners, sitting in the seat of the scornful.

Given the power of the basic opposition which most fundamentalist Christians posit between sinner and saint, it is to be expected that the transition from childhood to being born again will be marked by a crisis, and celebrated by a rite of passage.[21] This is indeed what happens: the crisis is the conversion experience, and the rite of passage, baptism.[22]

A general outline of the conversion experience, as gleaned from the literature, is of interest here.[23] The conversion experience is often, although not always, preceded by a state of wretchedness. The individual perceives himself to be worthless, submerged in sin, beyond recourse. This state is often termed "being under conviction." With conversion comes tranquillity, acceptance, peace, surrender. The individual often has a new and marked clarity of vision concerning existence and the existential self. Outward appearances seem changed so that there is a sense of newness about everything. Some individuals see luminous visions similar to Saint Paul's on the Damascus road (Acts 9:3–9, 22:6–11).

The convert is overwhelmed with happiness, so intense that frequently its only outlet is in tears, also in embracing those nearby. However much or little conversion thereafter affects an individual's life, the impact of the experience is dramatic, and most converts seem to retain a clear and detailed memory of the experience. This account of conversion is consistent with accounts from the Great Awakenings in the nineteenth century, when the Baptists converted more black people than any other denomination. The Baptists still retain the largest number of black Christians as members, particularly so in Mississippi.[24]

None of the members of Clear Creek M.B.C. with whom I talked dwelt at all upon their wretchedness prior to conversion. Most of them simply presented a decision to accept Christ as their personal saviour.

> It's whenever you decide. . . . It's whenever you feel that now's the time for me to make a change in my life. I know that there's one day I'm goin' have to answer to Somebody, and I need now to make a change in my life (Gregory Thompson, interview, November 25, 1987).

"Well, I just decided that it was time for me to go on and accept Christ before my life was over" (Pam Thompson, interview November 22, 1987). Pam was twelve years old when she made this statement.

This decision or change of mind sets the stage, as it were. The conversion experience itself is marked by a new certainty and peace, but above all an overwhelming sense of joy, "a good feeling."

> It was just a feeling, just like I was not moving myself. I got up and I walked off the bench and I shook his (the pastor's) hand and I was cryin'.[25] I remember I was cryin'. It was just a feeling of gladness it was a good feelin'. It's something that you really can't describe (Gregory Thompson, interview, November 25, 1987).

The feeling is embedded in what is usually a very specific and detailed description of external reality as it was at the time. It is as if the heightened emotional state has frozen the scene in time. As an illustration, I quote in full here an account Rochelle Thompson gave me of her conversion.[26]

> It was in 1971. I was in the house. My grandmother was singing the song that she usually sings every year, "Come on Mourners to the Army of the Lord." She only sings it at revival. I was nine years old and it was in June. My grandmother's a very religious person and she just sings whatever she feels. And she was just singing, and I was sewing when I was nine. I was sewing a pair of pants. Because I had to

learn how to sew. You know I can't get all the clothes that I want to. My grandmother sews a whole lot. She just began to sing the song and I was just sitting there listening and, it just happened. You just have this funny feeling here [she indicates her heart]. It's just a tingling all over. You get this funny feeling in you heart; you just get this feeling all over. And it's a really good feeling of course. And I just got the feeling, and it just happened, you know (Rochelle Thompson, interview, November 23, 1987).

When I asked Rochelle how she knew what the feeling was, she replied without hesitation. "I had been told you know, what it feels like. My pastor, he preaches that all the time. And I knew what it was and it just happened" (ibid.).

One significant variation in the personal accounts that the church members told me of their conversion came from Lee Earl Robinson, a deacon of the church and Superintendent of the Sunday School. (I talked frequently with Lee, as I found him to be a thoughtful and articulate informant. He is held in high esteem by both the pastor and the church membership, and he seems to reflect frequently on religious questions.) Where everyone else with whom I talked narrated as one continuous event the decision to dedicate his/her life to God and the resultant conversion experience, Lee separated them very deliberately in time and space as two distinct events. The feelings of intense joy predominant in the accounts of the other church members are not present in Lee's account of his conversion. These occurred a full year later when he first received the Holy Spirit.

I was converted probably a year before I received the Holy Spirit. Conversion is a change of mind. Receiving the Holy Spirit is the power of Jesus comin' in. A person cannot receive the Holy Spirit unless he is converted. My conversion came with age and a little bit of knowledge. A growth process: day by day, little by little, I wanted to be more and more like Christ, to do the things like He does for us, to help peoples to love one another, and to be able to forgive my enemies and help each other along the way. And then after I decided that I wanted to live like Christ, then I prayed and I tarried for the Holy Spirit (Lee Earl Robinson, interview, November 11, 1987).

What Lee describes as his conversion parallels the "decision" recounted by other church members to dedicate one's life to God that immediately precedes the joyful feelings associated with the coming of the Holy Spirit. Lee's account of first receiving the Holy Spirit closely parallels the typical account of the conversion experience. It is significant that in this account Lee is the only member to refer to the characteristic newness generally considered typical of the awakening. Lee's conversion occurred, as do most, during revival, during the first night of revival services, which continue every night for five days. Service started at 9.30 p.m., two hours later than it does now, because farm work, in which most of the members were involved, had first to be completed.

> I received the Holy Spirit in church. I used to walk to church. One Monday they was havin' a evangelistic service goin' down there. I was already converted, but under the traditional things at that time you see, prayer services and so forth was not offered because it was a time when we lived mostly off the farm. . . . And I was down there at the church. I guess they was singin' and prayin' and doin' the usual things, but my mind at that time was not on the things that was goin' on in there. My mind was on bein' saved. And there was a certain transition that came about, and I can, I think when I last recall my action, of me deeply meditatin', it was something like about 10.30 p.m. There was a transition or somethin' that came over me and I don't remember or recall any particular things goin' on until about thirty minutes later. Whether I was layin' out on the floor kickin' or goin' on or somethin', I don't know. But that was a particular thing that came over me and the joy or the excitement in which the Holy Spirit filled me seemed to have overcome my consciousness. And when I returned to myself my eyes were filled with tears of joy and there was a newness or difference in the way I really view life or how I looked upon people. Not physically different, but spiritually difference [*sic*]. And all the things in which, from that point on, which I had developed or had a negativeness about, I was always able to see, and still is able to see, a positiveness, a side about anything. And right now, and I still feel there is nothing in the world that is really bad (ibid.).

As can be seen in this account of the coming of the Holy Spirit, the beliefs of the Clear Creek members include some that are closer to Pentecostal than to Baptist doctrine. Many, if not most of the church members, were converted during revival. The church holds two revivals, in April and August. Services are held every weekday night for a week, and one guest preacher usually preaches throughout. There is such a strong expectation that there will be converts during revival that potential converts are given a special place in the church.

> During the revival in traditional time, and it still happen at Clear Creek, we reserve the first two pews, and we call those the Seeker's Seat (Mourner's Bench). Those of them who desire prayer of the church, hoping that they would at that time receive the Holy Spirit [sit there]. Or any of children who twelve and haven't converted (ibid).

Revival is a very special time of community. It reinforces the collective identity of the saved and at the same time usually brings new members into the fold. Conversion is at its core, for it is the crisis of conversion that is the critical boundary marker between saints and sinners. Reverend McKinney, pastor of Clear Creek M.B.C., explained it to me thus. "If they been born again, the time will come when they'll come back to the Lord. But if you haven't been born again, you ain't got nothing to bring you back" (interview, November 17, 1986). He is quick to fault those who do not believe that one must be born again of the Holy Spirit (converted) and stresses its critical importance.

> But some of us don't believe that now. Yeah, even some Baptists. They think it's folkalism. A lot of them believe now that I could just sit and the Spirit does nothing, and I just get up and join the church and I'm saved. But that won't work! You remember Paul said on one occasion that when he was talking to some of the mens [*sic*] that was baptised by John the Baptist, and he said, "Have you received the Holy Ghost as you believed?" And they said no, they hadn't even heard of it. And this is dangerous ground to be on! They had took the baptism under John the Baptist but they had not received the Holy Spirit. So, you cannot have salvation without the Holy Spirit having active role in our lives. Now, according to my understanding—and I don't have to be right. I don't claim to know everything—when Christ left, according to the Bible, and on the tenth day of Pentecost the Holy Spirit was poured out to all believers. And the Holy Spirit is in action now, and there's no way to be saved unless the Holy Spirit comes and abode in the seat of your mind. I like to say it like that, because sometime we get mixed up and get to patting up there [pats chest] and this thing don't do anything but pump blood. It [the Holy Spirit] works with the seat of your mind. So you must be born by the spirit of God to be saved (Rev. Grady McKinney, ibid).

As I observed it, music functions during revival both to nudge potential converts towards conversion and to reinforce the solidarity of the Christian community. Until Friday night there is nothing but unaccompanied congregational singing. From the time of the slaves' first encounter with Christianity in the camp meetings of the eighteenth century, communal singing has been at the heart of the African American religious experience. As noted by religious historian Milton G. Sernett "the communal song, not catechetics, has been the principal hermeneutic of the African-American religious experience" (1991: 135). Without choir or accompanist to lead them, the members must rely on each other. The near symbiosis that results is powerful. This is readily understood if one pictures a small church, finished entirely in wood inside (floor, walls, and ceiling), and the resonance that this gives when the church is filled and everyone is singing out strongly and with spirit (see figure 9, p. 22). The effect is described by Gregory Thompson from his own conversion experience.

> During revival it's really no piano. It's just everybody blending in their voices and uniting. And I guess that's what make the whole service so powerful. And when they come into that lil' pool there, they stand, and everybody's standin' up singing, and everybody's united; it's just so much, I guess, fire there, I don't see how anybody could set on that bench when I came off. . . . It was about eight of us on that bench and I believe about seven of us came off that night, People were cryin' and shoutin' everywhere. It really was real powerful (Gregory Thompson, interview, November 25, 1987).

During revival, after the preaching, all attending preachers, the deacons, and the mothers of the church come down and stand in a semicircle around the Mourners' Bench. This is the "lil' pool" to which Greg is referring above. All the members also stand and everyone sings. All energy and attention is focused on the mourners. The "shout" mentioned is one kind of behaviour which is characteristic of the Holy Spirit's possession of an individual. During the shout the person seems to lose control over his body. Usually he/she will fling his/her arms about and shake, and the effect is often so violent that the ushers try to hold the person down to prevent him/her from hurting him/herself or those in the immediate vicinity.

"And then he dips them"

If the conversion experience is what separates the lost from the saved and reinforces community identity and integration, baptism is the ritualisation of this event for the community and for the outside world.[27] The members distinguish between a sinner and a child who has not yet reached the age of reason. While neither has accepted Christ and been saved, the former is responsible for his condition, but the latter is not.

> To a child who has never committed any sin, there is no sin to be forgiven. As a child, until he reach that ripe age of understanding, you are responsible for that child. Because if you don't teach that child, if that child should happen to die and you haven't taught him anything, then that child's sin is upon you. . . . I do not believe that even from a newborn, that God will condemn him to Hell (Lee Earl Robinson, interview, November 17, 1986).

The whole passage from lost to saved can be seen as a tripartite rite of initiation paralleling initiation into totem groups amongst Australian peoples described by Arnold Van Gennep (1960: 74–75), for example. The congregation of seekers or potential converts on the Mourner's Bench dramatises the initial period of separation: it is the rite of separation (ibid: 11). Admission of the new convert to "all rights and privileges of the church," is the positive holding stage. This is the transition stage (ibid: 11). And baptism is the final act, the religious ceremony, the rite of incorporation (ibid: 11).[28]

At Clear Creek M.B.C., baptism is usually performed only once annually. There are two reasons for this: first, it is traditional in this church that baptism is always followed by worship service. Because the church has only a part-time pastor, worship service is held only once a month: as scholars have repeatedly noted, this is not an unusual situation, particularly in the rural South. (There is also a Communion service on the evenings of the first and third Sundays.) This effectively limits to twelve the suitable occasions in any one year. Second and more important perhaps, the church has no baptismal pool. Whereas some of the members, the younger ones especially, would like to have a baptismal pool in the church, others oppose it. "I just don't like pools in church. It may be all right. Don't like it because we have no Scriptoral uses where it was carried on in those days. It's too immodest. That's why I just don't like it" (Mr. Charles Campbell, interview, November 20, 1986). Because baptism must be by immersion, i.e., the whole body must be submerged in water, the members must usually use some outdoor pond. Baptisms, therefore, cannot take place in cold weather.

The annual baptism at Clear Creek M.B.C. is generally on the first Sunday following summer revival, as revival usually yields the majority of converts for a particular year. This precise scheduling is characteristic of Clear Creek M.B.C.: it is not the case at Main St. Baptist Church in Lexington, Kentucky, for example, where a pool is always available within the church building. Many Baptist churches have their pool underneath the raised platform where the podium is located. Second Baptist in Oxford, Miss., is typical in this respect. If a person comes forward during the Altar Call (which follows the sermon), the pastor, Rev. Leroy Wadlington, may perform a baptism immediately. While he and the convert change out of their Sunday best into older clothes, the deacons remove some of the boards in the platform and the pool is revealed. (Several sets of old pants and tops are kept in the church offices so that baptism may be performed immediately following conversion. It is immaterial whether or not the clothes fit well as long as they are not immodest). At Main St. Baptist Church in Lexington, Ky., however, which, as I have mentioned, is a large, affluent church, the pool is in a separate chamber set into the wall of the church behind the podium, about midway between the platform and the ceiling of the church. Most of the front wall of the chamber is glass so that everyone in the congregation can observe the ceremony (see figures 11 and 12).

In situations described above, baptism can, of course, be performed at any time. At Clear Creek Missionary Baptist Church, however, such is not the case, and, in general, anybody who converts at a time other than summer revival must wait until the annual baptism after revival to be baptised. (The convert is sometimes baptised at another church if a baptism is held there during this time, but this is an unusual occurrence.)

Although baptism is an important ritual for the church community, many members perceive its importance as secondary to the conversion experience.[29] One of the deacons expressed this opinion thus: "To us, baptism isn't the saving factor, conversion is. Baptism is the ritualisation which Jesus done and which He required of us" (Lee Earl Robinson, interview, November 11, 1987). Given this and the necessity of trekking across an overgrown field to reach the pool, attendance at the ceremony is not as large as one might expect. The baptismal candidates dress in old clothes, typically jeans, a T-shirt, and sneakers, and the girls (and sometimes the boys too) cover their heads to prevent their hair from getting wet.

Figure 11. Baptism at Main Street Baptist church in Lexington, Ky. The Baptismal pool is in a separate chamber set into the wall of the church behind the podium, about mid-way between the platform and the ceiling of the church.

Figure 12. Most of the front wall of the chamber is glass so that everyone in the congregation can observe the baptism ceremony.

> I was baptised in the mud. You wear something that you don't mind getting wet, like bluejeans, tennis shoes and a T-shirt; something that you don't mind getting dirty and muddy. I had plastic towels and everything on my hair. I said no, I would not get my hair wet. I had just had it done (Rochelle Thompson, interview, November 23, 1987).

Pamela Thompson, who was baptised in the church pool at Second Baptist, dressed in a similar fashion. "We wore jeans and a long-sleeved shirt, and something over your head, 'cause you really didn't want your hair to get wet. The water was real cold" (interview, November 22, 1987). Pam was pleased not to have been baptised in an outdoor pool because "you have all that slime and stuff down there" (ibid).

In the summer of 1987 the church moved the baptism from where it had traditionally been held at the "Patton pool"—a pool that belongs to Rochelle's grandmother and her siblings—to a pool of their neighbour Hewitt Mullins, because the Patton pool was considered unsafe (see figure 13).

> Because, it's snakes in the water. And I said "uh-uh, I'm not goin' nowhere near that pool!" And the pastor was saying, "Well, it's slick," you know, it's real slick!" And they were afraid, you know, that a snake might come and wrap around someone's leg, and afraid they might slip

Figure 13. The Baptismal pool for Clear Creek Missionary Baptist church.

off the bottom of the pool. I was told there was water moccasins [deadly venomous snakes] in that thing (Rochelle Thompson, interview, November 23, 1987).

Baptism is scheduled in the place of Sunday school on the particular Sunday, i.e., at nine-thirty a.m.; afterwards the members proceed directly to church. Everyone but the officiating deacons and pastor, therefore, is dressed in his Sunday best, attire not altogether suitable for tramping across the fields.

Those of us who have been baptised, we go in dresses and heels, like I did this year, of course tearing up stockings and scuffing up shoes. We just kind of gather up on the other side [of the pool]. And once you get over there and then they start, sing the traditional song which is "Take Me to the Water" (ibid).

The members sing two verses of the song, which are repeated as long as the baptism lasts. (See example 2.4 for a transcription of the members' rendition of this song). This is how Rochelle describes the ceremony:

Pastor McKinney goes down in the pool, him and about two or three other deacons, so when he dips them, if they slip, they won't fall. (Because my foot slipped off the bottom.) Pastor McKinney, he stands out in the water, and the deacons, they assist the person back to the

♩.=64

Take me to___ the wa - - - - ter. Take me to the___

wa - - - - - - - ter. Take me to the

wa - - - - ter___ to be bap - tised.

No - thing but___ the right - - - - - - teous,

no - thing but the___ right - - - - - teous,___

no - thing but the righ - - - teous shall see___ God.

= slide up to note

= glissando between two pitches

= pitch lower than notated

Example 2.4. "Take me to the water," the hymn that accompanies Baptism, as performed by the Clear Creek M.B.C. congregation.

> bank, and then they bring the next one in [. . .] Pastor McKinney he says (it's in the Bible, of course), he says, "Obedience to the great head of the church. I baptise thee my brother or sister in the name of the Father, Son, and Holy Ghost," and then he dips them (ibid).

Since Baptist churches are independent churches (which trace their history to the unlawful dissenters who founded the denomination, and thus place a high premium on religious freedom[30]), the ritual of baptism differs from church to church.[31]

To me it seems—and I could be wrong, and I always pray for understanding and I pray that if I'm found wrong that God will not hold these things against me—to me it seems, and I'm sure it seems the same way with any other synagogue, to me it seems the Baptists have the most liberal religion of all.[32] We are not governed by any organization. Baptist churches are independent churches. The Convention is a place where we are brought together and taught different concepts, but the statement is always made that these things may not work in you synagogue. [. . .] They don't teach you that you should do this or you should do that because Baptists try mostly to govern themselves. I would like to see our synagogues mostly governing themselves by the guidelines which Christ has laid down for us (Lee Earl Robinson, interview, November 17, 1986).

At Main St. Baptist Church, baptism is usually incorporated into the service, either at the beginning, or occasionally after the Altar Call, if someone has come forward and the spirit is strong in the church. The traditional song at Main St. is the spiritual "Wade in the Water," and in similar fashion, the refrain of the song, sung by the congregation, is repeated as long as the baptism lasts. The congregation sings the song in compound time (12/8), rather than the simple time (4/8) given in the hymnal (see example 2.5). This "compounding" of time found in many African American Baptist churches, is generally used for slow songs, sometimes for faster ones. It makes for greater rhythmic interest and it is significant that the "twos" of simple time are also retained along with the "threes" of compound time (see m. 4), as the incorporation of both additionally engages the listener. This two versus three ambiguity, sometimes referred to as horizontal hemiola, typical of much African American music, is generally thought to be an African retention (Lazarus Ekwueme, 1974; Wendell Logan, 1984; Richard Waterman, 1952; Olly Wilson, 1974).
The congregation stops singing while the Pastor, Rev. Benjamin Baker, pronounces the baptismal formula.

We come this morning in obedience to our Lord's command to "Go ye therefore unto all the world, to baptise all nations and teach them to

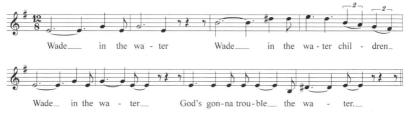

Example 2.5. "Wade in the water," "compounded" by the Main Street Baptist Church congregation.

observe all things." I baptise now this my brother/sister, upon the confession of his/her faith in Jesus as the Christ, in the name of the Father, the name of the Son, and the name of the Holy Spirit. Amen.

The congregation resumes the song once the pastor stops speaking.

It is significant that with the ritualisation of the rite of passage, Baptism, at this time of incorporation into the community, the singing is congregational, unaccompanied (at Clear Creek M.B.C.), and at most, sparsely and informally harmonised, for it affirms in action what the members told me about the power of this type of music. It is just this kind of music that musician Greg Thompson characterised as moving, powerful, and especially, as a uniting force for the community. Such uniting power is critical at this moment of integration of a new member. If successfully accomplished, the incorporation of a new member strengthens the unity and identity of the group. If imperfectly realised, however, the new addition (for in this case that is what the newcomer remains: he is added to, but not integrated into the group) disrupts the unity and integrity of the group. The type of music described above functions in the final stage of this rite of passage to reinforce community solidarity, thereby also reinforcing separation from outsiders as the community's boundary is more clearly and tightly drawn.

3

Concepts of Time

"Total good aspect comes from the Lord"
"We not in charge of time"
 —Members of the Clear Creek M.B.C.

"Only children live in the present while the mature live simultaneously in the past, present, and future. The sense of identity, of self comprehensibility, is thus dependent upon this experience of temporal continuity"
 —Michael Kearl, 1983: 159

How we conceive of time, the degree to which we try to measure and control it, says a lot about our approach to life, how we perceive our identity. Time, after all, is the one certainty that life offers us: our life is the time-space between our birth and our death. We know our starting point, but very few of us have any clear indication of our finishing point. At various stages or periods in our lives, we perceive time to be dragging, at others, running. To give ourselves the illusion of control, we monitor time, we measure it in quantifiable amounts and schedule our waking and our sleeping, our work and our play, our coming and our going. We move the whole system forward in spring and back again in autumn, arbitrarily assigning numbers to hours of daylight and darkness. As Michael Kearl asserts "Individuals and social systems are alike in that both seek continuity, and hence identity and meaning, through selective recollections. There are personal and collective rituals for forgetting and remembering" (1983: 159). Passing time is the reality of our lives. How we confront this issue goes a long way towards determining our worldview.

Southerners are generally regarded by northeasterners, at least, as being slow-moving, "laid back," and virtually always late. Such generalised stereotypes, while hardly to be embraced, carry some grain of truth. One New Yorker who moved to Mississippi several years ago gave me the following advice: "Always go thirty to forty minutes late, and you'll likely be right on time." Time does seem to pass more slowly in Mississippi. There is time to stop and talk with friends and strangers, time to slow-cook a turkey for twelve hours for a special barbecue, time to sit by the creek and fish on weekends or long summer evenings, time to watch and listen.

As I became more familiar with the community of Clear Creek M.B.C., I perceived them interacting with time on three different levels. These I have designated existential, social, and musical time. I have chosen not to explore a potential fourth area, that of work or job time, for several reasons. First, most of the members now work outside of their community and in the larger white community. This work/job time, therefore, is not a community experience; the members refer to it specifically as "going out into the world." Second, for many of the members, their job is what earns them sufficient money to survive and be relatively comfortable, but it is not necessarily a part of themselves. (This, of course, parallels their compartmentalization of "devil's music," as discussed in chapter 2.) That which intrudes into the members lives, but of which they do not approve, or that which they choose to incorporate, but do not necessarily embrace, they put aside from the core which they consider to be themselves. While on the job, they perceive themselves as working for "the man" (a common African American usage denoting the white power structure), and although they believe in working hard and doing the best that one can, this does not mean that they identify with the work or with the system. As I listened to different individuals, they spoke as though they shift into a different mode when they go out to work, relaxing again into the community when they come home.

These designations of specific kinds of time are, of course, my analytical framework, not those of the church members. They believe that all time is God's time, and regard that fact as central to their lives. I selected the categories, however, as an efficient way of "capturing" time for the purposes of analysis.

"When we sing the lazy tune . . ."

Sunday morning service at Clear Creek M.B.C. accommodates a tremendous range of musical styles, the two most dissimilar being lined hymns and gospel pieces. The lined hymns, or "Dr. Watts" (so called after the most famous and prolific author of the same, Dr. Isaac Watts, 1674–1748), are a tradition brought to North America by the English immigrants in the seventeenth century.[1] They have their origins in the Psalters (books of Psalms set to music) of the Calvinist churches of the sixteenth century. The Calvinists generally distrusted the adornment of services with music, and specifically forbade their members to sing texts not found in the Bible. The Psalms from the Psalters were originally sung in unison and unaccompanied in church services. As Donald Grout and Claude Palisca note, the French Psalter influenced

> the most important English Psalter of the sixteenth century, that of Sternhold and Hopkins (1562), and was even more influential for

the Scottish Psalter of 1564. A combination of the English and the French-Dutch traditions, embodied in the Psalter brought out by Henry Ainsworth in 1612 for the use of the English separatists in Holland, was brought to New England by the Pilgrims in 1620, and remained in use many years after the appearance of the first American Psalter, the Bay Psalm Book of 1640 (1988: 316–17).

It was with the rise of Presbyterianism, however, that a new technique called "lining out" was introduced. As described by Nicholas Temperly:

> The Westminster Assembly of Divines, set up by Parliament in 1644, published *A Directory for the Publique Worship of God Throughout the Three Kingdoms of England, Scotland, and Ireland* (London, 1644), which included a section "Of Singing of Psalms":
>
>> That the whole congregation may joyne herein, every one that can reade is to have a Psalme book, and all others not disabled by age, or otherwise, are to be exhorted to learn to reade. But for the present, where many in the Congregation cannot read, it is convenient that the Minister, or some other fit person appointed by him and the other Ruling Officers, do reade the Psalme, line by line, before the singing thereof.
>
> It is clear that this reform had nothing to do with music. [. . .] Its avowed object was [. . .] making sure that the people heard, understood, and sang the biblical words (1981: 532–33).

The settlers who landed in Jamestown, Virginia, in 1607 brought with them the *Este psalter*, and perhaps some copies of the *Old version Sternhold and Hopkins psalter*. After the publication of the *Bay Psalm Book*, lining out was quickly introduced in the Northeast, and "it was defended by J. Cotton (one of the editors of the *Bay Psalm Book*) in 1647" (ibid: 533). The Watts psalter was first published in England in 1719, and the first American edition in 1729. It was, however, Watts' *Hymns and Spiritual Songs* (England, 1707, and Boston, 1739), that ensured Watts' popularity and saw his hymns introduced into the devotions of American Protestants (see Don Cusic, 1990: 19–25).

Lining out has survived "among two kinds of people in the United States, among certain Baptists in Appalachia, particularly eastern Kentucky, and among black Baptists and some Methodists throughout the country. Because of immigrants from the South and from Appalachia, the white lining out can be heard in Indiana, Ohio, and Michigan, and the black lining is found throughout the country [i.e., the United States] wherever there are black Baptist congregations" (Terry Miller, 1987). The practise of lining out seems to have arisen in response to two problems facing church congregations in the seventeenth century. First, hymnbooks were scarce and it was not possible for everyone to see the text. Second, much of the congregation was illiterate and would not have been able to read the text had sufficient books been available. A leader would, therefore, line out the song one line at a time, the congregation singing each line after him in call-and-response fashion. Now, even with hymn-books and literacy, the style continues as a tradition among black Baptists and others.

At Clear Creek M.B.C. and in most black Baptist churches I have visited, lined hymns are usually sung during the Devotion, which comes at the beginning of the service, is usually led by the deacons; it consists of alternating spontaneous prayers and songs. One deacon (at Clear Creek M.B.C., Lee Earl Robinson) usually begins the Devotion by calling up a song in which the congregation joins. The Dr. Watts are composed of rhyming couplets that form the musical and textual unit.

> Father I stretch my hand to thee, No other help I know
> If thou withdraw thyself from me, Whither shall I go?

As each couplet is self-contained, the song may continue for as long as the leader knows, or wishes to compose text. The leader always signals the final couplet by rising to his feet, followed by the congregation.[2] When I questioned the members as to how this tradition arose, none that I asked could explain it. Their responses typically posited tradition as an adequate explanation.

The structure of the Dr. Watts incorporates a call-and-response (leader and congregation) within a call-and-response (the first line of the couplet answered by the second). Call-and-response is, of course, common in African American music (see, for example, William Tallmadge, 1986), and is generally agreed to be a West African retention. When other hymns are called up during the Devotion, they too are shaped in the above fashion, so that on the final chorus (in the usual verse-chorus structure) the person who has called up the hymn stands and the congregation follows suit. When the hymn is finished everybody sits down and someone, usually a deacon, kneels and starts a prayer. At the conclusion of his prayer, the deacon who is leading the Devotion, or perhaps someone else, will call up the next song. Because music of worship is considered to be "a ministry through song" (be it congregational singing, a gospel chorus, or an a cappella quartet), it is important that participants and audience be seen to respond to the music.[3]

> Normally when I'm doing Devotion, the songs or things they come to me according to the way I feel. As far as me outlining which songs I'm goin' to sing next and next and next, I don't do that. The songs I try

to sing, if I am doin' it on my own—and sometimes when people come in, they just help, and sometime they sing a song it's not on my mind to do right then—it's just, I have an initial song I start with, and all the others come with the way I feel, and I just gradually move into it. If the first song I sing the peoples not responding to it, then I'll try to move to change the tempo to something else. Usually if the congregation joins in with you and sing fluently with you, then you know that they are with you, and if they're not, you change to something else (Lee Earl Robinson, interview, November 21, 1987).

Although lined hymns are most typically called up during the Devotion, they may be called up during other parts of the service, sometimes after the sermon. Unlike other songs, they are never strictly "scheduled": I have never seen a lined hymn mentioned in the service bulletin, nor, in my experience, has one ever been called up where a "selection" is indicated in the bulletin. As currently performed a cappella by black church congregations in northeast Mississippi, the repetition of each line of the hymns is considerably elaborated, drawn out in mellismatic chant fashion. On the elaborated lines the hymns have no leader or conductor. Their articulation is a consensus of the congregation. While melismas are generally agreed upon (as to their placing, but not their shape), and the contour of each line is understood, the shape is a flexible one that fades and blurs more than it crystallises. The rendition is heterophonic. The music, while it flows in certain directions, lacks clear metric organisation.

This is important: for it is the only music I have heard in these churches that has no readily identifiable beat. (Even prayer and sermon chant become quite regular and punctuated.) On this point, my findings are opposed to those of Ben Bailey who states: "A superficial listening to the lined hymns may lead to the erroneous conclusion, because of the extremely slow tempo, that the songs are unmetrical. Deeper study reveals, however, that there is a steady pulse which, once established, is likely to be unerringly maintained" (1978: 6). For Clear Creek M.B.C. and other black Baptist churches in this area of Mississippi, I have not found this to be so. It is significant that the church members also regard the lined hymns as unmetrical. "The Dr. Watts are not a tempo or beat song. It's a kind of meditation hymn" (Lee Earl Robinson, interview, November 21, 1987). The rendition of the hymns by these churches is also different metrically from the type of lining out described by Joy Driskell Baklanoff in regard to black Primitive Baptist congregations (1987: 381–94) and my transcription reflects that difference (see example 6). Although there is often overlap between the leader's call and the congregation's response, I have notated the two separately. I elected to do this for two reasons: because the extent of this overlap is not consistent, and because the components are clearer this way. I have transcribed the opening couplet of this hymn as it is representative of subsequent couplets.

The hymns described by Baklanoff are clearly metered. "All songs performed during the foot-washing ritual range from slow ($\quarternote$ = 60) to very slow ($\quarternote$ = 40) in tempo. A strict steady pulse is maintained throughout the singing" (ibid.: 386). While I could attribute approximate time values to specific pitches, the values are precisely that, approximate, and should be interpreted thus. I could not justify, in this case, imposing the structure of bar lines, for they carry too many strictures of meter. Stresses are "naturally" indicated, almost invariably, by long notes. Baklanoff's description of the singing style, however, closely parallels that of the Clear Creek M.B.C. community.

> Each individual sings his or her version of the melody, sometimes an octave lower or higher than the leader. . . . The highly mellismatic melody frequently contains improvised embellishments. The group produces sounds with a relaxed glottal region and a relatively wide opening of the glottis. This results in a considerable amount of resonance and richness (ibid.: 385).

It is the amorphous nature of the rendition that gives the Dr. Watts their beauty and power, their slow but not "draggy" movement (this is an important distinction), that lends itself to individual expression (see example 3.1). This issue of meter in the Dr. Watts is critical, for not only does it point to a particular and very free way of conceptualising musical time (as well as a certain relinquishing of control), which also carries over into other areas of the members' lives, but the essence of the unmetered, heterophonic singing is imbued with significant meaning by at least some of the members.

> I guess it may have to do with culture. All of our's way of doing has a two-fold culture in which to take from; part of it is American and part of it is things that were brought over from Africa, just kind of mixed together. And from the mixture of our culture, tends to form probably a lot of things that other people are unable to relate to. Also the negro spiritual songs, the black gospel songs years ago, used to carry a message, and those messages at that time were foreign to the white slave owners, and they understood them not. So that may be another cause why the songs are sung in a babble-type form. To us as black Americans, and to us who was brought up with a lot more, or bein' reared in a lot more of a black atmosphere until the sixties, 'til the total integration caused us to try to change to the American white culture, many things at that time was probably strange to the white man, but for those of us who come up before that time, still understands [sic] and

appreciate the true value of what black culture was all about. When we sing the lazy tune, the people from without us (that's not within us), become bored of the way it's bein' sung and think that there's not anything bein' said in it.[4] But there's a lot (Lee Earl Robinson, interview, November 21, 1987).

Example 3.1. Dr. Watts Hymn, "I love the Lord," lined out by Deacon Lee Earl Robinson and elaborated by the Clear Creek M.B.C. congregation. (See CD track 1.[5])

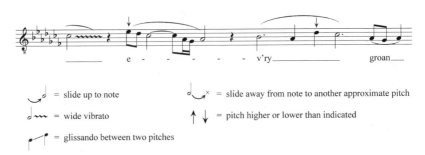

Example 3.1, cont.

This thought is echoed by Greg Thompson, and again the parallel is drawn with spirituals used as code songs during slavery.

> That's Dr. Watts. I think he's long gone. . . . But all of his tunes, there was a meaning. He gave like, there was a story through all of his songs. . . . It's something about the words in the songs that makes you think. . . . And just like the songs that the slaves used to sing, there were always messages. They used to sing songs to people because the slave owners wouldn't let them talk to each other. So they used to sing songs to tell them to "meet us down under the hall tonight. We goin' try to escape." It was a song that they could sing (interview, November 25, 1987).

The style of the lined hymns as currently performed by the Clear Creek M.B.C. community is, moreover, strikingly similar to this description of the style of performance of secular songs performed by slaves, quoted by Dena J. Epstein (1977: 169–70).

> A line was sung by a leader, then all joined in a short chorus; then came another [improvised] solo line, and another short chorus, followed by a longer chorus. . . . Little regard was paid to rhyme, and hardly any to the number of syllables in a line; they condensed four or five into one foot, or stretched out one to occupy the space that should have been filled with four or five; yet they never spoiled the tune (quoted in Portia Maultsby, 1990: 198).

Lined hymns are part of the tradition of Clear Creek M.B.C., even young members see them as powerful. Twelve-year-old Pamela Thompson told me that these songs were special: "They kind of pick up the Spirit" (interview, November 22, 1987). The Dr. Watts are not taught to the choir or congregation; rather they are absorbed by hearing them every Sunday. Choir director and pianist Herbert Bonner sees them as meaningful and also as evoking "feeling" in the congregation, arguably the two most important and most critical characteristics of African American church music.

As a way of structuring time, a non-linear, unity-oriented way, the Dr. Watts are particularly free. The members of Clear Creek M.B.C. sing them very slowly and elaborately. There is a perceived relationship between slowness and expression, especially if the rendition is also unmetered. The members often equate slow tempo with "feeling," as though slow songs are by their very nature expressive. There is no underlying beat, no precise rules as to what note comes when. Their movement is felt by the congregation, and its amorphous nature directs the congregation inwards, obliging the members to synthesise with each other, to listen and respond to one another, so that the performance may be cohesive. There is no metric referent outside themselves. Paradoxically, this way of structuring time also gives the members a high degree of freedom because the desired aesthetic is a heterophonic rendition of the hymn. Greater integration as a congregation, therefore, also allows greater individuation amongst the singers.

"I guess this goin' to be our new way of singin'"

Gospel pieces, on the other hand, are a twentieth-century phenomenon. Thomas A. Dorsey is generally credited as the "father of gospel music" because of his seminal role in the early history of the genre.[6] His highly successful "Precious Lord," is still a favourite in churches today, and was written by Dorsey upon the death of his wife and first child, a son. (On August 26, 1932, Dorsey's wife, Nettie, died in childbirth, while Dorsey was on the road: the baby, Thomas Jr., died the following morning). Dorsey had spent his earlier years as a bluesman, "Georgia Tom," and accompanist to blues singer Ma Rainey, and it took tragedy in his personal life to bring him back to the church. His story is a perfect illustration of the "devil's music" – "good music" opposition discussed in chapter 2. Despite the often verbalised and philosophically important dichotomy between devil's music and good music, therefore, the two are in fact very much intertwined. As Portia Maultsby remarks, "principle, rather than practice, has separated and continues to separate the secular from the sacred musical traditions" (1985: 37).

The large body of gospel music embraces many traditions and styles that extend from spirituals, hymns, and blues to contemporary jazz, pop, soul, disco, and funk. [. . .] Perhaps the greatest secular influence on gospel has been various instrumental styles. Former blues and jazz musicians were among the first to become instrumentalists for gospel singers. Orally transmitted from generation to generation, the style and musical vocabulary, first introduced by Dorsey, was combined with contemporary secular genres to create a new form for gospel style.

Thus, [. . .] modern gospel uses the musical vocabulary and instrumental styles characteristic of jazz, soul, disco, and funk (ibid.: 41–42).

Many black popular musicians "got their start" in the church, but few managed to retain a church audience once they crossed over into secular musics.

These two musics are often seen as so opposed that one must renounce one in order to embrace the other. While the switch from the profane to the sacred and vice versa carries with it a concomitant renunciation (voluntary or "forced") of one's previous affiliation, the very fact of the apparent facility and frequency of the switches attests to the strong connections between the two musical systems. Aretha Franklin is one of very few singers who managed to keep both a religious and a secular audience, and the fine standing of her father, the Rev. C. L. Franklin, was surely influential in this matter.[7] On two consecutive dates in January 1972 (13th and 14th), then soul singer Aretha featured in services in a California church. The recordings which resulted therefrom, and which also featured the gospel giant James Cleveland and the Southern California singers, as well as Aretha's father—one of the most famous black preachers of the twentieth century—were subsequently released as a double LP *Amazing Grace* by Atlantic, and made the Billboard top 10. On one of the album tracks secular and sacred are integrated in a very striking way (and in a fashion reminiscent of "Lord Lift Us Up" discussed in chapter 2). The performance, which is preceded by Aretha's introduction by her father stating "She has never left the church" (a remark that was retained, significantly, on the album) opens with the famous gospel piece "Precious Lord" (discussed above). In the Franklin/Cleveland rendition, as the song progresses, the Carole King popular song "You've Got a Friend"[8] is superimposed upon and integrated into the fabric of the gospel piece, to the appreciation of the congregation/audience, betraying both the musical and lyric affinities between these genres. Thus, the African American church, by its strong musical and sometimes even textual identity with secular music traditions, on the one hand retains the holistic view of religion embraced by West African ancestors, and on the other hand whole-heartedly espouses the strict dichotomy between worldly and spiritual spheres which is the Reformed Protestant inheritance of the New World.

Nonetheless, this opposition of musical genres (sacred vs. secular) has continued and developed into an opposition of musical styles in African American gospel music today. That opposition is most often expressed within the gospel community as an antagonism between gospel music and artists who have become "too commercial" and those who have remained traditional. As Don Cusic remarks:

The Christian artist trying to reach the secular world is forced to appeal to secular companies and outlets—who are generally not interested in promoting the Christian message. The Christian culture often casts a jaundiced eye at those who would become immersed in the world of unbelievers. It is generally an either/or situation and the Christian culture is very possessive of its own. It fears that the sheep will stray. They will go to great lengths to discipline and bring back to the fold those they believe have erred in their ways with musical adventurism. Therefore, in order to survive artists must either subjugate their Christianity and become a secular act or direct their energies and efforts to the Christian culture. Even those exceptions who find acceptance in both worlds must have a firm commitment to one world while they make forays into the other (1990: 226–27).

As Cusic implies, some traditional singers and audiences see buying into the trappings of the "star" scene as selling out traditional values in favour of the financial gains and widespread fame that can come from crossing over into the commercial market. They believe that gospel must remain a ministry, and that it is not possible to evangelise and minister in the commercial world. Other (commercial) artists and their audiences believe that gospel should reach out to the greatest audience possible, and that this can be accomplished only by going outside the traditional church.

> The tension existing between tradition and innovation (or, as Susan McClary has recently characterized these dialogical terms, convention and expression) is one of the reasons the church has remained a hotbed of musical creativity through the years. While church leadership has generally guarded and cherished the notions of tradition and convention, forces from within the church (more often than not the younger generation) have defied the older heads, as Thomas Dorsey called them, [. . .] and claimed stylistic change as an artistic priority. The interaction of these two impulses (tradition and innovation) has provided a creative framework through which musicians have continually pursued new musical directions, despite the inevitable controversies that these innovations are sure to inspire (Guthrie Ramsey, 2003: 191–92).

Surprisingly, some scholars are still very critical of the performance of gospel music in church. Amongst these critics is Wendell Whalum, who has stated rather scathingly that "Gospel choirs today, though often very talented and entertaining, sometimes turn the act of worship, which is at best well-planned drama, into a religious circus in which the profane often exceeds the religious" (1986: 17).

In contrast to lined hymns, gospel pieces are generally upbeat and rely heavily upon clear metric organisation. (There are, of course, very slow gospel pieces that are looser in the articulation of meter, but even these frequently incorporate a faster section based in driving rhythms.)

The presence of a strong, clear beat is part of the essence of the music, and even where the soloist confounds the meter, plays with the beat (as, for example, in "Lord Lift Us Up," transcribed in example 2.3), it is still the expectation of the metric structure that gives the solo meaning by contrast. Gospel choral style is a tightly controlled genre, reliant upon an accompanist and choir director. In contrast to the ever more elaborate melismas which result in deceleration of lined hymns, gospel pieces tend to accelerate as tensions builds, and when they are most affective, their expression is likely to culminate in a short, sharply defined ostinato. The very short and rhythmically defined ostinato that generates such excitement and intense emotion is probably a structural retention from a West African heritage whose extended drum pieces are built on such repeated patterns. The soloist, improvising against this rhythmic backdrop is, in gospel music, the solo singer for the particular piece, in West African drumming, the master drummer. The constant repetition of a simple pattern is also analogous to the imagined repetitive action suggested by psychiatrists to patients in whom they wish to induce trance. Depending upon the church and the tenor of the service, members may become possessed of the Holy Spirit at this point and go into a shout.

At Clear Creek M.B.C., it is primarily the youth choir that sings contemporary gospel. While the senior choir also sings gospel songs on occasion, hymns and spirituals form their more usual repertoire. When the latter choir sings gospel pieces, it is usually older and slower pieces. It is generally Herbert Bonner who brings songs to the choirs. He seldom buys gospel music (either sheet music or a recording). He has a particularly good memory and will remember any gospel song that appeals to him if he hears it once. Herbert refers to this ability as a gift from God, as do the other church members. He usually gets his songs from the radio, particularly from the very popular black gospel programme, *Highway to Heaven*, which was broadcast from Holly Springs, Mississippi, every weekday night.[9] Many of the church members used to listen to it, but it was unfortunately discontinued during 1987. Bonner generally likes the songs of James Cleveland, the Williams Brothers, and the Jackson Southernaires. Close harmony is his preference and he usually arranges the song in parallel sixths and thirds as far as possible, for three voices, Soprano, Alto, Tenor (SAT). The bass he will take on the piano, because he is not enamoured of bass voices.

Once Herbert has figured out the parts—or sometimes his sisters, Sheila and Janice, and his cousin Greg Thompson, will "catch" their own parts (S, A, and T, respectively) off the radio—the song is brought to the choir and each part is taught by rote, starting with the sopranos and working down. (This teaching method is common in the tradition of gospel, both in local communities and at the national convention level. I have rarely seen choirs use scores, except as rudimentary guides to the lyrics. In gospel, in particular, texts of all types are generally discarded in performance, partly because of what Mellonee Burnim describes as "the visual dimension of performance," whereby musicians, in communicating with their audiences, display total physical involvement with the music through use of the entire body [1985: 150–65]. Scores would be a hindrance to this type of physical engagement.) The youth (choir members range from about eleven years old to about eighteen years old) pick up their parts quickly and have little difficulty fitting them together. (This ease is, of course, facilitated by the parallel motion.) Focus is then directed to the words and their enunciation, and to the rhythms and accentuation of the piece. Precise rhythmic articulation not only delivers the words clearly, it also adds to the life of a song. Herbert insists on appropriately accenting the song, quite beyond keeping it in time and together. While accentuation is frequently syncopated, the force of the meter underlying the song gives it coherence.

Below is my transcription of a gospel song, "You Oughta Take Some Time Out," as performed by the Clear Creek Youth Choir (see example 3.2).[10] The song illustrates the stylistic characteristics delineated above and discussed in chapter 2. As is clear from the notation, the chorus is set in syncopated, homophonic style, and articulation of meter is unambiguous (in mm. 10 and 12, however, there is ambiguity because of the duple rather than triple subdivision of the beat). The soloist's line, by way of contrast, is more free-flowing, ambiguous in its articulation of meter (subdivisions of the beat into twos alternate frequently with subdivisions into threes), embellished, and extended upwards in pitch at the climax (m. 26, f^1). When the choir resumes singing, taking their parts as before, the soloist, as is typical in this style, adds interpolations at points where the choir is not singing. While these interpolations do not generally add to the textual dimension of the piece, (the soloist may anticipate or repeat an important portion of the choir's text), they are musically and aesthetically significant. They fill in "holes" in the musical structure (otherwise the accompanist will take this role); they maintain the free-flowing, improvised, and personalised essence of the soloist's role, adding another dimension to the strictly timed, fixed, and formalised rendition of the choir; and, according to the soloist's talent, they continue to stretch both musical time and shape, and occasionally even texture as the soloist may exploit a wide range of vocal timbres for aesthetic variation.[11]

The third facet on which Herbert focuses is volume. A large sound becomes part of the aesthetic of the music, so that even congregations with very small churches insist upon an amplifying system.[12] This is very striking, especially if one is unaccustomed to boisterous singing. Everywhere I went, people were quite comfortable with microphones, which in some ways facilitated my recording. The problems that I ran into with recording, however, were also as a result of this familiarity and ease with microphones. When my recording microphones did not produce the amplified sound

Example 3.2. "You oughta take some time out." Gospel piece performed by the Clear Creek Youth Choir.

Example 3.2, cont.

expected, soloists frequently came right up against a microphone and sang directly into it as loudly as they could, thereby peaking well above the recording level I had set based on the opening, not to mention the shock to my ears monitoring the recording on headphones. If this still did not produce the desired effect, a soloist would generally tap a finger against the microphone, trying to ascertain whether or not it was working. As to the choirs, it took several sessions for me to adjust my expectations of the level of sound that about twenty-five eleven- to eighteen-year-olds could produce. The level of sound at the climax of the song was much higher than I had initially anticipated. As previously mentioned, singing out power-fully with all one's might, is generally interpreted as a total involvement in and commitment of the singer to his ministry. This submersion of the singer in the song convinces the congregation of his or her faith and dedication.

Not all members, however, appreciate a big sound. This "loudness" is perceived as a characteristic of gospel music and of the young people, and occasionally it can reinforce the division between "our music" and "their music" between young and old. Criticism at Clear Creek M.B.C., how-ever, is rarely levelled at their own youth choir because they have not crossed that fine line between having a "powerful sound" and "screaming at people."

But I tell you, I can't go and listen to choirs, screaming in your ear! All of a sudden you hear they blastin' out "Pass Me Not." Oh my goodness! But they sing some good. They really do, but . . . I guess this goin' to be our new way of singin'. And when one church get it, they all goin' to. It's mostly the young people. But I don't see what they get out of it. I don't know what's the difference. I guess I think they really care too much for that music, the younger people. It's just because a set of young people started it and they like to be like 'em. I don't think they really care too much for that music. But it's one choir that come out of Memphis when we was in Harrisonville, they had drums, they had horns and everything and it was about one hundred of those children, and they didn't need a mike, they definitely didn't.[13] They blast, they sing from the top of their voice. I got up and left. I can't stand it. You got to have a great big . . . I said those kids must have been used to singing with a church so big. They definitely did not need one [a microphone] (Shirley Fox, interview, November 10, 1986).

All of the characteristics of gospel music discussed here point to a tightly controlled genre. Precise rehearsal of accentuation and enunciation, syncopated rhythms against a clear metric backdrop, all delivered for the most part in a loud and confident voice, all make for, and can only be products of, very precise articulation of time. Juxtaposed against this, and this is a discrete and crucial element of the style, is the improvised and more free-flowing line of the soloist. Unlike lined hymns, however, which are independent of meter in their flow, the flow of the gospel soloist's line earns its distinction by direct contrast with a metric backdrop. In this case, "unmetered" exists only as a by-product of meter.

Both styles of music (lined hymns and gospel) emphasize, albeit in different ways, what Portia Maultsby has identified as central to the aesthetics of African American singing: "[T]he aesthetics that govern the singing of Black Americans derive from a key cultural value, one that emphasizes free expression and group participation" (1993: 522). But whereas the heterophonic performance of lined hymns at Clear Creek M.B.C. simultaneously facilitates both individual free expression and group participation, the more controlled nature of gospel music places group participation with the choir (and not the entire congregation), and free expression with the soloist. (There are, of course, exceptions to this, but this reflects the fundamental allocation of roles within gospel music.) Both, significantly, preserve the antiphonal, call-and-response structure that is so characteristic of the African American aesthetic.

"Now Baptists, black Baptists believe that Sunday is the Lord's day"

Just as Sunday service at Clear Creek M.B.C. accommodates two such opposite expressions of musical time, so also the social concepts of time that govern the service are in some ways contradictory. Baptist churches differ in their approach to the Devotion (a short song and prayer service, usually led by the deacons of the church). Some churches do not have a formal Devotion service at all, but start directly into worship service. Such is the case at Congdon Street Baptist Church in Providence, Rhode Island. Service begins at eleven a.m., immediately following Sunday School which convened at nine a.m., and starts with a prelude (organ or piano music), the processional, and then the Call to Worship. Other churches print up the Devotion in the service bulletin, but have the Devotion precede the service, as relatively autonomous. This is the case with many of the Missionary Baptist churches in the Oxford area (Second Baptist, for example) and with Main Street Baptist Church in Lexington, Kentucky. In the latter case, the Devotion is listed as "10:45 a.m., Prayer and Praise Services led by Deacons" (church bulletin).

In these churches, most members seem to conceive of the Devotion as separate from the service, i.e., they generally arrive at church around eleven a.m. and are admitted to the sanctuary when the Devotion ends. Black Baptist churches usually have ushers who act as doorkeepers to the sanctuary and welcome and seat people. In some cases, as at Congdon Street Baptist Church in Providence, they also take the names of visitors and give them to the pastor so that he may recognise them at the "Recognition of Visitors." One may not walk into the sanctuary at whatever time one arrives. There are specific points in the service when the ushers open the doors to admit those who have gathered outside. There is a five- or ten-minute break between the end of the Devotion and the beginning of the service, while newcomers find their friends and are seated, bulletins are distributed, and the pastor takes his place. The result is that one perceives the "real" beginning of the service to be at eleven. The timing of events in this instance also predisposes one to think of the Devotion as a prelude to the service, not an integral part of it. In Western society, we are accustomed to events beginning on the hour, or perhaps on the half-hour. This is how we structure time, as though every hour were a unit unto itself. The effect of scheduling the Devotion for 10.45 and the service for eleven, is to designate the Devotion as preceding the service, rather than as a part of it. As Michael Kearl notes (drawing on Emile Durkheim, 1915), the structuring of time, particularly in relation to religious ritual, carries implications beyond the hours and minutes involved.

On the cultural level, the role of time in religious knowledge and rituals is to assist in the demarcation of the sacred and the profane. What is sacred is the order that links our activities with an overarching meaning. To accurately repeat the rituals of one's ancestors, for example, is to participate in sacred time. Sacred time is the collapse of the past and future into an eternal now: the heroics of our ancestors and our descendants will forever be part of the present. Profane time is passing time, time as decay or entrophy, time without immortality (1983: 163).

At Clear Creek M.B.C., members conceive of the Devotion as an integral part of the worship service. In contrast to Main Street Baptist Church in Lexington, Kentucky, for example, where the Devotion always precedes the Call to Worship, at Clear Creek the Devotion is always after the Call to Worship, and perhaps also after a song from the choir, and thus undeniably embedded in "sacred time."

It [the Devotion] is a part of the service. It is the starting of a service. Lots of churches start off with what we call a "Call to Worship," where a portion of scripture is read. Then the choir will come with an inspirational song, to, for the settlement of the people, in order to get their minds off of whatever they was doin' and to get them to think along the line of getting into service. It's kind of a traditional thing. And then the Devotion follows (Lee Earl Robinson, interview, November 21, 1987).

Sunday morning worship service at Clear Creek M.B.C. is scheduled for eleven a.m. (which is quite usual for most Baptist churches), although from year to year the time may vary to 11.15 or 11.30 a.m. It may be late, consistently between ten and twenty minutes late, but never early. But if the time of service is clear, the length of service is not. It may run anywhere between one hour and four hours and thirty minutes, depending on the working of the Holy Spirit in the people, and also on other more mundane factors such as a second service that night, or an afternoon programme, or a big football game on television. The pastor of Clear Creek M.B.C., Rev. Grady McKinney, recognises that Sunday is no longer dedicated exclusively to the Lord, as he remembers it used to be, and laments that fact.

Now Baptists, black Baptists believe that Sunday is the Lord's day. It's set aside for the purpose and wishes of God. Now we done got so modern we'll go to church Sunday, we get back early enough we put on our hunting clothes and go to hunting, go to fishing, Sunday evening. But when I was coming up, black Baptists didn't do that on a Sunday. Even sinners, and of course there wasn't many sinners then in the community, even sinners had respect for Sunday. Even sinners would come to church. Some of 'em came to church and never did accept Christ, but they'd come to church on Sundays. But now, we kind of running loose now (interview, November 17, 1986).

Service length at Clear Creek M.B.C. generally varies between one hour and thirty minutes and three hours, and anywhere within this range is quite comfortable. While the members feel that service should start at a particular time, there is no comparable expectation of its conclusion. Time allotted to service is thus elastic, but only in one direction. It is not even that it is not important when service ends; what is important is that one not try to control its duration and thus run the risk of interfering with the working of the Holy Spirit.

A similar sort of control/non-control can be seen in the sequence of events within a service. A bulletin detailing "order of service," amongst other things, is printed up for every service. The members buy the covers, which generally have some idyllic scene and a quote from Scripture on the front, and into these they photocopy their own text. Nonetheless, the order of service, however concrete it may appear in black and white on paper, is but an indication of how service may be expected to proceed. While pivotal structures such as the sermon are rarely moved, anything else may be changed. Songs are frequently added, as are spontaneous prayers; they may be moved forward or delayed; a spontaneous testimonial may generate a whole subsection of prayer and song; while the recognition of visitors, announcements, and the financial report may occur almost anywhere. This fluidity in the order of the service is, as Hans Baer and Merrill Singer remark, quite typical of both Baptist and Methodist services. "The Sunday preaching service, regardless of whether it occurs in a Baptist or Methodist church, almost invariably includes certain ritual events such as prayer, hymn-singing, testifying, 'penny' and regular collections, the sermon, and the benediction, but the exact sequence in which these occur varies considerably from congregation to congregation" (1992: 33–34).

In parallel fashion, in less formal or official temporal situations, there often exists a tension between control and non-control. I have heard members of Clear Creek M.B.C. refer to themselves one day as "timely people," priding themselves on their punctuality and expressing the opinion that punctuality is a common courtesy and should be observed by all, even for a barbecue. On another day the same member(s) may, in a similar situation, joyfully embrace the concept of CPT, or Colored Peoples' Time, i.e., a sophisticatedly cultivated stance to the effect that "people make the event" and that to try to govern an event by hours and minutes is artificial. Whether or not one is "on time" in any given social situation (or indeed whether one's guests are on time for a particular occasion) is, of course, more than simply a detail of what is commonly referred to as "good manners" but, as Kearl acknowledges "implies an awareness of social structural time, and reveals the institutionalised bases of projects that make up one's *life plan*" (ibid.: 160).

"There is nothing we can do without God"

But it is not simply in greater and lesser details of life that the members of Clear Creek M.B.C. mediate between diametrically opposed poles. It is not only in their sense of musical and social time that the members embrace opposites. This is also true of their sense of existential time, i.e., their view of their lives' progression. Because of an existential viewpoint that grants a superior being all power, wisdom, and knowledge, the members embrace a state of relative helplessness. They believe that man can be saved only through God's mercy and grace, and not by an infinity of "good works" without them. "Within all and all, if you really believe in God, in Christ, you can realise all things that happen to you that benefit you, total good aspect comes from the Lord" (Lee Earl Robinson, interview, November 11, 1987).

> This world has already been condemned. Ever since sin first entered into this world, it was condemned. God himself made several attempts in a sense to try to get man to get a hold on things, when He sent his prophets and so forth, try to get man to live better. At one time, grieved God that He made man, so He destroyed him. After started again with Noah, man became wicked again. This when Christ intervened. Christ Himself spoke to disciples and told them about His kingdom, not of this world and they understood not. In new world that is to come, it shall be sin-free, for man has corrupted everything in this world from the smallest atom to the biggest rock. There is no purification in this world (Lee Earl Robinson, interview, November 17, 1986).

Jessie Orange presented much the same belief at the Harvest Day programme on November 11, 1987. "We of course know we only achieve because God see fit to bless us. For everything that we receive, we should of course be thankful. Not just one time of the year, but every day of our lives, because there is nothing we can do without God."

While the members of Clear Creek M.B.C. certainly make efforts to direct events in the direction in which they would have them flow, there is also a certain sense that even the smallest happenings are outside their control. One mother, Shirley Fox, shook her head unhappily in telling me that her twelve-year-old son did not yet understand that only God could get him such things as a new bike. While she would eventually be the one to go into a store and make the acquisition, God alone could give her the financial means and the will or desire to do so.

From a child's point of view of life's progress to the adults' estimate of the progress of their church, the same tension exists. As I have mentioned before, Clear Creek M.B.C. (in common with many other rural black churches), has a part-time pastor, but the members want a full-time pastor.

I would like to see him [Rev. McKinney] get more involved in the church, I really would. It just like leaving your sheep running on their own for a whole week, and you come in and preach the sermon to 'em and try to tell them something. Uh-huh, it's not going to work! You see him once a month, it's not, basically I think I need more. We need, o.k. if you goin' have someone leading you, they should be there to lead. All the time (Shirley Fox, interview, November 10, 1986).

Although the church does have services two Sundays of the month, morning worship is held only once a month. Quite a few of the members do not turn out for the evening services, and this has been a bone of contention in the church. On the other Sunday mornings, many of the members attend another church's morning service, and they do not go out again in the evening.

The biggest difficulty seems to be that because of his commitment to other churches, Rev. McKinney cannot come to Clear Creek M.B.C. full-time. Yet the members value him highly and are reluctant to part with him. On the one hand, they are frustrated because of their apparent inability to secure the church's forward movement by employing a full-time pastor. On the other hand, they bow to the will of God, realising that although they think that it is time to move on, it must not be or God would ensure that they did. "But, I guess it's not time for us to change yet. If it was, it'll come along. But I guess it's still not time, because if it was, it would have happened. It's some reason that we bein' held back" (ibid.). One must not only try one's best to rectify a particular situation, one must also wait on the Lord. "It's not impossible to find another minister, or a pastor to do a full-time church service. But at the same time, we are obligated to go into prayer and to ask God to send us a minister suitable for our congregation" (Sam Jones, interview, November 23, 1986). In effect, because of the part-time nature of Rev. McKinney's pastoring, he cannot fully meet the burden of pastoral care, which is one of the two principal practices (the other being preaching) by which black pastors help to maintain and nurture congregational culture (Molefi, 1987: 268).

"You must be born again"/"I know I got religion"

It is in the conversion experience, however, that the congregation's mediation between control and non-control is arguably most arresting. All seem to agree that this is the single most important event in their lives. Their belief is that unless one is reborn in Jesus Christ, one cannot be saved: once saved, one can never be lost again. There is a critical difference, for members, between backslider and sinner. It is to be expected, if lamented, that almost every church member will backslide at some stage in life. "And this I believe about anyone that been born again: that don't mean you won't get corrupted sometime, or mess up sometime, because in our churches most all our believers come in when they are young. They haven't had no experience of life, and naturally when they get a certain age, they goin' do some of those things" (Rev. McKinney, interview, November 17, 1986). Or again, as Deacon Jones expressed it:

> So even after bein' saved, if you want to lead a sin-free life, it's very difficult, if not impossible. And to me it's basically impossible, because of our emotions and our mind in itself. Plus, we not in charge of time. We don't know, where we goin' be next week (interview, November 23, 1986).

The most important thing is that the person who has been born again will always come back to the church. He cannot help but, because the Holy Spirit residing within him will eventually bring him back to the Lord.

> If they been born again, the time will come when they'll come back to the Lord. But if you haven't been born again, you ain't got nothing to bring you back. A lot of us sometimes, "We ought to go and get Lee Earl and bring him back to the church."[14] But if he been born by the spirit of God, God will bring him back. When he get through flirting around out there, the spirit of God will bring him right on back to the church. But if he haven't been born again, he'll never come back. . . . You don't have to get anyone if they been born by the spirit of God, you don't have to go get 'em. It'll bring you back home. I been just as young as anybody. I [con]'fessed hope in Christ when I was eleven years old and I don't tell nobody how to live like I live now. But it was something on the inside would reason with you when you did wrong, but it just took a little time to bring you back home. So now I'm satisfied. I don't need none of the woolly stuff. And that's the way God work if you been born again . . . that inward spirit will bring you back to God (Rev. McKinney, interview, November 17, 1986).

In order to ensure that I understood this concept, one of the deacons cited a Biblical example.

> All right, let me, let us deal with it like in the Old Testament. Deal with David, a man after God's own heart. David slew Goliath, the giant of the Philistines, and all this matter. David was a king of the children of Israel. But David went on and made a certain mistake in his life, situation he had with Bathsheba. And having Uriah sent off to war, and all of a sudden Orias [sic] was out of the picture and David was free to deal with Bathsheba. But David paid a price for that. After he realised how wrong he was, he spent the latter part of his years repenting and

trying to get right with God. We are here and we don't know how long we goin' be here. Really we don't know how much we goin' do. And what we goin' get involved in. Nor what circumstances we goin' be involved in. In being said that you are saved, you will seek the guidance and you will know where to get your guidance from, rather than succumb to the pressures of the world. I'll try to compare it with the world situations. Before I give a dime to a counsellor about a problem that I'm having, I'll give a dime to a mender to repair my clothes from bending on my knees so much.[15] To get into some sincere prayer to God to help me. If He directs me that-a-way, He will make funds available, through the strength given me to go to work everyday, to make some monies available to pay someone to help me (Sam Jones, interview, November 23, 1986).

These explanations prompted me to ask whether being saved meant that one could then lead a bad life, secure in the knowledge that one could not be lost because the spirit of God would eventually reconcile one with God. The members feel, however, that a true conversion will preclude premeditated sin, at least for a protracted period of time.

The statement of repentance, salvation, and what have you to the Christian community is absolute. It's not a relative statement. Once you are saved, you are saved. It does not excuse you, nor give you an excuse from doin' wrong, in that respect (ibid.).

Salvation is the most mysterious of life's events. It comes of God's goodness and not of human efforts. It is neither predictable not controllable. At every service there is an "Altar Call," or a particular time (usually immediately following the sermon) when people are invited to come and acknowledge Jesus as their personal saviour. Yet it is not within the context of this invitation that most of the members of Clear Creek M.B.C. acknowledged Jesus Christ as their personal saviour. In the ten months that I have spent at the church at different times, I have never seen anybody come and be saved at this time, although occasionally people will come forward and rededicate their lives to God.

This difference between Clear Creek M.B.C. and other black Baptist churches in which I have done fieldwork is largely the result of the close-knit, familial character of the membership. At Main Street Baptist Church in Lexington, Kentucky, people respond to the altar call. But it is a large church and attracts college students as well as newcomers to town. The same is true, albeit to a lesser extent, of Second Baptist in Oxford, Mississippi. Because the current pastor at Second Baptist, Rev. Leroy Wadlington, is also a chaplain of the University of Mississippi, and also because the church is close to campus, college students attend the church and frequently bring friends. Again it is not unusual for one of them to come forward at the altar call. Consequent to the familial structure and the comparatively small size of Clear Creek M.B.C., strangers attending the church are rare. Children usually convert once they reach the age of reason (generally between the ages of nine and twelve).

Two revivals are held at the church during the calendar year, one in spring and the other in summer. During revival there is service every night of the week and a guest preacher usually preaches throughout. As the reader will remember from the conversion narratives of chapter 2, the two front pews on the right hand side of the church are designated as the "mourners' bench." Those seeking Christ are seated here. At Clear Creek M.B.C. seekers are almost invariably children between the ages of nine and twelve years old. There is such a high expectation of children of this age, by their parents, their siblings, their aunts, uncles, and cousins, that they will convert, that it is unusual for anyone to be older than twelve when converting. Nobody is generally left on the mourners' bench at the end of revival.

During revival attention is focused on the mourners' bench. A great deal of the preaching and praying is directed towards the mourners. The hope and expectation of the church is that they will acknowledge Jesus Christ as their personal saviour and be saved. The altar call during revival is expanded considerably in density and length. Instead of one preacher giving the invitation, the attending ministers, the deacons, and the mothers of the church also extend the invitation. It is important to remember that each of the mourners will have at least one relative in this group, be it a parent, grandparent, aunt, or uncle. The invitation is thereby rendered much more personal at Clear Creek M.B.C. than at non-familial churches. What is usually one song, the invitation hymn, becomes an unspecified number of songs. As long as someone is moved to call up a song, the singing will continue. The physical space of the invitation is expanded with the number of people extending it, and it is concentrated around the mourners. I will quote in full here an account Greg Thompson gave me of his conversion, as it illustrates all of the above points.

> I was nine years old. It was a Wednesday morning at Clear Creek Missionary Baptist Church. They had a, it was a summer revival. We were out and we had revivals in the morning and at night; two times a day for a week. I was sittin' on the mourners' bench. . . . The pastor[16] was a man, Rev. Hoof. I don't know where he is now. Hardly even remember some of the people were on the mourners' bench with me. I have a cousin named Tony, he was on there. Herbert's sister [Herbert Bonner, choir director and accompanist at the church], Janice, she was there too. It's a very personal and private thing. 'See salvation and religion, that's something that's very personal. That's something that Mama cannot do for you and Daddy can't. Being saved is a very personal thing, and

your relationship between you and God is a very personal thing. And that's something that Greg, or anyone else, just has to make up on their own, something that I have to do, and something that no one else can do for you.

It ended up all of us did at the same time, stood up and, it was right after the preaching, and I think Rev. Hoof started singing "I Know I Got Religion." Rev. Hoof had just got through preachin'. It's a congregational song. He started off and everybody else joined in. During revival, traditionally, after the preacher gets through preachin', everybody in the pulpit comes down in front of the mourners' bench, the deacons and the mothers of the church, and it's just like a pool. They make a pool around the mourners on the mourners' bench, and all of 'em are singin'. And that's when Rev. McKinney came down, all the deacons— my father, Lee Earl, Sam, my grandmother, all of my aunts. All the mothers of the church, they come up and make a little oval shape right in front of the front bench there, the mourners' bench, and they start singing and everybody in the congregation joins in. And they stand pretty close. And whenever you feel that you have accepted God in your life, you can get up off the mourners' bench. That's when you're "saved."

It was just that willingness to make that first step. I felt that no longer was I alone in this world, that I had someone with me. And I felt that I believed that God had died on the cross for all of my sins, and that by Him dying for me, that if I kept His commandments, that I'd be able to live with Him. You know this has been instilled into you by bein' in church all those years. You know I was brought up in church, so it wasn't as hard for me to accept all of those things, believe all this, because this has been instilled into me all my life.

It was just a feeling just like I was not moving myself. I got up and I walked off the bench and I shook his hand, and I, and I was cryin'. I remember I was cryin'. It was just a feeling of gladness. It was a good feelin'. It's something that you really can't describe. It might be that way for me. Some people shout when they get happy, some people cry, some people laugh, some people don't do anything, they just sit up and it just be something feeling good on the inside. You know it's the Holy Ghost, it works on people different ways. No which way to say, "Well, if you don't come off the mourners bench shoutin' you ain't got nothing." That's not true! It works on people different ways, and it's just a personal thing, that only you know and your God knows.

They'll sing, they'll usually sing, oh about three or four songs. Like Rev. McKinney might sing a song, and then after he get through singin' that song, somebody else will sing what they call "traditional" revival songs. Like they might sing, "I Know I Been Changed," "Certainly Lord" (interview, November 25, 1987).

Conversion is arguably the most mysterious and spiritual event in the members' lives. It comes from God's goodness, yet it is, in effect, submitted to the constricts of a human timetable. It is expected that individuals will be saved between the years of nine and twelve years old if they are children (which is by far the most usual case at Clear Creek M.B.C.), and most probably during the course of one of the two revivals held annually. The members believe that the Holy Spirit is with them in a special and powerful way during revival. The amount of control that the church members exercise in "scheduling" conversion contrasts sharply with the relatively helpless existential position that they embrace. "Time has a constituent role in shaping our apprehension of 'reality.' There is a temporal order implicit in our roles, interactions, histories, and cognitions" (Kearl, 1983: 166).

At all levels of time, the members of Clear Creek M.B.C. mediate between diametrically opposed poles. Taken together, the two genres of music that I discussed earlier—lined hymns and gospel pieces—can be interpreted as a symbol for the members' lives. The resultant whole is a composite (but never a fusion) of ancient and modern, of fluidity and sharp definition, of control and letting go. The framework that results can absorb a wide diversity of events and styles, and is thus tremendously resilient. Tensions are embraced, but not defused or dissipated, so that interwoven with the calm and secure warp of a close-knit community, there is also the weft of considerable latent energy.

4

Tradition

"Have you ever seen Jackson State marchin' band?"

As it is to the lives of most of us, the ability to synthesise or move between different time frames is fundamental to the worldview of the Clear Creek community. Their collective past extends back through desegregation and post–World War II industrialisation, to slavery and, in a necessarily more vague and idealised vein, back to Africa. (While it is true that the members recognise and embrace their origin in the life and death of Jesus Christ, and even before that in the story of Genesis, these events seem not to have the immediacy and "reality" of those previously mentioned.) Their future extends to a life after death and the Day of Judgement. Their present is a mix of tradition and modernity, frequently laced with a measure of nostalgia. Through all these temporal dislocations they hold constant a close relationship with God. Religion is the tie that binds.

The ability to call upon the past and the future, in order to enrich our understanding of the present, is uniquely human. On it depends our capacity for learning, for abstract analytical thought, even for creative imagining. This gift of simultaneous past, present, and future is one of our greatest sources of meaning, encouraging us to cling to life, giving us a sense of belonging, and enabling us to extrapolate reason and meaning from what might otherwise be a futile, irrational, and momentary dance. Paradoxically, it can also be used to negate the present. Too often, perhaps, we flee the present for dreams of beauty or memories of love, seduced by the power of illusion. To tell our story, we need to "know" our past (at some level and in some fashion, no matter how mythological), and hope for our future.

This chapter examines the Clear Creek M.B.C. community's understanding of the present and its place on the continuum of past-future. I also discuss two related, but subsidiary, oppositions (old-young and rural-urban). The harvest ritual on which the chapter centres, symbolically brings together tradition and modernity, old and young, rural and urban. All these oppositions are crystallised in the musical forms spiritual and gospel. Through religion the members transform the agricultural significance of harvest, which is dying in the community, to a spiritual significance that is at the centre of the community's worldview. The past is retained in the present and propelled into the future through reinterpretation in religion.

"Yeah, cotton used to be pretty, a long time ago"

Many, if not most, of the adults of the community grew up farming, their parents typically sharecropping, sometimes moving about considerably as they tried to make a living. The family was largely self-sufficient, growing most of their own food. Children helped out on the farm according to their age and strength. During harvest season parents often kept them out of school to help harvest cotton, wheat, and other crops. Deacon Lee Earl Robinson, typical in his history and in his ready invocation of that history, briefly described his childhood.[1] The interview took place at Lee Robinson's home in Springhill. Place names are necessarily vague in his account as on occasions when I asked members to be more specific as to the place where they grew up, or even where they now live, it was frequently not possible because red dirt roads are not named. It would be impossible for a stranger, such as myself, to locate specific places without a guide. When such places or areas are named, it is frequently after the person who owns them, and these names may persist despite the property changing hands.

> I was born about one mile north of here, a mile and a half north of here. They used to call it the old Standback Place, which was recently purchased by a relative of mine by the name of Charlie Bates. I was born in the year 1950, on a hot summer afternoon, Wednesday, September thirteenth, 1950. We were sharecroppers at that time. [. . .] In the year of 1953 we moved from what we call the Standback Place to a place we call Woodson Ridge. And we lived there and sharecropped out there for almost a year, I believe. [. . .] After the year of 1955 we moved to, in a place called St. John, over there in Cottage Hill area. [. . .] I don't know the real reason we left the Standback Place, but we left Woodson Ridge because of the unfairness in which we were share-cropping. My daddy decided to come back home in the latter part of the year of 1956 and '57. When we came back here, this was our home land. My uncle used to farm this land. He died in the year of 1955. Also in November, my grandfather died, in the year of 1955. [. . .] And my father lived out his year of contracting which he had made with Tanksley over there, and then we moved back home. And in the year of 1957 his family took over this land and begin to farm it. We grew cotton, corn, peanuts, watermelons, all types of vegetables and such. It was for ourselves and we hardly bought any grocery, because we had our own meat. We had our pigs, cows, and so forth. We used to own something like one hundred acres in here. We no longer own that. Again,

somehow or another—to be realistic, my father was not a very good businessman—and in order to make crops again we [. . .] borrowed money and stuff to make crops and so forth, and the man he was dealin' with, even in those times, was running thirty percent interest on the money which we borrowed. It was a white man. It seems as though that from the first two years we had to borrow money to make crops with, we never seemed to get out of debt. And in the year of 1968, my grandmother, my father's grandmother,[2] died and word got around to us, to my father, some kind of way that the man who he had owed a debt to, he had planned on foreclosing on the land. So, in desperation, to save some, most of the land, my father sold off some of the land to pay off the debt (Lee Earl Robinson, interview, November 17, 1986).

The pastor of Clear Creek M.B.C., Rev. Grady McKinney, a contemporary of Lee Robinson's father, raised most of his nine children by farming, supplemented with construction work. Because of health problems, he had to abandon construction work in 1961–62. He has witnessed the gradual demise of farming in the community and tries to grapple with the practical contradictions of late-twentieth-century life.

Yeah, cotton used to be pretty, a long time ago, when back in the forties, small farmers could live pretty good [see figure 14]. Now they didn't have much money, but they could live pretty good. But those big folks got so grouchy, they started working all the land and producing too much. And they mad at the Government, but they need to whip them own selves. If he have a hundred acres of cotton this year, he want two hundred acres of cotton next year. And it just pushed all the small peoples out of business. All through this country, in Mississippi, white and black was farming. And that's the reason the cost of living is so high. Back then we didn't buy butter, you didn't buy eggs, you didn't buy meat. And if my hen was laying and your's wasn't, you still had eggs. But then after they pushed everybody off the farm, the poor white well so the poor black, them big mens took it all and pushed 'em all off, and took tractors and pushed some of the houses down with bulldozers, just so some of 'em burnt and some of 'em up, and they went to working five hundred and six hundred acres. And they brought the price down 'til the little people that was able to farm on their own little farm, they just couldn't survive, because you couldn't get anything for what you produced. So you just had to let it go. And so that's what got the thing in the shape it is (Rev. Grady McKinney, interview, November 17, 1986).

As time went by, economic pressure forced many small farmers off the land. Increased mechanisation and falling crop prices sent the next generation of the Clear Creek community towards the cities and factories.[3]

Figure 14. Yeah, cotton used to be pretty, a long time ago, when back in the forties, small farmers could live pretty good.

Some moved north to Detroit and Chicago. Of Lee Earl Robinson's nine brothers and sisters, for example, five now live in Michigan. Others found jobs in a couple of local factories, in Oxford, or on the University of Mississippi campus. (A large proportion of the service people—maintenance, cleaning, cooking—at the University of Mississippi are still black. Compared to the percentage of black faculty and staff, the number is disproportionate.) Although the Robinsons still have some land, none of those who remain in Mississippi farm it. Unable to compete with the big farmers, Rev. McKinney also abandoned farming.

I don't farm at all now. I got 'few cows. I don't farm. It's not worth it. You'll put more money in the ground than you'll get out, because long as those big farmers producing all this cotton, you not goin' get anything for it. You take like soy beans. I tried soy beans two year. [. . .] The price is up while you're planting 'em. When you're done planting and you start to harvest, they start to coming on down, on down. Now, no way in the world you can raise soy beans at little old five dollars a bushel and make money. You can't make no money that way! It's not enough in it. Now when soy beans was selling for ten dollars and eleven dollars a bushel, you could come out with it. So, 'bout the onliest thing a little fella can have now is two or three cows. That's about all he can have. You know you might raise a little corn feed them, or a little hay, but far as talking about ploughing making a living [. . .] if I fool 'round out there trying to plough it out of the ground, I'd starve to death. It's not anything in it. But it used didn't be that way. You could make a pretty good living. Now, I said now, you didn't have a whole lot of money, but you could live comfortable because you raised just about everything you did have. And light bill—when we did eventually get lights; we haven't always had lights—you know it was down cheap, people's light bills, fifty cents, a dollar and a half, two and a half dollars. But now they charge you ten dollars even if you cut the switch box off. It's goin' cost you ten dollars that month, even if you don't even use the thing! You can get ready to go out of town if you want to, and unplug all your stuff and cut it off, you still goin' have a light bill when you get back. But now, you think now, the average person, if he don't have hardly anything plugged up, his light bill goin' run about thirty dollars, forty dollars a month. Your telephone bill steady goes up. So that's just the way it is (Rev. Grady McKinney, interview, November 17, 1986).

The demands of producing enough food to feed the family obliged the parents of Rev. McKinney's generation to keep their children out of school during some of the harvest season.

At the time when we was coming on, school was running a regular nine months. And what our parents would do was keep us out of school two days a week and we harvest our crops September to, we sometime would finish in the latter part of November. Then if we started late, it could be mid-December before we finish. We mostly done our, the corn and grain harvests on the weekdays and Saturday and stuff. 'Round August, just before school started, it was time for those who grew sugar cane or sorghum; harvest time came around mid-August. And it was taken to the mill and all that was done before school started (Lee Earl Robinson, interview, November 17, 1986).

The role of agriculture has been so attenuated in the community that those who raise animals simply raise them for market. The general introduction of pasteurised milk to the community during Rev. McKinney's lifetime meant that even cows were not milked any more. The bitter weed that the cows would occasionally eat gave a bitter taste to the milk, and the taste of pasteurised milk was preferred. Cows thereafter were raised only for sale. Of the families of the Clear Creek community, only the Simmons family now farms for a living.

Despite the demise of farming in this community, ties to the land and to a traditional and simpler way of living remain strong.[4] If the children are no longer kept out of school for the harvest, some are likely to spend a part of their summer vacation helping out with the crops. Rochelle Thompson, for example, whose grandparents' farm has now been reduced to a rather large field, is less than enamoured of peas, especially come harvest time.

> My grandparents used to farm. We have a, I want to say a garden, but it's bigger than a garden. It's a *field* out there, out back. . . . We plant the field, we chop the field. We plant [black-eyed] peas, yes peas mostly, peas, and corn, and tomatoes, sometimes onions, and okra, watermelons, you know, things like that [. . .] [I get tired of them] especially when I have to pick them in the hot, boiling sun. It's like June, July, August, in the boiling heat of the day, it's like we pick peas. They be ready by end part of June, first part of July. We pick peas for three or four weeks straight (interview, November 23, 1987).

While Rochelle complains of picking black-eyed peas for three or four weeks straight in the summer when it is very hot, her complaints are lightened with laughter. Although farming is now much less central to the members' lives than it used to be, they are still attuned to the natural phenomena that affect farmers. They are aware of local and national weather patterns and seasonal changes: an early frost or an unusually mild spell causes concern, usually voiced in Sunday school, for the crops.

"Sinner, please don't let this harvest pass"

Consonant with their past, the members' celebration of Harvest Day at church is one of the most important annual feasts, second only, perhaps, to Homecoming. Celebrated in mid-November, it of course coincides with the completion of harvesting, and for the occasion, a small table at the top of the church is decorated with samples of the members' produce. In their ritualisation of the harvest, the members re-create their past, bringing together young and old, modern and traditional, urban and rural, in the symbolic ritual. Some are acutely aware of the potential tension in this union.

> I would say probably about twenty to twenty-five years ago, it [Harvest Day] was probably a lot more significant to most of you. Probably about that time, you all were *more* on farms, working on farms than you are now. I would probably guess that the majority of you are working in town, or in some other aspect of public work, instead of on the farm. So people older than I would definitely know what the true meaning of harvest day is about. People younger than I am probably have no conception what it's about (Jessie Orange, remarks at Harvest Day programme, November 15, 1987).

Resolution of this tension, as of so many others, is found in religion, the primary meaning-structure of the members' lives.

A particularly beautiful example of the synthesis of tradition and modernity, old and new, is the choir's rendition of the spiritual, "Sinner please don't let this harvest pass" (Johnson, 1925). In the Johnson collection, the spiritual is arranged in straightforward western style, like any number of arrangements of folksongs in "art song" settings. I recorded Clear Creek Choir's rendition of the spiritual at the eighty-second annual Tallahatchie-Oxford Missionary Baptist Convention on August 29, 1982. The chorus of the spiritual is first sung by each of two soloists in slow, unmetered style ($\downarrow$ = 60).[5] I have transcribed the second soloist's rendition (see example 4.1).

This slow, free, and highly embellished style is characteristic of slow gospel solo style, and indeed sometimes of the gospel soloist's style against the backdrop of a rhythmically articulated choral number, although the degree of embellishment generally decreases as the overall tempo increases. It is significant, however, that it is also reminiscent of the style of the Dr. Watts hymns discussed in chapter 3. This is in many ways the "old," "traditional" expression of the church, particularly when it is presented, as here, without the backdrop of the chorus. While in the transcription I have grouped the notes in "beats" to facilitate reading, the performance is freer than the transcription indicates: there is not a clear beat referent, rather, one can hear a grouping of notes into somewhat heterogeneous units. The soloist ornaments the melody, confining herself, however, to the melody's pentatonic structure. Scalar runs (pentatonic) are typical ornaments and fulfil two functions.

1. They fill in gaps in the melody (see line 2 of the text, "please don't let this").
2. They extend the range of the melody (line 1, "this"). This soloist's rendition, in fact, considerably extends the range of the original

Example 4.1. "Sinner please don't let this harvest pass." Spiritual, performed solo, in slow, unmetered style.

melody in each phrase: (in line 1, the original minor sixth is extended to a perfect octave; in line 2, the original perfect fifth to a major ninth; in line 3, the original perfect fifth—implied major sixth, see Ex. 4.2—to a perfect octave; and in line 4, the original perfect fourth to a perfect octave).

In the same way that this style of singing (Dr. Watts) unites the church, this style of ornamentation "unites" the melody by filling in any downward leaps ("harvest pass," 1.2, is the only exception). The most significant melodic extension is always around either "harvest," emphasising the theme of the song, or "please" stressing the plea to the sinner to repent. Overall, however, the range of the song as it is performed by the soloist in this elaborated style is almost identical to that of the original (the only exception is the addition of the lower leading tone and lower dominant in line 4): the soloist's exploitation of that range creates a more wide-ranging impression. The soloist stretches the melody in time also, both by singing it very slowly and by the addition of more "events" (notes) in time: her rendition is three times longer than the choir's, which is to follow.

The organist accompanies the melody with sustained chords (on the electric organ). Part of the attraction of the organ is undoubtedly the variety of timbres available, and also the possibilities of rapid *crescendo* and *decrescendo*, none of which is available on the piano. His harmonisation introduces the second (G$\sharp$) and the sixth degrees (D$\sharp$) of the diatonic scale omitted in the pentatonic melody, and also the sharp seventh (E$\sharp$) so that flat and sharp seventh both appear in the accompaniment. Occasionally the accompanist's sharp seventh is sustained against the flat seventh in the melody (see "this," line 1), but the dissonance is not prominent.

The unmetered solo section gives a sense of timelessness and tradition, especially as the congregation had sung several Dr. Watts earlier in the service. This rendition carries with it all of the associations of feeling, Spirit, tradition, and timelessness discussed in chapter 3 in relation to lined hymns. The soloist seems to move with time, not paying it any particular attention or giving it any clear articulation. The congregation adds cries of approbation and encouragement, claps their hands, and chuckles with approval and enjoyment during this first part of the performance.

Having thus engaged the listeners (congregation and preachers respond enthusiastically to the soloists with shouts, cries, and laughter), the mood is moved up tempo to a very different time frame, musically and historically. The two soloists are followed by the choir, although it is not the choir which carries the weight of melodic expression: for much of the rendition the melody (on-time, bare, and unembellished) remains with the soloist. It is shared between soloist and choir for only the last two lines. The song has now been transformed into an upbeat ($\textit{J}$ = 172–208) gospel piece. The gospel choral arrangement is SAT, with the snatches of melody which the choir shares with the soloist in the last two lines voiced in the sopranos, and the other two voices harmonising mostly in parallel motion. The arrangement, however, is unusual: many chords are in root position, occasioning parallel fifths and thirds as opposed to the choir's more usual harmonisation in parallel sixths and thirds. (My transcription is of the choral rendition as first presented, i.e., without the soloist's typical interjections. Variations from one repetition to another by the choir are, in fact, minimal in this instance: there are some minor textual modifications, but no significant changes in the musical line.) The keyboard accompaniment (not transcribed) also becomes upbeat, percussive, and wide-ranging, in "typical" gospel style (see example 4.2).

This is the church's "new" musical expression (although in this somewhat attenuated version it is not an altogether typical instance), with the first soloist now the gospel soloist in the call-and-response structure. Paradoxically, however, with this move to up-beat gospel style, the soloist abandons all of the traits of improvisation, personalisation, and freedom typically associated with gospel solo style (and so much in evidence earlier in this version when the choir was not present), and reverts to what we might term gospel chorus style (on-time, very clearly articulated—whether syncopated or not—and rather bare), while the chorus adds an ostinato-like pattern that one might more readily associate with the latter stages of a gospel song. This ostinato pattern would normally, of course, be embellished by the soloist. The relationships between the various singers here are, thus, atypical, and the reaction of the congregation reflects that.

In the gospel version, rhythmic articulation of time is very precise, focus of attention has moved to a large extent from pitch (spiritual) to meter and rhythm (gospel): this change is emphasised by the addition of percussive elements (foot tapping and hand clapping, as well as percussive piano style). After a couple of verses the accompanist taps a steady rhythm (Example 4.3a) $|^4_4 \; ♩ \; ♩ \; ♩ \; ♩ \,|$ with his foot, the congregation joins in with off-beat hand clapping (Example 4.3b) $| \, ♯ \; ♩ \; ♯ \; ♩ \, |$ and occasional more $| \, ♯ \; ♩ \; ♫ \, ♯ \, |$ complex interlocking rhythms (Example 4.3c).

This shift of orientation points up two things. In the "spiritual" rendition, there is considerable response from the congregation—vocal interjections and hand clapping. While the derivation of general behavioural patterns from musical structure is always problematic, this style is, I think, indicative of the community's social style: it is flexible, not fixed; complex, but not laboured; improvised (interpreted), not exact—were there more than one singer the rendition would undoubtedly be heterophonic—and despite its elaborateness, it is predominantly contemplative rather than showy. The increased response from the congregation to the climax in the third line, however, must express appreciation of technical skill as well as aesthetic beauty, because the religious message remains constant throughout the song, i.e., "Sinner please don't let this harvest pass." As Portia Maultsby remarks,

Example 4.2. "Sinner please don't let this harvest pass." Spiritual, performed in gospel choral style.

[W]hen performers create and interpret songs within the aesthetic boundaries framed by black people, audiences respond immediately. Their verbal comments and physical gestures express approval of both the song being performed and the way it is performed. This type of audience participation is important to performers; it encourages them to explore the full range of aesthetic possibilities, and it is the single criterion by which black artists determine whether they are meeting the aesthetic expectations of the audience (1990: 194–95).

Although one might expect increased participation from the congregation when the style moves to gospel and the choir joins in (in response to the upbeat rhythms, tighter sound, and enthusiastic performance), the opposite is true. After several verses the congregation joins the choir in off-beat hand clapping, but the "feeling" that lined hymns evoke and that was present during the "spiritual" soloist's performance is absent. The congregation seems to enjoy the gospel section, but the section contributes little of significance to the performance on any of the three levels of text (message), melody, or rhythm. The song text (a single line repeated four times), now on its third repetition, has yielded its message and repetition, unless newly improvised and aesthetically beautiful, is redundant. Although the gospel version formulates a new musical expression, both the soloist and chorus parts are unimaginative and, critically, as mentioned previously, there is no true gospel solo style in evidence, the soloist having abandoned that style. The speed of the rendition ($\downarrow = 172$–208) to some extent precludes an embellished or highly improvised solo, yet one would expect some degree of personalisation and innovation from the soloist, and neither of these is the province of the choir.

The gospel section, in fact, has very few characteristics of the Clear Creek community's social and cultural style. It is not improvised or individualized; it is tightly controlled, but not flexible; the leader-chorus relationship, particularly in the rigid fashion presented here, is not strongly mirrored in the church—Clear Creek is more an egalitarian group wherein different individuals and smaller groups have influence. Many individuals have effective power at Clear Creek, and most can conceive of the church as separate from Rev. McKinney: church leadership is not concentrated exclusively in the figure of the pastor, as is sometimes the case.[6] The members gather together as a church community as frequently without Rev. McKinney as with him, and spend a considerable amount of informal social time together when he is not present.

Although the leader-chorus structure of the gospel section is characteristic of lined hymns, in that form it is a more integrated structure. The leader lines the hymn, but also joins in with the group, so that he is both separate from them and a part of them. The congregation's response is not subsidiary to the leader's call: textually it is on an equal footing and musically it is more important. The response realises the melody in individualised, heterophonic fashion that is melodically and rhythmically complex, whereas the leader barely sketches a skeletal melody.

A significant problem with the gospel section of "Sinner please don't let this harvest pass" is the atypical nature of the relationship between soloist (leader) and chorus. Usually, when a gospel soloist joins with the chorus, the relationship is a complementary one. The chorus generally carries most of the significant meaning—in the rhythmic and melodic shape, and especially in the spiritual message of the song. The structure of the chorus's presentation (homophonic, straight, and quite inflexible), however, is not significant for the community: it is not a structure that is mirrored in other aspects of their lives. The soloist, on the other hand, usually contributes meaning to the performance primarily in the aesthetic and structural spheres where improvisation, individualisation, and flexibility are essential. Because the soloist adds interjections between the end of one line of the song and the beginning of the next, she generally contributes little additional spiritual or textual meaning.

In this performance of "Sinner please don't let this harvest pass," however, this complementarity of soloist-chorus has been upset. The chorus' role is subsidiary to that of the soloist who now carries the melody, and neither component (soloist or chorus) is very significant aesthetically. The only significant addition in this section, it seems, is the percussive elements described above, to which the congregation responds accordingly.

Despite all the problems discussed above, this rendition of "Sinner please don't let this harvest pass," offers a synthesis of tradition and modernity, old and new. Yet the weight of aesthetic investment lies with the former. One comes away from the performance with a sense of two different but complementary modes and feelings. If neither subsumes the other, it is clear which is more satisfying. Both stand alone, yet are reasonably effectively integrated in the rendition. Old and new are joined in the textual theme of harvest.

"We don't have service now like we used to have"

The members not only give the community greater coherence through the synthesis of diverse understandings of harvest in a symbolic celebration, they then also create from this celebration a communal sacred reality through the transformation of the profane harvest of crops into a sacred harvest of souls.

> The meaning of Harvest Day is all about gathering. But instead of gathering crops, I want you to think of gathering newcomers for Christses [*sic*] kingdom. Whether we accept it or not, we all, as Christians, have an obligation to try and influence non-believers to follow Christ. We don't all have to be preachers, deacons, or teachers to do this. We can do this simply by living a life that will influence others. There are many people that could be saved, but there are so few of us that are willing to work towards that end (Jessie Orange, remarks at Harvest Day programme, November 15, 1987).

As evidenced by Jessie Orange's earlier statement about the differences between the older and younger generations' comprehension of Harvest Day, the community's past and future is, in some sense, represented in church every Sunday. The membership encompasses four generations of family, from people who lived through the latter part of the nineteenth century to those who will probably live through a good portion of the twenty-first century. But living memory goes further back, enriching the present with ancestors from a more distant past. Where there is still time to talk and reminisce, ancestors are given life in the present tales of the community. Deacon Lee Earl Robinson not only has a picture, garnered from the memories of his elders, of a native American great-grandfather, he also carries his grandfather within himself because his elders have recognised his grandfather in him.

> My grandfather done a lot of things. I don't know, nothing that I can say for sure that he done, but I know he was a handy man. Many elder people say that I have lots of the same talent my grandfather had: anything I put my hand to I can do. And he made a lot of medicine and other stuff, something I wish I had been around. He was part Indian; I supposed to have a bunch of people somewhere in Oklahoma.[7] His father was Indian. My grandfather was about ninety-two years old when he died, and that was in 1955, so he was around in the eighteen-hundreds. He could go in the woods and get different types of roots and stuff, and he made medicine and stuff. Over in Springhill we have, well they call it the sorghum mill, where they made molasses and stuff. He could do that kind of stuff and I don't know what all. Actually my grandfather used to do, from what my grandmother used to, well she never really said exactly what he used to do, but I got a feeling he used to do some things that weren't quite legal either (interview, November 17, 1987).

In contrast to this historical past of symbiosis with nature, herbal medicine, and self- or community-healing, the members now find themselves dependent upon modern medical bureaucracy and technology, administered by strangers whom they may not trust. There is no black doctor in the Oxford area; to consult a black doctor one must be willing and able to travel twenty miles or more to Batesville or Holly Springs. There is a perception that credit is generally not extended to black people and that black doctors, who might otherwise practice in the community, therefore lack the capital to set up a practice in the Oxford area.

> It's awful hard for a black person to get established when his people don't have any money. To a white person, he can get a whole bunch of money, just on signature alone. Whereas me, I would have to mortgage my house, my land, my cars, and everything else, and I still wouldn't get the money that I would need to set my business up right (Lee Earl Robinson, interview, November 21, 1987).

As the members are conscious of their agrarian past and its juxtaposition with what will in all likelihood be an increasingly urbanised future, so they contrast the financial poverty of their past with the comfortable standard of living that several now enjoy. Once again, religion is the receptacle wherein experiences are reinterpreted and transformed into a communal sacred experience. More often than not, the members see greater wealth in material things as paralleling and responsible for the loss of religious fervour. Rev. McKinney sees this as a major problem in contemporary churches.

I wish you could have been down in here about thirty years ago. We don't have service now like we used to have. Back, and I know why, there was a time when poor folks, whether you white or black, you didn't have anything to depend on but the Lord. 'Cause see the man had the money, he didn't care what color you was; in a sense of speaking, everybody was a slave. You just put out there to make that man some money. And you got bad treatments, I don't care what color you was. People was 'pending on the Lord. But after World War Two, that's when black people started to change. And a white man told me about his church. [. . .] He used to live down the road here and he used to talk to me about his church. And that's what happened at they church. They church changed. After the Lord started blessing everybody, it changed. And he said his church used to be spiritual, but it had gone bad. And that's what happened to the most of our black churches. Since everyone got ninety-eight cents—don't mean he got forty thousand dollars, but he got ninety-eight cents—he got a check book in his pocket. He can buy might near what he want to eat. The Lord fix it so you can get a forty-thousand-dollar house, and get thirty years to pay for it. You can buy a new car.[8] Well, one man now probably end up having more shoes than the whole family used to have; because we had a pair of work shoes, and we didn't have dress shoes, we had Sunday shoes, and that meant you wore them shoes Sunday. And when you came back from church, you pulled them off and put them up, your dress clothes too. 'Cause if you had two outfits, as we call Sunday clothes, that's about all you had! But now the Lord blessed us. We better clothes through the week than we used could wear on Sundays. Mens now got more suits than they can keep up with, and there was a time we didn't have but one. And we enjoyed goin' to church, praying and singing and having a glorious time. But now when the Lord blessed us, and black-and-white TV came out and we got one of them, and the Lord blessed us and we moved on up and got a color TV, and the Lord just have blessed us and it have kind of did like a suck on something. It kind of drawed [*sic*] some of our dependence on God from us, and we kinda feel like we can make it on our own, and that'll dry you up. Any time you feel like that you got all this thing together, that you can make it by yourself, that make you spiritually dead (Rev. McKinney, interview, November 17, 1986.).

That there is a difference in social and cultural identity between the vast majority of African Americans and the prosperous few is indisputable. It is an opposition illustrated by the research of black psychologists (Guthrie, 1976; Jenkins, 1982; Jones, 1980), reiterated time and again in the literature, and by all of the "disadvantaged" African Americans with whom I have worked (that affluent African Americans are not "really black" because they identify with the dominant culture and adopt that culture's norms), and played out quite consistently in the religious context.

> So respectable you can't touch her with a ten-foot pole, that's Tempy! Anjee's all right, working herself to death at Mrs. Rice's, but don't tell me about Tempy. Just because she's married a mail-clerk with a little property, she won't ever see her own family any more. When niggers get up in the world, they act just like white folk—don't pay you no mind. And Tempy's that kind of nigger—she's up in the world now! (Langston Hughes, *Not Without Laughter* (1930); reprint, New York: Alfred A. Knopf, 1962, 44–45).

It seems generally true that as one climbs toward the higher echelons of the socio-economic spectrum so the style of worship used by congregations becomes increasingly formalised and restrained. A rise in social status seems to bring with it a shift in worship style. African Americans of high socio-economic status, especially if northern in orientation, seem to adopt much of what is traditionally associated with mainstream white worship traditions—restraint, emotional detachment, increased formalisation. "Unlike independent Black churches, the Black 'folk church' did not evolve from white Protestant denominations. Its musical repertoire, therefore, is distinctly different from that of Protestant churches, representing a continuation of *age-old musical traditions and practices, adapted to reflect twentieth-century attitudes, values, and life-styles of the poor and uneducated*" (Maultsby, 1985: 39) [my italics].

As mentioned earlier in relation to musical style and the performance in spiritual/Dr. Watts style during the opening choruses of "Sinner, please don't let this harvest pass," tradition is valued at Clear Creek M.B.C. It is a traditional church, and is regarded thus by other churches in the area. Preaching and praying are frequently chanted in the traditional manner, and traditional songs are an integral part of services. But the church is also seen as progressive; it has a large percentage of young members, and the youth choir is known for the contemporary gospel they sing. While young and progressive do not necessarily go hand in hand, in this instance gospel is both a progressive musical form and one that is explicitly identified with young people. There is an awareness amongst the members that their church is more expressive in its emotional style, a trait that is seen as traditional and "down home," than are some others in the area, but concomitant with that is an awareness that it is not as expressive or as overtly emotional as it used to be.

In the 1960s and 1970s black theologians selected emotional expressivity as a gauge to measure the "blackness" of a particular congregation. This characteristic became the measure of the "authenticity" of a particular black service, where conservatism, emotional suppression and formalism were associated with white traditions.

> You see, the Black Church became very self-conscious and like individual black people she as an institution began to seek her legitimacy in the white community. She started to judge herself by white standards and her values became increasingly white as she sought authenticity in the community, forgetting that she was authentic because black people are authentic; and in seeking approval from the broader white community the fires of liberation were dimmed, and she became increasingly more conservative. Her conservatism was seen in many ways, from the changing of her music to her emphasis on dignity, quietness in worship (Calvin B. Marshall, Jr., 1974: 159).

Albert B. Cleage, Jr., also refers to "the dead emptiness of white folks' service; the little rhythmless songs with nothing to pat your foot to all through the service" (Cleage, 1974: 174).

As black theology began to come of age in the mid-1970s, it asserted its distinction from, and yet its complementarity to white theology. "Black theology is in some sense what is missing from white theology. To the degree that it fulfills its own best intentions, it is the restoration of a deficit incurred through the habitual malfunctioning of a racist calculus" (William Jones, 1974: 145). In the 1980s and 1990s, however, scholars of black religion began to challenge the notion of a single, monolithic black church. The noted historian Milton J. Sernett, for example, asserted that "recognition of differences, of varieties of African-American religious identity and expression, 'problematizes' the notion of a single entity conceived of as the Black church" (in Dayton and Johnston, eds. 1991: 136). And Hans A. Baer and Merrill Singer's important 1992 study highlights in its title, *African-American religion in the twentieth century: Varieties of protest and accommodation*, a new celebration of the diversity of black religious expression. Detailing several reasons why the diversity of African-American culture has, until relatively recently, been largely ignored, Baer and Singer conclude that "as a consequence, the myriad expressions of

African-American religiosity have been compressed in scholarly under-standing into a number of major types and a few peripheral and largely unattended variants, a pattern that can be seen in the tendency to equate African-American religion with the 'Black church' " (1992: xv–xvi).

Nonetheless, in a society as racially preoccupied and racially divided as the United States, awareness of the distinction of African American religion persists. As remarked by Albert J. Raboteau, "[T]he segregation of black and white churches signified the existence of two Christianities in this nation and the deep chasm that divided them demonstrated the failure of the nation's predominant religious institution, the major source of its common symbols, images, and values, to achieve meaningful, sustained community across racial lines" (2001: 198). Contributing to the Wind and Lewis 1994 collection, *American Congregations*, Robert Michael Franklin tries, not altogether successfully, to supplant the icon of "the Black church" with that of a core black religious culture.

> There are varieties of black congregations which share a common core culture. This culture is an amalgam of symbols, practices, and ideas drawn from numerous traditions [. . .] Amongst the most significant constitutive practices of the culture are the full engagement of the senses in worship, intimate prayer, cathartic shouting, triumphant singing, politically relevant religious education, and prophetic preaching (1994: 2:259–60).

As are members of black congregations throughout the United States, members of Clear Creek M.B.C., are clearly aware of perceived differences between what are termed black and white worship styles. Obviously sensitized to the topic, deacon Leroy Thompson offered these remarks during the course of an interview:

> Somebody asked me one time why it is that black services were different. Well, a person asked me why is a black service very emotional. And my only answer to that is that, you know, black people had no release for the tensions and the problems. The only source of release—we knew nothing, and I'm saying as a people we knew nothing about counselling and psychology and psychiatric treatment, we knew nothing about those things—and the only release was a worship service. And so the worship services became very emotional, because of the things that I couldn't say and the things that I couldn't do, I can release it and emotions on Sunday, you know, Sunday services and all. And the sermons were preached that way, as a means of getting at this binding inside of me and it's tearing me apart, you know, getting at that and bringing it out in the opening [sic]. And I felt better because I got it in the opening [sic], you know. I didn't tell it to a counsellor, and I didn't really have

to tell it to anybody else, not even to the guy next door or to the guy sitting right next to me. I just let it go. So, because of that, black services are . . . not so much as they used to be! I can remember when this church, you talking about very emotional and very together as far as singing, and loud! . . . I think it's evolving into a thing where the need for, again, the emotional release is not there as much as it has been in the past. Because if you go to a counsellor, it's slow, but as a result you don't have. . . . And plus, I think more and more we are learning to go to others and talk to them about problems, whereas that wasn't the case. You know, you just didn't do things like that! You didn't talk about things that are happening in your family, or problems that you're having. You didn't do things like that. But you did let it out, you expressed it (interview, November 22, 1987).

Deacon Thompson also delineates other reasons for what he perceives as the decline in emotional expressivity in black churches. He notes that because many members are not as poor as were their parents, they have access to other avenues of release for suppressed emotions.

You may go off on a trip, vacation with the family, go do things. You may go to a ball game or anything, you may go to a show or a theater or something. You have a lot more means for releasing the tensions and the emotions than you did in those times. In the past we never did that, we never had those things. Two places you went, or actually three places: you went to school, you went to church, and sometimes you would go to town.[9] That was it! And that was a routine. You didn't have anything to do, and so when you came out on Sunday, all of this over the week has been built up to an emotional fervor. I mean like binding again inside, and it's released (ibid.).

In black Baptist services in general, the sermon is seen as the climax of the service. Everything that precedes it is intended to prepare the congregation for the message that the preacher will bring. More than any other event, the sermon is expected to intensify the emotional state of all participants. As Baer and Singer assert, "[T]he sermon, which occurs in the latter half of the service, functions as the focal ritual event of the service. Whereas ritual events prior to it collectively serve as a prelude to the climatic sermon, which may last over an hour, events afterwards are anti-climactic" (1992: 34). The sermon's culmination in the Invitation Hymn is an attempt to reach people, to bring them to salvation when they are likely to be in a heightened emotional state. For this reason, the primary difference pointed to in contrasting old-time services and contemporary ones is the difference in preaching style. Leroy Thompson cites the direct, emotional appeal of many preachers as a distinctly black characteristic.

Given the importance of preaching in the mainstream black religious traditions, it was to be expected that black theologians of the 1960s and 1970s would also identify this style of preaching as iconic of black religious expression. Albert B. Cleage, Jr., highlights this by contrasting this style of black preaching with a picture of "white" worship, or black congregations trying to sound "white":

Have you ever heard a black preacher trying to sound white? He gets up and tries to whisper at you and tell you how nice everything is. That's only in churches for well-to-do black folks who don't go to church often, anyway. This is the most ridiculous black church there ever was because it doesn't have any relationship to the needs of black people at all. We don't like the music. We don't like the preaching. We don't like anything about it and the only black people who attend are black people who have a need to pretend that they really like to do things the same way white folks do them. A black church which is a copy of the white church cannot meet any of our needs. [. . .] Now, the old down-home churches, Baptist, Methodist, or what have you, were in a sense a replica of white folks' religion. But there we took white folks' Christianity, twisted it around and made it fit at least a few of our needs. When you worship in a down-home black church, at least you feel good. The music is good, you can jump up and down, you can shout and feel free—free like you are home. To help you feel good and release tension is meeting at least some need. You caught hell all week. The white man was driving you, and all week you have wanted to tell him off but you couldn't because you didn't want to lose your job. You took insults because you didn't want to get whipped up and go to jail, and on Sunday you just let yourself go (Cleage, 1974: 175).

Note the close parallel between these remarks and those made by Leroy Thompson earlier in the chapter (see pp. 102–3). An extroverted, emotional style of worship (which may, but need not necessarily, lead to shouting and falling out) becomes a valued characteristic of the black church, a characteristic used in conscious opposition to white traditions. (See also the comments by Randy J. Sparks in chapter 2 (p. 31). It is important to bear in mind, however, that this difference between black and white worship styles has a more profound basis. "The emotional ecstasy of black Protestant worship symbolizes a profound religious truth: the preeminent place of God's presence in this world is the person. [. . .] Moreover, it is the whole person, body as well as spirit, that makes God present" (Raboteau, Albert J, 2001: 199).[10]

The theme of emotional release is also emphasized repeatedly, and there is a return to the assertion of the black church as the retreat where black people could behave as they wished and experience necessary release.

And you notice that a lot of the, no matter how much most of the ministers, black ministers, want to get into the Scriptures and to be as sophisticated about the Scriptures, and to use all the rhetoric you can possibly use with Scriptures, most of them are going usually get to the thing where you start dealing with personal problems. And that's when the church responds, when he starts talking about things they can identify with—not that I can't identify with the Scriptures—but things like "It's been hard this week, and I been talked about this week, and things have happened to me this week, and I been sick," you know; and to talk about "But hey, look, God will stand by me!" That brings out the emotional side, and for the first time, I can release that. And nobody has to know that it has happened to me this week. They may know something is wrong, but they don't have to know what it is, because I can release it in this term and nobody's gonna ask me, "What's wrong with you?" either. If I'm doing it at home or if I'm riding along the road and I do it, or if I do it on the street, now somebody's gonna ask me, "Hey, something's wrong?" But if I do it here, nobody's gonna ask me what's wrong (Leroy Thompson, interview, November 22, 1987).

Rev. McKinney also cites emotional intensity as a traditional characteristic of the black church, but he is more critical of it than is Leroy Thompson. Inherent in the emotional sermon, he sees the danger of there being a lack of substance or teaching. He faults those preachers who, in his youth, preached only emotion-evoking, or "loving" sermons, because they failed to educate their congregations. Such sermons rely for their power solely on exposition and reiteration of God's love for every individual, ignoring the individual's obligation in the relationship.

But when you get on this loving sermon, how much God love us, and I have known this to happen back when I was young, some of the preachers just lived on them kind of sermons, and every time you go to church, them peoples was knocking over pews, they were shouting. But you shouldn't get your congregation built upon that type of sermon all the time. You use them sermons sometime. . . . You see, it's a bad policy for a minister to keep his people shouting all the time. If you keep people shouting all the time, they'll come the place where they don't know nothing to do but shout. And every time they come to church, they expecting to shout. And if they don't shout, they go home disappointed. But see, it's a time for shouting. But you need to know something (Rev. Grady McKinney, interview, November 17, 1986).

Many black Baptists equate this type of preaching with "down-home," traditional worship. At Clear Creek there is also a perception that responding very emotionally to such a style is old-fashioned and somewhat unrefined, and should be left in the past where it originated.

> In the old, traditional thing, a minister used to preach emotional sermons. . . . And that kinda stuff was probably alright in its time— hellfire and brimstone and stuff like that, what I call graveyard dogma. It did nothing to help the people. And what we need now is for us more teaching on what the Holy Spirit is all about, and what livin' a true Christian life is all about, instead of preachin' about Daniel in the lions' den and relatin' it to some emotional things that happened years ago, to bring on what I call a "shout," not for joy, but a shout of sorrow. When you get people emotionally disturbed you can get 'em to shout and they really haven't learned anything. Key things I like to emphasise and would like to see in many of our black churches, to learn what the Scriptures are saying and how to read and understand about (Lee Earl Robinson, interview, November 11, 1987).

In many instances, this sort of preaching and response is seen not only as passé, but also as unacceptable socially and as somewhat ignorant. "You are told that it's not culturally accepted to be that way, that's not intelligent to act a certain way" (Leroy Thompson, interview, November 22, 1987).

Partly because the members of Clear Creek M.B.C. value both tradition and progress, neither subsumes the other; old and new co-exist at Clear Creek. This co-existence is not without its tensions, but it is not as divisive as it might be. Because the community's worldview is flexible enough to accommodate them, both poles can co-exist. "We have a traditional church. There are those of us who would like to move away from the old tradition that has been goin' on for a hundred years or more. And there are those who are contented" (Lee Earl Robinson, interview, November 11, 1987). In some senses the wide age range of the membership precludes a unanimous style. At the same time, however, the close-knit, familial nature of the community ensures bonds that will not break under the tension.

"Well, we are more so equal now than has been"

But this community does not exist in a vacuum; there has always been interaction with the larger white community. The Brown v. Board of Education Supreme Court decision (1956) to integrate the public schools (finally overturning the 1896 Plessy v. Ferguson "separate but equal" justification for segregation) and the civil rights movement of the 1960s have meant increased interaction between black and white. Nonetheless, social segregation is still virtually a way of life in this part of Mississippi. Integration of the University of Mississippi campus, for example, has meant the admission of black people to the university and, as the number of black students has increased, the two communities mix socially to some extent. This, however, is very much a campus phenomenon and seems not to apply at all to the residential communities. This mixing is also true of educational establishments at all levels, but I am referring to "social time" as time when one is not obliged to remain in a certain place or to engage in a certain activity. Primary and high schools do not in general have this type of interaction, as the students usually leave each other's company once the school day is ended. School desegregation in Mississippi, moreover, as Bolton has asserted,

> occurred largely on white terms. Black teachers and administrators lost their jobs and the black community saw an erosion of the control they had exercised over their children's education. In the years that followed, as federal support waned, efforts in Mississippi [. . .] to create unitary school systems usually floundered, in many cases leading to a resegregation of the schools (2000: 781).

There are diverse attitudes towards desegregation within the Clear Creek community. Some are glad about the progress the black community has made since the sixties. Although they may be acutely aware of how limited their situation still is, they tend to be optimistic, happy with gains made, and looking forward to a future of greater freedom. Others are more conscious of the losses they have suffered with desegregation: they regret the loss of an isolation that made them strong, which fostered a "black" culture that was largely independent. I did not find in the Clear Creek community, however, the separatist stance that I encountered in other places in Mississippi and elsewhere. It is, of course, not uncommon for individuals to become disillusioned with the reality of desegregation, which is sometimes far from the ideals of the sixties. Individuals who, in the sixties, risked their lives to integrate restaurants and other buildings in some instances withdraw into separatism because attitudes lag so far behind legislation. In their own words, "Why should we bother to go where we are so clearly not welcome?"

It may be that their perceived helplessness precludes, for the more pessimistic members of Clear Creek, a separatist future, and so they take refuge in the past. Or it may be that they are pragmatic and see the near impossibility of creating such a community. It is also possible that, having developed a reasonably close relationship with me, the church members did not wish to isolate me by advocating separation. I think that this is unlikely, however, as I believe that those with whom I talked most had come to accept that I do not consider myself white, but Irish: white being a category not yet operative in Ireland. I do not think that it is because of any inherent virtue that the category "white" is not operative for Irish people: the Irish have other out-groups. Contact with dark-skinned peoples has not been extensive enough to necessitate categorisation of them. (Closer ties with the European Union and the resultant contact with non-Irish peoples are, however, beginning to change this in recent years.) For whatever reason, when the members of Clear Creek M.B.C. envision a more ideal community, they look backwards rather than forwards. To the extent that the members alternate between these two positions, loss and gain, they move between past and present/future.

Mr. Charles Campbell, who at 99 [in 1986] was one of the oldest members in the church (the oldest member at that moment was Mary Penamon, who was one hundred and six), told me that he had seen considerable improvement in the treatment of black people in his lifetime. He taught school for between fifteen and twenty years after he married, and he also commented freely on the differences between school then and now.

> We as black folks are more recognised today than we were years back, but there have always been mix. Much better to getting along now, because the black man don't serve under the white man like he used to. More considered as equal. We are equal people in all things. Every man should have equal rights in every thing. All is human. If we just consider, we are all human, and every man has the same right. Well, we are more so equal now than has been. We are getting along together more. We are not oppressed. The black man, they don't oppress him now like they used to. He is more respected and considered as human than it has been. Well, there's lot of 'em don't consider us now. They think the color has something to do with it. Well it's not the color, it's the principle of a person what rules. Because we have some sorry of each kind, in each of 'em. Now, they is allowed to marry! But used to be, the white man, he was the one done the mixing. But now, it's the black man, he's trying to do what the white man used to. . . . Well now, you take it, there's been just as many poor white people as there were poor black folks, back in those days. And a poor white man, he stood just as bad a hack as a poor black man. They doin' the same work. A black man, he doing the same thing that a white man doing today. Because we got black folks in school, I don't know about the men folk, it's not too many black menfolks as teachers now. But the black mens [*sic*] holding the same jobs as the white men hold. It's the brains and the money which promotes a man nowadays (interview, November 20, 1986).

Deacon Lee Earl Robinson, on the other hand, feels that things have not improved dramatically for black people.

I don't really feel that the hearts of people has really changed to some extent. For there are some still die-hard racists . . . white people who still, it was, I don't know who to blame, it was just brought up in them. And likewise, hostility is still found in many of the hearts of the black people from the way they have been treated. So the trend look as if it is changing, but things 'far as the hearts of men, really as an overall, it's really not changed that much. These things are done because the law says you have to do. It's not because it's something that mens are willing to accept (interview, November 17, 1986).

Some of the members feel, as does Deacon Robinson, that there has been considerable loss to black people in desegregation, and that the gains, not as extensive as hoped, have exacted a substantial price. Some members of Clear Creek, and other black people in different areas of the state, feel that any move towards integration has been largely at the expense of black culture, i.e., that it is always black people who must become "more white," and never the reverse. There is a perception that, because of this, black people have lost a tremendous amount through integration, perhaps more than they have gained.

To any given generation, even for yourself . . . there's a certain amount of pride you take in just bein' Irish. But when total integration came about, and all the culture and the pride was bein' stripped from the black generation or the black people, then there was a sense of "don't give a durn" about it. So when you take all of a person's pride, he has nothing left. And from this brought about many problems, and the generations that come on now are not taught the pride and dignity in which one should have within hisself and within his own nationality. Integration, to an extent, was a bad thing, because you was forced to give up all the things that you had, that meant a lot to you. For instance, have you ever seen Jackson State marchin' band? . . . You know, you could tell me all day what it means to you to be an Irish, and the things that you miss that meant a lot to you, and the traditions and things that you would like to keep goin'. And if you was forced to give up all these things, you see, to take a new life, and then there was a limited amount of things that you was able to participate in, because you was rejected from bein' in things simply because of the color of your skin. And these things have a great bearing on the outcome of a person's life. Only those who are strong and are able to look beyond those things, only those people who can accept the change in life and still continue to deal from that, are the ones that are able to survive (Lee Earl Robinson, interview, November 11, 1987).

It is clear from Deacon Robinson's comments that integration has caused a considerable amount of pain, probably more so in Mississippi than in many other places because of the ugliness of the fight there. Even the positive black movements of the 1960s, such as Black Power or the Black is Beautiful movements, are seen as only mildly successful struggles to keep black culture alive. "All of those things was the quest and the fight to keep black power and black pride alive. Even with the cry to keep our culture alive, in many instance it was being chipped off little by little" (ibid.).

Such overwhelmingly sad comments hardly give rise to hope, no more than do the racist attitudes of some white people, contemporary Ku Klux Klan rallies, or the vast economic discrepancy between rich and poor. Mississippi has, in some ways, led the way in the nationwide deterioration in race relations that continued in the 1990s. Black churches in Mississippi were being burnt to the ground before church arson became a matter of national concern in 1996. And the trend continued. As Sparks eloquently points out, "in June 1996 two black churches [. . .] in the northeastern part of the state went up in flames one night within minutes of one another. While many residents of both races found it difficult to believe that the fires were set by local residents, others pointed out that a Ku Klux Klan rally had been held on the steps of the nearby Corinth courthouse only two months before" (2001: 276).

But there have also been moments of hope. In 1992 the pastors of two very separate churches in Oxford, Mississippi—St. Peter's Episcopal (white), and Second Baptist (black)—began concerted efforts to bring their congregations together, both in worship and socially. The leaders of each of the two churches—Duncan Gray III, and the Reverend Leroy Wadlington (who grew up as a member of Clear Creek M.B.C.)—preached in each other's churches, with each congregation listening to their very different styles. As Charles Reagan Wilson points out, although both pastors grew up in Oxford, "coming of age in the 1960s and both living through the turbulent violence and social instability in Oxford during James Meredith's entrance as the first African American student at the University of Mississippi. Yet, as part of racially segregated communities, they never knew each other growing up" (2001: 215–16).

After Wadlington's lively Baptist sermon, the associate rector, representing the congregation, thanked him, noting that even though he was an Episcopalian, he had almost yelled out "Amen." Several of us met afterward in small groups at neighborhood houses to reflect on the experience. No one had prepared the Baptists to rely on the Episcopal Book of Common Prayer to guide them through the service. Some members of Second Baptist had been surprised, moreover, to taste real wine in the Episcopal communion, rather than the grape juice they were accustomed to taking. Since then, the congregations have had joint summer picnics in the town park, visited each other's services, sponsored youth retreats, and even tailgated together before a football game in the once all-white Grove of the University of Mississippi (ibid.: 216).

In some ways the comments of Lee Earl Robinson (above), keep the past alive by prompting a nostalgic and sometimes desperate flight back in time to a more secure, homogeneous society. As an outsider, looking at race relations in Mississippi today, I found that I needed to make a conscious effort in order to avoid being drawn into an affective state of frustration and hopelessness. Habitual negative attitudes are so strong that it is difficult not to fall into a position of helplessness. Such a position, of course, influences one's present actions and thereby moulds the future.

This, however, is not the only or even predominant feeling in the community. There is also happiness and gratitude for the substantial gains that the black community has made, and a sense of optimism about a future that can only improve because black people, and some white people, will not allow it to deteriorate, or even to stand still. Deacon Sam Jones, who is politically active in the community, is of this group.

Bottom line to me, the two communities, black and white communities, goin' have to come together. It is inevitable that they will come together, because I still believe in the fact of this, irregardless of how long a man lives, he still goin' die. The powers that be, regardless of their age, they just can't be in power forever. There are several people that are being groomed, and not necessarily by me, to do certain things. It does not take a whole lot of folks in this state to do anything but mess up (Interview, November 23, 1986).

One significant political development in Mississippi has been the election of a black man, Mike Espy, to the U.S. House of Representatives in the Fall of 1986. Deacon Jones points to this as "fantastic for the state! It's the first black we've had in the U.S. House of Representatives since the eighteen hundreds" (ibid.). And as Mozella Mitchell remarks "Mississippi today has more Black elected officials than any other state: and more than twenty of the ninety-six legislators in Mississippi are Black" (1994: 2).

Tradition is strong in the Clear Creek M.B.C. community. The past has a very real and important presence in the community's life. It is present in the past of the older members of the church, in the remembrance and in the curtailed present of an agrarian life, of farming the land. It survives in stories and notable ancestors, memories of a strong, if isolated, black culture, and in traditional expressions in the church. But the community is also a forward-looking one. The children and young people of the church are the community's future. They are pursuing college education and learning about modern technology. They have hopes of becoming professionals, as do their parents for them. They are creating a new, but still distinctly black culture, one of whose expressions is the contemporary gospel that they sing in church.

Embracing both their past and their present/future, the members create for themselves a community that is strong and resilient. History evokes for them their communal past, which grounds them in who they are and from whence they have come. The community's direction, where the members are going, is indicated and fostered by the community's present choices, and takes flight in the dreams and hopes of and for the young. "To everything there is a season, and a time to every purpose under the heaven" (Ecclesiastes 3:1).

5

Moving in the Spirit

"If it ain't no shoutin', no Spirit in it"

Before proceeding any further with our exploration of religious expression in African American Baptist communities, and the Clear Creek M.B.C. community in particular, it is essential to consider what the members believe is the intervention of the spirit world in their lives. Briefly alluded to in description of phenomena such as the "shout" and the conversion experience, surrender of one's consciousness to individual and intimate experience of the Holy Spirit is a central and often essential focus of church members' lives. Because the issue of spirit intervention in the natural world is a complex one, it is useful, for the sake of clarity, to consider the categories established by Gilbert Rouget in his book *Music and Trance: A Theory of the Relations between Music and Possession*. Rouget broadly defines trance as "a state of consciousness composed of two components, one psychophysiological, the other cultural" (1985: 3). The psychophysiological component is what accounts for the universality of trance, as it would seem that trance issues from and is dependent upon "a psychophysiological disposition innate in human nature" (3).[1] The cultural component accounts for the culture-specific characteristics of trance behaviour engendered by different cultures.

Proceeding from this definition, Rouget distinguishes between ecstasy and trance, a distinction that he details on p. 11 by a listing of opposed characteristics (see table 5.1). The characteristics seem self-explanatory and describe the context necessary to engender each state, the climax of the experience, and the resolution state of the individual. In table 5.2, I have rearranged the characteristics in order to more clearly illustrate these three stages.

Rouget describes the crisis in trance as "a convulsive state, accompanied by cries, trembling, loss of consciousness and falling" (8). Although opposed, ecstasy and trance may be experienced by the same individual at different times or in different ritual contexts. Trance is an unusual and temporary state of consciousness; the individual frequently withdraws from temporal reality and seems to enter another space. He returns from this altered state of consciousness at the end of the trance and generally

Table 5.1. Characteristics of Ecstasy and Trance I

Ecstasy	Trance
immobility	movement
silence	noise
solitude	in company
no crisis	crisis
sensory deprivation	sensory overstimulation
recollection	amnesia
hallucinations	no hallucinations

Table 5.2. Characteristics of Ecstasy and Trance II

Ecstasy		Trance
	Context	
solitude		in company
silence		noise
immobility		movement
sensory deprivation		sensory overstimulation
	Climax of the Experience	
hallucinations		no hallucinations
no crisis		crisis
	Resolution	
recollection		amnesia

has no memory of the time lapsed. Rouget divides the characteristics of trance into two categories; symptoms and behaviour. Symptoms are defined as "the simple, unelaborated expression of a certain perturbation experienced by the subject at, let us say, the animal level" (13). These include shuddering, swooning, and falling to the ground, amongst others. The category of behaviour includes:

> those signs that no longer constitute a simple reaction, as do symptoms, but a positive action, endowed with symbolic value [. . .] Ultimately they all seem to be merely the various "signifiers" of one and the same "signified."[2] One could say that in practice they always symbolize the intensification of some particular faculty by means of an action endowed with certain extraordinary or astonishing aspects. Thus trance may be recognised, among other signs, by the fact that one can walk on burning coals without being burned, pierce one's flesh without bleeding, bend swords one would normally be unable to curve [. . .] handle poisonous snakes without being bitten, [. . .] speak a language one has never learned, swoon or die of emotion, be illuminated by the Eternal. [. . .] Thus trance always manifests itself in one way or another as a transcendence of one's normal self, as a liberation resulting from the intensification of a mental or physical disposition, in short, as an

exaltation—sometimes a self-mutilating one—of the self. [. . .] These behavioral signs can vary [. . .] from the very spectacular to the extremely discreet, just as the symptoms [. . .] can vary from the extremely visible to the barely perceptible (13–14).

Taking into account these various aspects of trance, Rouget draws a thumbnail sketch of the individual who is in trance, a sort of quick checklist for the trance state. The picture, of course, will be more or less complete in individual cases.

The individual in a trance state is thus recognisable by the fact that (1) he is not in his usual state; (2) his relationship to the world around him is disturbed; (3) he can fall prey to certain neurophysiological disturbances; (4) his abilities are increased (either in reality or otherwise);[3] (5) this increased ability is manifested by actions or behavior observable by others (14).

Although trance may occur in other situations, it is overwhelmingly a phenomenon associated with religion.

Rouget further distinguishes different types of trance. The first distinction is between shamanism and possession. Shamanic and possession trance differ most importantly in the way they relate to the invisible. In shamanic trance the shaman's soul leaves his body and journeys into the spirit world. In possession, on the other hand, it is the spirits who come and join the individual: it is they who make the journey. It is an inward journey rather than an outward one, not only in the direction which the individual's soul takes, but also in the sense that whereas the shaman goes to a larger space (the spirit world, or some part of it), in the case of possession, the spirits move into a much smaller space (the body of an individual).

In examining how the relationship between the subject in trance and the divinity responsible for that state is conceived, Rouget proposes three sub-categories of possession, (1) possession, (2) inspiration, and (3) communion (25). In possession, the possessee becomes the spirit in question; the spirit in effect substitutes its own identity for the subject's. In the case of inspiration the subject does not become the deity; instead he is "filled with" the deity, under his influence. "Rather than having switched personalities, the subject is thought to have been invested by the deity, or by a force emanating from it, which then coexists in some way with the subject but nevertheless controls him and causes him to act and speak in its name" (26). Finally, communion does not involve embodiment at all, but a meeting of the subject and the deity. "The relationship between divinity and subject is seen as an encounter which, depending upon the individual, is experienced as a communion, a revelation, or an illumination" (26).

In this study, clearly, it is inspiration that is involved. The Holy Spirit controls the subject's actions, but the subject does not become the Holy Spirit.[4] Black Baptists do not image a human form to fit the Holy Spirit, and even should they do so it would be considered blasphemous to thus identify with the Holy Spirit.

Rouget concludes from his research that non-identificatory inspiration and communion trances are typical of transcendent religious traditions. "Non-identificatory trance inspiration or communion trance appear to be characteristic of Islam, Christianity, and Judaism. In other words, it seems to be linked with the logic of religions of transcendence" (28). However, in contrast to many traditions of shamanic, possession, and inspiration trances, the inspiration trances of black Baptists are not generally, in my experience, divinatory (see Rouget: 3), i.e., the subjects are not looked to for insight or prophecy as an effect of the trance state.

I have dwelt thus long upon Rouget's definitions because, in contrast to earlier studies, (Bourguignon, 1973; Eliade, 1960; Lewis, 1971), he has made a consistent attempt to differentiate and classify different types of altered states, and also sketched their different relationships to music. Scholars acknowledge that trance behaviour (or 'shouting' as it is generally called) is one of the most controversial aspects of the African American worship experience (see, for example, R. M. Franklin, 1989), yet rarely is any attempt made to proceed beyond description to analysis, nor is trance generally considered as normative in a cross-cultural context. Hans A. Baer and Merrill Singer, for example, describe their approach as 'methodological agnosticism' (1992: xiii). While acknowledging the reality that the supernatural has for church members, they choose not to engage with that reality. "As social scientists, we recognize that religion is an integral part of socio-cultural systems and as such often motivates human beings to act *as if supernatural forces have a reality of their own*" (ibid.: xiii) [my italics]. Yet a study of religion that fails to seriously consider what church members embrace as the intervention of the spiritual in the physical world, omits what is at the heart of the religious impulse: the desire for an encounter with the holy, whatever the culture-specific understanding of that is.[5] Without becoming entangled in metaphysical discussion or evangelistic proselytising, I have tried to present the members' understanding of what they consider to be the core of their religion: the personal experience of the entry of the Holy Spirit into their bodies.

"Some folks cry, some folks laugh, some folks jump up and down, and some folks holler"

According to Rouget's scheme, two kinds of altered states occur in the Clear Creek community, 1) ecstasy and 2) non-identificatory inspiration trance which is also non-divinatory. This latter type of trance, frequently referred to as "possession," will be referred to more precisely as "inspiration" in the remainder of the text. These two types seem to hold true for all the black Baptist communities that I have studied. I have never seen an individual in the Clear Creek M.B.C. community in the altered state of ecstasy (this, of course, is largely due to the state's prerequisite of solitude), but individuals have told me about their experience of this state and their descriptions include most of the characteristic traits Rouget lists— solitude, silence, immobility, sensory deprivation, no crisis, and recollection. None of the individuals, however, described anything that could be considered a hallucination. All of these points are illustrated in the following account that Lee Earl Robinson gave me of his experience of ecstasy.

The Holy Spirit moves in many different forms, and sometime when I'm lonely, into feelings, that comes upon me that gives me comfort. And sometime when I have doubt about things there is this inner being that moves in me that reassure me that things will be alright. And sometime when I'm worried, I can kneel in prayer and talk, or not necessarily kneel in prayer, kind of tune everything else out. And then I begin to meditate and then the Holy Spirit, again if I am troubled, if I am worried about something, then the Holy Spirit itself reassures me that everything will be alright. . . . And you can sometime, and if you really believe, concentrate or meditate on the Lord in such a manner that even you can be by yourself and sometime you find yourself crying and no one has ever said anything to you. Or you can get so wrapped up in the Holy Spirit, you can find yourself in laughter, and no one has said anything funny (interview, November 11, 1987).

Because of the solitary context of the state of ecstasy, it has been little researched. It is not of great import to me in this study because it is not, in essence, a community experience. The members do not reify it through testimony in service, although Rev. McKinney sometimes refers to it in his sermons.

Inspiration trance, on the other hand, is a community experience and is readily accessible. I have observed it frequently in Southern churches (and churches in the North which have a "Southern orientation," or a membership drawn partially, at least, from the South), but much less frequently in Northern churches. Where, for instance, the Holy Spirit moves upon an individual at Congdon Street Baptist Church in Providence, Rhode Island, the individual is likely to weep quietly or issue several cries of joy, but less frequently does an individual go into a "shout," or lose control of his body, behaviour that is quite usual in Baptist churches that I have visited in Mississippi. Black Baptists with whom I talked generally referred to

these more extravagant behaviours as "traditional," if the informants
were Southern and in the deep South, or "down home," if the informants
were Northerners and in the North, or even in what I think of as the
"transition" zone around Kentucky. Shouting is generally looked upon as
a traditional form of expression, and it is but a small step from "traditional" to "old-fashioned." Although nobody in any of the churches that
I visited told me that they personally thought shouting to be "unseemly,"
"illiterate," or unsophisticated behaviour, several people told me that
"some people" (generally referring to white people) think it is so. Leroy
Thompson told me that "you are told that it's not culturally acceptable to
be that way, that's not intelligent, to act a certain way" (interview,
November 22, 1987). In a similar vein, Charles Campbell related: "Some
folks thought that when folks got to shouting going on, why they was
drunk! But one Scripture says they are not drunk. They are filled with the
Holy Spirit" (interview, November 20, 1986). Acts 6:8–15, relates that
Stephen was accused not of being drunk, but of blaspheming.

> Then they suborned men, which said, 'We have heard him speak blas-
> phemous words against Moses, and against God.' And they stirred up
> the people, and the elders and the scribes, and came upon him, and
> caught him, and brought him to the council. And set up false witnesses,
> which said, This man ceaseth not to speak blasphemous words against
> this holy place, and the law.

It is likely that in his own day, Mr. Campbell had heard people inspired of
the Holy Spirit accused of being drunk, or he might have heard it as a
common story.

At Clear Creek M.B.C., the Holy Spirit "inspires" members not only at
special times such as revival or conversion, but regularly at church services
and programmes.

> The Holy Spirit isn't something that comes (only) during revival. God
> is a momentary God. The Holy Spirit is a momentary being, and when-
> ever we in our minds believe and decide that we are goin' to accept
> Christ as Lord and head of our lives, and sincerely believe this and do
> this, then the Holy Spirit is able (Lee Earl Robinson, interview,
> November 11, 1987).

The members believe, in fact, that all true believers must be inspired by the
Holy Spirit at some time. During my most recent visit at the church, the
members prayed that I too would feel the Holy Spirit moving upon me, a
prayer that I appreciated although it is not part of my tradition.
Inspiration is such a central part of their religious experience that it is difficult for them to imagine faith without inspiration. Lee Earl Robinson

posited it as a necessary part of Baptist experience, as do Rev. McKinney and many of the members.[6]

> It is belief among vast majority of blacks, especially Baptists, that if you cannot feel the Holy Spirit moving upon you sometime, or moving within you, and if it does not sometime make you act unseemly to other people, then what good is it? If you don't have, if the Holy Spirit, if you cannot feel Holy Spirit sometime within you, then is it the Holy Spirit that you have? "With the heart, man believeth, with mouth confession is made unto salvation," Romans 10. There should be some sign, not necessarily outbursts and jumping all over and running benches and so forth, running pews. Maybe that's not necessary, but them who am I to judge how the Holy Spirit moves on that person, when I only know how it moves on me? (Lee Earl Robinson, interview, November 17, 1986).

When I returned to this topic with Lee one year later, he explained to me that there is a state of heightened experience to be attained in the Lord, and that naturally this state has a physical expression. "There has been said by Pentecostal ministers, 'There's a higher height in the Lord.' Which means that you can become so wrapped up in the Holy Spirit that your physical body is not able to contain the excitement in which, or contain the joy, possesses" (November 11, 1987).[7] The necessity of feeling the Holy Spirit in this fashion is not mainstream Baptist doctrine, although an emphasis on religious experience is (see, for example, Eric H. Ohlmann, 1991), and so I asked Lee whether living a 'good life' would not in itself attest to being saved.

> Even a sinner man can live a good life. If I never do anything wrong or harm you, and everything I've done has been pleasing in the eyes of man, but I have not accepted Christ as my personal savior, or do not believe in Christ . . . Even atheists do good. Except you accept Christ as your personal savior, you are condemned (ibid.).

Inspiration by the Holy Spirit is considered an indication that one's conversion has been a true one and not just empty words. Don Cusic similarly describes how it may occur: the "initial religious experience must be followed by a series of experiences with god so that the person may 'know' him. It usually culminates in a second decisive experience, the baptism of the Holy Ghost" (1990: 94). The members believe that inspiration of the Holy Spirit is "the power of Jesus comin' in" (Lee Earl Robinson, interview, November 11, 1987), and that it happens as a result of faith. "Faith [is] what makes the Holy Spirit come in" (Rev. Grady McKinney, interview, November 17, 1986).

"This wrongness was in 'em, and they exploded!"

Although I have not seen examples of it in the community, the members believe that it is also possible to become inspired by the devil.[8]

> The devil has the power for everybody. It's a spirit. The devil was an angel and he got threw out of Heaven, so, it's a spirit. Do you remember this Scripture, in one of Gospels, that this man when Jesus came across him he said his name was Legion? And this man, he had more than one evil spirit in him, that was many spirits in him. And He said, Legion—now I don't know which book right on this, 'cause if you get one book, say this guy now say this, and I looked in it, said it's probably three thousand or four thousand. I have read some other books where it's six or seven different spirits, so I don't know who right—but I do know that mean you are possessed by the devil. He done implanted his spirit in you. And he will usually get in all of us some time, if we don't watch ourselves. And the devil will get in you, and it will make you say to yourself, "Well, I do this, ain't nobody goin' know it." That's what the devil tell you. "Go on, do it! Won't nobody know it." And you notice in studying your Bible, the devil always get you in trouble, but he never get you out. He gets you out and gets you messed up, and leave you right there. So that's what we have to watch. Devil is powerful. There's no way in the world that I can overpower the devil with my own power. It have to be the Holy Spirit. And without it, we just can't make it (Rev. Grady McKinney, interview, November 17, 1986).

Although the devil seems to be a very real and defined figure to the members of Clear Creek M.B.C., they do not usually talk about him inspiring somebody in as demonstrable a fashion as does the Holy Spirit. Concrete imaging of the devil is common in most forms of Christianity, although it is currently becoming unfashionable. In 1957, Carl Jung, suggested that it is one of Christianity's greatest strengths that it posits an evil force—the devil—which is given responsibility for the proclivity towards evil in man. If one accepts Jung's analysis, it is to be expected that Christians will image the devil in a concrete fashion. Jung sees evil as equally integral to the human psyche as good, "[I]t is lodged in human nature itself" (reprint, 1959: 110), and sees Christianity, therefore, as in some ways resolving the resultant psychological split in man: "[In] the Christian view, one is willing to postulate a metaphysical principle of evil. The great advantage of this view is that is exonerates man's conscience of too heavy a responsibility and fobs it off on the devil, in correct psychological appreciation of the fact that man is much more the victim of his psychic constitution than its inventor" (110–11).

Instances of inspiration by the devil are, however, rare. More often it is through subtler temptations and yearnings that the devil makes his presence felt.

A lot of times I think about we believers in Christ, we may not be drinking, we may not be running around, but sometimes even our wants of material things gets us in trouble. You build you a nice house. And I come over there and look at it, look at your furniture, and I've just got to have me one of them houses. And the Bible already told me to be content. Be thankful what the Lord have given you. If the Lord wants you to have something else, He'll give it to you. But usually I get in a rush and won't wait until the Lord fixes it so I can get it. I get in a rush and go and get it because you got it, and then the next thing I know, I'm in trouble. But whatever's for you—I'm a firm believer in this—you goin' get it 'fore you leave here. So you need not hurry. Just take your time. As the old folks say, do like the blindman, kinda feel your way. Just don't jump over the mountain, 'cause sometime when you jump over the mountain, you won't be able to come back on top (Rev. Grady McKinney, interview, November 16, 1986).

Not only do the members of Clear Creek M.B.C. distinguish between "possession" by the Holy Spirit and "possession" by the devil, they also distinguish between a "real shout," i.e., one that is caused by the Holy Spirit, and a "false shout," i.e., one that has lost its spiritual basis and continues only out of excitement or habit.

You see the Lord says this, now it's kind of difficult to explain. A person can be a shouter and it can be real from the start. And then he start to living so he corrupt his life, but he is still shouting. And it is really not the Holy Spirit making him shout. You see what I'm saying? You know, the dress you have on, now if you go get something on it, it's the same dress, but it's not clean. And the Bible says that God's spirit will not dwell in an unclean temple (ibid.).

It is possible, however, for the shout of someone who is not at the moment leading a Christian life to become the crisis of his reconciliation with the Lord and thus be, at this crisis point, a "true" shout.

And then sometime, if your life isn't right, and you think you're happy and you're Godly sorry (see everybody has a conscience, whether they want to face it or not), and when you know what you done did, and you know it's wrong, then sometime that's our way of confessing that we're wrong. I have saw people just get tore up in the

church, and I saw 'em, just as you come to the close of service, say
"let me say a word." And then they talk, and they never come out and
just confess, but in that talking you can detect, they is confessing they
been wrong, and that's what had 'em tore up. This wrongness was in
'em, and the Gospel was working with this wrongness, and they
exploded! (ibid.).

The members in general believe that worship has a purpose other than
"moving in the spirit," one should also be learning and growing. Because
of this, they feel that one should not always be shouting, that there is an
appropriate place for it (if one can so civilise a spirit force!).

But see, it's a time for shouting. But you need to know something. And
this is what I've been trying to get over to the congregations where I
am, that if your life is not in harmony with your shout, you just might
as well quit shouting. If you been out all Saturday night doin' the
wrong thing, and you come to church Sunday and shout, then you need
to be reminded that your shouting is in vain. You have to have a life to
back up your shout (ibid.).

Yet the members also believe that learning and shouting, although complementary, are in some senses the two poles of an opposition. While they
believe that worship that consists of nothing but shouting is somewhat
empty, they also believe that worship without any shouting at all is empty,
as was remarked by Lee Earl Robinson (above). This was also the essence
of Charles Campbell's message when he said that the members felt that the
white man who used to visit them was an "upstairs believer," i.e., that he
believed only with his head, but not with his heart. While one must lead
a life commensurate with inspiration by the Holy Spirit, study cannot
teach one to shout. That is outside man's control.

When Spirit strike you, that ain't you. You not of yourself, no longer
myself that's the Spirit.[9] You don't shout from everything that you
understand. You just admire it. If it ain't no shouting, no Spirit in it
(Charles Campbell, interview, November 20, 1986).

"I will send you a comforter"

As I talked with the members of Clear Creek M.B.C. and tried to understand
how they conceptualised this spirit that can overwhelm them, I perceived
three different, but interrelated, views of the Holy Spirit: 1) a comforter, 2) a
good feeling, 3) a state of mind. The Holy Spirit as comforter, having scriptural origin and sanction, is probably the most usual view.

And Holy Spirit is one thing; as Christ said, "I will send you a comforter," and a comforter can be defined to do many things: again, to
cheer you when you are lonely, and make you feel wanted when no one
around you love you, and make you love even the ones who persecute
you. . . . In Christ's last commission, where He commissioned the one
hundred and twenty before he ascended back into Heaven . . . he stated
that "All power in Heaven and earth is given unto me, by the Father."[10]
And another statement that He made, "I will not leave you alone: I will
send you a comforter,[11] who will keep you in the remembrance of, and
also to keep you in remembrance of all the things which I have told
you."[12] So what He was telling us then; He was going back to be with
the Father, and if there anything that we need, the Holy Spirit was there
to assist us. And we could still petition Him through the Holy Spirit—
"No one cometh unto the father but through me"[13] (Lee Earl Robinson,
interview, November 11, 1987).

As was already mentioned in relation to the conversion experience, the
Holy Spirit is often described as "a good feeling," one that cannot really
be described but must be experienced in order to be understood. Indeed,
members also use the phrase "getting happy in the Spirit" to refer to inspiration by the Holy Spirit. Inspiration seems to be a happy experience even
when it moves people to tears because, as Leroy Thompson explained, the
tears are a form of release. Powerful verbs are used to describe inspiration
by the Holy Spirit. Rev. McKinney uses "explode" quite consistently:

That's the work of the Holy Spirit. It makes you feel good. Otherwise,
you can't hardly explain it. It's really beyond our understanding how it
work. But it make you feel good. It's just something explode on the
inside, and if a person haven't been born again, they wonder what is
wrong with you. But it just something happens on the inside you can't
explain and that's just the way you express yourself see (interview,
November 17, 1986).

When I mentioned being somewhat shocked and frightened at the rather
violent physical expression of the shout the first time I witnessed it, Rev.
McKinney explained further.

In other words, it's kind of like boiling water. Now you can put water
on the stove in a kettle or a pan or something, and you can turn it down
and the water just stay warm. But once you turn it up, the water's goin'
boil. It will not be still, you know, and that's the way the Spirit is, you
know. Now you can feel the Spirit without being overwhelmed sometime. But sometime you just can't help it, it just make you act that way.
And you feel good when that goin' on (ibid.).

Other members conceive of the Holy Spirit as a state of mind rather than a spirit-force. Deacon Leroy Thompson is amongst these. He sees the Holy Spirit essentially as a liberating state of mind, which allows one to release everything that one has had to suppress in order to survive. To this extent, the Holy Spirit allows one to feel, to feel even more extreme emotions which, if expressed in a different context, might get one in trouble or, at least, certainly provoke unwanted attention. As with many experiences, Leroy Thompson traces the tradition back to slavery, a traumatic, shared past.

> We interpret the Holy Spirit as something that's going to be a guide and a comfort for me, and I don't know whether we can describe the Holy Spirit as something that's goin' cause me, like . . . putting something into me, like say LSD, it's goin' make me act a certain way. Well, that's because it has a certain physical effect on me. I don't know that we can consider the Holy Spirit as being that! The Holy Spirit is more to us, is more like a thing where again it allows me and it guides me to the point where I know I can release my emotions in a certain way, and I don't have to be degraded for it, I don't have to be talked about for it. To me, rather than being something that's gonna say "boom," the Holy Spirit is more of a state of mind. You're talking about a state of mind, that's all it is. Rather than being a force. Holy Spirit is a state of mind. . . . It goes back to the time of slavery when the only means of outlet again, after having been treated the way you were treated in the fields, and having to sneak off to a certain place to have a worship service, this is the only freedom of expression that I have. And can you imagine the emotion that must have boiled over, in a place where, you know, I can say what I want to say? And I can say it the way I want to say it, as loud as I want to say it, and I don't have to worry about anybody around me beating me for it, or screaming at me for it.[14] So regardless as to how loud I want to be, and the expression of black churches is that, you know, you do it the way you want to do it, however you want to do it (interview, November 22, 1987).

Despite differences of expression between Leroy Thompson and Rev. McKinney, for example, the analogy to boiling liquid is fairly constant amongst the membership. It is a powerful image. The power attributed to language is significant. The slaves, once alone and "free" in some sense, are pictured not as doing anything, but as saying whatever they want to say, in whatever way they choose. And, of course, there is a recurrence of emphasis on loudness, a quality that I posited as part of the aesthetic of black gospel music.

The three different perceptions of the Holy Spirit described above are but three perceptions among many, but they seem to be perceptions that predominate amongst the members of Clear Creek M.B.C. More than anything else, perhaps, the people with whom I talked reiterated that the experience of inspiration by the Holy Spirit is above all a personal thing. No two people, the members believe, experience the Holy Spirit the same way because no two individuals are exactly alike. "The Holy Ghost, it works on people different ways. . . . It works on people different ways and it's just a personal thing that only you know and your God knows" (Greg Thompson, November 25, 1987). It follows from this that people will also express themselves differently when they are inspired by the Holy Spirit.

> People don't all express themselves the same. Some of them just sit there and cry. And some peoples, when the Spirit get on them, they wouldn't sit down for nothing. They get up and walk just as fast as they can, walk right on out the church. So, when it dealing with us, all of us don't have the same reaction, you know, we act different. Some folks cry, some folks laugh, some folks jump up and down, and some folks holler.[15] So, everybody don't express their feeling the same, but it's really a good feeling (Rev. Grady McKinney, interview, November 17, 1986).

The individual expression of the shout is the cultural correlate of the psychophysiological component of trance to which Rouget refers. The most dramatic version of the shout was consistent in its characteristics in all of the churches that I visited where it occurred, from the Northeast, through Kentucky, to the deep South (Mississippi and Arkansas). Typically, individuals who are inspired begin with short exclamations such as "Jesus, Jesus, Yes Jesus, Thank you Jesus." They may then begin to laugh or to cry and their body will often begin to shake or twitch with short, jerky movements. These movements soon expand to a flailing of the arms and then the whole body is flung about as individuals rise to their feet, fling both arms out rigidly to either side while at the same time arching the back and throwing themselves backwards. As one can imagine, the person who is shouting, and also those seated close by, are at this stage in real danger of being hurt.

William Wells Brown (1816–1884), cited in Sernett (ed., 1985), gives a somewhat humorous, if accurate, account of a shout.

> The church was already well filled, and the minister had taken his text. As the speaker warmed up in his subject, the Sisters began to swing their heads and reel to and fro, and eventually began a shout. Soon five or six were fairly at it, which threw the house into a buzz. Seats were soon vacated near the shouters, to give them more room, because the women did not wish to have their hats smashed in by the frenzied Sisters. As a

woman sprang up in her seat, throwing up her long arms, with a loud scream the lady on the adjoining seat quickly left, and did not stop till she got to a safe distance.

"Ah ha!" exclaimed a woman near by, "'fraid of your new bonnet! Ain't got much religion, I reckon. Specks you'll have to come out of that if you want to save your soul."

"She thinks more of that hat now, than she does of a seat in heaven," said another.

"Never mind," said a third, "when she gets de witness, she'll drap dat hat an' shout herself out of breath" (Brown, 1880: 190).

The seemingly increased strength and abandon of the shouter must be contained to avoid injury. The persons nearby, depending amongst other things on how comfortable and familiar they are with this rather violent expression, may try to restrain the shouter until the ushers or nurses come.

In black Baptist churches where this form of shouting is a fairly regular part of worship, structures for coping with it have generally been formalised. In smaller churches, ushers are usually trained to restrain the shouter and it is considered a part of their routine responsibilities. This is usually the case also in Holiness and Pentecostal churches. Such is the case at Clear Creek M.B.C. In the event that such shouting occurs at the monthly youth programme, the deacons, mothers of the church, or adult ushers (or simply someone who is close by) will help the young ushers, as it is usually adults who shout at Clear Creek, and their strength when they are shouting is more than the young ushers can contain. (Indeed, this is generally true of other Baptist churches where I observed the shout also. It seems to be an adult phenomenon, and perhaps requires a certain spiritual and emotional maturity.) It frequently takes two or three adults to restrain one shouter. At larger churches, such as Main Street Baptist Church in Lexington, Kentucky, trained nurses are present to attend to shouters and there is a small first aid station at the back of the church. At Main Street Baptist Church special seats, marked with red crosses on white, are reserved for the nurses, who come to the church in uniform. If the shouter is close to where they are seated, they attend and try to restrain him/her. If, on the other hand, they are too far away from the person, ushers who are close by will help, and the nurses' only responsibility in this case is to give medical attention to those who may need it.

Shouting is not as unpredictable as one might think. There are individuals in a church who consistently express themselves in this fashion, and there are others who never seem to do so. It is also true that as one becomes more familiar with it, one can anticipate the occurrence of inspiration from the "feeling" in the church. A shout does not happen out of the blue. Certain people (usually older women), in a certain context (most frequently during preaching, especially if it is chanted, but also during the ostinato section sometimes at the end of a gospel song), usually combine to produce it. In black Baptist churches, women are more likely to shout than men, although men also shout. (Similarly, Hans Baer, in referring to the work of Hortense Powdermaker [1939], asserts that "in the Cottonville area of Mississippi, the large majority of blacks who attend services and revival meetings, 'shout,' and 'get religion' are women" (1985: 12–13.) Deacon Leroy Thompson, for example, told me that there used to be men who shouted at Clear Creek M.B.C. "One of the Burts used to shout constantly" (Interview, November 22, 1987). The Pentecostal minister to whom I referred earlier, who attends Clear Creek M.B.C. regularly, is also of the same Burt family. He shouts frequently during services, but he is the only man that I have seen do so at the church. Other men may laugh, or even cry, but I have never seen them shout.

"Look among you and find seven mens"

This is quite to be expected if one bears in mind the context of this cultural expression. With Turner, I believe "social structure to be closely related to ritual structure and process" (1968: 8). In North American society in general, men are raised to be circumspect in the expression of any "weak" emotions, e.g., sorrow, pain, fear, or compassion. These emotions are held to be feminine. Baptist tradition also conspires to place men in positions of authority and strength, although these received ideas are beginning to be challenged.

> The idea that black men feel entitled to leadership in the Black Church grows out of many years of a patriarchal tradition wherein black men and women became accustomed to this entitlement for men. As black women begin to compete for some of these policymaking positions, it is understandable that men will view this movement as an erosion of their power and control. Coupled with the fact that there are few other opportunities for black men to inherit leadership outside the Black Church, resistance against women moving into the hierarchy emerges as a strongly embedded, intransigent barrier (Carpenter, 1989: 20).

Ministers are generally male: of the twenty churches in the Tallahatchie-Oxford Missionary Baptist Association, only one (New Hope M.B.C.) has female ministers (1981–1990), as far as I could ascertain, and they were both associate ministers (Rev. Joanne Nelson and Rev. Annie Ruth Hickinbottom) serving under a male minister, rather than pastors in their own right. This is in keeping with Scripture as interpreted by the church members.[16] "The only thing that Scripture says, that a woman is not to exercise authority over a man. 'Let the woman learn in silence with all subjection. But I suffer not a woman to teach, nor to usurp authority over the man, but to be in silence' (1 Timothy 2: 11–12)" (Lee Earl Robinson, interview, November 17, 1986). While Deacon Robinson concedes that a woman may be called to preach, he clearly does not expect it to happen:

> Many times people may say that I'm chauvinistic, but I never fight a person. If a woman say that she has been called by God to preach the Gospel, I don't say that she's a liar. . . . I hope that my Lord wasn't selfish when He chose twelve men as disciples and later made them apostles. And when Judas was out, the apostles brought in two more mens, and they took a vote and chose Matthias. And even when James was killed and Phillip went off to some place else, and they called all them Paul and Barnabas and made them apostles (interview, November 17, 1986).

Because Clear Creek M.B.C. follows Scripture's guidelines with regard to deaconship also, women are not expected to become deacons.

> The Scripture says, "look among you and find seven mens." And he must be the husband of one wife. Certain qualifications, you see.[17] I have heard of churches with women deacons, but then I don't find any Scripture to back them up. So I can't go around saying they're wrong. All I can say is I can't find any Scripture to support them (ibid.).

Male and female roles are quite clearly defined in the church. A woman may become a church mother, usher, secretary, or choir president, but she may not hold a position in the primary authority structure of the church, i.e., pastor or deacon. The members believe that the subsidiary role of women, not only in church, but also in secular life, is clearly proscribed in Scripture. (This is, of course, a common belief in many similar church communities. As Dolores C. Carpenter remarks, "Biblical texts are interpreted to prescribe women to certain roles, prohibiting the pastorate" [1989: 21].) For the church members, of course, secular and spiritual life are inseparable. Their total life is dedicated to God, in the same way that "all time is God's time."

> If Christ is the head of the church, man is the head of a woman. Then how can your bottom part lead your head? This is all Scripture: woman was made for man's helpmate, not to exercise authority over man. Although society has dictated that, this is not saying that God approve of it. For He said, "I changeth not. I am the same today as yesterday, and forever more." But [because of] man's negligence and disobedience

has dictated to the way the world is now. People say things changes, but God does not. Man changes things to please himself. So, where's a woman's place in life? Where does the Bible put her? Where is a man's place in life? Where does the Bible, or does God, put him? And if we would remain, or try to stay in position or in places in which God has placed us in the first place, undoubtedly the world would be in a better situation. But because man has run off and left woman, left her in a situation where she must look after herself, dictates to her how she must run her life (Lee Earl Robinson, interview, November 17, 1986).

The formalised subservience of women at Clear Creek M.B.C., combined with societal norms, ensures that women are not perceived as occupying positions of strength.[18] The correlate of this, of course, is that men are confined to "strong" roles. The image to which men must conform is no less rigid and is quite pervasive. On one occasion a guest minister gave the following advice in a sermon which he preached at Clear Creek M.B.C. during the "Pastor and Wife's Appreciation" programme in October, 1987: "You cannot be wishy washy, not only because you're a preacher, but because you're a man. God made you a man first, before he called you to preach, and a woman don't want no wishy-washy man. She want a man that's goin' be a man" (October 18, 1987).

Consistent with their weaker positions, women are perceived to be subject to expression of "weak" emotions. It is to be expected that they will readily be overcome or overwhelmed by emotion. "Some people become very emotional when the Holy Spirit moves upon them. Just like, most times, a lot of women get hysterical when they are frightened. . . . Womens have a tendency to show their emotion much greater than mens" (Lee Earl Robinson, interview, November 11, 1987). This is not to say, however, that church members are unaware of the role socialisation plays in such perceptions and behaviour. Many of them recognise that men and women play out certain stereotypical roles because they have been socialised to do so, rather than because of an innate predisposition.

I don't think you can possibly separate the macho thing from the church. And see, that's the reason I'm saying it [Inspiration by the Holy Spirit] is a state of mind. Because you see, guys have suppressed that, [they have] the idea that you just don't do that, looks kind of strange. You're not macho to do that. Women are more emotional, supposedly, than men, so naturally the Holy Spirit is going to deal with them differently than it will with men (Leroy Thompson, interview, November 22, 1987).

It is not only men who perceive women to be weaker and more emotional than men, nor is it a perception unique to older people. Some of the younger women were appalled, for example, that I had driven alone from Rhode Island to Mississippi (a distance of about 1,290 miles). They told me that they would never drive alone from their homes to Jackson, Mississippi (a distance of about 130 miles), lest something go amiss. They do not perceive themselves as capable of protecting themselves in such an eventuality, and they stated that they would have no idea what to do should the car get a flat tyre.

"There's a higher height in the Lord"

Having established the background and some context for inspiration, let us proceed to the shout itself and the importance of its musical context. Rouget, unfortunately, does not pursue inspiration trance and its relationship to music. He is more interested in possession, which the trance of black Baptists is not, because they do not identify themselves with the Holy Ghost. They are invested with the Holy Ghost, but the latter's personality is not substituted for their own. Nonetheless, it is possible to sketch the relationship between inspiration trance and music by drawing on Rouget's characteristics, albeit in a different combination. In my research at Clear Creek M.B.C., I frequently found what appears to be a direct link between inspiration by the Holy Spirit and music, that is, it was very rare for someone to become inspired outside of a musical context. However, before proceeding any further with this discussion, it is necessary to point out that Greg Thompson, for example, (who is a gospel soloist and pianist), having prefaced his remarks by saying that he had never really noticed or thought about it, refuted the idea of a direct relationship between inspiration by the Holy Spirit and music.

> I don't know if you can say music is the key to the Holy Ghost, or you seeing the effects of the Holy Ghost, because I've seen preachers get up and pray a prayer and people just shout all over the place. I've seen my cousin Kenneth,[19] like when they have the offering, and he comes up and bless the offering and everybody stands up, I've seen people shout.[20] And the piano's not playing, he's not singing, he's just praying his heart out. He can move people. They say his membership is identical to his ability to preach too, because he's drawin' 'em in every Sunday. But I don't know if you can pinpoint that music is what people shout off of, or that's the fire, or the ignition, to get people started (interview, November 25, 1987).

As I observed it at Clear Creek M.B.C., however, inspiration most usually occurred during the sermon, and specifically during the chanted portion of the sermon. As such, it was induced, not conducted, as the person who was inspired was not the musicant of his own trance.[21] The trance was generally invocatory. Immediately before the onset of trance the individual often called upon Jesus in invocatory fashion, e.g., "Jesus, Jesus, Yes Jesus, Thank you Jesus, Oh Jesus." It seems that although the members speak of inspiration by the Holy Ghost, Jesus is the figure with whom they move into trance, he is, perhaps, the mediator of the trance. If we accept this explanation, the citation of Scripture by Lee Earl Robinson (above), becomes clear ("No one cometh unto the Father but through me."). His citing this line of Scripture in relation to possession by the Holy Spirit seems to be a non sequitur unless Jesus is the mediator. In short, it appears that although the spirit force which inspires people is the Holy Spirit, the spirit acts not on its own but is sent and controlled by Jesus. This, of course, has scriptural support in John's Gospel.

> But when the Comforter is come, whom I will send unto you from the Father, he shall testify of me (15:28).

> If I go not away, the Comforter will not come unto you: but if I depart, I will send him unto you (16:7).

The shouter most frequently responds to singing: in the sermon, the preacher's chant. It is precisely this kind of music, vocal music, that Greg Thompson described as especially powerful and uniting. Music is thus inextricably bound up with text. There seem to be two fairly predictable triggers for trance. The first is repetition: in sermons, sequences, and invocatory passages; in gospel, the improvised sections built upon a short ostinato that generally comes at the end of a song.[22] The second is the introduction of a religious song, particularly an old favourite, into the sermon or prayer text. Rev. Carter, pastor of Congdon Street Baptist Church in Providence, Rhode Island, often moves into heightened speech during the course of a sermon, but he does not use the considerably more elaborate, melodic chant that preachers in northeast Mississippi do. He will, however, at the climax of a sermon, integrate song titles or lines into his sermon. The response from his congregation always intensifies at this time. Rev. Benjamin Baker, pastor of Main Street Baptist Church in Lexington, also frequently introduces song titles or lines from songs into his sermon at climactic points. While Rev. Grady McKinney, pastor of Clear Creek M.B.C., only rarely introduces song texts into his sermon, almost every time that I witnessed it, at least one member of the congregation immediately went into trance.

On one occasion only did I see a musician go into trance while performing. At the "Pastor and Wife's Appreciation" programme (October 11, 1987), Jackie Vaughn stepped forward to sing a solo, "When the Gates Swing Open," an old song which all the congregation seemed to know. She is a powerful, if often understated, singer and the members seem always to respond to her enthusiastically. She was not long into the song on this occasion when one of the women went into a shout. Shortly afterwards Jackie herself began to shout and could not continue singing. Several ushers came to restrain her, the congregation picked up the song and the pianist took the solo line. Jackie was taken into an adjoining room until she became herself again. Not only was the song (which was a tribute to the pastor and his wife) interrupted in this case, Jackie was also unable to make the presentation from the choir to Rev. McKinney and his wife. There was some confusion afterwards as to what had happened to the presentation (an envelope containing a cheque) that Jackie had had in her hand when she began to shout, but it was found, and Jackie eventually made the presentation. This incidence of shouting is unusual because it seems to have been conducted (i.e., the musician was also the musicant of her own trance). It seems likely that the shout of the other member also contributed to triggering Jackie's shout. When the members believe that the Holy Spirit is physically present in the church, it is not unusual for more that one of them to become inspired.

I have transcribed in example 5.1 one incident of shouting that involved two women, Because I am not primarily interested in characteristics of chanted preaching here, transcription of Rev. McKinney's chanting is prescriptive (Seeger: 185): it is not exact. The context was a chanted portion of a sermon delivered by Rev. McKinney on Harvest Day, November 15, 1987. Each of the women uses one of the two most common shout patterns I heard at Clear Creek. The first is a staccato "uh-uh-uh" that is usually disjunct: movement is in jumps across several pitches. The second is a sustained cry, sometimes static, but usually sliding across several pitches. This is the "sharp, piercing cry" generally referred to in descriptions of shouting. In both instances I have notated pitches with an "x" as, because of vocalisation, pitches are somewhat "distorted." Because of the nature of the shouting patterns, I have located them spatially in relation to Rev. McKinney's chant, rather than attempting to assign rhythmic values to slides. Their duration is clear from the time space they occupy in relation to the chant. If, as Bruce Rosenberg asserts "we murder to transcribe" (1971: 429), chanted sermons then that is even more true for shouting. It is impossible to convey on paper the complexity of the shout, but I have elected to make an attempt to do so here because I have found no instances of any scholar attempting to engage with the musical complexities of shouting. Yet until we do, we can only talk in broad generalities. In order to gain a fuller understanding of this transcription, the reader is referred to track 2 ("Shouting": "Gabriel is comin' out that mornin'") on the accompanying CD. It should be borne in mind, however, that to excerpt a section of shouting (such as this one) from the context of a thirty- to forty-five-minute sermon is to do it a certain violence. What cannot be appreciated

from either the transcription or the recording is the gradual progression of
the religious utterance that finally culminates in this expression.

"Gabriel, is comin' out that mornin'
With the trumpet of God
And my Bible say
He goin' blow it calm easy
And that goin' wake up the saints of God   5
I heard him
Say they goin' meet God in the air
Oh Gabriel
You goin' have to blow again
Oh Gabriel   10
Blow your horn
I want you to blow it
Loud my friend
I've sent claps of thunder
Wake up the wicked   15
That midnight rambler
Goin' come blunderin' in
That drunkard
Goin' stumble his way in
Goin' hear the Master say   20
"I never knew you
Depart from me
Ye that . . . [unclear]"
But I'm so glad
That I signed up   25
Did you sign up?
A long time ago
I'm so glad
The Holy Ghost is my witness
Ain't God alright?   30
And in this Book of Life
One thing about it
Men write sometime
And over a period of years
The writin' begin to fade out   35
And sometime
If you don't catch it in time
You won't have a active record
But one thing about it
When the Holy Ghost   40
Signed my name

I don't have to worry
About it fade out on me
The older I get
The brighter my name shine   45
Oh at harvest time . . .
God goin' gather
Up all of His children
Somebody said
All of those that cried   50
And didn' know why they cried
He said you goin' understand it then
Ain't God alright?"

Whether it is by intent of the shouter, or because of the aural context of
Rev. McKinney's chant, I hear the shouted pitches as directly related to the
musical scale of the chant. I believe that the relationship between the two
is too consistent to be the result of coincidence. At no stage during the
fairly lengthy section transcribed do the shouters vocalise anything that
violates the pentatonic scale of the chant: even when covering an extended
pitch range (g to c^2, for example), the notes selected en route belong to the
selected pentatonic scale.

This consistency of tonality between the preacher and the shouters is
not so surprising if one examines the role of music in African American
Baptist churches. As will have been appreciated from earlier discussion,
music is vital in the services of these churches. It does not simply adorn
the service, it seems rather to be its life breath. There are few moments in
the service when music—either congregational or choral singing, or instrumental music of some sort—is not being performed; in fact, especially in
Southern churches, the whole service may be underpinned by a coherent
tonal system. (See the Introduction, pp. 24–25, for my discussion of the
82nd Annual Convention of the Tallahatchie-Oxford Missionary Baptist
Association service in Mississippi, August 29, 1982.)

When one examines the relationship above between Rev. McKinney's
chant and the shouting, the women seem to be responding to two things
in the chant: its melodic shape, and the textual message. A strong
response to images of a familiar or favourite event (past or future), often
prefigured in spirituals, is usual even when it does not lead to shouting.
This sermon extract is essentially an evocation of a single apocalyptic
event: the Day of Judgement (Gabriel blowing his trumpet on the Lord's
command, God's rejection of sinners, and inscription of the saint's name
in the "Book of Life," are parts of this event). In this case, both the
sound of Gabriel's trumpet and Rev. McKinney's question to the membership as to whether they had signed up, serve as a "trigger" for one of
the women.

Example 5.1. "Shouting," in relation to sermon excerpt, November 15, 1987: "Gabriel is comin' out that mornin'," Rev. Grady McKinney, Clear Creek M.B.C. (See CD track 2.)

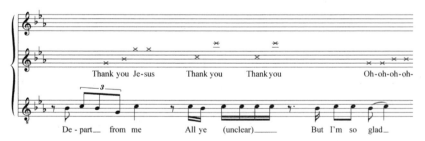

Example 5.1, cont.

The first woman's shout begins just after McKinney chants that the saints of God are going to be woken up by Gabriel's trumpet, and coincides with McKinney's "say they goin' meet God in the air.. From that point (line 8 ff., "Oh Gabriel, You goin' have to blow again"), the woman's shout comes initially at the end of every two lines of chanting, increasing to the end of virtually every line at line 14 ("I've sent claps of

Example 5.1, cont.

thunder"). The placing of the shout in this instance is analogous to a gospel soloist's interpolations between lines when singing with a choir. The density of the shout then increases from the end of line 21 ("I never know you") until the entry of the second shouter at line 26 ("Did you sign up?"), when the first shouter drops out.

Example 5.1, cont.

The second shouter uses a sustained cry, sometimes static, but usually sliding across several pitches, initially (from line 26 to line 32 "One thing about it") across a descending perfect fifth. As mentioned above, this is the "sharp, piercing cry" generally referred to in descriptions of shouting, and, unlike the first woman's shout, it does not seem to relate spatially to the structure of McKinney's chanting. Just before the re-entry of the first shouter at line 32, the second shouter's range increases to one octave (a^1

Example 5.1, cont.

up to c^2, and octave descent to c^1), which is sustained until the return to the original perfect fifth at line 45 ("the brighter my name shine"). We have now reached the 'cooling down' period of this excerpt, and both range and density decrease for both shouts from this point on.

Despite the close relationship between McKinney's chanting and the shouts of the two women, the melodic shape of his chant does not seem to evoke an analogous melodic shape from the shouters. The first woman sometimes covers an extended range when Rev. McKinney's chant is little more than monotonic recitation (see line 19, "Goin' stumble his way in"). Because the melodic shape of the second woman's shout is quite consistent (generally a falling fifth or octave), it appears that she is not responding to the melodic shape of the chant either. It should be borne in mind, however, that because both women pitch their shout so high, one does not get the impression of any clear melodic contour on first hearing the shout.

While shouting is, therefore, in this instance closely tied to its musical context (restricted to the same melodic scale, for example, as the chant), in other respects it pursues an independent musical logic, and develops its own shape. Yet the climax of shouting and chanting coincide in this extract (see, lines 24–26, "But I'm so glad, That I signed up. Did you sign up?"). Where Rev. McKinney's words are most meaningful, in his articulation of what is for the community a primary identificatory opposition (lost versus saved), there also is the melodic climax of the first woman's shout (lacking words, melody is a primary source of meaning in the shout), and the climactic addition of the second woman's shout. Each shout, on the other hand, has its own internal logic and, while the climax of the extract (and of the sermon) occurs here, the climax of the second shout occurs later, with the addition of an ascending shape and the expansion of range to one octave (see line 32, "One thing about it," ff.). Music, text, Spirit and meaning are fused in this communal expression of the community's apocalyptic vision.

The members' understanding of religion is a holistic one in that it permeates all aspects of their lives. Inspiration by the Holy Spirit is a dramatic enactment of this understanding. Through inspiration, the members believe, the Holy Spirit is physically present in their midst. It is a penetration of the material by the spiritual.

6

Prayer

Prayer will build a bridge across deep waters
Prayer will bring mountains low
Prayer will lift you out of the valley
Prayer will take you off of Broadway and put you on the straight street
Prayer will
Prayer will change your condition
        —Rev. Grady McKinney, Sermon, October 18, 1987

Some have to have prayers written so that they can say them at the proper
time, having no words of their own. We stand in the tradition of the free
church that says that everyone should examine his own heart and see
what God done for him. Our prayers should never be the same repetition
of meaningless words. Our prayers should be spoken from our heart, in
thanksgiving to our God.
        —Pastor, Congdon St. Baptist Church, Providence, Rhode Island,
        addressing his congregation during Sunday service, December 22,
        1985

Chanting is not a stylistic feature unique to prayer in African American
churches. It is a stylistic expression common to many cultural and religious
traditions from Roman Catholicism to Buddhist monasticism. But the formulation of spontaneous chanted prayers is a special characteristic of
African American churches because improvisation or personalisation is
uniquely central to the African American aesthetic. Chanted prayers embody
many aesthetic values of African American culture: a holistic approach to
life, an emphasis upon collective consciousness, the expression and sharing
of emotions and their expression in improvised, personalized form. What I
refer to as chant is an intermediary form between speech and song. George
List stresses that both speech and song have certain characteristics in common that differentiate them from other forms of communication. "Both
speech and song are 1) vocally produced, 2) linguistically meaningful, and 3)
melodic" (1963: 1). List's definitions are cited here for the sake of clarity.

Speech is defined here as casual utterance, as in conversation. Other
types of speech, those found in more socially structured situations such

as dramatic representation, the delivery of sermons or the telling of jokes and tales will be classified as "heightened speech," a form somewhat intermediate to speech and song. Song itself will be defined [. . .] as a form exhibiting relatively stable pitches, possessing a scalar structure at least as elaborate as the heptatonic, and showing little, if any, influence melodically of speech intonation (ibid.: 3).

While there are several different traditions within the African American Baptist denomination—American, National, Missionary—these differences do not seem to be of critical concern between churches and have relatively little effect on worship style.[1] The style of worship and the prevalence of chanting in prayers is influenced, rather, by two other features: first, the geographic location of the church and/or the geographic origin of its members; second, the socio-economic status of the church.

In chapter 5 I discussed the shout as a traditional phenomenon associated with "down home" churches. Chanting is another traditional phenomenon associated with "down home" churches. The movement from speech to chant in prayers is generally more characteristic of Southern churches (where African American communities have traditionally been more separate) and/or of churches that have many members of Southern origin. Thus, it is no contradiction that chanted prayers are a feature of several churches in Detroit, Chicago, and New York City, cities that continue to draw African Americans from the South. This characteristic is valued as "traditional," "down-home," "getting in the Spirit." Traditional Northern churches, on the other hand—such as Rhode Island's Congdon St. Baptist Church, which celebrated its 150th anniversary in 1986, established by "freed blacks" and sustained by their descendants—are less likely to feature chanting. Where it does occur, it is frequently little more than a single recitation tone and lacks the rhythmic and melodic complexities of Southern chanting. A second factor that may influence the prevalence of chanting in prayers is the relative affluence of the church. While this factor is heavily dependent upon the geographic composition of the congregation, it is true that more affluent churches tend to be more restrained in worship style and spontaneous chanting is less likely to occur. This restraint, which is often seen as synonymous with sophistication, seems to be related to the extent to which the church congregation has adopted the values of the dominant culture. Certainly, it is derided by some African Americans as evidence of "buying into white middle-class values" and a betrayal of the race. Such churches are seen as "white" or "oreo"—black on the outside but white inside. In short, I have found chanting to be most prevalent in small, rural Southern churches that are, perforce, at the bottom of the socio-economic ladder, or in urban churches which have drawn their population from this geographic area.

In chapter 5 I also discussed the relationship between music and inspiration by the Holy Spirit, my conclusion being that music facilitates inspiration, the most direct and most intimate contact with God. The most successful prayers—those that seem to establish the most intimate contact with God within the context of the service—move increasingly towards a musical expression. To quote William James: "Music is the element through which we are best spoken to by mystical truth" (1902: 420). In her study of John Maranke's Independent African church, Jules-Rosette remarks that the Apostles intentionally use song to enter into a spirit world (1975: 103). It is thus not unusual for music to be granted this power. While such behaviours as falling out and possession are traits generally associated with Pentecostal churches, their occurrence is not unusual in Baptist churches, especially in Southern Baptist churches (Southern referring to "of the South," as opposed to Southern Baptist Convention). While the Rev. Baker jokingly chastised his congregation one day for such manifestations of the Spirit—"Y'all better cut that out. Y'all don't act like Baptist folk. Y'all act like yo' done got religion" (October 12, 1985)—these characteristics of a "hot" church are, in fact, much appreciated. A few minutes later Baker remarked: "Our God is alive. You'd better believe it. . . . It's a kind of glory that has come in here." Such occurrences are viewed as the active participation of God in the service. On a similar occasion (August 18, 1985) Baker shouted joyously: "Something is happenin' here. The Holy Ghost is in charge. . . . He's runnin' from every heart and from breast to breast."[2] These very occurrences were commented upon, however, as somewhat if not particularly unusual. Marion Rogers, Music Minister at Main St. Baptist Church, elaborated:

Main Street is not considered an emotional church. In fact, we might be considered an "uppity Black church." We're known for our budget, and our ability, our capability of doing what we need to do. A few prominent folk are here. The church has always been stereotyped as being a "well-dressed church." You haven't really had the opportunity to see the furs and so forth because it hasn't been that cold, but you will see full-lengths in here. But yet there are a couple of churches in town that are very emotional. So people that enjoy that go there. I enjoy feeling the presence of the Lord, and that does not need a lot of whooping and hollering to do that (interview, January 8, 1987).

In all the churches in which I have worked there are at least three structural points in the service which are occasions for personalized prayer: the first in the context of the offertory (some churches have two prayers here, one directly before the offering and another after), the second in a specific musical context, and the third to close the service. If it is a Communion Service, a fourth, Communion prayer is added.

The offertory prayer concentrates, of course, on the offering and as such is frequently didactic and exhortatory. Scripture is often cited to remind members of their duty of tithing to the church and while God is usually thanked for his goodness in so richly blessing the congregation, the thrust and emphasis of the prayer is monetary. As a result these prayers are generally rather formal, direct, and short. They do not usually have any musical accompaniment—the accompanist is rarely moved to join in—nor do they become very poetic or tend toward chant. Money seemingly does not call forth the same imaginative and poetic powers as does the love of God.

The second occasion for personalized prayer can be anywhere between the formalised text of the call to worship and the sermon—the climax of the service. At Clear Creek M.B.C. the Devotion offers several opportunities for spontaneous prayer. The prayer is generally preceded and followed by music that may, in a more or less structured form, continue in the background to the prayer. At Congdon St. Baptist Church in Providence, this prayer is invariably preceded by the chant "Let the words of my mouth," and followed by the chant of "The Lord's Prayer," both performed quite faithfully to their respective scores in the Baptist Standard Hymnal. Because this is the score used by the accompanists, and because the congregation adheres very closely to it, I elected not to transcribe the actual rendition by the church. The differences are on the detailed descriptive level (Seeger, 1958: 185), and vary from service to service. Although prayers rarely move into chant at Congdon St. Baptist Church, the accompanist generally plays some unobtrusive chord sequence in the background during the prayer and this music then leads directly into the chant of "The Lord's Prayer."

At Main St. Baptist Church in Lexington, the prayer is embedded in the meditation hymn. The hymn precedes the prayer and is continued very slowly by the accompanists (piano and organ) and frequently by humming from the congregation, as a background to the prayer. The hymn is picked up again at the end of the prayer. The prayer, therefore, in such a context takes its tonality, perforce, from the hymn. At Clear Creek M.B.C., because there is such a strong musical underpinning to the whole service, the prayer is inevitably affected by the tonality of the previous musical piece. In this context chanted prayer comes into its own: an improvised musical and poetic piece which facilitates the entry of the Holy Spirit into the church, calls for considerable artistry and creativity, and demands the integration of rhetorical, poetic, and musical skills.

Chanting in general in African American churches has received little scholarly attention. What little research has been done has concentrated on sermons. Yet this from Bruce Rosenberg, in relation to sermons, might equally well be applied to prayers:[3]

> Especially during the chanted portions of the sermon, the audience is actively involved in the service. The congregation sings, hums, yells, and joins in the service as it chooses, and almost always its tone and timing is musically correct. The quality of the congregation seems to have a great effect upon the sermon, influencing the preacher's timing, his involvement in the service, and sometimes even the length of his performance. A sermon of this type often fails or succeeds according to how well the preacher can stimulate the congregation's rhythm by his own chanting. Clearly, chanting builds up the emotions of the audience as no other means can, and it is at such moments of emotional intensity that the Spirit of God is said to be most noticeable (1970: 5).

Chanting has the apparent function, then, of bringing the people closer to God. (This is the language that Jeff Titon describes as "in the Spirit" or "anointed by the Spirit" [1988: 198].) The Rev. Darryl M. Smaw (Associate Chaplain at Brown University, 1978–84) acknowledges the effect and calls the experience a transcendental one of the type described in scripture. He sees the movement into chant as a movement to a different level of being and surmises that this is how other preachers see it, also. He says that he himself is frequently unaware of his surroundings at such times. Despite this transcendence, the chanter's "movement to a different level of being," there is, at this point, an intimate and dynamic interaction between him and the congregation and also between him and the accompanist (if the accompanist joins in). There is here an apparent inherent contradiction. While the prayer is undoubtedly spontaneous and dynamic, and while the person praying seems totally wrapped up in his prayer and unaware of his accompanist, he would never stop in the middle of the accompanist's phrase, any more than the accompanist would stop before the prayer had finished. This phenomenon cannot be explained by the fact that prayers have a set duration, for their length varies from week to week. Occasionally, however, a particularly zealous deacon, or the pastor himself, might continue for an extended length of time. If such is the case, the pianist might play the final cadential phrase two, or even three times (even the most zealous speakers seem to get the message by the third time) until the prayer finally winds down.

Prayer is usually led by the pastor, a visiting minister, or a deacon. The prayer leader steps forward and turns to face the congregation. Closing his eyes he begins to pray aloud (see figure 15). In the Baptist churches where I conducted my fieldwork the prayer leader was usually male. Women and girls lead prayers exceptionally, on special occasions, "Youth Sunday," for example, or "Mothers' Sunday." This is in keeping with the previously outlined male authority structure of the church.

Figure 15. Deacon Sam Jones leads a prayer.

The prayer is "spontaneous," generally begins in unmetered prose, and gradually becomes more measured and repetitive. As rhythm and repetition assume a more prominent role, the voice moves to "heightened speech," distinct pitches emerge, and a tonal centre is established. By this time the person praying is well into his prayer, and the congregants, if the prayer is at all successful, add comments of agreement and encouragement. From all the occasions that I have observed it seems clear that this transition from speech to chant is a two-way process: the congregation encourages and stimulates the person praying, frequently to the same extent that he is affecting them. On one occasion at a revival meeting at Congdon St. Church, when the spirit of the congregation was particularly high, both the congregation and other ministers outdid themselves humming and chanting words of encouragement to the visiting minister who was leading the prayer, all to no avail. When the minister did not pick up on their leads, they then returned to speech and finally all interjections died out.

At the transition stage to chant, the vocal range covered by the deacon or minister may be very large, narrowing typically to a fifth or less often to an octave, as the chant crystallises. The introduction of the melodic element may come during the congregational responses, prior to its appearance in the prayer. It is not unusual for this to happen at Main St. Church in Lexington. The Rev. Baker, while a dynamic preacher and a beloved pastor, is not exceptionally gifted musically and himself refers disparagingly to his singing. Yet the church is strong in music and some deacons and congregants move with greater facility into musical expression than does their pastor.

The importance of this transition stage was highlighted by its absence in a prayer delivered by the pastor of Jefferies M.B.C. on 5 September 1982 in Abbeville, Mississippi.[4] This prayer was remarkable because there was no transition between speech and chant, either at the beginning or at the end. Formalised opening and closing phrases were stated and the body of the text was uniformly chanted. The abrupt movement to chant negated any feeling of accomplishment: as no tension had been generated, there was no feeling of resolution. Throughout the prayer both the rhythm and the contour of the chant remained regular and predictable.

These physical and spiritual circumstances give rise to the chant which can be recognised by its specifically musical characteristics. Several principles form the basis of the melodic system. The scale used in chanting is pentatonic, most commonly based on a minor triad, in my experience in Mississippi, but a major triad seems to be more usual at Main St. Baptist Church in Kentucky. Typically the chant begins with the lower third and gradually expands to include the whole fifth. At this stage the upper and lower third of the triad are often juxtaposed within the two halves of a single phrase, as in example 6.1. If a wider range is desired, the lower dominant may be included. Once the range of the chant has been clearly established, the two thirds of the triad usually coalesce, and phrases (usually in descending motion) typically outline the complete fifth (dominant-tonic, descending) or narrow it to a fourth (subdominant-tonic, descending, or lower dominant-tonic, ascending).

Example 6.1. Juxtaposition of upper and lower thirds of the triad within two halves of a single phrase: "Not because Father, that we did all you told us to do."

Once the basic pulse is established, chants usually proceed at a fairly even tempo. Often in the transition from speech to chant the tempo is slow, but picks up as more repetitive rhythmic elements are introduced. A pulse or beat to measure the chant having been established, it becomes apparent that the pulse has typical African American ambiguity in its subdivisions into two or three units. Generally syllabic, the chant does not tend to be elaborately ornamented. Ornaments, where used, are usually in the form of slides, usually up to a note, but also falling away. Melisma occurs at a moment of heightened intensity, or set to an exclamation (Wo-oh, Yeas, Ooh, etc.) produced by the person praying or interjected by a member of the congregation. These more melismatic moments are sometimes standard melodic formulae. The most common of these (taking in descending motion degrees 5, 4, 3, and 1 of the scale) I have found in all of the chanted prayers. Rosenberg describes it as the most common melodic formula found in the chanted sermon, as does Titon in reference to C. L. Franklin, a fact supported by the sermons I have heard.

Specific examples will illustrate the preceding points. Below is a complete textual transcription of a prayer; only a small portion of the melodic content is provided (lines 22–35 of the text, see example 6.2).[5] I recorded the prayer on 29 August 1982 at the 82nd Annual Session of the Tallahatchie-Oxford Missionary Baptist District Association and Auxiliaries, in Abbeville, Miss. The music transcribed is taken from the prayer at its most strictly musical in the Western sense, i.e., metrically regular and using relatively discrete pitches. The transcription (below), is prescriptive, not descriptive (Seeger, 1958: 185): "bent" notes, slides up to and away from notes, rhythmic anticipations and delays, are all characteristic of this style (and of most African American music), rendering the finished product much more complex than it appears in this notation. I have elected not to notate these complexities for two reasons. Our Western system of notation does not allow for an accurate representation of the complexities of pitch, i.e., it cannot accurately represent pitch distinctions smaller than a semitone. But more importantly, these complexities are highly personalised and vary greatly from leader to leader. They express the individual's artistry. I have sought instead to extrapolate from one particular prayer a basic representative structure. (In all transcriptions I have beamed notes in pulse groups to facilitate reading, rather than separating notes for each syllable.)

The man who led the prayer is Rev. Kenneth Bonner, a young minister who is clearly respected by the community for his spiritual and personal qualities. Both his praying and preaching are dynamic and elicit great response from his congregation. He is the older brother of Herbert, Sheila, Janice, and June Bug Bonner, and at the time I recorded this prayer he had not yet moved to his church in Tennessee. Because Rev. Bonner grew up in the Clear Creek Missionary Baptist community and still lives in the community, despite pastoring a church in Tennessee, I consider his style representative of the community. As I recorded the prayer at a convention of the Tallahatchie-Oxford Missionary Baptist Association, the congregation was a heterogeneous one drawn from the twenty churches that comprise the association. The degree of response that Rev. Bonner received, even though no habitual communication system existed between this preacher and this congregation, says much about both his dynamic force and the spirit of the people. The recurrent patterns commonly used by all who prayed or preached at the convention that day and the unanimity of the congregational responses (and even anticipations) exemplify a coherent and well-defined system of chanting which makes this particular transcription both representative and individual.

One further interesting characteristic of this prayer, as illustrated in the transcription, is a reinforcement of the duple-triple ambiguity or tension already mentioned as inherent in the pulse subdivision, i.e., ♫ as against ♪♪♪. Unlike the Rev. Brown of Bakersfield, who, according to Rosenberg "is happiest with a tetrameter line" (1970: 6), the Rev. Bonner seems to favour a line with three metrical feet, but preserves a sense of tension by interposing lines of either two or three feet. Thus, he exploits a duple-triple ambiguity not only in the pulse, but also in his phrasing.

The Eighty-Second Convention of the Tallahatchie-Oxford Missionary Baptist Association and Auxiliaries. Abbeville, Miss.: Project Center, August 29, 1982.
Prayer: Rev. Kenneth Bonner.

Our Father in Heaven

It us again
That a few of your children
First, we have met out, at this appointed place
We have had a chance, to sing thy sweet Zion songs   5
We have had a chance, to study, your words
We have a chance, this mornin', to stand and call your name
We just want to take this time this mornin', and give you the praise.
Bright early this mornin', you were so good.
Not because Father, that we kept the commandments so well   10
Not because Father, that we did all you told us to do.
But just because Father, that you love us so well.
Wo-oh Jesus, wo-oh Jesus.
Still somebody here this mornin', too mean Jesus, bow down
   and call your name   15
Oh-oh Jesus, I'm so glad this mornin'.
I know you this mornin', in a part of myself.
Ooh Jesus, I'm so glad this mornin'.

When I rose from my sleepin' couch
I had a chance this mornin', bow down on my knees   20
Just tell you I thank you this mornin'
Oh Jesus, we need you this mornin'
Can't get along without you
All in our homes
All on our jobs   25
Even in the church house, yeah
We can't get along without you.
Now Lord, oh my Lordy
Somebody here this mornin', have trouble in their home
Somebody here this mornin', mind is all confused   30
But oh Jesus, we know you can this mornin'
Touch their mind right now
Oh somebody family this mornin'
Oh have been broken this mornin'
Oh Jesus, come right now   35
Touch our minds
Remember that girl this mornin'
Don't forget about that boy this mornin'
That man or that woman this mornin'
Gone astray Jesus   40
Have turned their back on you this mornin'
Oh Jesus, oh Jesus
Please sir right now Jesus
Come on in the building right now
Somebody heart is too mean   45
Somebody mind is too cold
Lord Jesus, we just love you today
We gonna praise your name today
I don't care, what mens do or say
I'm gonna praise your name   50
I don't care this mornin'
I'm goin' if I have to go all by myself
Now Lord, oh we thank you right now
We just like to feel your spirit
When we can feel you Jesus   55
Everything is all right
We love you today
Come on in
Bless our souls
Somebody sick today   60
Somebody family discouraged
Somebody's in the hospital

We know you's a doctor
Somebody done give you up this mornin'
I know this mornin', if we just have a lil' patience   65
And give you time to come in
Go with us throughout this day

This is my prayer in Jesus' name and for thy sake.
Amen.

When this prayer is examined within the context of the African American church, a textual framework underpinning African American chanted prayers in general can be extrapolated.[6] Each prayer begins and concludes with formal standardized patterns of address (in the above example, "Our Father in Heaven," and "This is my prayer in Jesus' name and for thy sake") which frame the more personal and individualistic language of the body of the prayer. The temporal movement from beginning to end of the prayers traces God's influence through the preceding night into morning, this particular morning. The spatial movement converts a sense of God's permeating influence in all aspects of the church members' lives to a specific request that He enter into the church with them now.

Besides having qualities of spatial movement, the prayers are rich in symbolic meaning. The prayer leader, for instance, usually sets his prayer in the morning, even though it may be late afternoon. The "morning" setting allows for a symbolism which works on numerous levels: the dawning of a bright new day; the reawakening of the Christian to a new dawn, both literally and figuratively speaking; the Resurrection of Christ "bright and early" in the morning, etc. Additionally, the opening of the prayer deals with the passage from night to day (line 9 above), from darkness to light, a passage occasioned by the active participation of a caring God. Frequently, reference is made to the fact that even the darkness of night was relatively secure, for God was vigilant. The Lord is thanked for his goodness; there is open avowal of the members' dependence upon Him, help is asked for those who have deviated, and, finally, the Lord is asked to come directly to the person praying or to the congregation. A favourite elaboration on this basic structure is the successive mentioning of man, woman, boy, and girl—not necessarily in that order, (see lines 37–39)—which serves the dual purpose of integrating the congregation and also of giving each person a sense of individual mention.

Choices from a set repertoire of textual formulae help the leader in the formulation of his prayer. These formulae are of three types:

1. Exclamations such as "Oh Jesus," "Now Lordy," etc., which are not elaborated but serve essentially as stalls allowing the leader time to formulate his next line(s). On occasion these "stalls" serve

Example 6.2. Prayer excerpt, August 29, 1982, Rev. Kenneth Bonner, 82nd Annual Session of the Tallahatchie-Oxford Missionary Baptist District Association and Auxiliaries, Abbeville, Miss.

a much more important religious function. When spun into an invocatory sequence, they can lead to inspiration by the Holy Spirit (see chapter 5).

2. Standard turns of phrase such as "(Right)/Bright and early this mornin'" or "We just love you today," which do not further the immediate development of the prayer but can serve as "stalls," what Rosenberg designates "refrain formulas," or as transition phrases to a new idea;

3. Short generative phrases such as "Somebody here this mornin' . . ." or "Touch our minds/hearts, etc.," which the leader uses as a base for a whole section (see lines 29–30 and 60–64).

Similarly, there exist stock melodic and rhythmic formulae which not only allow the person praying a break to formulate his next line, but serve as the key motives on which the individual builds his prayer (see example 6.3).

Deacons and ministers seem to be aware of these formulae or "aids" and exploit them, even if not consciously. When questioned about the existence of rhythmic and melodic formulae, the Rev. Darryl Smaw immediately affirmed their use. Similarly, Rosenberg found an awareness of the "stalls" among the preachers he interviewed, although they might initially be reluctant to admit using them. He quotes one Rev. Brown as describing these formulae as a rest "on the highway, where you could pull off and regain your strength to drive on" (1970: 9). It will be noted, however, that in keeping with the pentatonic nature of the chant, the excerpt of music transcribed generally outlines the minor triad (B flat, D flat, F), occasionally filling in with the fourth degree of the scale (E flat) but consistently, in both the prayer leader's chant and the congregational responses, omitting the second degree of the scale (C).

An individual's sincerity is underscored by imaginative and spontaneous teasing and moulding of the basic framework. It is significant that this moulding very closely parallels the role of improvisation in African American music traditions in general. The general framework and shape of these prayers seems to be quite old.[7] A prayer of this type is transcribed in the 1899 publication, *The Watch Meeting*. The similarities between the

Example 6.3. Stock melodic and rhythmic formulae.

two prayers (separated in time by almost a century) are striking. Furthermore, as the practice of chanting still persists in Scottish congregations of the Outer Hebrides, which have also preserved the lined hymn tradition, it seems reasonable to postulate that this tradition of chanting prayers was brought to the New World at the same time as the hymnody, i.e., in the early seventeenth century. The contemporary Scottish rendition of chanted prayer, as described by Breandán Ó Madagáin (1993), is strikingly similar to that of the contemporary African American church.

> We then stood for prayer by the Minister. He closed his eyes and commenced to pray with great emotion, his voice for the full duration of the prayer (about twenty minutes) in marked recitative. The prayer (which my landlady [. . .] assured me was quite impromptu) was entirely in a kind of chant, which varied however. The first half consisted of a series of invocations to God [. . .] on roughly the same melodic pattern. Then the prayer changed to a kind of litany of needs or requests [. . .]. In addition to the manner of delivery the poetic style of the language was very noticeable, particularly in the use of litany [. . .]. His eyes remained closed to the very end of the prayer, when he dropped his voice in the closing appeal to God (1993: 265–66).

At Clear Creek M.B.C., although the deacons lead the prayers in the Devotion and also the Offertory prayer—it being one of their duties to take up the offering—Rev. McKinney always leads the final prayer, but none of the prayers that I have heard lasted for the twenty minutes referred to by Ó Madagáin above. The final prayer is preceded by a short song, the chorus of "Reach Out and Touch Somebody's Hand" or "Remember Me," for example. All the members frequently join hands while singing to emphasise their unity before dispersal. The singing leads directly into the prayer, which is generally short and often beautiful. The pianist continues to play as a background to the prayer, sometimes a continuation of the song, at others an unobtrusive chord progression. Rev. McKinney concludes the prayer with "Let the church sing! . . ." and everybody sings "Amen." He has a particular phrase that he sometimes adds after this: "Now turn around and look at the person next to you and—now don't say this unless you mean it—tell them 'I love you.' " This, or course, leads to laughing and talking, and the members gradually disperse.

I have transcribed below an example of one of these prayers. The complete text is provided, but again only a short portion of the chant, at its most melodic and metered (lines 26–35, see example 6.4, p. 158, and track 3 on the accompanying CD). When chanting, Rev. McKinney frequently punctuates each line with a "ah" expulsion of air at the end. While it is much softer and less accented than the "hah" of the white preacher John Sherfey, pastor of Fellowship Independent Baptist Church (Titon, 1988), for example, it is noticeable. Rev. McKinney usually vocalises his "ah" on the tonic and I have indicated it in parentheses. On this occasion, the prayer was preceded by a very slow rendition of "Remember Me," which the congregation sang in the unmetered, heterophonic, and ornamented style of the "Dr. Watts." The unity and cohesion that this type of singing promotes was reinforced by the handclasps of the members.

As one would expect, the tonality of the hymn carried over into the prayer although, in keeping with the characteristics of chant in this region (outlined above), the tonality switched to the minor. The minor triad (built on A, as the prayer was transcribed at pitch) forms the framework of most of the melodic structure, but it is filled in as before with the fourth degree of the scale (D). As one might expect from Rev. McKinney, however, and indeed from the final prayer of the service, the range of the chant is further expanded here to included the fifth note of the pentatonic scale (G, i.e., the fifth distinct note of the scale, but seventh in relation to a septatonic scale built on A), which initially appears as an unobtrusive under auxiliary at the end of the first line of the musical transcription ("And its board of members," line 26 of the text). As McKinney builds towards the climax of his prayer, however, ("We got to go in the dyin' room, ain't goin' come out no more," line 32) he also expands the range of his chant upwards to that fifth note of the pentatonic scale, the minor seventh (G) above the tonic. As the climax is reached in dying (with the expectation of joining Jesus, who will "stand by my side," line 34), this seventh appears as the highest note of the prayer in three successive phrases, resolving in each case down a minor third to E. The final resolution is reached in the last chanted phrase ("And everything will be alright," line 34), contained within the perfect fifth (A to E), which is at the core of the prayer. Resolution in Jesus is symbolised in the aesthetically convincing resolution of the melodic line back to the perfect fifth from which it was generated.

Clear Creek Missionary Baptist Church, October 18, 1987.
Concluding prayer: Rev. Grady McKinney (see figure 16).

Oh Eternal God,

We come again to say we thank you
For 'llowing us to 'ssemble at this appointed place
We thank thee for all our sisters and brothers
Who have bowed in prayer with us   5
Father, 'realise many names was read off on the sick list
Father, there are many more that we don't know anything about
But by you bein' a universal God
You know wherever the sick might be

Figure 16. Rev. Grady McKinney preaches at Clear Creek M.B.C.

Father, we comin' now aksing [*sic*] you to heal the sick, wherever
    they might be   10
We come now aksing you to bind the broken-hearted
We aks [*sic*] you to remember those behind the prison bars
Father, we aks thee to bless every one that stand in the need of
    blessing
Father, we aks you to bless every church door that renders service
    unto your name
Father, bless every individual who are being a livin' witness
    for you   15
Now father, bless every one under the sound of my weak voice
I don't know the needs but all of us stand in the need of something
Father, but by you bein' a almighty God, you know our every need
Father, when you get through blessin' them, stop by and bless
    your servant, according to your holy will
Now Lord, somebody have confusion in their home, and we
    know you can bring peace to confusion   20
Now Lord somebody in their home, may not have sufficient
    clothes to wear, but you can provide a way
Please sir have mercy this evening
Somebody might be sick today, and doesn't have any money to
    go to the doctor
But we know you can this evening, and we know you will
Now Lord, now Lord   25

Bless this church and it boards of members, if it is your holy will
Now Lord, take out the stoney heart, and place in a heart of
   reasoning
Now Lord, when it's all over, and we can't sing no more
Now Lord, when we're done prayed our last prayer
Sung our last song   30
Thy servant done preached their last sermon
We got to go on in the dyin' room, ain't goin' come out no more
I'm not goin' to aks you to make up my dyin' bed
But oh, stand by my side, and everything will be alright

This we come aksing in thy son Jesus' name   35
Let the church sing! . . . Amen.

A discussion of chanted prayers would be incomplete without some consideration of congregational responses. While the prayer is led by an individual, it is most certainly effected by the response of the congregation. The first prayer examined (pp. 148–52) was led by a minister who is recognised to have exceptional musical talent. Members told me that the Patton family has always been exceptionally gifted musically. Many of the Patton descendants have inherited that talent and it is particularly evident in the Bonner family. The second prayer (pp. 154–58) was led by a mature pastor and preacher whose services are in demand by several congregations. But both of these prayers were built around a minor triad and so explored only one of two possibilities.

The third prayer that I will examine was delivered by the Rev. Benjamin Baker of Main St. Baptist Church in Lexington, Kentucky, on 13 January 1985 (see figure 17 and track 4 on the accompanying CD). It is a good contrast to the first prayer because of the disparity between the musical skill of Rev. Baker and some of his congregation, and also between Revs. Baker, Bonner, and McKinney. In this prayer I have transcribed both the minister's text and the congregational responses. The picture is thus more complete. Moreover, while Baker does not move into chant until line 38 and thereafter moves freely in and out until line 118, already by line 26 the congregation has introduced one of the most elaborate chanted responses (see example 6.5). (Single note responses were evident from the congregation almost from the beginning.)

Embedded in the hymn "I Trust in God," this prayer, despite the complex of pitches evident around the third degree of the scale, is built on a major triad. The prayer is unusually long, but then it is delivered by the pastor who is also to deliver the sermon. Note especially the exceptional length of sections built around a single phrase (for example, see lines 4–12 and lines 118–135) and the smooth transition between sections (see lines 34–74). The text, as before, is transcribed in full, this time complete

♩=80 The rendition is rubato

Now Lord,_____ Now Lord____ Bless this church_ And it boards of mem-bers,

if it is your ho - ly will Now Lord,___ Take out the ston - y heart

and place in a heart of reas-'ning Now Lord,____ When it's all o - ver,____

and we can't sing no more Now Lord,__ When we done prayed our last_ prayer_

Sung our_ last song_ Thy ser-vant done preached their last_ ser-mon We got to

go on in the dy - in' room__ Ain't goin' come out no more__

I'm not goin' to ask you to make up my dy - in' bed__ But oh, stand by my side,__

and eve - ry thing_ will be al - right__

⌣♩ = slide up to note   ↓ = pitch lower than indicated

Example 6.4. Prayer excerpt, October 18, 1987, Rev. Grady McKinney, Clear Creek M.B.C. (See CD track 3.)

Figure 17. Rev. Benjamin Baker preaches at Main Street Baptist Church, Lexington, Ky.

with congregational responses. The musical transcription that follows is taken from lines 119–141 (see example 6.6). The transcription, again, is prescriptive, not descriptive. This prayer is, in fact, even freer than the Rev. Bonner's: the basic pulse varies considerably even in this short excerpt; it is slowed considerably on one occasion by three slow foot taps from one of the deacons sitting behind Baker (see the * in the transcription, "In His name, Thank yo' sir," lines 135–136), again showing an awareness of his surroundings on the part of the preacher, despite "movement to a different level of being." Although this chant never becomes quite as "musical" as Bonner's, for example, some few indications of variance have been given. Slides between two pitches are indicated by joining the two with a line; pitches which sound considerably sharper than indicated have this indicated thus, ↑, and notes which are almost spoken are indicated by an x on the note head, thus ♩. Finally, there is a musical transcription of the most characteristic congregational responses (see example 6.7). It will be noticed that these parallel the formulas or "aids" referred to earlier.

Example 6.5. Relatively elaborate congregational response, Main Street Baptist Church.

This prayer, additionally, offers further illustration of the complementarity between the chant of the preacher and that of the congregation. At line 117, a congregant introduces a response "In the name of Jesus," which is taken by Rev. Baker at line 118. In the following line (119) Baker shortens this to "In his name," and in response to this, the members shorten their response identically (line 119). Rev. Baker then builds the following section (lines 119–141) upon it. This close interaction opens the section where Rev. Baker's chant becomes most clearly defined musically, and it is this section that I have transcribed.

Main St. Baptist Church, Lexington, KY.
Pastor: Benjamin Baker
Sunday Service, January 13, 1986: Theme "Jesus Shows Us the Father"
Prayer: Rev. Benjamin Baker. Following hymn "I trust in God."

Preacher	Cong. response	Line
Our Father	Yessir	
Our Father	Oh yeah	
Creator and Sustainer	Yes	
	Oh yeah	
You're a Redeemer	Yeah	
You're a Judge	Oh yeah	5
You're a Keeper	Oh yes	
You a Shepherd	Yes	
You a Bridge	Well	
You Breads	Ooh yes	
You're Water	Well	10
You all that we need	Oh yes	
In this life and even in the life yet to come	Oh yeas	
Father, we thankful that we are your children		
We thankful, our father, that you watch over us	Thank you sir	
We thankful that there's no mountain too high	Ooh	15
No valley too low	Wo-oh	
No road too rough	Oh yes Lord	
No going too tough	Well	
	Thank you Jesus	
That we don't have that inner 'ssurance	Yessir	
In knowing that you watch over us	Well	20
Take our hand Father	Take our hand	
And lead from one degree of grace unto another	Alright	

Give us faith — Ooh
Give us courage — Yes Lord
Give us humility — Oh yeas — 25
Give us sincerity — Sincerity Lord
We need you Father — Oh yes we do
More than silver or gold — Well
We need you Father — Oh yes
To be our help in ages past — Yes Lord — 30
We need you to be our hope in unknown — Ooh yes
and uncertain days of future
We need you Father — We need you
Father

To take our weak hands and lead us on — Yes Lord
We pray our Father for healing for those — Oh yes Lord
that are sick
We pray in the name of Jesus that you — In the name — 35
might . . . set those in bondage free — of Jesus
We pray our Father this morning for those — Wo-oh yes
that are discouraged
We pray for those that have crying eyes — Yes
We pray for those that have troubled hearts — Oh yes Lord
Pray for those that have confused minds — Yes
Let 'em know you a mind regulator — Oh mind — 40
regulator

Let 'em know you still a heart fixer — Heart fixer Lord
Let 'em know you still a problem solver — Oh yes lord
Let us all know if we have the faith — Well
You sure 'nough got the power — Yes Lord
Let us know our Father if you . . . would — Well — 45
stand ahead of us
Stand behind us — Oh yes Lord
Stand under us — Oh yes Lord
Stand all around us — Oh yes Lord
You are greater than anything that is — Oh yes Lord
against us — Thank yo' Jesus
Father we pray this mornin' — Thank yo' Lord — 50
For the sinner man and sinner woman — Oh yes Lord
We pray our Father for the power of — Oh yes Lord
your word
And we pray for the 'nointment of your — Ooh yes Lord
Holy Ghost
That he might convict — Yes
That he might convey — Yes Lord — 55
That he might convert — Oh yes

	In the name	
	of Jesus	
That men and women would fall out	Oh yes Lord	
With the weightings of this old world	Yeah	
Realising that this world ain't no friend	Well	
of grace		
But come crying "what must I do to	Well	60
be saved?"		
Let 'em know Jesus	Jesus	
Is the Christ	Oh Jesus	
Jesus	Jesus	
Is Saviour	Oh Jesus	
Jesus	Oh Jesus	65
Is Lord	Yes	
We pray our Father for your power upon	Yes Lord	
the church		
We pray Heavenly Father your will be done	Ooh yes Lord	
Your name be glorified	Ooh yes Lord	
We pray Heavenly Father for those that	Yes Lord	70
discouraged		
We pray Heavenly Father for those that	Well	
feel weak		
'Pray for those that feel like they're least of	Oh yes Lord	
the children		
But let us know our Father that you are	Yes	
more than the whole world is against us		
And if we will call on yo'	Call on yo'	
	Yeah	
In sincerity	Oh yes Lord	75
Call on yo'	Call on yo'	
In honesty	Jesus	
Call on yo'	Jesus	
In holiness	Yes Jesus	
Call on yo'	Jesus	80
And believe your word	Ooh	
We shall receive your promise	Oh yes Lord	
Now Lord bless us	Please	
Anoint this choir	Yes Lord	
And hide me behind the cross	In his name	85
Let me not preach for fame nor fortune	Oh yes Lord	
But let me preach for the end that	Yes Lord	
somebody might believe		
And believing they might be saved	Well	
And then Father	Yes Lord	

When we go down from this place	Oh yes	90
When we leave praying ground	Well	
When we stood the test of time	Oh yes Lord	
Been 'buked been scorned	Yes Lord	
Been misunderstood	Yes Lord	
Take us down from this place	From this place	95
That we might go into that city	Ooh yes	
That Abraham didn't find	Well	
Let us go down from this place	Oh yes Lord	
That old man Elijah left the world	Yes	
And walked on into that city	Well	100
Let us go down from this place	Yes	
	Go Lord	
That we might leave this world of tears and sorrow	Yes Lord	
Open our eyes upon celestical shores	Yes	
See Jesus Christ	Yes Lord	
See him in Lord	Oh yes Lord	105
See him as conqueror	Oh yes	
See him as victor	Yes	
See him in reigning supreme	Ooh	
Until that hour	Ooh	
Watch over us	Well	110
Keep our hearts	Yes Lord	
Keep our souls	Oh yes Lord	
Steady our feet	Yes	
Hold our hands	Well	
Keep our eyes on you	Oh yes Lord	115
Make our hearts turn toward you	Well	
And we'll give you the praise	In the name of Jesus	
In the name of Jesus	In the name of Jesus	
In his name	In his name	
In his name	Yes	120
Woh in his name	Alright	
In his name	In his name Lord	
In his name	In the name of Jesus	
Bad men get good	Yes Lord	
In the name of Jesus	In the name of Jesus	125
Weary folk go restful	Yes	

In the name of Jesus	In the name of Jesus
Folk that can't sing make music	Well
In the name of Jesus	In the name of Jesus
Folk that can't speak . . . talk in tongues	Well 130
In the name of Jesus	In the name of Jesus
In his name	Hey
In his name	In his name
In his name, in his name	Alright
In his name	In the name 135 of Jesus
Thank yo' sir	Thank yo'
Thank yo' sir	Thank yo'
Thank yo' sir	Thank yo'
My soul	Oh yes Lord
My soul	Oh yes Lord 140
Want to thank yo'	Thank yo' Lord
Want to thank yo'	Thank yo'
All the redeemed in the Lord thank yo'	Yessir
The saints thank yo'	Thank yo'
The born again thank yo'	Oh thank yo' 145
The double dipped thank yo'	Oh yes Lord
Those that been covered by the blood	Well
Washed in the redeeming blood of the Lamb	Well
We thank yo' sir	Thank yo' Lord
In Jesus' name	In Jesus' name 150
Amen	Amen
Amen	Yes
Amen.	Yes

Besides characteristics already discussed in relation to Bonner's prayer—formal structure and movement, the three types of textual formulae, melodic and rhythmic formulae, etc.—this prayer, partly because of its length, highlights several other characteristics, any one or more of which may be incorporated into chanted prayers, but the combination of which is more characteristic of sermons. Absolutely characteristic of both is the juxtaposition of pairs, usually with rhyme and/or alliteration, for example, "No mountain too high, No valley too low, No road too rough, No going too tough," (see also lines 23–26 and lines 45–48). Even when spoken these pairs are usually clearly indicated by intonation, voice inflection

Example 6.6. Prayer excerpt, January 13, 1986, Rev. Benjamin Baker, Main Street Baptist Church. (See CD track 4.)

In the name of Je-sus   Oh yes Lord   Oh mind re-gu-la-tor   Oh yes Lord.

Example 6.7. Characteristic congregational responses.

rising considerably at the end of the first line and falling at the end of the second. Closely related are short sections built on anaphora or alliteration (see lines 54–56; this particular sequence is a favourite one of Rev. Baker's).

Three other characteristics exhibited by this prayer are more typical of sermons. The first is the incorporation of lines from sacred songs—spirituals, gospel pieces, hymns, etc.—or even secular songs. See line 15: "There's no mountain high enough," Diana Ross and the Supremes; line 93: spiritual, "I've been 'buked and I've been scorned"; lines 147–148: there is a whole series of hymns which tell of the saving power of the blood of the lamb, "There is power in the blood," "I am coming to the cross," "Jesus saves," "His blood atoned for me," etc. These references considerably enrich the associative power of the prayer and add another level of symbolic significance. During a sermon, reference thus to hymns may move the accompanist to pick up the tune, and if it is particularly apt, the whole church may burst into spontaneous song. Rev. Carter, pastor of Congdon St. Church, rarely moves into elaborate chanting in his sermons but frequently, at the climax, intersperses lines from song texts. Second, Rev. Baker makes reference to passages from Scripture (see lines 96–100). Third, Rev. Baker's prayer on this occasion leads to inspiration by the Holy Spirit in at least one member of the congregation. It is interesting that this occurs at line 130—"Folk that can't speak . . . talk in tongues." As will be further discussed later, the occurrence of inspiration is much more usual in the context of chanted sermons.

The musical section of the prayer transcribed is typical of chant in general and also of any one of a number of sections in this prayer. It is interesting to note first that the three prayers transcribed cover almost exactly the same pitch area around middle C (1. B flat–F, 2. A flat–E flat, G added at the climax, and 3. A flat–F), one built on a B-flat-minor triad, the second on an A-minor triad, and the third on a D-flat-major triad. Prayers have been transcribed at pitch, and this pitch area seems to be typical of chanting. The key used in example 6.6 above, despite its five flats, offers no surprise, since the keys most commonly used in African American Baptist church services—partly influenced no doubt by the notation of hymns in Baptist hymnals—are the "flat keys": E flat, A flat, and D flat (B flat and F less commonly). Two "sharp keys" are infrequently used: G and D. Thus in learning gospel piano, which is almost exclusively taught orally, one is likely to be introduced first to keys with at least three flats. There is, of course, no difficulty in reading, as one learns by ear. And it is relatively easy to play in these keys, in a style that features broken chords the length of the piano. I think that most pianists would agree that it is far easier to play a fast, even D-flat arpeggio over several octaves than a fast and even C arpeggio. One clue to the relative facility of the "flat keys" is clearly the ease of passing the thumb because of the different heights of black and white keys.

One further intriguing aspect of the chant as seen in example 6.6 is the further reinforcement of the duple-triple ambiguity already mentioned (accents/line, and pulse subdivision) by an alternate grouping of the pulses themselves into twos and threes. While most of the excerpt pulses are grouped into twos (thus giving a feeling of duple meter), in the middle section—from line 128, "Folks that can't sing," to line 134, "In his name, in his name"—Baker groups his pulses in threes (thus giving a feeling of triple meter).

Finally, it should be kept in mind that the full complexity of this particular chant cannot be appreciated without remembering the hymn "I trust in God," which continues in the background throughout, sustained by the accompanists and by the humming of some of the congregation. The 4/4 meter of the hymn is switched to a slow 12/8 during the prayer and offers yet another layer of rhythmic interest and ambiguity. This "triplication" of the meter is quite usual in African American Baptist performances, partly because it adds interest to a hymn performed at the slow tempo, which is preferred especially at intense moments of the service. (This prayer and the hymn in which it is embedded are found on track 4 of the accompanying CD.)

While the preceding discussion shows that there are similarities between chanted prayers and chanted sermons—the dynamic interaction between congregation and preacher or prayer leader, the use of standard textual and musical formulae, the transcendental experience of the deacon or minister—there is one crucial distinction. Sermons build toward a definite climax—the sermon is itself the climax of the service—which is in a sense a cathartic resolution of the tensions generated, and this resolution is often expressed in a spontaneous hymn. Chanted prayers, on the other hand, have no such climactic resolution. The function of the prayers is to generate those tensions, to "move" the people, to make them "feel the Spirit." The tension is never brought to a peak and so is never resolved, it is relaxed but not released. This difference can be partly attributed to the large discrepancy in length between a typical chanted prayer and a typical sermon. Yet the distinction has a more fundamental basis than that. Without question the sermon is the highpoint of the service. It is the climax and its realisation is in climactic terms. Prayer should never upstage the sermon.[8] One function of chanted prayers, as indeed of most music in the service, is to prepare the congregation for the preacher, to make them receptive to his message, to generate a certain amount of spirit in them so that the preacher is not addressing a "cold" congregation.

Chanted prayer in the African American church thus allows personal and individual expression, but along established lines, which the congregation can readily follow and even anticipate. It places a premium, therefore, on the spirituality and creativity of the person praying and is an important expressive challenge. It allows the congregation maximum participation in the form of interjections, responses, and vocal and percussive expressions of appreciation and approval. Consequently, it increases the community's sense of solidarity and its sharing of a common artistic form with which to approach the deity; yet the fluidity and individualistic interpretation of the form ensure against its becoming too familiar as well as boring. One never quite knows which turn the prayer will take. In this sense it parallels the "withheld information" practise of gospel music.

Because the problems and wishes expressed in the prayers are adapted to each situation and are the immediate concern of the person praying at that time and, most likely, of the majority of the congregation, each prayer has a certain freshness and is stamped with the hallmark of sincerity. If the person praying is not truly feeling what he is saying, his insincerity is communicated very quickly to the members of the congregation, who express their disapproval with ominous silence. On a more specific level, it is an established principle of rhetoric that repetitive formulae are important devices in arousing an audience emotionally. The repetitive rhythmic, melodic, and syntactical formulae of chanted prayers are certainly more effective in "moving" these congregations that unmetered prose could be.

It is the aesthetic of this African American church tradition that the service should be a "whole" worship experience. The move from unmetered prose to chant in the prayers makes increased demands upon both the person leading the prayer and the congregation. By the time the prayer has become chant, the concern is not only with the sentiments to be expressed but also with their eloquent expression in terms of rhythm, melody, and syntax. The demands are greater, the degree of self-immersion deeper, and the integration of leader and congregation more cohesive.

Sermon

"Now Lord, You know more than I know"

In every society, it would seem, there are those who are recognised as being especially gifted with regard to language. Oral discourse is arguably the primary mode of discourse around the world. Its primacy is no longer confined to "folk" or "pre-literate" societies. The blossoming of the radio, phonograph, movie, television, cassette, and video tape industries has transformed Western culture to the extent that high-school literacy in the United States is alarmingly low. The majority of people in the United States now glean most of their information not from newspapers or books, but from radio and television.[1]

Although it is not always fashionable to say so, individuals are variously gifted with and variously develop different abilities. Those whose strength is oral language have and will, I believe, continue to possess considerable power within society. That power need not express itself in political or financial terms: it can be the power of an Irish seanachaí to move his audience to tears or laughter; the power of a counsellor to instil hope and belief in someone who has lost all desire for life; the power of a revolutionary to ignite a struggle for justice. Language is arguably our most valuable tool. With it we deride or praise, belittle or aggrandise, comfort or injure. Language allows us to "control" our environs; it gives us the power to recognise or ignore, define and label. It is the paradox of language that it can not only incite us to action, but also trap us in inaction. All too frequently, perhaps, "talking about" displaces and substitutes for "doing."

Linguists have found a considerable degree of variance in the importance accorded language from one culture to the next. "Language is not everywhere important in the same way, to the same extent or purpose. Communities vary grossly in the sheer amount of talk, in the place assigned to talk in relation to touch or sight, in trust or distrust of talk, in the proportion and kinds of roles dependent on verbal skill" (Dell Hymes, 1971: 81). African American culture is one of those that accords language great importance. African American communities set a premium upon effective speaking, and recognise it as a noteworthy skill. As Roger D. Abrahams remarks, "[I]n such communities, the eloquent speaker is capable of garnering a great deal of power, respect, and in many cases admiration through his artful speaking" (1983: 21).

Recognition of the emphasis African American communities place upon effective speaking, however, is not new. Many earlier writers in the slavery and reconstruction periods remarked upon it, although not always in a positive tone.

> Although the proverbial sayings of the Negroes have often much point and meaning, they, however, no sooner begin to expatiate and enter more minutely into particulars, than they become tedious, verbose, and circumlocutory, beginning their speeches with a tiresome exordium, mingling with them much extraneous matter, and frequently traversing over and over the same ground, and cautioning the hearer to be attentive, as if fearful that some of the particulars and points on which their meaning and argument hinged should escape attention. So that by the time they arrive at the peroration of their harangue, the listener is heartily fatigued with it, and perceives that the whole which has been said, though it may have taken up half an hour, could have been comprised in half-a-dozen words (Stewart, 1832: 264, quoted in Abrahams, 1983: 31).

Stewart's writing here is hardly concise: it is deliberately tedious, as by example, perhaps.

Research indicates that the emphasis on spoken language referred to above has been retained in contemporary African American culture, and it seems to have survived best in African American communities that are most separate from white communities. Ardener remarks that "lower-class black children in the U.S., for example, are probably much more sensitive to the aesthetic and interactional uses of language than are many middle-class white children" (1971: 56). Abrahams in turn brings this argument a step further by citing the commonly accepted paradigm that the more affluent an African American community becomes, the less "black" or traditional is its expression. "The more middle-class a black community becomes, the more its observances tend to conform to white norms (because it is whites who dictate the middle-class forms of behavior). However, when dealing with features of lower-class or peasant behavior [. . .] there is often a superficial resemblance to European practices, while the manner of performance, especially of interactional expectations, is more characteristic of African performance practices" (Abrahams, 1983: 33).

In African American scholarship, behaviour that is perceived as "black" is generally traced back to Africa, and scholars such as Melville Herskovits (1941), Lazarus Ekueme (1974), Cheryl Gilkes (1997), Joseph E. Holloway (1990), Holloway and Vass, eds. (1993), Portia Maultsby

(1985), Sidney Mintz (1976), Mozella Mitchell (1994), Kete Molefi (1987), and Robert Farris Thompson (1983), have identified many African retentions in African American culture in the New World.[2] Through comparison with African studies, scholars such as Abrahams trace the African American emphasis on eloquence to African roots. "Recent description of African village life and expressive culture encourage us to look to that continent as the primary source for the Afro-American valuing of eloquence. There has surely been a continuity between New World speechmaking practices and African expressive patterns" (Abrahams, 1983: 21). Abrahams substantiates this assertion with relevant quotes from various Africanists, including the following from Ethel M. Albert's writings on Burundi:

> Speech is explicitly recognised as an important instrument of social life; eloquence is one of the central values of the cultural world-view, and the way of life affords frequent opportunity for its exercise. Sensitivity to the variety and complexity of speech behavior is evident in a rich vocabulary for its description and evaluation and in a constant flow of speech about speech. Argument, debate, and negotiation, as well as elaborate literary forms are built into the organisation of society as means of gaining one's ends, as social status symbols, and as skills enjoyable in themselves (Albert, 1964: 35, in Abrahams, 1983: 22).

Music is the non-verbal correlate of speech and, as a non-verbal form of communication, it is in some ways more direct than speech. One institution in the African American community has been a training place and a showcase for these two skills, music and oratory, i.e., the African American church. Music and oratory are most closely allied in chanted prayers and sermons. Each of these genres articulates one side of the dialogue between God and humankind and they are, therefore, extremely important expressions of the black church.

Much of the information discussed in chapter 6 relating to chanted prayers also pertains to chanted sermons. However, where prayer is a form that may be realised by any church member (although it is usually the deacons who lead prayer in black Baptist churches), preaching is a far more restricted form available only to a special class of individuals—preachers. The preacher, even where he is not a pastor, is set apart from others. His mission is a special one and his commitment is generally a lifetime one.

"Ordained of God to preach"

As mentioned before, Clear Creek is a traditional church. Some members believe that God selects certain individuals to be preachers even before

they are born. In referring to Rev. Kenneth Bonner, for example, Lee Earl
Robinson told me: "Kenneth was ordained before he was born. Even
before Kenneth was born, he was ordained of God to preach" (interview,
November 11, 1987). This calling from God, or ordination before birth,
seems to be quite a widespread belief amongst African American congregations. When Gerald L. Davis questioned Bishop Cleveland (one of the
three preachers whose sermons are examined in his 1985 study), he
received much the same response.

> Preachers are born. They are not called, they are born. . . . When you're
> born, preaching is in you. And when the time comes it stirs, God stirs
> it up. Bible says, "Stir up the gift that is within you, which are given
> you from God." So when I begin praying and I really got converted,
> why then it started up and I began preaching (1985: ix).[3]

This "ordination" is succeeded by a call to preach when the individual
comes of age. This call to preach is essential, for the members believe that
one must be called by God in order to be a true preacher. It is not something that one can choose to be, or become simply through training.
"Some people go to school to be preachers, trained to be a minister. I have
no objection to that, but I'm a Baptist, and we believe men is called by
God to preach. Now it's good to go to school, after the Lord have chosen
you, but we don't believe in going to school to be something the Lord
didn't choose you to be" (Rev. Grady McKinney, interview, November 17,
1986). Charles Campbell made more explicit the danger in deciding to be
a preacher unless first called by God. "It is evil to get up and preach if you
not called by God. . . . For instance now, Robinson go up and start to
preaching and he not called by the Almighty. He may be assigned to it by
humanity, but that's evil" (interview, November 20, 1986). Nor can any
other person convince you to become a preacher. As Rev. McKinney
explained to me, it would be wrong for a parent or another preacher to
"make a preacher" out of an individual.

> An individual asked me once if I was gonna make a preacher out of my
> baby boy. I said, "No, I don't think so. If he be a preacher, let the Lord
> send him." I ain't gonna send nobody to preach. 'Cause if the, you can't
> hold up 'til the end. That's why we have a failure with a lot of our min-
> isters. . . . If the Lord have anointed you to preach the Gospel, then
> you're gonna continue. But if you just decide "I can do it," because
> Brother Robinson is a preacher, now you might go out there and draw
> a big crowd. But you gotta have more than a big crowd. When it comes
> down to preaching, they are peculiar peoples. And if his life style is just
> like anybody else's, the Lord haven't sent him. That's why a lot of us
> fail on the road somewhere. We can't stand up and act like a leading

man ought to act like, we'll fall down in the gutter. So a person just need to be sent by God. And if he sent by God, he'll hold on, don't care how rough it's getting (ibid.).

Rev. McKinney also faults preachers who try to promote a son who is a preacher, on the grounds that preaching and a commitment to ministry are things that have to come from within an individual.

> I have a son a minister. I said, "Now when you get a 'pointment, you go preach. Next thing—you not goin' ride on my coat tail. You will have to make it on your own." You know, some ministers have a son preaching, and he just bore his folks to death with his son; every time he come he got his son up there preaching. But you gotta let that person make it on them selves, and if they make they own record, they can stand on it (ibid.).

The decision to become a preacher without being called by God may, the members believe, account for the poor quality of some preaching. Rev. Kenneth Bonner is referred to as a "dynamic" and "powerful" speaker, but Rev. Bonner did not enter the seminary until after he had been called to preach.

> Kenneth never entered into seminary until after the Holy Spirit had chosen him to minister to his people. . . . Scripture tells us these things. Many mens has chosen themselves to become leaders or ministers for God and have gone to many schools of theology and are unable to expound in the Word and to explain the Gospel and the true meaning of what the Scriptures is all about (Lee Earl Robinson, November 11, 1987).

The call to preach is as distinctive as the experience of conversion. Often, the individual's first reaction to this call is to resist it. There is a reluctance to accept the challenge and often, a sustained struggle. "It's an inward thing. Have you ever had anything that constantly comes to you? It's continuous, on the inside, and so you'll fight it for a long time. I fought it for a long time" (Rev. McKinney, November 17, 1986). This resistance seems not to be unusual in Christian traditions. Jeff Titon remarked on it among the white Baptists and Pentecostals he studied (1988),[4] and Davis quotes remarks from Bishop Cleveland in much the same vein. "They said, 'Preach!' Oh when they said that, I'd say, 'Oh, oh, that isn't the way I want it' and I'd stop. And it just went so bad so long 'til I had to do it, you know" (Gerald Davis, 1985: ix). Bauman (1983) also notes a similar reaction amongst seventeenth century Quakers, and quotes an account, from the journal by William Caton, of a resistance that ultimately leads to acceptance.

About that time I begun to know the motion of his power, and the command of his Spirit by which I came to be moved [. . .] against the deceit of the priests, and the sins of the people, and to warn all to repent, for I testified to them that the day of the Lord was a coming. But, Oh the weakness, the fear and trembling, that I went in upon this message, who shall declare it? And how did I plead God concerning this matter. [. . .] Howbeit, whatsoever I alleged by way of reasoning against the Lord, concerning the weighty matter, I could not be excused, and must go (1689: 9, quoted in Bauman, 1983: 132).

For different individuals, the call is more or less dramatic. Rev. Grady McKinney gave me this account of his call, or what he describes as an "ultimatum" concerning his call, for he had been struggling with the call for a "a long time" before this moment. He was thirty-one when he went into the ministry, married, with "a whole truckload of children." "I didn't want to be no preacher. I was doing fine just like I was. And being a good 'bench member' as they call it, I was doing fine. But that was the Lord's plan" (interview, November 17, 1986). The call, however, was not to be denied, and the experience was a dramatic one.

One day I was laid down across bed, and I don't know was I asleep or awake, and something appeared and said unto me, "If you don't preach, you won't be here long. I ain't arguing no more." That settled it! I said to the Lord, "Now Lord, you know more than I know." And I was ready to go. I been ready ever since, but sometime I feel like quitting I get so discouraged. If the Lord 'nointed you to do something, you can't quit (ibid.).

"You preach the Gospel and let the Lord work it out"

The following is a delineation of the process of becoming a preacher, as Rev. McKinney explained it. Once the individual has acknowledged and accepted his call to preach, he approaches his pastor with this knowledge. The pastor and board of members set a date for his "trial sermon," and if that is good they give him a preacher's licence. Formerly in the "old Baptist rule," one was not ordained until called by a church. Main St. Baptist Church in Lexington, Kentucky, for example, has seven assistant ministers. Of these, however, only one has been called by another church, and he was ordained at that time. The other six have their preacher's licenses. In other churches nowadays, however, ordinations are generally performed once the individual is ready. Then, depending upon one's perspective, one either seeks a church or waits to be called.

Rev. McKinney has little patience with ministers who cater too much to the body of the membership, and feels that instead one should wait upon the Lord.

> You preach the Gospel and let the Lord work it out. Now, if the Lord give you a church, then the Lord let you stay there 'til He get ready to move you. But when you go out, as I call it "politicking." I talk with a lot of these young preachers and I'm too old-fashioned for them. Now they believe in it. They believe in going 'round wanting to find out where the deacons live, and talk with them and make a bargain. But I don't believe in that. I'm a firm believer in that the Lord send you to do something, he goin' give you something to do. And you just ought to wait until the Lord give you something. And if the Lord give you something, you got something. But if you go out and coat up on it, you might say, then them same people that you dealt with will be the first folks to turn against you (ibid.).

Central to a preacher's role in the black Baptist church, and central to the religious expression of the church, is the sermon. The sermon is the high point of a service and everything that precedes it is intended to prepare the people to receive the message. It is in the sermon that the symbolic and ritual expression of the church is realised, often in a concrete way, for it is during the course of preaching that the Holy Spirit manifests itself most frequently in the church through expressions such as the shout. As Hans Baer and Merrill Singer put it:

> Following [Van] Gennep (1960), it can be argued that pre-sermon events separate worshippers from the profane world whereas post-sermon ritual events reincorporate them back into this world. Separation is best exemplified in the testimony session, during which various members, especially women, review recent hardships in their lives and express their joy in being able to discard them, at least temporarily, since they are in the process of entering a sacred liminal period. More so than any other portion of the service, the sermon or "message" constitutes a liminal period during which the preacher may act out the journey to heaven or various members of the congregation become ecstatic or "shout" (1992: 34).

Members understand the Holy Spirit to be involved in all stages of preaching, from the calling of the preacher, to the conversion of the unsaved, and the reconciliation of the backslider.

While it is a preacher's obligation and responsibility to prepare his message, the members do not believe that this will necessarily produce a good sermon or make a good preacher, just as knowledge will not make people shout. The message, the members believe, must come from God.

> Now that's the way preaching is, with me and many other black preachers that I know. We have, many times I have sit down and worked on a message a whole week and when Sunday came I couldn't even do nothing with it, because that was my message, it wasn't God's message. And the best thing to do is get you a little ('least I believe in doing it. I won't say it the best because other person have a right to their opinion), is to study, and whatever you think you'll say, get you a little sketch over here on it, or an outline which way you think you goin' go. But if the Spirit change your mind, you better lay it down, because if you don't lay that down, you not goin' preach. You goin' get up there and mess it up! I don't care how hard you done studied and if you get up Sunday morning (and I usually look over what I goin' talk about it, and I even do it when I get to church. I go back there in the study, and if they just stop bothering me, and I goes kind of back over what I goin' talk about). But if you don't get some sense of feeling Sunday mornin' from this you studying, you better start talking to the Lord, 'cause you need something. You ain't got nothing that Sunday! (Rev. McKinney, interview, November 17, 1986).

No more than one can be a true preacher without being called by God, can one preach a sermon without God's approval.

> In other words, preaching a message, it's like food,[5] it's got a taste to it when you get it. And if you can't get a taste of this, you better do something right quick. And if the Lord don't give you nothing but two words, you done went through all this work getting this thing ready and you cain't get no feeling for this message, and if the Lord give you "Jesus wept," you better take it. You can take "Jesus wept" and do more with it than that whole week's work you done did on that sermon (ibid.).

Nonetheless, as discouraging as it may be to work on a sermon and not have it come together Sunday morning, Rev. McKinney is confident that all he has to do is to call on God and he will get all the help he needs. "It takes a lot out of you when you study like that and prepare a sermon and then when you get up Sunday morning, all the taste is gone, you ain't got nothing. 'Oh Lord, what I'm goin' do?' And you say that question, you already know what you goin' do: you know what you gotta do 'cause this message you have is no good to you, so you gotta talk with the Lord" (ibid.). With a flexibility that allows him room to move to a more advantageous viewpoint, Rev. McKinney sees not loss of his time and effort, but a lesson in humility and a reassurance of help.

> Here what I think happen is. The Lord have to prove to us that He still rules, because we kind of wants to be self-sufficient. Whatever we do we wants to be an expert on it. And the Lord just have to show us sometime, "This is not your Gospel, this is my Gospel. You made your plan what you goin' preach, but I'm goin' tell you what you goin' preach." And the best way in the world for a preacher to get a message is to pray over it. And I believe in that. . . . But I must constantly pray. I don't mean in the sense of praying all day and long as you woke at night, but we must constantly ask God for His leading and His guiding, and God will supply our needs, if we would only allow Him (ibid).

These ideas about finding a sermon message are not unique to Rev. McKinney, but are shared by many preachers. They are also causes of concern to music ministers of larger churches (such as Main St. in Lexington) who seek to correlate the Invitation hymn with the sermon topic. A sudden change in sermon topic, therefore, generally necessitates a parallel change in the choice of Invitation hymn. Jeff Titon quotes Rev. Henry Snyder, a white minister of a Pentecostal church, expressing the same sentiments as Rev. McKinney.

> I prepare every week for my sermons. I—sometimes I spend ten hours on a sermon; sometimes I spend twenty minutes. Because I'm prepared. Because preparing for a sermon is not getting down and studying and all that. I do a lot of that; I have books in my office up to here. And I read books and I study and I study and I study. But if you just pray. And say, "God, God, I need Thy will. God, I need Thy wisdom." Then you're prepared. That's why I can come out here if I have the whole message ready, like last Sunday, and God says [claps hands], "Not that one this morning, Henry, you're going to preach another one." And He shows me a scripture. And I preached that for forty minutes. I can't do that out of my own being. But that's God! (Excerpt from "Be Prepared," sermon preached by the Rev. Henry Snyder, Bucksport [Pentecostal] Church of God in Christ, Bucksport, Maine, August 10, 1975. Collected and transcribed by Jeff Titon.)

Thus, contrary to all principles of war, there is peace, not shame, to be found in surrender. This idea of freeing the mind, of acceptance but not of helplessness, is, of course, an ancient concept in many of the world's religions, from Buddhism to Christianity. It is also at the heart of such contemporary movements as the New Age movement and self-healing groups.

To the church members, of course, surrender is valuable for them only
when it is surrender to God.

"When the Spirit come it feeds you"

And so to the preaching itself. The art of preaching an oral sermon is in
many ways analogous to telling a tale. A good preacher is an artist/per-
former in the best sense of those words: he creates, in performance (see
Bauman's definition of "performance" in relation to oral narratives), an
"object" that is culturally acceptable and aesthetically pleasing.[6] The sermon must also be accessible to the congregation. In the words of Walter
Benjamin: "The storyteller [read "preacher"] takes what he tells from
experience—his own or that reported by others. And he in turn makes it
the experience of those who are listening to his tale" [read "sermon"]
(Benjamin, 1969: 87, quoted in Bauman, 1986: 2). The sermon has the
potential to add another level of sustenance to the performance that is not
available in the same way to the tale. At its best, the sermon is spiritually
nourishing. Spiritual nourishment occurs on two levels: 1) the citation and
explication of Scripture and Biblical events; 2) the entry of the Holy Spirit
into the physical body of the church. (See Baer and Singer's comments above,
p. 175 [1992: 34].)

The preacher is believed to quite literally become the mouthpiece of the
Holy Spirit. As Rosenberg remarks: "The belief is deep and widespread
that the words of the sermon come directly from the Holy Ghost, that
while the preacher is behind the pulpit he is merely lending his speech
organs to the Holy Spirit. Hence the words are not his, but the Lord's"
(Rosenberg, 1971: 426). Titon remarks on a similar belief "At such times
the worshiper is understood to be possessed by the Spirit. He or she then
becomes a mouthpiece for the Spirit, is 'led by the Spirit,' and speaks,
chants, or sings the words of the Spirit" (1988: 199). At Clear Creek
M.B.C. the members believe that this is especially true of the chanted portions of the sermon. Rev. McKinney explained to me that he starts off on
his own, but that when he begins to chant that is the Holy Spirit speaking through him. It is not he who is preaching at this stage, but the
Holy Spirit.

> You see, that's the mystery of the Holy Spirit. You see when you doin'
> something for the Lord, when you start off, you might start off on your
> owns doing your best, but when the time come the Spirit goin' come in
> and then that's goin' lift you. And then you begin saying things that you
> hadn't even planned on saying. The Lord feeds you. Have you ever saw
> a sausage mill, what you grind up sausage? Well, a sausage grinder is a thing
> you grind, you make sausage; like this hog sausage you buy. Alright, you

put it in there and you grind it and it come out. And that's the way it is by preaching the Gospel. When the Spirit come it feeds you. It feeds you whats to say, and it has power with it. Now just on your own you don't have no power. You just have to get up and just do the best you can. But when the Holy Spirit come, you don't have to worry about nothing. It all falls in place (Rev. McKinney, interview, November 17, 1986).[7]

The Holy Spirit also literally "fills" the members: "[I]t renews and reassures the saints who re-live Holy Ghost ecstasy" (Titon, 1975: 2).

Moving the focus from performer to audience, Bauman delineates other aspects of performance:

From the point of view of the audience, the act of expression on the part of the performer is thus laid open to evaluation for the way it is done, for the relative skill and reflectiveness of the performer's display. It is also offered for the enhancement of experience, through the present appreciation of the intrinsic qualities of the act of expression itself. Performance thus calls forth special attention to a heightened awareness of both the act of expression and the performer. Viewed in these terms, performance may be understood as the enactment of the poetic function, the essence of spoken artistry (1986: 3).

The members of Clear Creek M.B.C. distinguish between two styles of preaching: "explaining" and "emotional." Although the distinction is, in one sense, based upon content, e.g., whether the preacher cites Biblical illustrations of God's love for humankind, or simply reiterates in different ways that "God loves us," it is also based upon style. The focus of the former proof is primarily rational and logical in the fashion of a mathematical theorem—Q.E.D. The focus of the latter is primarily intuitive and emotive: it is real because "I can feel it." As the members are ambivalent about shouting, depending on its source and its pervasiveness, so they are ambivalent about emotional preaching. Some of the members believe, as does Charles Campbell, that "emotional" preaching is lacking because it does not instruct the congregation.

Preachers who teach the text ought to explain it. Not emotional but explaining, what it really means. I could put on this radio and there may be some jazz on it. It tickle you, sort of stir you up. It's not what's said what stirs up a lot of folk, it's how it's said. Now I don't approve of this here whooping.[8] I don't like for a man. . . . Take a text, explain what's result of those words in the text. It what a man says that stirs me up. Now I don't ask the preacher to go ahead and preach to suit me. It's just like a cook. If I hire somebody to do my cooking, why I want 'em to cook like I like it done. But if I go to they place, I eat just like they usually. Just put the stuff in there that really need to be in there (interview, November 20, 1986).

Campbell makes some important points here, points echoed by the scholarly community, and the comparisons with food and sustenance which were prominent in Rev. McKinney's explanations are also evident here. As to his argument that manner of delivery rather than content is what moves people, Bruce Rosenberg touches on essentially the same point:

> We murder to transcribe: in print the sermon does not seem to have rhythm, and certainly lacks the music and the cries of the congregation. If in this art the medium is the message, that message is in many ways non-verbal. James Weldon Johnson recalled that in his youth he attended services where the congregation was "moved to ecstasy by the rhythmic intoning of sheer incoherencies" (James Weldon Johnson, 1948: 5; quoted in Rosenberg, 1971: 429).

As to the "whooping" that Campbell mentions, it is a style of preaching, usually chanted, that specifically aims to provoke shouting. As I illustrated in chapter 5, certain contexts (favourite myths, based on Scripture), as well as certain phrases (such as "Ain't God alright?" or "You don't hear me!" for example), elicit response from the congregation. Artfully combined and manipulated, preachers can use these to "make people shout." Because shouting is such a good feeling, and also considered an indication that the Holy Spirit is present in the church building, it is possible for a preacher to earn the loyalty of his congregation in this rather effortless and superficial manner. It is this abuse that earns "whooping" a bad name.

This is not, however, to assert that African American congregations can be effortlessly manipulated by preachers to produce a particular response. As was noted before, for chanted prayers, chanted preaching depends on a dynamic interaction between preacher and congregation.

> It is the preacher's task and duty to charge the preaching environment with dynamic energies and in so doing to induce the congregation to focus oral and aural mechanisms on the content and structure of the sermon performance. Preacher and congregation are locked into an aesthetic environment dependent on the continual transmission of messages between the units of the performing community for the successful realization of the performance. An African-American congregation listens attentively and critically to a sermon and can instantaneously withhold assent and response if a preacher fails to speak acceptably. Tradition merely offers a framework, a structure, and organizing principles for the dynamic performance of the African-American sermon (Gerald L. Davis, 1985: 17).

There is, however, partly as a result of the perception that preachers can manipulate their preaching so as to "make people shout," a segment of the African American community who believe that "emotional" preaching is a traditional thing, but a tradition that should be left in the past.

> Folks used to shout more so. We don't have the shouting like we used to. There's quite a difference in way a man preach. He don't preach like he used to. The ones he was preaching to didn't know what preaching was, and one was doing it didn't know how to do it and so, it was just a racket. Is more understanding now. In many cases today we just go by sound not by the words: not what the preacher said, but just how he said it. Now that's more effective than anything else. It's not what he said, but how he said it. It's just like, I can say a vexed word and you won't be able to stand it. I can say it in a way make you mad. That's just the way the preacher did. It's just how he said it. They understand more better now. Used to be, all he had to do was have a good sound (Charles Campbell, interview, November 20, 1986).[9]

Despite his negative attitude towards it, Charles Campbell hit here upon an important aspect of the sermon that has received scholarly attention. "In many cases today we just go by sound not by the words: not what the preacher said, but just how he said it" (ibid.). Gerald L. Davis first commented on this aspect of the sermon in 1985 taking it one step further to consider non-linguistic sound but, unfortunately, did not pursue it to any extent: "articulated sound, as distinguished from articulated words, carries semantic affect in the context of African-American narrative performance. Frequently such sounds would be responded to by a congregation as if, or in the same manner as if, the sounds were words" (1985: 7).

While some of the members hold this negative view of "emotional" preaching, others see it as a positive thing. On occasions when Rev. McKinney's preaching does become emotional, I have heard members make such comments as, "We done had service today!" The response to these two different styles of preaching is tied in with many points raised before: "head religion" as opposed to holistic religion, tradition as opposed to modernity, Spirit as opposed to learning. Contrast between the two styles is not always so clear-cut in performance. As Albert J. Raboteau has remarked "to identify ecstatic behavior with the style of the preacher, and instruction or edification with the intelligible content of his words, is to misunderstand the complexity of the sermon and the religious ethos from which it springs. Ecstatic religious behavior is central to the religious tradition in which the chanting preacher stands" (1995: 149). And as always, it would seem, the members' worldview is flexible enough not only to accommodate all these perspectives, but also to allow individual members to shift from one position to another, depending on the occasion. As Henry Mitchell has remarked, "the preaching tradition of the masses of African American Christians is to be distinguished [. . .] by its warmth and spontaneity, its graphic portrayals, and its holistic involvement of the entire personhood of preacher and audience (emotive and intuitive, as well as intellectual, or cognitive) in the preaching event" (1993: 606–7).

Rev. McKinney is, of course, aware of both styles of preaching, and feels that both have a place. He cautioned his congregation in the sermon he preached on January 19, 1986:

> Now just cool down now. Y'all think I'm goin' crazy, 'cause I tell you "don't shout" every now and then. But I done learned if you shout and doesn't have a life to back up your shouting, all of you shouting is in vain. Yes. Most any of us can learn how to sing like a mocking bird, that gets up early in the morning and find a light-line, a tree limb to get up on and flop his wings, dance and sing, 'til it'll draw your 'ttention. But after the dancing is over—this what we got to watch—do I have a life? Do my life corresdespond [correspond] with my singing? Do my life coincide with my preaching? Do my life stand approval call to my deaconship? This is a very important part.

The critical point is learning how to balance both styles of preaching, because as Charles Campbell remarked: "If it ain't no shouting, no Spirit in it" (interview, November 20, 1986), and people generally shout in the context of "emotional" and not "explaining" preaching. Rev. McKinney also makes a distinction between "loving" sermons and "sin" sermons. Whereas people shout during the former, they do not shout during the latter, although the preaching style of both may be "emotional."

> This is what we talking about—You preaching the Gospel to satisfy people's minds. You see, the Gospel—I don't care who you are, preacher, deacon, or whatever—the Gospel goin' hit you somewhere. If you preach sound doctrine, it's goin' hit you somewhere, 'cause we even sin when we don't get up and do what we're supposed to do, by omission. This is what we be talking 'bout when we say "make people shout," when we just get us a sermon and just preach all the good side of it, how loving God is—which He is!—and we never tell peoples that to be a Christian then it requires something of us. We must live according to God's teaching. And that's what we be talking 'bout. When we leave that off, when the Bible tell you that no liar shall enter the Kingdom, no whoremonger, no backslider, and this what we talking about. You see, when we get to preaching this kind of Gospel, you

hitting some folks, and they can't shout. But when you get on this loving sermon, how much God love us—and I have known this to happen back when I was young, some of the preachers just lived on them kind of sermons. It's best, what I always found for myself was, I always try to let God give me a message, what I'm goin' preach. And which way He guide my mind, that's the way I preach. If the Lord guide my mind to talk about the goodness of God, I'm goin' talk about that that Sunday. Now next Sunday, if you come back, if He tell me to talk about sins, now I'm goin' elaborate on sins that Sunday, and there's not goin' be any shouting (interview, Rev. McKinney, November 17, 1986).

Christianity itself, especially in more fundamentalist congregations, embraces distinct opposites. It posits a very strict God—even if one does nothing wrong, one can sin simply by doing nothing—and yet a lenient and compassionate one—a God who suffered and died for humankind. It confronts one with the ultimate principle of good—God—and the ultimate principle of evil—Satan—and leaves one susceptible to both. Both are necessary, because without sin there can be no forgiveness, and without rupture there can be no reconciliation. The members believe, however, that once saved, one can backslide, but one cannot be lost again. This would imply that backsliders must go to Heaven as, unlike Catholic theology, Baptist (and most Protestant) theology does not recognise an intermediate place (Purgatory), but only the clear opposites, Heaven and Hell. The assumption on Rev. McKinney's part is that the Holy Spirit will always bring the backslider back to God, and so he will repent before he dies.

One final comment before we proceed to examine specific examples of the sermon and its context. While the members of Clear Creek M.B.C. (and some scholars) emphasise that in the "emotional" sermon, people are responding not to what is said but to how it is said, I think that even on those occasions, the congregation is responding, perhaps in general terms, but nonetheless responding to the content of the sermon. While I have not empirically tested this, I believe that the members are grounded so deeply in their particular belief system, and apply it with such consistency in their everyday lives, that it would not be possible for a preacher to preach contradicting that belief system, without their registering it on some level. The belief system of such congregations precludes the preaching of certain texts. In studying the method of composition, we must take into account the method that informants tell us that they use, i.e., that the Holy Ghost actually speaks through the preacher and that, thus, it is He who composes the sermon. As it is for Hamlet's Horatio, so it is for all of us: "There are more things in heaven and earth, Horatio, than are dreamt of in your philosophy."

"Moving in the Spirit"

He died, to make things work
He died, that He might claim you
He died, that He might lift you
He died, that He might save you
Out yonder on Calvary
Do you know He died?
Do you know He died?
He died out yonder, the sun wouldn't shine
He died
He died out yonder, the moon dripped it down in blood
Kept right on dyin'
Stars moved outa, their silver socket
Kept right on dyin'
The wind rose that day
Kept right on dyin'
Lightning licked out a tongue
Played a number game
Kept right on dyin'
Yes He did (Rev. Grady McKinney, sermon, November 1, 1987,
6 p.m. service). (See track 5 of accompanying CD.)[10]

Before Rev. McKinney preaches at Clear Creek M.B.C., everybody stands and sings "Amazing Grace" (see track 6 on accompanying CD).[11] The song is sung very slowly, in the melismatic and heterophonic manner of the Dr. Watts, with the important difference that "Amazing Grace" is metered ($\quarternote = 24$), but still sung rubato.[12] The members generally sing only one verse of the song, although occasionally somebody calls up a second verse, in which case everyone joins in. When they have finished singing, everybody but Rev. McKinney sits down, even the ushers. This is usually the only time that the ushers leave their posts as doorkeepers in the house of the Lord. (Psalms 84:10. This seems to be general Baptist practise and is also true of all other churches I visited.) Rev. McKinney comes forward to the lectern and generally reads a few lines from Scripture to introduce his theme, for example, "You might notice from St. Luke's Gospel, the tenth chapter and verse two. . . ." This is sometimes followed by a rather elaborate greeting such as the following, while the congregation finds the appropriate passage.

We thank God for allowing us to come on another Lord's day. To our M.C. [Master of Ceremonies],[13] to the ministers on the platform,[14] to all our officers and visiting officers, if there be any; to all the saints of God and sinners, if there be any. We thank God for the privilege of being able to come and share with you in another service. And if you notice the tenth chapter and the second verse. . . . (Rev. McKinney, sermon on Harvest Day, October 19, 1986).[15]

Rev. McKinney uses the citation from Scripture as a springboard for his sermon. From it he draws a title that runs through his sermon, but depending on the Spirit, the body of the sermon may make several digressions.

At the evening service on January 19th, 1986, for example, Rev. McKinney moved back to the Scripture after the greeting:

You might notice for our Scripture from the Gospel according to St. Matthew, chapter one and verse twenty-one, and it read as follows: "And she shall bring forth a son, and thou shalt call his name JESUS: for he shall save his people from their sins."

There then followed some introductory remarks—several sentences thanking God for being back in service together and commenting on the attendance.

We thank God for being able to be back tonight; sorry that it seems like that we getting a little slack in our communion service.[16] With what all God has done for us, this ought to be one service we ought not to miss. Not because I'm here, because if you coming just because I'm here you have already flunked that course, but you come because Christ is our saviour.

As will be noticed from the above remarks, Rev. McKinney confronts the church with any problem that he perceives. He does not mince words, and the members value this quality in him, i.e., "telling it like it is." The third part of this introductory passage presented the title of the sermon:

We want to talk briefly tonight I hope, "If Jesus Had Not Come. If Jesus Had Not Come." Let me hear you say it. [The congregation repeated the title of the sermon.] Say it again! [The congregation had not responded with sufficient enthusiasm the first time.]

Rev. McKinney almost always opens his sermons using this tripartite form, although he may vary the order of the sections. Sometimes he also comments generally on the mood of the congregation. On this particular occasion everybody was rather quiet and he talked for a few minutes about this feeling in the church, probably in order to change it.

Sound like you all feel at least as well as I do. I know that it's usually thought of that the minister don't ever feel bad, he have sunshine every day. But we are human just like you are. And we have to deal with some of the same problems that you deal with. We get sick, we have pains, we have headaches, we have whatever you have. But however, I don't think the Lord work with us in the way that we feel. I think God bless us whenever we do our best in his service.

The ambiguity of the word "service" as used in this context, implies not only a general life-message, but also an immediate one. The implication is that not only will the members be judged on how well they serve the Lord in their daily lives, but how they respond to the Word of God in this particular service.

Rev. McKinney then proceeds with the body of his sermon. There are several facets to his presentation here.

1. He contextualises the opening passage of Scripture, drawing in other biblical events that are pertinent and that appeal to him. Bruce Rosenberg comments that this "text-and-context" sermon structure is that most usually found in the chanted sermon. It is possible that it is derived from the structure of the Puritan sermon. "The preacher begins with a quotation from Scripture ('the text'), and then explains its relevance ('context'); doctrine is then raised from the passage and finally, is applied to every-day affairs. . . . This pattern was popular, though by no means exclusive, in New England for over a century; it is the structure that we most often find in the chanted sermon" (1969: 192).

Significantly, it is also the structure still used in chanted sermons on the Outer Hebrides, as described by Ó Madagáin:

> The sermon was in the same style [as the chanted prayer], both language-wise and in the manner or tone of delivery. He kept his eyes open all through but had no script or notes of any kind. He preceded it with a reading in declamatory style from a chapter of the Old Testament; then, for the sermon he re-read a couple of verses as his text. The kind of chant-like recitative was just as in the prayer, except that there was more variety of tones which prevented any monotony [. . .] The poetic and dramatic style was no less marked than in the prayer, so that the whole constituted the most extraordinary and moving performance for the best part of an hour (1993: 266–67).

Ó Madagáin, unfortunately, does not provide us with any musical or textual transcription of the sermon, nor does he give us any indication as to whether the congregation participates, as in the African American tradition. He provides one transcription of a section of a chanted prayer which was collected on these islands in 1953, but again without indication of congregational participation. As transcribed, however, the chant is considerably more limited in pitch range and melodic expression than are African American examples.

Although Rev. McKinney does not proceed sequentially with the text-and-context structure described above, the various elements are there, but they are generally intertwined rather than sequential. It is essentially this structure that Titon also describes as typical. "And, of course, not all oral sermons are chanted; but, chanted or not, they follow the same basic structure: the reading of a passage of scripture, the explication of its doctrine, and the application of the doctrine to clarify life" (1975: 2).

On the occasion in question (6 p.m. service, January 19, 1986) the biblical context given to the passage of Scripture is divided into six sections:

a. The background to Christ's coming: the Garden of Eden and the creation of Adam and Eve, Adam's temptation by Eve, and humankind's resultant rupture from God.

b. The Heaven's search for a redeemer and Jesus' willingness to comply.

c. The birth of Jesus: an account of all that He went through in order to be born (forty-two generations, fifty-two burning worlds, and nine months on "nature's train"); Satan and Herod's search for Jesus.

d. Jesus' ministry in his adult life: the ministry of John the Baptist and his baptism of Jesus; reference to three of Jesus' miracles—giving sight to a blind man, curing a woman of "issue of blood," and raising Lazarus from the dead.

e. Jesus' Passion which is to redeem humankind: the Last Supper; the Garden of Gethsemane; trial before Pilate; crucifixion and death on Golgotha.

f. Jesus' resurrection which ensures life for all.

2. On occasions when the subject of the sermon does not invite immediate contextualisation, when it does not call for narration the way "If Jesus Had Not Come" calls for a narration of Jesus' coming, Rev. McKinney first relates the Scripture to the members' lives, sometimes with very brief references to Scripture, but it is in his subsequent presentation of witnesses from the Bible who lived their lives according to Scripture's dictates that he really explores biblical events. In his sermon "Trust in the Lord" (11 a.m. service, January 19, 1986),[17] for example, it was not until he was about one third through the sermon that examples from the Bible were presented. In sermons with this structure, the move to Biblical examples is usually indicated by a set phrase, "Well, let's see here can we find a few witnesses that . . ." (whatever the topic of the sermon is, in this case, "that put their trust in the Lord"), and it is generally at this juncture that Rev. McKinney makes the decisive break with speech and moves into

chant that it precisely rhythmically and melodically defined. In this sermon, for example, Rev. McKinney's first and only example is Job, a striking witness to illustrate trust in God because, despite all that Satan subjected him to, he never wavered in his trust. The narrative of Job's trials by Satan and his constancy with God seems to be a favourite with the church. They refer to it frequently and always respond to it. They certainly see parallels between Job's trials and their own lives, both generally in a racial context, as black people in a predominantly white area of Mississippi, and individually in the daily human frustration of their lives.

3. Within this framework, Rev. McKinney relates each event to the church members' everyday lives. (This correlates to the " 'weighted-secular' factor" which Davis describes (1985: 61–64).) He draws a parallel, for example, between Herod's fear that Jesus would take his throne and the action that he takes to prevent this, and the members' attraction to "positions" and status and the conflict that can result from this.[18]

> Jesus come on into the world. And when Satan realised that Jesus was coming to redeem man, Satan got on His trail, chased Him on down to His birth place, even had Herod looking for Him, "I'm goin' stop him right now. I've heard it said that this is the king of the Jews, and I'm the man that sit on the throne 'round here." Now if you want to start a conflict, you just put me in a position and let me stay there fifteen years, and I'll get mad at the world because I own this position and I don't want nobody else to have it. But in our churches we ought to learn that all members have the same right. If you can serve as a secretary for five years, what wrong with somebody else serving sometime? You have served on the Board as a officer for ten years, what wrong with getting down and letting somebody else serve? But folks get mad when you talk about moving them out of one place. But I believe that God want us to let everyone have a chance. You don't know. Maybe you doing your best, but maybe that next person can do greater than you have ever did. But he can not do anything until you 'llow him a chance (Rev. Grady McKinney, sermon, January 19, 1986).[19]

4. Within this context Rev. McKinney also explicitly states some facets of the community's worldview, some of their central values. In this particular sermon, for example, the Creation of Adam and Eve served as the basis for delineating the societal roles men and women occupy in relation to each other. "But God saw that man was there by himself and God made him a helpmate. He didn't make him a boss, He made him a helpmate" (ibid.). Adam's subsequent temptation by Eve and his realisation of his nakedness brought Rev. McKinney to a commentary on the indecency of contemporary dress.

And ah she didn't say this word, but let me say it like this, she said, "Adam, if you try it you'll like it." Ain't that right? "If you try it, you'll like it." And Adam tried it and he must have liked it. But after he tried it, he found out that his understanding was more widely. And he realised that he was naked. And ever since then until nineteen hundred and eighty got here, folks tried to hide their nakedness; but since then they done stopped putting clothes on (ibid.).

Although it is not explicitly stated, Rev. McKinney is also articulating here the community's emphasis on modesty in dress as an antidote to man's lust. And he is reinforcing the community's solidarity and their separateness from the world. In similar fashion, the Nativity, which realises Jesus' coming, serves to present the community's dichotomy of sinners versus saints as expressed through music (track 7 on the accompanying CD).

If you remember, Satan was one of God's angels.
Yes, and he was the director of angelic choir in Heaven.
Choir members, you ought to watch yourself
Yessir, Satan can so easily misuse you, and have you walkin' round all puffed up
But don't you know that voice you sing with,
Jesus He came that you might sing.
You see here, if, it had a been left up to Satan,
You'd be singin' bout "blue moon."
And if it had a been left up with Satan,
You'd probably be singin' . . . ,
Yeah, I ain't goin' mention that,
But you'd probably be singin' something else.
But by Jesus comin' into the world
He fixed it so you can sing about a saviour.

5. Rev. McKinney has certain sequences that appear frequently in his sermons, although their form varies. "He died . . . ," quoted earlier in this chapter, is one of these. Another example is a litany of titles for Jesus.

Oh, I know a man from another land
They call his name Jesus
Somebody else call Him, my prince for peace
Somebody else call Him, the rose for Sharon
The lily of the valley
The bright and morning star
Oh I call Him, I call Him, my everything
Somebody else said He's a leaning pole
He's a sky-riding king

He's a heavy load carrier
He's a burden bearer
Yes He is (Rev. McKinney, sermon, January 19, 1986, 11 a.m. service).

Sequences such as these often vary considerably from sermon to sermon, not only in their elaborateness, but also in their surface structure. John Blacking distinguishes between deep and surface structures. Deep structures are those at the level of concepts—"the workings of the human mind." Surface structures are the "signs and symbols" of these, as in musical notes (Blacking, 1971: 91). In the evening service of the same day as that quoted above, the sequence appeared as follows:

Let's see here now
I can see my Jesus
Maybe a little baby
That my little lamb of God
That prince for peace
That war-horse that Job talked about
That pond in the valley
That wheel Ezekiel talked about that was right in the middle of a wheel
Jesus, that my little lamb of God.

The deep structure of these sequences (the generating concept) remains constant, giving Rev. McKinney time to consider what will follow.

6. As with most chanted sermons, Rev. McKinney's are built upon a series of climaxes. (These are the "units" to which Davis refers: "a fundamental or basic unit of sermon organization. And most African-American performed sermons are composed of these units cast in a serial structure" [1985: 4]) During the climaxing section the chant is typically well defined and the expression is often sequential. Tension is then relaxed and expression moved back in the direction of spoken prose before building towards the next climax.

The apex of the sermon can be at either of two points: a) about two thirds to three quarters way through the sermon, or b) at the very end of the sermon. In the first case Rev. McKinney moves from speech/heightened speech to chant for the middle section of the sermon, and then a "cooling down" period that subsides into normal speech rhythms and intonation follows. Generally about half to two-thirds way through the sermon, Rev. McKinney states that he is about to finish: "As I close this message . . ." or "Let's hurry now and try to close this thing." This indication to the congregation that the sermon is almost over, usually calls forth greater enthusiasm from them and the apex of the sermon is often reached shortly thereafter. It is as though the threat of imminent closure calls forth greater effort from both congregation and preacher. (One must bear in mind, however, that as this is a habitual occurrence in Rev. McKinney's sermons, the threat cannot be taken too seriously. Rev. McKinney generally extends his sermon for almost as long again after this utterance.) But the sermon continues for a substantial period afterwards. At the 6 p.m. service on January 19, 1986, for example, Rev. McKinney introduced this "closing phrase" after about twelve minutes. He continued to preach, however, for a further fifteen to seventeen minutes.

In the second case, the sermon builds from beginning to end. This structure is a little more unusual, but Rev. McKinney uses it frequently. In such instances he moves straight into the "Invitation hymn" which the congregation picks up immediately. Here, the climax of the sermon can sometimes be seen to occur after the sermon and within the invitation hymn. It is also possible in this case, of course, to view the sermon as expanding to encompass the invitation hymn, and this seems more satisfactory. The addition of the rhythms and harmonies of the piano (with the hymn), the text and music of a familiar song that has "meaning" for the members, and the complete immersion of the members in the experience through singing, often combine to produce shouting. A choir number is never called up here. If one is scheduled after the sermon, it may follow the song, or it may simply be omitted. In his "Harvest Day" sermon of October 16, 1986, the sermon evolved as described above. The Spirit was strong in the church, Harvest Day being a very important feast for the members, as previously discussed. While the sermon moved through a series of climaxes, the apex was not reached until the very end. The following is the closing section (track 8 on the accompanying CD).

> This is at the annual harvest day when every sick will leave the earth, when every little slick thing you thought you got by with, Sam, every little tiny thing you thought you hid, God is goin' bring it up. It's goin' be on your record. You know the old song, said, "You may slip and slide, but I declare you ain't goin' get by"
> 'Cause God got your record.
> He know where you live.
> He know everything you do.
> That's why the church is so cold
> You know I'm glad that I know God
> And I even know why Grady get cold sometimes.
> When I 'llow the world to filter in on my soul, it takes my spiritual strength, and I have to go back and call on God. When you busy on the telephone running other folks' business, gossip and lying on other folk, and when you get off the 'phone you get the TV, and put forty hours in a week looking at TV, and put nine hour in prayer, you cain't help but be cold to save your life. If you don't crank automobile up,

the motor never will get warm. Ain't God all right? You crank the
thing up and let it run a while and I declare it get warm.
But I'm goin' to leave you now.
But every once in a while,
I have to crank mine up and let the Holy Ghost warm it up
Every once in a while
I steal away and get all by myself
And I tell the Lord
"Now Lord, I don't feel your Spirit
Now Lord, I know I been born again
Now Lord, I know you the same God
Set my soul on fire
Now Lord, come on and see about me."
Ain't you glad today?
Ain't you glad today
He is that kind of God?
Oh yeah
If I don't get back no more
Hold on
[Sings] When all [congregation joins in] God's children get together
(Rev. McKinney, sermon, October 19, 1986).

It is interesting to note how throughout the course of this excerpt, Rev.
McKinney moves in and out of sequential, regulated passages in which
sentences become parallel in structure and in length. On this occasion,
Rev. McKinney moved straight into the song "When All God's Children
Get Together." The quotation of song texts at the apex of a sermon is, in
my experience, common among black Baptist preachers. It is also
remarked upon by Jules-Rosette in relation to the African Independent
church of John Maranke, where the usage is more elaborate. "The
cadence of preaching is sustained by 'interruptions' of song that result in
its intensification and acceleration. Although not prescheduled, the songs
pick up and elaborate on themes of preaching" (1975: 100). This occurs
twice in the above extract from Rev. McKinney's sermon. The first is made
explicit: "You know the old song. . . ." The second time it is implied:
"Every once in a while, I steal away."

Even those preachers who never move beyond heightened speech
or monotonic recitation (List, 1971: 259 and 261–62), quote song texts
at climactic points. Rev. Carter of Congdon Street Baptist Church in
Providence, for example, never moves into elaborate chanting, but
almost invariably introduces lines from familiar hymns at the apex of
his sermons. It is very effective (and it must be a familiar song to be
effective), for the text carries with it a specific musical context and both
shared and unique meanings. The "meaning" that we attribute to songs

derives, I believe, not so much from the subtext of the song as from the subtext of our first notable encounter with the song and, indeed, from our association of it with particular individuals who are or have been important in out lives. Thus, a favourite song may conjure up not just past images and feelings, but in a very real way, the ghosts of people past. In the sermon quoted above, the song, in its past and present manifestations, and in its old and new meanings, becomes an integral part of the sermon. The apex of the above sermon occurred, in fact, during the final lines of the sermon and continued into the song. Shouting had occurred at other places in the sermon, but it was most pervasive here, especially following the phrase "and let the Holy Ghost warm it up." As with prayer, it is not unusual for shouting to be cued by phrases relating specifically to this expression, particularly in the chanted portions of the sermon.

The preacher's switch from conversation prose to the metrical and tonal chant, the rhythm holding steady as a drumbeat, sets the stage for the divine possession that everyone expects. Moreover, there are recognizable cues that announce the Spirit's arrival. The preacher's harsh vocal sound, the constriction of voice, the audible gasp at the end of each line, the tonal quality, the participatory claps, shouts and noise of the congregation all announce the onset of possession and instigate it in others. In this sense, the preacher's style itself speaks, at least to those who understand the language of his sermonic tradition (Raboteau, 1995b: 150–51).

"Most any of us can learn how to sing like a mocking bird"

It remains to consider the rhythmic and melodic characteristics of chanted sermons. It is not my intention to provide a structural model for chant. However, I will sketch certain broad outlines.

1. Transition to chant: at the transition speech moves towards monotonic recitation.
   a. Some words are intoned, while others are half-spoken.
   b. Settled monotonic recitation.
2. Chant is typically pentatonic and built on a minor triad.
3. Phrases generally cover a fifth (tonic-dominant) or a fourth (lower dominant-tonic).
4. Return to speech: this is a reversal of the transition.

Rev. McKinney's chanting is the most beautiful that I have heard. When he settles into sequences at climactic points, the lines become quite regular, almost metric, and he punctuates them with his fist striking the podium. This sound provides a pulse referent, and one can generally subdivide it with the internal accentuation of the phrase.

It is unfortunate that most studies of chanted sermons have concentrated almost exclusively on structure and the use of language, and have failed to deal in any detailed manner with the musical text produced. Even Gerald Davis' excellent 1985 study is guilty of this omission. When, for example, he defined the principal morphologic unit of the African-American sermon as "a group of hemistich phrases shaped into an irrhythmic metrical unit" (1985: 49), he referred purely to the spoken level of sound. He took no apparent account of the musical underpinning that, overtly or in a more covert fashion, may be seen as the guiding pulse behind rhythm in the genre. This is, perhaps, reflective of an academic division where one group of scholars typically deals with verbal texts and another with musical texts, particularly when those texts are chanted as opposed to full-fledged song. Where chanted, musical texts are transcribed into primarily verbal analyses (as, for example, in Ó Madagáin, 1993); the musical transcriptions have frequently been completed by a person other than the primary author, and they tend to be oversimplified and lacking in detail. As a consequence, what little musical analysis is presented is not very instructive. A critical element of chanted sermons is omitted, however, if the musical chant is not transcribed: a whole layer of structure, meaning, form and aesthetics is thereby ignored. Yet few would argue that a chanted sermon (or the chanted portions of a sermon) would be just as effective if spoken.

I have transcribed below a rather lengthy section of chanting (see example 7.1). Notwithstanding difficulties in transcribing a musical structure that is not always discrete in terms of duration and pitch, I have endeavoured to provide a transcription that is as close to descriptive as possible (Seeger, 1958), while not so burdened with detail as to be unreadable. On occasion, rather than complicate the score with minute subdivisions, I have, for example, added pauses above rests. Read with some use of rubato, the transcription should yield a fairly accurate picture of this particular instance of chanted preaching.

The sermon title is "You must be born again." I recorded it at the morning service on Sunday November 16, 1986.[20] The transcription is taken from the latter part of the sermon, which was structured so that the apex came almost at the end. The song that was introduced (a Dr. Watts hymn, "That awful day will surely come"), became the climax, and Rev. McKinney moved the sermon directly into it. During the transcribed section and the succeeding hymn, several people went into a shout. I have indicated this in the transcription thus: (s). Sometimes the cry is sustained (s___), occasionally it is broken (s_ _ _). The subject of this sermon—being born again of the Spirit of God—is, of course, one that one would expect to relate to shouting.

The extract transcribed is rich in textures:

1. Scriptural reference: "I heard Paul said," (line 6).
2. Sequential composition: "I been borned again," (lines 4–9).
3. Reiteration of one word which builds suspense: "everything," (lines 18–20 and 21–22).
4. Song quotation: "One thing I know," (lines 33–36).
5. Elaborate congregational responses: "That man is alright" (lines 53–54).

Throughout the musical transcription I have indicated Rev. McKinney's "thump" with an "X." Initially he uses it simply to punctuate his lines, but as intensity builds, he uses it to underscore a particular moment, and then, during a cooling down period, he omits it altogether. Members clap to reinforce climactic points, and I have indicated this thus (////) (track 9 on the accompanying CD).

I don't claim to be a great philosopher	
I don't claim to know a whole lot	
But it's two things I do know	
I been borned again	
I been 'nointed to preach the Gospel	5
I heard Paul said	
I been commanded to preach	
I been anointed to preach	
I been ordained to preach	
Them two things	10
I can brag about	
And then I maybe so	
I can brag about something else	
If I hold out	
Stand on His Word	15
Hold out	
Until tomorrow	
Everything	
Everything	
Everything	20
You don't hear me	
Everything	
Everything, everything	
Is gonna be alright	
Goin' be alright	25
It's goin' be alright after a while	
They used to sing a old song	

They used to moan
in our revivals
When we was filled with the Holy Ghost   30
Didn't we hear,
some old sister over in the corner say
"One thing I know
I been born again
One thing I know   35
Been born again"
Y'all excuse me today
But I wonder do you know,
you been born again?
Sometimes I wonders about it   40
I see folks goin' to church
All the year long
Don't ever shed a tear
Don't ever smile
Don't ever wave their hand   45
Dear Lord
Seem like to me
You're not sure
This thing
That got on to me   50
Won't let me act right sometime
Every once in a while
    Oh that man is alright
    Oh the man is alright
We're gettin' ready to close now.   55

The chant is typically (as previously discussed in relation to chanted prayers) in a minor pentatonic scale; C minor, in this case. In the transcription, musical phrases coincide with lines of text; these are signalled in the text by line breaks, in the music by rests. At the beginning of the extract Rev. McKinney's phrases are short and regular: two beats (an occasional one- or three-beat phrase). Pitch range is restricted and typically centered around the tonic (C), falling at the end of the first line to the lower dominant (G). In the second line the minor seventh (B flat) is introduced as the under-auxiliary to the tonic, and these three notes provide the melodic material of the first nine lines (within the range of a perfect fourth).

As we move into a new section at line 10 ("them two things"), McKinney expands range upwards to include the minor upper mediant (E flat), an upper expansion that coincides with his "bragging" about his selection by God to deliver God's message through preaching. As his text then becomes

Example 7.1. Sermon excerpt, November 16, 1986: "I don't claim to be a great philosopher," Rev. Grady McKinney, Clear Creek M.B.C. (See CD track 9.)

Example 7.1, cont.

more "otherworldly," more anticipatory of resolution in Jesus ("If I hold out, Stand on His Word," lines 14–15), Rev. McKinney expands his pitch range upwards again, now to the upper dominant (G, line 14). In a parallel fashion, he expands the phrases in time and they become less regular (two and a half beats, "Hold out, Until tomorrow," lines 16–17): and a new musical note is introduced, the upper subdominant (F) on "Until tomorrow." Musical expression is further stretched by a couple of other

Example 7.1, cont.

additions: the tempo is slowed (see decel., "Everything," line 18), the tone is expanded (see wide vibrato on the sustained upper dominants ("Hold out," "Everything," "Everything," and "Everything," lines 16, 18, 20, and 22), and coincident with these expansions, one member goes into a shout. It is no coincidence, of course, that the first of these sustained upper dominants with a wide vibrato occurs on the phrase "Hold out": musical

Example 7.1, cont.

expression reinforces linguistic meaning. And it is the musical line that carries the most meaning at this juncture as the text, while significant, is highly repetitive. (This parallels what I have referred to earlier as the "withheld information" practice in gospel, a repetitive, delaying tactic that is an established principle of effective oratory.)[21] The punchline ("Is goin' be alright," line 24), is delivered almost casually, in small note values

Example 7.1, cont.

(quickly) and with an anti-climactic return to the pitch material of the opening phrase (tonic-lower dominant, C–G), but in this case inverted (lower dominant-tonic, G–C).

Rev. McKinney now draws back and "cools down": he contracts the pitch range (back to the lower dominant-tonic of the opening, typically, with an occasional lower seventh or upper mediant); density of sound is diluted, the introduction of the first extended pauses/rests here serves to

Example 7.1, cont.

loosen the tension that has been built; rhythmic articulation, which had become very pronounced (fast taps of his fist increased the tension considerably, lines 14–18), is halted—he stops tapping his hand.

The members, however, are not as willing to cool down. One woman continues with fast handclapping and another continues shouting. The relaxation of tension, however, allows Rev. McKinney to build a bigger climax in the song passage ("One thing I know, I been born again. One

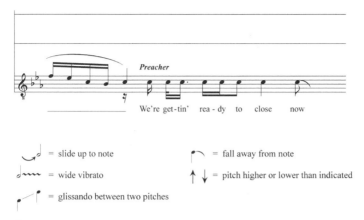

Example 7.1, cont.

thing I know, Been born again," lines 33–36). The phrases expand in pitch and in length: line 33 is built around tonic-upper mediant, line 34 adds to this the upper subdominant (F), which had been entirely omitted in the preceding section. The apex of this excerpt, and indeed of the whole sermon, is reached in the third phrase ("one thing I know," line 35): tonic-upper seventh, C–B flat, including all the notes of the pentatonic scale in sequence, and featuring the single appearance in this sermon of the upper seventh. This is, additionally, the longest phrase in this chanted excerpt, lasting five beats. As with the previous climax, it is the statement of knowledge ("One thing I know"), rather than the fact ("Been born"), that draws forth the most elaborate expression. Tension is resolved somewhat in the closing phrase of the song (line 36), which contracts back to a descending perfect fifth (G–C), but with the important inclusion of the subdominant (F).

Smaller peaks round out the sermon and, after some elaborate responses from the congregation (lines 53–54), lead into the lined hymn "That awful day will surely come." The style of the hymn is so close to Rev. McKinney's chanting that the transition is a successful and unifying one (in that all the members now participate fully), and there is some more shouting before the hymn subsides. This is an extraordinarily effective piece of chanted preaching, the musical chant reinforcing, uplifting, and elaborating upon the quasi-poetic text.

There is, however, more to the texture of this extract than can be conveyed on paper, or indeed on the accompanying recording: the visual and emotional impact, which ally effectively with the aural stimuli, create a very intense experience.[22] The Clear Creek M.B.C. building is a small one, completely panelled in wood, and it was on this occasion quite full. The evening darkness that wrapped itself around the church insulated and integrated the experience within the sanctuary. Besides the sounds of chanting, clapping, and fist-banging, the steady drumming of feet resounded on the wooden floor, and many members added interjections, shouts, and laughter. Shouting and calls from the choir members in the stalls behind Rev. McKinney, meeting with those of the congregation from the opposite direction, directed most of the energy inward. Concentration of that energy within the group reinforced feelings of community, of separateness from the world, and of union with the spiritual.

The members believe that preaching, and especially chanted preaching, is a gift from God.[23] Regardless of how long one spends in Seminary, it is not something that can be taught.

> That's a gift of God. Now that ain't something you learn. Nobody can learn you how to preach. I attend seminary about nineteen years, they can teach you the letter, they can teach you how to pronounce a lot of them 'fisticated name, as I call 'em, in the Bible. They can teach you that, but no one can teach you how to preach. Now, if you want to be a failure, you decide to preach and come over here and let me teach you how to preach. And you never will preach, you'll be a failure. But you must be as David did, you know when he went out to catch a glimpse to his brothers, and he got out there and this big giant was up on the hill, challenge them. And he wanted one man to come out for Israel, and he would stand for the Philistinians [Philistines], Goliath. And er-ah, all the mens in the camp was afraid to challenge him, and here David was, a untrained lad, you know. But he had faith in God. And he went and got him a few stones, and took an old sling and killed that big John; cut his head off and brought it on back. So what I'm saying is, you can be taught the letter, but no one can teach you how to preach. And you really cannot preach until the Spirit of God start to working with you (Rev. McKinney, interview, November 20, 1986).

Chanted preaching is, I believe, the most powerful expression of the African American church. It creates an intersection of the material and spiritual worlds, not only in presenting the Word of God, but in bringing the Holy Spirit into the church, into the body of the preacher and of the members. "The chanted sermon is the product of a religious imagination in which experience is primary and is so because it validates religious truth. [. . .] In the chanted sermon, African-American Christians did not merely talk about God, they experienced his power, and found that in the experience their own spirits were renewed" (Raboteau, 1995b: 131). The alliance of music and text integrates the melodic, rhythmic, linguistic, and emotional levels of human experience; and the introduction of such experiences from the past into the sermon, through quotation of a familiar song, unites past and present in a single "event." The focus of preaching is ultimately the future, the afterlife. The aesthetic is the successful integration of all of these facets into culturally acceptable and pleasing form. Chanted preaching like that examined above is not only very powerful, it is also very beautiful.

Conclusion

In the Afterword to their two-volume 1994 publication *American Congregations*, Wind and Lewis concluded:

> Much more needs to be learned. Moreover, the ways that congregations serve as tradition bearers and creators and their capacity to serve as communities of moral and practical theological discourse also demand attention. [. . .] Through historical and ethnographic investigations of individual congregations and through larger thematic and interpretive studies of them, we can begin to approach a full appreciation of what is really going on within America's major institutional form of lived religion (2:285).

The Clear Creek M.B.C. community gives us a good picture of at least some of what is really going on in one of America's major institutional forms of lived religion—the African American church. It also offers an antidote to what Don Cusic has identified as the "bigger is better" syndrome in American Christianity. Writing in relation to the Christian music industry, Cusic asserts that "it is not acceptable to have a small, local ministry—a ministry must be national in scope and reach the far corners of the USA to be considered truly effective" (1990: 226). The present study vividly illustrates that the creation of a strong and vibrant religious community in America may be most effective at the congregational level. The study makes no pretence, however, to make a definitive statement about African American religion, congregational religion, or indeed the Clear Creek M.B.C. community. Its strength lies in the fact that, as I stated in the introduction, it is an in-depth study of "a particular community at a particular point in time." For, as Wind and Lewis remark, "[T]he American religious experience has been predominantly a congregational one in which leaders and members share authority in a varied and complicated fashion. [. . .] [C]ongregations represent an essential religious link between past and present. Congregations have been part of American history from the first page" (1994: 1:9).

One person who read an earlier version of this manuscript commented that it is the very ordinariness of the Clear Creek M.B.C. community that gives this study its strength. And while this is true—there must be hundreds of such small, familial churches throughout the rural South—it is in equal measure true that it is the exceptional quality of this community that is the strength of this study. It is sometimes easier as an outsider to approach a particular topic because one is not assailed with divided loyalties, socially and culturally conditioned assumptions, or ingrained expectations. And because of my position not simply as an outsider, but as a foreigner, it was possible for me to ask the most basic and direct questions without causing offence or seeming to challenge elements of a belief system. This study, therefore, is also in many ways "my study" and is inevitably coloured (as many scholars in both the Humanities and the Social Sciences now recognise) by my interpretations. I have, however, tried to balance this outsider's view with insider's perceptions, particularly in relation to spiritual experience, most importantly through the inclusion, in the member's own words, of their interpretations of particular phenomena.

I came to the United States to study African American religious music and, as my knowledge deepened over the course of ten years living there, I found the subject growing ever more complex, more challenging and rewarding, and more fascinating. But despite years of study, visiting many churches, and listening to hours of recorded services, religious programmes, and sermons, nothing that I encountered matched the beauty and integrity of expression that I encountered in the Clear Creek M.B.C. community. Which is not to say that it is an idyllic community: in many ways it is not, it has its problems as all communities do. But nowhere else did I encounter such a close-knit, yet dynamic structure: great-grandmothers sitting beside great-granddaughters, mothers next to sons, brothers and sisters side by side, uncles, aunts, nieces, and nephews.

The church was additionally blessed, not just in its strong spirituality, but in two other areas that serve to reinforce the former: music and preaching. The church has some exceptionally fine musicians who contribute enormously to the aesthetic enjoyment and the spiritual power of church and community life. And, partly because of the age range of the community, the musical expression of the church almost seamlessly covers a very broad range of musical traditions. In the person of their pastor, Rev. Grady McKinney, Clear Creek M.B.C. has an exceptionally gifted preacher. At its best, McKinney's preaching rivals any that I have heard, from the celebrated sermons of the Rev. C. L. Franklin, to the earlier recorded sermons of the Rev. J. M. Gates, for example, to those of any of McKinney's contemporaries whom I heard preach. With an intimate knowledge of this small, familial community's concerns and hopes, an earthy ability to "tell it like it is," and superlative poetic and musical improvisational skill, all underpinned by a strong biblical grounding and a rocklike, if sometimes vulnerable faith, Rev. Grady McKinney delivers sermons that are compelling, poetic, and lyrical.

If, as Cusic asserts, "[T]he Puritans of early America relegated music to a position that was secondary to preaching. They stifled musical creativity by insisting that only Psalms be sung to a handful of tunes" (1990: 227), it is in the African American church that that disjuncture has been repaired. Not only does music permeate African American religious expression, chanted preaching brings music back to the forefront of preaching, indeed to the centre of the worship experience. And the evidence presented here further supports the argument that the physical entry of the Holy Spirit into the body of the church, is most likely in a musical context. For the Clear Creek M.B.C. community, and others of which it is representative, in chanted preaching the preacher literally sings the words of the Holy Spirit or, rather, the Holy Spirit uses the voice of the preacher to sing to the congregation. Surely music can assume no more central role in religious expression than this.

With the development of Black Theology in the 1960s and 1970s, one concern that came to the forefront in the writings of black theologians was whether Christianity served as a liberating reality in African-American life or as an oppressive ideology. Although less foregrounded in current scholarship, this issue remains a concern (see, for example, Mark L. Chapman, 1996: 3). Examined "on the ground" as it were, rather than in theoretical or historical overview, this study, based in ethnographic documentation, reveals that the religious community serves to deliver to African American people a distinctive voice. The African American church (in all its diversity), which as so many scholars have remarked, is central to African American identity, serves not only to forge that identity but to facilitate its free expression. Or, as Baer and Singer put it, "[I]n this interplay of worldly and otherworldly images and attributes [in African American religion], African Americans constructed their identity as a people" (Baer and Singer, 1992: xvii).

The African American church is not, and perhaps never has been as otherworldly in its thrust as was hitherto thought. As illustrated by the Clear Creek M.B.C. community, the church meets virtually all the needs of its congregation. Gerald Davis has found that in sermons, which are arguably the primary didactic vehicle of this church, the weighting of the message tends toward the secular rather than the sacred (see Davis, 1985: 61–64). Addressing topics as diverse as politics, weather patterns, race relations, and crop harvests, church services facilitate the articulation not just of black people's religious quest, but of their daily struggles and aspirations.

My primary interest in this book has been the examination of one community's worldview and its articulation in expressive culture, music specifically. But I have also sought to situate that community in a series of larger contexts: the black community outside the church, the predominantly biracial community of Mississippi, the community of "the black Church" or African American religion, etc. To this end I have also incorporated data from other churches, two primarily, Main St. Baptist Church in Lexington, Ky., and Congdon St. Baptist Church in Providence, Rhode Island. Yet Clear Creek Missionary Baptist Church remains unmistakably the focus of study.

As I stated in the introduction to this book, my interest in religion is not in its institutional forms or denominations, but as a system that serves to situate self, world, and the relationship between them. My interest, in other words, is the realm of the spiritual and its intersection with the material. I have tried to present the Clear Creek M.B.C. community's intersection of existential, social, and aesthetic spheres, because I believe that it is at the congregational level that these complexities can most effectively be examined. In-depth, congregational ethnographies such as the present one facilitate such study because "under the seemingly petty conflicts that turn so many people away from these places of worship are fundamental questions about human identity and purpose, about meaning, about right and wrong, about the ultimate character of human life and the universe" (Wind and Lewis, 1994: 2:6–7). The resultant picture, while complex (and it must be complex to convey faithfully the complex reality that is life) is, I hope, cohesive and integrated. It is important, I believe, that we try to create and examine such complex pictures because, although they carry the risks of generalisation and imprecision, they are nonetheless mirrors of an important part of our being, uncomfortable though we may be with its murkiness and ambivalence. If we do not sometimes return to a more generalised complexity, we run the risk of ploughing diligently down a highly specialised path, knowing more and more about less and less, until finally, as popular expression would have it, we know everything about nothing. It is, perhaps, ethnomusicology's greatest strength that contextualisation, the messy complexity of life, is its focus.

The Clear Creek M.B.C. community challenges us in many ways: the members' tolerance and flexibility force us to question popular perceptions of fundamentalism: their comments on racism and their relative isolation compel us to examine race relations in late-twentieth-century America: their spirituality and expression of that spirituality challenge us to look to worldviews outside that of Aristotelian rationalism. Above all, their warmth and friendship impressed me deeply. I never was saved, nor did I ever experience spirit possession, to the disappointment of the church membership. Although as to that, the tenets of their fundamentalist Christianity allowed them a retreat to a position of resignation "the Lord knows best" that allowed them to preserve their conviction. I am sure that when I next return to this community, it will be to encounter their evangelistic zeal.

While we sometimes bemoan the lack of one central definition and theory of ethnomusicology, diversity is also, I believe, ethnomusicology's strength. We are naive if we assume that the conduct of fieldwork does not involve us in dynamic processes over which we may have little control. The questions that we ask (or omit), the songs that we request (or do not), the ideas, beliefs, and objects in which we express interest (or ignore) all potentially effect our findings. Additionally, these findings are ultimately refracted through the lens of our individual subjectivity, rendering undeniably "ours," but also "theirs," the "reality" that we present. Complexity can foster a wonderful sense of curiosity that always pushes us further in our search for knowledge.

Appendix 1

Outline of a Black
Baptist Service

As Baptist churches are independent, with a strong emphasis upon congregational autonomy, the "events" outlined below may vary in position in the service from church to church, and also from service to service in one church. The events themselves, however, generally comprise (albeit in a different order) the services of many black Baptist churches.[1]

As described in chapter 3 ("Concepts of Time"), Sunday morning worship service at Clear Creek M.B.C. is preceded by Sunday School, and generally starts around 11.10 a.m.
The order of the Service is:

1. Call to Worship, a short passage of Scripture. Although Rev. McKinney is consistently assigned the role of reader in the church bulletin, it is almost always Deacon Robinson who reads the call.
2. A Selection by the Choir may follow. A "selection" is a choral piece rather than a solo or a congregational piece. Although some members may sing along if they know the song, most sit and listen, adding interjections and other indications of their approval.
3. The Devotion opens as one of the deacons (Lee Earl Robinson, usually, at Clear Creek M.B.C.) calls up a hymn (Dr. Watts or congregational), which the congregation picks up. Throughout the Devotion spontaneous prayers, which may be chanted, alternate with hymns. The number of hymns and prayers depends upon the Spirit in the church. Anybody who wishes may call up a song or begin a prayer, but it is most usually the deacons who do so; and four songs with three interspersed prayers is about average. Both prayers and songs generally last between three and four minutes, although this varies considerably with such factors as congregational response and how many verses of a song the leader knows or wishes to sing. The Devotion usually lasts about twenty minutes. At the end of the Devotion, Rev. McKinney comes on the altar and reads a short passage of

4. Scripture, usually Psalms 1, which is read in responsorial style: Rev. McKinney and the congregation read alternate verses and join together to read the final verse.

5. A selection (or perhaps two) from the choir follows. This part of the service may expand considerably if the occasion is a special one and other choirs are invited. Usually each invited choir sings two songs.

6. The selections are generally followed by the Offertory sequence: taking up the offering, the Sick and Prayer List, and the Offertory prayer. Depending upon a church's custom, the members may march around the church depositing their offerings on the plates, which are left on the offertory table. At Clear Creek M.B.C. the members usually march while Herbert Bonner plays and the deacons preside over the offertory table. Most churches have some congregational singing accompanying the offering: at Clear Creek a favourite song at this point is "The Lord is blessing me." As with songs for Baptism, the song is repeated until everyone has returned to his/her place. One of the deacons then composes an offertory prayer, an improvised prayer that may be chanted, often to the hummed accompaniment of the offertory song by the congregation, accompanied by the piano. The resultant texture is a complex one.

7. Recognition of Visitors and Announcements, and the

8. Financial Report generally follow the offertory sequence. All the black Baptist churches that I have attended incorporate a "Recognition of Visitors" into the service. At this stage visitors are invited to stand and introduce themselves, whereupon they are generally welcomed to the church.

9. Another selection (or two) from the choir follows.

10. "Amazing Grace" directly precedes the sermon. (Some church congregations sing a different hymn here, but "Amazing Grace" is usual in most churches.) It is sung very slowly in heterophonic Dr. Watts' style but, unlike the Dr. Watts, it is metered.

11. The Sermon is the climax of the service and is generally between 20 and 60 minutes long. At Clear Creek M.B.C., Rev. McKinney usually chants a substantial portion of his sermon, and the congregation responds with interjections and other expressions of agreement, such as hand clapping or laughing. On occasions when the chant is particularly successful and the Spirit strong in the church, Herbert Bonner also punctuates Rev. McKinney's preaching with chords and very short phrases on the piano.

12. The Invitation to Discipleship follows the sermon: the invitation hymn is sometimes the culmination of the sermon. The choir sings a song, in which the congregation usually joins, while Rev. McKinney exhorts the congregation to "Come to Jesus." Individuals may come

forward here and be saved (at Clear Creek, this usually occurs only in revival services), or come forward simply to ask for prayer, or to rededicate themselves to God. If the invitation hymn has been called up by the preacher, it is usually followed by a

13. Selection from the choir. If, on the other hand, the preacher is not moved to call up a song, he may say "The choir is coming with a selection," and make that the context for the invitation to discipleship.

14. Comments from the pastor follow (Rev. McKinney sometimes adds another congregational song such as "Remember Me" here), with a prayer and benediction closing the service. Rev. McKinney's closing formula is: "Let the church sing!" and everybody sings "Amen."

Transcribed Prayers

I

Eighty-Second Annual Convention of the Tallahatchie-Oxford Missionary
Baptist District Association and Auxiliaries
Project Center, Abbeville, Miss., August 29, 1982
Prayer given by one of the deacons.

Oh eternal God, creator of Heaven and earth
Our Father, we come this mornin' in the name of thy son Jesus

We come, O Lord, just to say thank you
Thank you Jesus, for just being God
Lord we come just now   5
Realising that we're weak creatures, thou art strong
Realising that we've sinned against thee, and against Heaven
Oh forgive us right now Lord
Create in us a new heart and a new spirit
A spirit that will allow us to serve thee   10
Now Lord, as we look back over our lives
You brought us from the rocking of a cradle, up until right now
Not only that Jesus, but you watched over us, all night long
Unconscious of the many dangers that are left around
You told your guardian angel to watch over myself   15
Early this mornin', I didn't need an alarm
You woke us up, and didn't let us sleep too late
We thank you this mornin' Jesus
Thank you for our food
Thank you for our clothing   20
Thank you for those that are in the sound of our voice
Thank you for the sinner man
Thank you for the sinner woman
For the sinner boy and girl
We ask you to touch the hearts, then come on in   25
I once was lost, but now I'm found

I once was blind, but now I see
Bless these thy servants, in the name of Jesus
Send down your holy power, that we'll love each other
Send it down, 'til somebody soul catch on fire   30
Send it down, 'til the church catch on fire
Send it down, 'til the preacher preach your word
Send it down, 'til the deacon pray your prayer
Send it down, 'til the choir sing your song
Oh Lord, Oh my Father   35
When it's all over, when it's all over Father
When we can't pray no more, want you to meet us somewhere
Oh Lord, I know there is somebody here, that needs you
      right now
Right now, in the name of Jesus
Bless the sick, bless the afflicted   40
Bless the abused, bless the accused
In the name of Jesus, repuke [rebuke], reprove, oh cast out sin
In the name of Jesus, bless us right now

These and other blessings we ask through Thy son Jesus and for his sake
Amen.

II

Jefferies Missionary Baptist Church, Abbeville, Miss.
Crouch Family Reunion Service, September 5, 1982
Prayer given by the Pastor.

. . . . .
So good and so kind to me
Oh Lord you watched over me all night long, last night
Why, as I lay unconscious in my home
Right bright and early this mornin' Jesus
You took a lil' time and stopped by my home a lil' while   5
Oh Lord and laid you hand on my head, and made me rise
      and run round and find my family well one more time
Oh Jesus you been so good and so kind to me
Oh Lord, I just love to call upon your holy name
Oh Jesus you touched someone this mornin' but they still
      weren't able to rise and walk 'round in your wonderful world
Oh Lord, I wanna thank you for being so good to let 'em
      know that you still care for 'em   10
Oh Lord, why as I bow down this evenin'
Please sir have mercy on me

Go with me and stand by my side long as I pass along your way
Oh Lord, mm mm, why as I bow down this evenin'
Please sir have mercy on each and every one, on the sound
    of my weak voice   15
Have mercy upon the one that could have been under my voice
    but they failed to be here
Go with me and stand by me

My prayer for Christ's sake
Amen.

III

Main St. Baptist Church, Lexington, Ky.
Sunday Service, August 25, 1985
Prayer given by one of the deacons, following hymn "Sweet Hour of Prayer."

Let us pray
Our Father in Heaven

Again we are thankful to assemble in thy house of prayer
Thanking you, O heavenly Father, for blessing us these
    one hundred and twenty-three years
Heavenly Father, we thank you for all the blessings that
    you have bestowed upon us   5
We thank you for this day, O heavenly Father
A day that we had never seen before
And a day that we will never see again
O heavenly Father, we thank you for your savin' power
We thank you for wakin' us up this mornin', O heavenly Father   10
You didn't have to do it but you did
Heavenly Father we thank you . . . we just wanna say
    we thank you
Heavenly Father we pray that you would strengthen
    this church family
That we would grow together in one strong band of Christian love
Let the love run from breast to breast and heart to heart   15
Heavenly Father we pray that you will bless this worship service
We pray that you will bless our Pastor
Bless his wife and his family
We pray that you will bless the preached word that
    will be preached here today
We pray, O heavenly Father, that someone will come to
    thee saying "What must I do to be saved?"   20

We pray, O heavenly Father, that you will bless . . . the
    deacon board of this church
Let every man know that he has a job to do for thee
O heavenly Father we pray that you will bless Br. Rogers
    and all the musicians of this church
Bless this choir, O heavenly Father, that they will sing your praises
Not for show or for fashion, but to uplift thy most righteous
    and holy name   25
O heavenly Father I pray that you will bless me each and
    every day
Strengthen me, O heavenly Father
Help me to grow in grace each and every day
'Pray that you will bless all the ministers of this church
    and all the churches, throughout the world
Heavenly Father we pray that you will bless the sick and afflicted   30
Let them know that you are still upon the throne
O heavenly Father we thank you for bringing us, over
    the . . . highways, bringing us here, O heavenly Father
Lord we ask thee that you would tenure to strengthen us,
    each and every day
O heavenly Father we have so much to be thankful about
Thank you for those that have gone on   35
That made this day possible for us, to worship in this
    house, calling upon your most righteous and holy name
Heavenly Father, strengthen us, from day to day
Let the world know that we are on this corner to serve
    a risen saviour
We thank You for Your son Jesus Christ, who died upon
    the cross for all of us here
I just wanna say I thank you   40
Thank you O heavenly Father

These blessings I ask in thy most righteous and holy name
For Christ's sake
Amen.

IV

Eighty-Second Annual Convention of the Tallahatchie-Oxford Missionary
Baptist District Association and Auxiliaries
Project Center, Abbeville, Miss., August 29, 1982
Prayer given by Rev. Kenneth Bonner.

(Spoken) *"Our Father in Heaven, it is us again, that a…"*

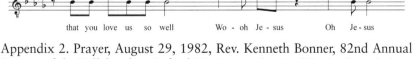

few___ of your child-ren   First   we have met out at this ap-poin-ted place

We have had a chance   to sing thy sweet Zi-on songs   We have had a chance

to stu-dy   your words   We have a chance   this mor-nin'

to stand and call your name   We just like to take this time this mor-nin'

and give you the praise   Bright ear-ly this mor-nin'___   You were so good

Not be-cause Fa-ther   that we kept the Com-mand-ments so well   Not be-cause Fa-ther

that we did all   you told us   to   do   But just be-cause   Fa - ther___

that you love us   so well   Wo - oh Je - sus   Oh   Je - sus

Appendix 2. Prayer, August 29, 1982, Rev. Kenneth Bonner, 82nd Annual Session of the Tallahatchie-Oxford Missionary Baptist District Associations and Auxiliaries, Abbeville, Miss.

Please sir right now Je - sus   Come on in the build - ing right now

Some-bo-dy heart___ is too mean___ Some-bo-dy mind is too cold Lord_ Je - sus

we just love you to - day   We gon - na praise your name to - day   I don't care

what mens do or say   I'm gon-na praise your name   I don't care this mor - nin'

I'm goin' if I have to go   all by my-self   Now Lord

Oh we thank you right now   We just like to feel your spi - rit

When we can feel you Je - sus   Ev - 'ry thing is all right___

We love you to-day   Come on in   Bless our souls   Some-bo-dy sick to-day

Some-bo - dy fam - ily dis-cour-aged   Some-bo-dy's in the hos - pi - tal

We know you's a doc - tor   Some - bo - dy done give you up   this mor - nin'

I   know this   mor - nin'   If we just have a   lil'   pa - tience

and give you time to come in   Go with us through-out this day.

(Spoken) *"...This is my prayer in Jesus' name and for thy sake. Amen."*

= slides up to note   = falls away from note

= slides up from note   × = approximate pitch

Appendix 3

Transcribed Sermons

I

Clear Creek M.B.C.
October 19, 1986, Harvest Day
Sermon by Rev. Grady McKinney:
"Harvest"

You might notice from St. Luke's Gospel the tenth chapter and verse two. We thank God for allowing us to come on another Lord's day. To our M.C., to all our officers and visiting officers if there be any, to all the saints of God, and sinners if there be any. We thank God for the privilege of being able to come and share with you in another service. And if you notice from the tenth chapter and second verse. We have heard so many wonderful things said about harvest today, I reckon I will just try to repeat what I have heard. I think everyone that was on this program have did excellent. I was listening—sometime when you don't see me, you think I'm gone. I don't be gone—and I was listening at all you, and all of you did wonderfully. And it's about time to eat, since all of you done said it all. They got a commercial on TV, and the guy said, "When you said Bud, you done said it all!' So we just have to repeat because it all have been said.

But I was thinking about what the old preacher said. He said something about there's a time to plant and there's a time to pluck up that which was planted. So we come today celebrating Harvest Day, a time of the year when it's time to gather up what you has planted or, maybe you didn't plant at all, maybe somebody else has planted. But it's reaping time, it's time to gather it all up. And I was listening this morning closely and I was wondering are we all sick today? We 'bout dead as a doornail. I was just wondering was all of us sick. Now last third Sunday I was serious sick, but I just got old folks' complaint today. But it seems like the most of all of us is sick. I was listening to the choir singing and when they got through you couldn't hardly get an amen. I was listening at those that had the reading. Things wasn't much better, and I asked one fella, "I wonder what's the matter. Everybody dead today." But this should be a day of rejoicing. Because you is being thankful for what God have done for you.

We realise harvest come more than one time a year. It just depends on what you are gathering. But to most farm states, we are in the midst of harvest. It's time to get the cotton out the field, and you don't want to hear that, 'cause some of you don't want nobody to know you ever picked it, but I know you did. It's time to get the corn out. It's about time to plough the sweet potatoes up. It's about time to get the peanuts up. And this is what we familiar with, in the state of Mississippi at harvest time, was a time and is a time to gather up your crop. And then it's a time of rejoicing sometime and sometime it's sad. Sometime, you have worked all the year long and when you get to the end, whatever you have planted fail to produce like it should. And then you be kinda sad at harvest time. But whenever it brought forth abundily [*sic*], then you rejoice about how good your crop has made. Even some of these peddlers that peddle peas and beans and so forth, when harvest time come and they made pretty good and they say, "I made six hundred dollar off this little patch, that I have here." So that's a time of rejoicing. But if the individual doesn't make anything he'll say, "You know, I lost money. I bought the seeds and I planted it, and come the harvest time it didn't produce anything."

But we ought not only think of the harvest of vegetables, and so forth, but we need to think in terms that there will be another harvest. And it's depending on each individual whether they be gathered up into the harvest of God or not. No one else can fix it for you, you must fix it for yourself. And Jesus said unto them, at this therefore He said unto them, "The harvest truly is great, but the laborer are few." Jesus was replying to man's salvation. And I believe, and I keep on saying it, and I'm goin' to keep on saying it, if we would quit out all this lil' yig-yag mess that we have, and get about doin' our Father's business, all of us could be better servants for the King. The Lord did not save us for us to just sit around and gossip. But the Lord saved us that we might go out into the world and draw others unto Christ. And in the community where I live, there is plenty of work to be done, and there is much work need to be done.[1] But the harvest is great, but the labourers are few. And I believe in this county, and in the community that you live in, there is plenty of work to be done. But we fail to do it. And I believe if we don't do it God goin' call us in question about the great harvest and all this was present to be harvested and you failed to go out and harvest it for the Lord. Now Jesus want us to go out and try to encourage others to come to Christ that our souls might be gathered at harvest time.

Let's see here, a man that labor for something down through the years, looks for something at the end, but sometime it doesn't come. So then when the Lord saved you and I, He expect for us to bring more than just ourselves. But you know we looks on the con side and we looks at material things with all our heart, until we fail to realise there is something more important than just our material things. There is a life beyond the grave. There will be a great harvest, when the Lord come again. And all of those who are fit for the Kingdom will be able to go home and live with God. But now, this is something we must work on. There be many will be gathered up at harvest time, but their reward will be very scarce, because they failed to work in God's vineyard. Now the Bible says salvation is free. You are saved by having faith in God, but your reward comes by your labours. So then, if you expect to have a great reward, then you ought to do great works. You see you may not be able to sing for the Lord, but you still can harvest for the Lord. If you're not able to do anything but be a good witness, witness until the Lord say "that's enough." Well, ah, you may not be able to pray like others pray, but the Lord fix it so all of us can pray. Because God says, "I know your needs even before you ask." So I'm saying, ah, we ought to work on ourselves so that we might be able to go out into the vineyards and labour for the cause of Christ. Well, ah, let's see here a man in the Bible that God was ready to send him to harvest and to gather up Israel to God. And ah, he cried out, "I'm not able to speak well." And ah, he began to complain about his tongue. But the Lord, ah, will take all of the excuses away from you because He have something else to offer. I heard Him say, "Moses," maybe not in these words, "since you're complaining about you not able to speak plain, I'll send Aaron along with you, and you talk to him and let him talk to Pharaoh."

Well this what I'm trying to bring out: harvest time is a time of gathering. But for you and I to have something to gather, mean we must go out and do some works. And ah, my Lord didn't say it was goin' be easy. There is some ups and downs working for the Lord. But the old song said, "If I can hold out until tomorrow, I know everything will be alright."

Well er-ah, Jesus was looking here on the condition of humanity.

He saw men goin' down in degradation.

Well ah, he saw mens and womens living according to the pleasures of this life, and they wasn't concerned about the hereafter.

And I heard the Lord said,

"Truly, the harvest is great, but the laborers are very few."

I believe this evening—and I'm getting ready to close now—we ought to go out in the vineyard and tell men about Jesus.

Tell them, He is a God you can 'pend on.

Tell them, He is a way provider.

Tell them, He is a friend in a time of trouble

Tell them, how Job said one day,

"A man that is born of a woman only have a few days and they full of trouble."

Tell them, that after a while this life goin' be over.

Tell them, they've got to stand before a righteous judge.
Tell them, every knee goin' bow and every tongue must confess.
Tell them, when they come down to life's end,
Cain't stay no more,
All we 'ccumulate, all our material things,
We goin' have to leave them behind for somebody else to enjoy.
Tell them, if they come over on the Lord's side at harvest time,
Yeah Lord,
When they come to life's end journey,
This what I love about the Lord,
Doesn't matter how much you have,
You still got to die like any other man
But I'm so glad the Lord saw fit to use me in his vineyard.
Said go out into the world about Jesus and how he died on Calvary.
Oh at harvest time,
Every individual got to come marching on in.
Come on in and give an account of your story.
Somebody had a chance, but they was too lazy work.
Somebody had a chance, but they was so busy trying to gain the world,
    they didn't have time to do the Lord's work.
Somebody goin' look back that day
"Lord, Lord, if I had another chance, I'd work in the vineyard."
Goin' hear the master say,
"Time have end sure ain't goin' be no more."
Oh servant,
Come on in it's harvest time.
But let's see here my friend,
To make this harvest price, to make this harvest true
Jesus came in a sin-cursed world
Died out yonder on Calvary for your sin and mine.
Died out yonder, the sun wouldn't shine.
Died out yonder, the moon dripped it down in blood.
Died out yonder, sinner man was standing by the cross
"Surely, surely, it must be the son of God."
But not only that my friend,
Early, early, one morning He got up out the grave and made it possible
    that you and I might have eternal life.
He got up out of Joseph's new tomb,
And I heard Him said one day,
When He was getting ready to leave here,
"I got all power."
He didn't say part of it.
But, "I got all power in the palm of my hand."
Oh wait a little while.

Harvest time is coming after a while.
And I heard John talking about it.
I heard John Divine said,
"Oh, in the morning,
When the Lord come,
He is coming out of glory with a rainbow 'round His shoulder
Eyes are like balls of fire
Feet like polished brass
Hair like lamb's wool."
Oh in that harvest day,
Oh Gabriel get your horn,
I want you to blow it this morning
Call all of my children,
Yes, been laboring somewhere in the vineyard,
Telling men the wages of sin is death,
The gift of God eternal life.
Oh servant, you can rejoice right now.
Oh servant, you worked in the heat of the day
You went when you didn't feel like goin'
Servant, servant, servant,
Come on up a little higher.
It's harvest time.
Servant,
You don't hear me
Servant, you won't have to cry no more.
Servant,
Come on up a little higher
It's harvest time.
Sit down at the table,
We won't eat bread of sorrow.
It's all over now,
And I'm so glad that harvest time is coming.
But as I close this message, if you haven't did anything, you won't see very
   much, because God is goin' reward us all according to our deeds. That
   make me go sometime when I don't feel like goin'. Oh I know after a
   while, I know after a while.
I know after a while,
Jesus said,
He will wipe all tears from my eyes.
I heard Him say that you can wait on the harvest time.
Oh if you can wait 'til Gabriel blow his horn,
Oh if you can wait 'til I get through building on the nation,
Oh if you wait,
Oh, I'll come again and then call you home.

And I'm so glad this morning Jesus not goin' call us by name. He gonna say "Servant," and you know one thing when the Lord say servant, somebody is not goin' answer, because some of us have not served.
Servant,
Servant,
Come on in.
Come on in servant.
You been on the battlefield.
Some of those old warriors,
Is coming up that morning,
"Lord, I lost my flag somewhere on the battlefield.
But oh my staff,
Oh my staff is my witness that I stayed on the battlefield.
Oh I stayed there."
Yes at harvest time, when each of us will have to give an account of our stewardship. When Jesus come, to gather up His children. He's not goin' to gather up the devil's children, but He's goin' to gather up His. And to all of you, let us practice what we talk about. It's easy to talk about Heaven, but it's goin' cost something to get there. Let us live so others can see Christ in our life. Let us do it daily—lot of folks likes to prove that they are Christian when they come to church. But we need to prove it when we 'way from the church. You don't have any problems acting like a Christian as long as you're with a crowd of Christians. But your problem after you leave the church, when you get out there with some folks that have decided, some haven't decided at all, this is when you goin' to have to stand up and let your light shine. And don't tell me it's easy. You might tell some of these young folks, you can't tell me. It's not easy, because to call you you don't have that dude.

Talk to me now! You know I never demands anybody to shout. Because if you haven't been born again you ain't got not business shouting nohow. And if you have been born again, you don't have to wait until you go to Green Gosha, Bluff Springs, Clear Creek, or Second Baptist. If you been born again, Lee Earl—now some folks don't know what I'm talking about because they haven't been born again—but if you been born by the Spirit of God, and it has come in and born it in your heart, you don't have to wait until you come here to shout.

Some of you may not have been around me much, but I don't leave none of the Bible out. And the reason why I don't want to leave none of it out, I thinks about what Matthew 23 and 23 says, the Pharisees tithed and did all that kind of stuff, but some of the very important things that they should have did, they left it undone. And when I stand before the Lord, I don't want to be accused of sticking my finger in one ear trying to make folks shout and then don't say nothing. If you does not preach all of the Bible, ain't no use in preaching none of it. Do you see what I'm talkin' 'bout? Most of us like the good part, but we don't want to hear the other part. But I don't plan on standing before God saying that I picked a certain part and this all I talked about. Because if you been born again, you don't need me to make you shout. I'm not the Holy Ghost. If you have the Holy Ghost you ought to be able to shout. But 'least, you ought to know what you shouting about. 'Lot of us shouting don't know what we shouting 'bout. I've been 'round here a long time. I been in the church ever since I was eleven years old.[2] And I done saw a lot of shouting, Beauford, and it wasn't a thing but a pharisee shout. Jesus said they love what the eye see, don't they? They love to stand on the corner of the streets and disfigure their face and keep up a lot of noise, and make somebody believe that they are something that they are not. But if you just be real at whatever you are, God will bring it out. You don't have to tell nobody you been born again. You just keep living. Your fruit will bear you out. Your life you live will tell your neighbors who you are.

So at harvest time there's goin' be a lot of folks goin' come in goin' be disappointed. Because Jesus said in his writing, that He's goin' say on that day, "Depart from me, those that work iniquity. I never know you." This is at the annual Harvest Day when every sick will leave the earth, when every slick thing you thought you hid, God is goin' bring it up. It's goin' be on your record. You know the old song, said, "You may slip and slide, but I declare you ain't goin' get by." That's why the church is so cold. You know I'm glad that I know God. And I even know why Grady get cold sometimes. When I 'llow the world to filter in on my soul, it takes my spiritual strength, and I have to go back and call on God. When you busy on the telephone running other folk's business, gossip and lying on other folk, and when you get off the 'phone you get the TV, and put in forty hours in a week looking at TV, and put nine hour in prayer, you cain't help but be cold to save your life. If you don't crank automobile up, the motor never will get warm. Ain't God all right? You crank the thing up and let it run a while and it get warm.

But I'm goin' leave you now. But every once in a while I have to crank mine up and let the Holy Ghost warm it up. Every once in a while, I steal away, and get all by myself. and I tell the Lord,
Now Lord, I don't feel your Spirit.
Now Lord, I know I been born again.
Now Lord, I know you the same God, set my soul on fire.
Now Lord, come on and see about me.
Ain't you glad today?
Ain't you glad today, He is that kind of God?
Oh yeah
If I don't get back now more,
Hold on.
[Begins song] "When all, God's children . . .

II

Clear Creek M.B.C.
January 19, 1986.
Sermon by Rev. Grady McKinney:
"Trust in the Lord"

It is said that the New Year brings in new ideas, and perhaps that is right but I would like to say it this way. Since all of us know we do not have long to stay here, we ought to not play church but we ought to try to live it every day. We need a well-adjusted life. We shouldn't be wobbling down the road. And I believe I heard Paul said on one occasion, "I press toward tomorrow for the prize, the high calling of God in Christ Jesus." Let that be our goal. Let us strive to do God's will. They that trust in the Lord shall not be moved. It is easy said that I trust in the Lord, but that don't mean it true all the time. One that trusteth in the Lord believe God is the answer to all our problems. One that trust in the Lord does not throw stone for stone. Jesus said on one occasion, in his inspired word, "If you're smoted on one cheek, turn the other." Jesus said, "Do good unto those that" do what?, "that spiteful misuse you." When we get so we can bring ourselves down to this level, then we can wave our banner high and say I know I am a child of God. But as long as we be mean-hearted, hard to get along with, talk when we ought to have our mouth shut up, it don't sound like God's children. If we could only remember what John 3:13 said, "For God so loved the world that He gave His only begotten son." I believe, you don't have to believe this, but I believe if we be begotten by God, then this love must be in us. And we must demonstrate it through the lives that we lead and not just through the words that we say. Now, if you have to roll on the stomp, you better come on down and start with me. I'm kinda tired, I ain't had much sleep. And I hope the Lord don't let nobody die this week. I done 'bout had enough funerals. They about to rattle my nerves. But God's will must be done. They that trust on the Lord will not go around saying that I'm not sure whether I'm saved or not. God cannot lie. And the Bible say that if you be faithful and hold out until the end, there is a crown of light laid up for you. We believe that Paul was a man that trusted in God. Because he said, "Be ye steadfast and unmoving." He was a man that had great experience with God. God had changed his life, and he became a disciple by Christ. And whatever he went out to do he did it with all of his might. Let us, if the Lord would bless us this year, come to church to do what is pleasing in God's sight. Sometime we get carried away with ourselves and want to be the superstar on the stage. But God doesn't have any superstar. Your heart must be right. It doesn't matter how well you can perform. If you're not steadfast, all of your performance is in vain.

The writer said, "Be ye doers of the word," so we must trust in the Lord before we can be steadfast. Because it's hard to hold on to anything that one do not trust. Is that right Sam? A man that has a wife and doesn't trust her has a miserable life to lead. He's always worried and always expecting something wrong to go on or something out of order to happen. Trust your wife. But if you trust your wife, you can go on to Australia and be satisfied. So then we must learn to trust and put all our trust in God.

A woman that doesn't trust her husband—y'all ladies, look at me now—usually when he goes off and come home you look at him funny, when he comes in the door. But if you trust your husband, your greeting will be with a smile. But Paul said, "Be ye steadfast and always abounding in the work of the Lord." Now sometime we gets confused. We thinks all of the works of the Lord stops at the place we call church. But I believe we come together at this appointed place to unite our voice and uplift God, that we might be better able to go out into the byways and tell mens about Christ. Then you ought to think about this sometime: I may be raggedy, but I am somebody, because I'm one of God's children. You 'member reading the message about Lazarus. He didn't have any material things, but he still was somebody, because he trusted in God. The Bible say when he died he was carried and placed in Abraham' bosom. You need not feel downhearted because you doesn't have all the riches of the world. If you have Christ in you life, you are still somebody. Stand firm on it and tell the world. "I might be humbly [*sic*], but I am somebody, because I trust in the Lord."

The Bible teaches us that if we trust in God and wait on him, He will fulfil the desires of our hearts. It has been said down through the years, that God's peoples supposed to be poor and not have anything. But if you think little—I'm almost through now—if you think little you goin' always be little. But if you stay steadfast in God you can realise that all things belongs to God, and if God is a big God, I am a big believer. Even if you wake up in the morning and decide that it's goin' be a bad day, it will be one. The Bible says, "So a man think," but let me say it this way, "so a individual think, so it will be with him." But if you stay steadfast in God's word, you can always look for a brighter future. Things will not remain the same because the God I trust in is able to make the mountain the valley, and move the stoney places out of the road. If you trust in God. If we trust in God, we will have that inner spirit. Let's see, they got a thing they call the turban drive. Y'all ever look at this supercar on TV? The guy push some buttons, the thing jump all out the side. Then you push another button and it takes off like a jet. Well, if you have God in your life, whatever you get in the low place it can not come out car lonely [? unclear]. There is an answer in God. Then He's able, if you put your trust in Him. Well, let's see here can we find a few witnesses that put their trust in the Lord.

Job was a man that put his trust in the Lord. When Satan got displeased with Job and he told the Lord that "Job are not serving you for nothing.

You got a hedge built all around him. And ah you allow me to come in Job' life, I'll make you cuss him to your face" [him cuss you is what is intended]. Yessir, but I heard the Lord said, maybe not in these words, "Oh I know Job, he is my servant. And, er-ah, I don't believe he'll turn his back on me." I heard Satan said, "'llow me a chance, I'll change his mind." That's the reason we act like we act sometime. Satan don't like for you to do right. And he'll try to turn you around. Yeah my Lord. The Lord moved back one step, said "Er-ah, I'll 'llow you to move in Job's life. Oh Satan, I got my eyes on you, not goin' 'llow you to go too far." Oh yeah, now, Job's children, yeas, was having a feast one day at the elder brother's house. Servant came running. "Oh Job, oh Job, you children are dead." Don't we almost die when we lose one child? Job lost all of his children. But I heard Job said, "The Lord giveth and the Lord taketh away, blessed be the name of the Lord."

If you trust in the Lord you can say some of the same words. Yeah my Lord. But that ain't all happen to Job. He lost all his cattle, he lost all his camels, he lost all his she-asses, everything he had. Job, things have got dark with you. You know every child of God, sometime the way get dark. Every child of God gets so I wonder sometimes. But oh, I heard the song-writer said, "I don't know why I have to cry sometimes. But oh, by and by we'll understand it, all after a while."

But not only that, my friend, Job trust in the Lord. And I heard Satan said, "Well, all that a man have he'll give for his life." Satan went out and made a deal with the Lord. "Let me touch Job now with boils and I'll make him cuss you to your face." Job broke out with boils from the crown of his head to the soles of his feets. And Satan walked in, come in between his love-life, and said unto his wife, "This man you married to don't you smell him? He don't even smell right. Why don't you tell Job, oh Job you ought to cuss God and die." I heard Job said, "Oh woman" (don't we get foolish sometime?) "Oh woman, oh woman, you sound like a foolish woman. You don't even talk like my wife." This what Job would say. "You know, 'long as we been together, I've always trusted the Lord. 'Doesn't matter what happen in my life, I hold it on God's unchanging hand. You just don't sound like my wife. You trying to tell me what good and what evil you must receive from the Lord." Eh my Lord. Trust in the Lord. He sure will, he'll sure bring you out all right. After Job's trouble was over, after Job's trial was over, after Job's tribulation was over, that same God stepped right on in and turned around, replanted [?] Job.

I'm glad this evening, that the Lord said in the Word, "Trust in the Lord, yeah, and ah you shall not be moved." If I don't get back on board, stay steadfast and hold unto God's unchanging hand. Tell the world out yonder, Oh I know a man yeah, I wonder do you know him. Oh, I know a man from another land. They call his name Jesus. Somebody else call him, my prince for peace. Somebody else call him, the rose for Sharon, the lily of the valley, the bright and morning star. Oh I call him, I call him, my everything. Somebody else said he's a leaning pole, he's a sky-riding king, he's a heavy load carrier, he's a burden bearer, yes he is.

Steadfast and unmoveable in God. Hold on a lil' while longer. You know I think deeper than I used to think. I used to think I had a long time to live. But Job said, "You only have a few days and then they are full of trouble." Then I heard him say, "You flee like a child. You ain't coming this way no more."

And as I close today, if you haven't decided to put your trust in the Lord, you ought to decide right now. Take me. Mould me. Create in me a clean heart.

Now just cool down now. Y'all think I'm goin' crazy, 'cause I tell you "don't shout" every now and then. But I done learned if you shout and doesn't have a life to back up your shouting, all of you shouting is in vain. Yes. Most any of us, can learn how to sing like a mocking bird, that gets up early in the morning and find a light-line, a tree limb to get up on and flop his wings, dance and sing, 'til it'll draw your 'ttention. But after the dancing is over—this what we got to watch—do I have a life? Do my life corresdespond [correspond] with my singing? Do my life coincide with my preaching? Do my life stand approval call to my deaconship? This is a very important part. You ought to shout because you got something to shout about. You ought to raise your hand and tell the Lord, "Oh I thank you, you been mighty good to me. Oh I thank you." Why I thank Him? You took nothing and made something out of it. Ain't God all right?

If it were left up to me, I'd be like any other man. I'd be gambling all night long. But something on the inside, the world didn't give it to me, Lord God. Now wait a minute. Somebody says that it's not anything to being born again. I want to give this over to you. If you haven't been born again, you don't have anything to lead you and guide you. I hear folks around talking about, you can be born and then be lost. No! You might believe and change your belief and be lost. But if you been born by the spirit of God, you are not what you used to be. You got something on the inside that the world can't give you. And once you been born again, the Lord not goin' take it. You might get wrong sometime. 'Long as I live, I'm goin' get wrong sometime. But oh, thank God, something down on the inside keep on reasoning with me. Yeah my Lord, this same God that Paul talked abut, He died out yonder on Calvary. Somebody said, the sun wouldn't shine. I heard, somebody else said, the moon dripped it down in blood. I heard, somebody else said, sinner man was standing by the cross, surely. . . .

This all I'm trying to say, stay steadfast. And stop telling folks that they been born again, and they still can be lost. No, if you just walk up and give me your hand, yeah you can turn around and take that back. But when something been put on the inside, Lord is not an indian-giver.

He don't give and take back what He give. But He let it work with you, yeah, 'til you get right. Is that right?

Look what David did, a man after God's own heart. But he got to looking at that naked woman, and she didn't even know that David was looking at her. Men, don't tell nobody that you don't like womens. All men like womens. Just the right one ain't come along yet. While he was there looking, his sinful eye, his lust and desire moved him in the wrong direction, and he had a heart after God.

You see, when God get on the inside, you might get wrong sometime, but you can't stay wrong. I heard David said, "Create in me a clean heart." Well, Clear Creek, I don't know your prayer you been praying, but I'd like for you to pray David's prayer. Tell the Lord, "Create in me a clean heart, so I can love everybody." Now some of these preachers say you can't love everybody. That's what they teach. They say the Lord wasn't intending for you to love everybody. Then I believe if Christ can lay His life on the line, since they made us, and man violated and walked from God, and if God could still have enough love to give His son that died for a no-good somebody like you and I, if God can have that kind of love, so can you and I. But what we need to do, get us a clean heart and then we can do these things.

We may not see you no more, but you stay steadfast. Don't worry about how much noise you keep up. Now the old folks told me this, and I live to be a witness that it's true, now some of you grey-headed folks know what I'm talking about. A loaded wagon doesn't make much noise, but a empty wagon coming down the road kicks up a whole lot of fuss. Do you know what I'm trying to say now? Yes, noise fool folks sometimes, and they think they serving the Lord. I'm goin' get in trouble now, Red. They got a thing out now they call the "Rock Gospel." White and black is acting the fool. Talking about they serving the Lord. And eh, if you want to dance, you just ought to go on and dance. And eh, when you get through doing your thing, you ought to bow down and tell the Lord, "I know I done wrong." You don't have to start to dancing in the church, when you don't have no reason to dance. If the Holy Spirit make you shout, you ought to shout 'til you get satisfied. If the Holy Spirit make you clap your hands, you ought to clap 'til you get satisfied. If the Holy Spirit make you run, you ought to run 'til you get satisfied. If the Holy Spirit make you cry, you ought to cry on 'til God wipe tears from you eyes.

This all I'm trying to say, don't put on. Be real in your heart and that's what the Lord want you to do.

Br. Thompson is coming. I want him to sing my favorite song. You just wait on him, he know what I want to hear. 'Cause with the ups and downs that I have dealing with church folks, Lord, nobody knows the trouble I bear. But I gets consolation out of this because it tell you that there will be peace in the valley. Oh yeah, yeah. There's goin' be peace after a while. Sing Br. Thompson. Come. You ought to come right now.

III

Clear Creek M.B.C.
November 16, 1986
Sermon by Rev. Grady McKinney:
"You Must Be Born Again"

You might notice from St. John's Gospel, the old Baptist favorite—You must be born again. We thank God for bein' able to come again on another Lord's day. Givin' honor to our officers and visiting officers, to all our members and visiting friends, and sinners, if there be any. This is the Lord's day. An' I'm quite sure all of us are thankful that we are able to come again on the Lord's day, to tell the Lord that we thank Him for all He has done for us. You know I'm so crazy, I even thank the Lord for bein' sick sometimes. 'Cause sometime, if I didn't have some sickness, I probably wouldn't have God on my mind. But just something to notify you once in a while that you still need God. That will make you pray when you not thinkin' about prayin'. Over the last, I guess it's been about a month now, maybe a little over, since I was missing, if I stay around much more longer, it's not goin' to be many left that went to school with me.

Folks are leaving here in hordes. They goin' to bury Horace Cookwood today at Shiloh at two or two-thirty. So that's four in about a month's time, or maybe about five weeks, that we come along together. They are crossed over the river. Now that let me know now that my time is winding up. I may be around fifteen or maybe twenty more years. But the fact remain the same, my time is winding up. Whether you believe it or not, all our time is windin' up. And that song writer that wrote that song that said, "The time is now to serve the Lord." And you know, whether you believe it or not, as the days go by you get a little closer to the grave. And all that you leave undone will remain undone.

But I feel like it's a need to talk from this Scripture. Because from the evidence that I can see and according to what the Bible say, there's a lot of us is not goin' to get in to the Kingdom. Now it doesn't mean anything to belong to Clear Creek, if you does not belong to Christses [*sic*] church. Because this is just where the church meet at. But you must be born into Christses church. You know, we take 'em in, don't we? But Christ teaches us you must be born into Christses church if you want to be one of His disciples. So we are sayin' whatever you are born, you will always remain that. Now a lot of folks don't believe that.

A lot of folks believe that you can be born again and then be lost. But, I'm sorry, you don't understand what you're reading. Whenever you been born by the Spirit of God, God put something on the seat of your mind that will lead you and guide you. Then if God is that weak, he is not worthy of praising. You see, I can catch onto a lot of things, but I can not hold

it. But whatever God binds, stays there. Now if you just came and decided you wanted to be a members of the church, yeah, you can turn around anytime when you get ready. But if you been born by the Spirit of God, it doesn't matter how you want to turn around, little still voice on the inside—Are you listening to me?—something on the inside will bring you back to God. Maybe, maybe, maybe, maybe we need to check our records. Maybe some of us haven't been born again. Sometime in our choirs, because some of us cannot have our way, we stop singing, and say, "I'm not not goin' sing any more." But if you been born by the Spirit of God, and have the gift of God to sing, no one can stop you from singing. They got a recording they got out, said the old man got old, and they didn't want him to sing with them, Lee Earl. Finally one day that he was missing they went to crying what become of the old man. And the story went on to say he have found him a choir, yeah, that he could sing with.[3] So if you be born again, you don't allow obstacles, to stop you from doin' God's work. Christ said unto this great man according to men's standards—but see what I really love about God, God can take a nobody and make a somebody out of him—you see, according to [begins chant] this man's standards, and accordin' to the standards of society, this man was a great man. He was a member of the Senheven council. And it is said this was, the highest court of the land, but still he didn't know Jesus. What I'm tryin' to say, sometime we may be gifted with a good voice and able to sing like a mockin' bird, but time, will prove whether it's real or not.
Because if God is not, in your heart,
You'll sing, long as the sea is calm,
But you wait until the lightnin' lick out its tongue,
You wait until the wind, raise the waves on the sea,
And start to tossin' you back and forth,
You'll 'bandon the ship and leave it alone.
But if you been born again
Doesn't matter how rough the sea get,
You'll say the God I serve is able.
He's able,
You don't hear me!
And I know he will take care.
If you've been born again on this old Christian journey,
It gets kind of ups and downs.
But let's go back to our text a little bit here.
This man had, all of this understanding,
But he had not been born by the Spirit of God
And er-ah, my Bible say, he came to Jesus by night
Now a lot of folks that know a whole lot
Say the reason why he came,
He didn't want the members of the Senheven council

To know that he, was goin' to Jesus.
And some claim, the reason why that he came by night, he was shamed to
   let the community know that the position he hold,
That he was goin' to a man like Jesus.
And Nicodemus came to Jesus by night,
And er-ah, you know this when Nicodemus
Came in the presence of Jesus
And began to talk with him, he said,
"We know that there are a teacher that comes from God."
He didn't even recognise him as the son of God.
But he recognised him as a teacher.
And er-ah, something was strange about the way Jesus talk
And er-ah, something about Jesus was different from other men.
And if you'll 'llow me to say this today,
Something is different about those that been born by the Spirit of God
Well, if I been lying and come into Christses fold,
But that don't stop me from lying,
I haven't had a change in my heart.
Ain't God alright?
You been born by the Spirit of God,
The thing you used to do, you don't crave to do no more.
Ain't God alright?
I heard the Lord said,
"Nicodemus, you must be born again.
Not only, you won't enter the kingdom,
But you won't even see the kingdom of God
Except you be born by the Spirit of God."
Well,
And I heard Nicodemus said,
"How can I enter into my mother's womb a second time?
Here I am, a grown man
I don't understand about bein' born again."
But I heard Jesus said,
"Nicodemus, you have felt the wind blowing
Tell me,
You don't know where it comes from,
Neither do you know where it goes.
So it is,
So it is,
So it is,
with everyone that born by the Spirit of God."
Aren't you glad this evening?
You got to be born again.
I heard some of the old warriors said, a long time ago,

They was born 'til their hand looked new
Born 'til their feet got light
Born 'til the world had changed
Ain't God alright?
Nicodemus, you got to be born again.
The same God is sayin' the same thing to you
Go to church, all you want to go,
Sing in the choir,
Serve on the Deacon Board,
Serve as a usher,
And in many other capacities.
But if you haven't been born again,
Oh by and by
You got to come to life's end journey
You got to stand before a holy and righteous judge.
And I heard one writer said,
"Every knee goin' bow and every tongue goin' confess"
In the morning
Oh in the morning
When I stand before the King
I want to come on in
I want to tell the Lord
I failed sometimes,
But oh grace,
Every time I failed
Grace raised me up
Grace turned me around
Grace started me
Back on the right road
Ain't God all right
Oh in the morning
Servant,
Who you talkin' 'bout now.
Servant, those that serve
Servant, those that care to earn
Servant, those that sung praises
Servant, those that help the poor and needy
Servant,
Servant,
Good God almighty
Servant,
Oh yes   (Yes my Lord)
Servant
Are you one of God's servants?

Or are you a busy-body?
Servant
Let me tell you today
If you haven't been born again
You can't sit with the servant
Oh I've seen, ups and downs
Standing by your name
Hangin' out on the highway
But oh I know a man
Do you know him?
Oh I know a man,
They call him Jesus
Oh I know a man,
They call him wonderful counsel
Oh I know a man
They call him a good provider
Oh I know a man
Say a shelter in the time of storm
Oh I know a man
He is my friend
In the time of trouble
Oh yes
I don't know how you feel about it
But I'm so glad
Aren't you glad today?
I signed up
On the heavenly roll
But oh I know after a while
God will
I said God will
God will, wipe all tears from your eyes
Lee Earl, I got a few more years
To hear God's words
Oh yes
Goin' hear him say after a while,
"Swing down chariot
Stop and let that poor man ride."
Yeah my Lord.
Jesus died, out yonder on Calvary
For your sin and mine
He died, 'til the sun wouldn't shine
He died, 'til the moon changed the image
And dripped it down in blood
He died, 'til the sinner man was standin' by the cross

Surely,
Surely, surely,
It must be the son of God
But not only that my friends,
They took him down from that
Old Roman cross
They laid him in another man's tomb
They got some mens
And then they sealed the tomb
Set a guard over the tomb
To watch it all night long
And somebody said,
They remembered what the Lord said
"This tabernacle tear down
and on the third day, I'll raise it up."
They were sittin' there in the morning
When a earthquake came
The angels came down
And rolled the stone from the grave
Jesus got up
Out the old tomb
Tell my brethren
"Meet me in Galilee
I gotta two more words,
I'm gonna have to share today
And then I'm goin' back to my father."
I heard on the last day
On that last day
I heard the Lord said
"Come and go out to meet
I'm gettin' ready
I goin' leave you now
But boys
I want you to go back town
And wait in the upper room
Until you hear from glory."
It start to ridin on up
They were standing looking
At the cloud was a chariot
Send him back up into heaven
Stand and gaze
But I heard a voice said
"Why stand ye here,
Gazing up into the heavens?

That same Jesus
Is coming back after a while
But you wait,
Down in Jerusalem
Until the tenth day."
They heard a mighty rumbling, like a rush of wind
Holy Ghost power
And as I close Clear Creek
You need a little Holy Ghost power
Power that make you love your enemies
Power, power
To guide your feets in the right paths
Power that make you speak good
Power to be as Abraham said,
"If you want the right, then I'll take the left
But if you want the left, then I'll go to the right"
I'm closin' now
I may not come back no more
But one thing I want to leave with you
Don't worry about me
I'm fixed up with Jesus
I'm tied up
I'm tangled up in His love [Shout_____]
Jesus
When I get lonely,
He's my company keeper
I don't have a friend
I can call on Him
Come see about you
Won't He keep you company?
You must be, You must be
Born again
And er-ah, as I come to a close
I'm talking to all of you now
If you don't ever feel the Spirit,
I better say that again
If you don't ever feel the Spirit
You just haven't been born again
Oh Sometime
It makes you act funny
Sometime, folks say you kind of looney in the head
Sometime, it make you cry, [Shout], when ain't nobody bother you
Oh sometime, make your feet get light
Sometime, make you raise your hand

Oh sometime,
Yeah
Yes
And kind of like the old song said,
I don't claim to be a great philosopher
I don't claim to know a whole lot
But it's two things I do know
I been born again
I been 'nointed to preach the Gospel
I heard Paul said
I been commanded to preach
I been anointed to preach
I been ordained to preach
Them two things
I can brag about
And then I may well so
I can brag about something else
If I hold out
Stand on His word
Hold out
Until tomorrow
Everything
Everything, everything
You don't hear me
Everything
Everything, everything
Is gonna be alright
'Goin' be alright
It's goin' be alright after a while
They used to sing a old song
They used to moan in our revivals
When we
Was filled with the Holy Spirit
Didn't we hear,
Some old sister over in the corner say?
"One thing I know
I been born again
One thing I know
'Been born again."
Y'all excuse me today
But I wonder do you know
You been born again
Sometime, I wonders about it
I see folk goin' to church

All the year long
Don't ever shed a tear
Don't ever smile
Don't ever wave their hand
Dear Lord
Seem like to me
You're not sure
This thing, that got on to me
Won't let me act right sometime
Every once in a while   (Oh that man is alright,
                                    Oh the man is alright.)

'Gettin' ready to close now
May God bless you
I want to sing a verse of a hymn, after which the choir will come
[Begins lined hymn] "That awful day will surely come"

Notes

Preface

1. These themes were at about this time coming to the forefront of discussions of American religion. See, for example, David Wills' 1987 article (reprinted in Fulop and Raboteau, eds., 1997: 7–20) in which the author asserts that "the gap between the races—a gap involving both the interpretation of the American experience and the degree of empowerment within it—remains one of the foundational realities of our nation's religious life [. . .] one of the crucial, central themes in the religious history of the United States" (20). And race has continued to be a central preoccupation both nationally and in contemporary scholarly writing on religion, as in the following from Albert J. Raboteau's article (in Boles, ed., 2001: 193–205). "The segregation of black and white churches signified the existence of two Christianities in this nation and the deep chasm that divided them demonstrated the failure of the nation's predominant religious institution, the major source of its common symbols, images, and values, to achieve meaningful, sustained community across racial lines" (198). As the field of Southern Studies has progressed, it has, ironically perhaps, emphasized the differences between North and South, scholars occasionally asserting that the North as a distinct, unified entity, has actually ceased to exist. Thus, Samuel S. Hill, Jr., for example, asserted, "[T]he South remains an identifiable cultural region (many subregions in one, of course); no North, as such, has existed for nearly a century. In Dixie, regional dialects, culinary tastes, styles of community life, interracial relations, and, not least, religious patterns still show a distinctiveness, sometimes bordering on a kind of quaintness, that reflects its peculiar history" (1980: 138).

2. Mississippi may, in 1994, have had more black elected officials than any other state (see Mozella G. Mitchell, 1994: 2), but it was, nonetheless, a state overtly divided along racial lines.

3. In 1922 the major record companies in the United States began recording large numbers of black musicians, marketing the recordings in specially segregated "race" series: for example, Columbia's 14000, Okeh's 8000, and Paramount's 10/13000 series.

Chapter 1

1. See above n3.

2. Dunbar Rowland, in his 1925 monograph *History of Mississippi, the Heart of the South*, asserts that these treaties were signed in 1830 and 1832. He cites the Treaty of Dancing Rabbit Creek, "made on September 27, 1830" (1925: 556), and "The Treaty of Pontotoc Creek, by which the Chickasaws ceded all their lands east of the Mississippi, [and] put an end to Indian ownership of lands in the State. It was made on October 20, 1832, at the tribal council house on Pontotoc Creek [. . .] between the Chickasaw nation in general

council assembled and General John Coffee, of Tennessee, United States commissioner" (1925: 579). See also Mary Elizabeth Young (1961), and James C. Cobb (1992). Mississippi had become a U.S. territory in 1798 and the twentieth state in the Union in 1817.

3. For a thoughtful discussion and history of the nomenclature used to depict black communities (with some reference to other geographic areas), see Joseph Holloway (1990) "Introduction." In *Africanisms in American Culture,* ed. Joseph Holloway, i–xxi. As Holloway remarks, with the backing of Jesse Jackson and Ramona Edlin, among others, in the 1980s "African-American" and now the unhyphenated "African American" became the accepted terminology in scholarly circles. "Thus this debate has come full circle, from *African* through *brown, colored, AfroAmerican, Negro,* and *black* back to *African,* the term originally used by blacks in America to define themselves. The changes in terminology reflect many changes in attitude, from strong African identification to nationalism, integration, and attempts at assimilation back to cultural identification. This struggle to reshape and define blackness in both the concrete and the abstract also reflects the renewed pride of black people in shaping a future based on the concept of one African people living in the African diaspora" (1990: xx).

4. Maryanne Vollers' (1995) description of the University of Mississippi as it was in 1961 when James Meredith sought to integrate it, while a little dated, is surprisingly applicable today.

> If there was one symbol of Mississippi's white heritage and a concentration of its oligarchic impulse, it was the University of Mississippi at Oxford, affectionately known as Ole Miss. The rolling green lawn, the stately columned mansions, and Greek revival buildings were artefacts from the mythical antebellum South. The school mascot was a character called 'Colonel Reb.' The Confederate battle flag was the school symbol. [. . .] This was white Mississippian society distilled (1995: 91).

5. Also at Piggly Wiggly, another local supermarket chain! By the early 1990s, these smaller, more local supermarkets were beginning to feel the pressure from larger chains such as Kroger.

6. As Hans Baer and Merrill Singer remark, "the common responses to the shortage of ministers in the countryside have been intermittent scheduling of Sunday services and greater lay control over church affairs" (1992: 31).

7. Although often popularly referred to as fundamentalist, churches such as Clear Creek M.B.C. are more essentially evangelical, as is characteristic of the South. "The religious tradition that has dominated southern culture is Evangelicalism. Both the Baptists and the Methodists are a part of this branch of Protestantism, the distinguishing feature of which is a concern for religious experience. The need is to be born again, to 'get right with God'" (Charles Reagan Wilson, 1995: 59).

8. As Baer and Singer remark, "Many of the Black Baptist churches in small southern communities are not affiliated with any of the national Baptist denominations" (1992: 30).

9. For a brief discussion of this matter, see ibid.: 16–18.

10. For some detailed discussion and reference to numerous other instances see ibid., 30–33. For more general discussion of the structure and congregational independence of Baptist churches, both black and white, and affiliations with various denominational bodies, see Frank S. Mead, and Samuel S. Hill (1990, especially 34–56).

11. "Gospel," in Paul Oliver, Max Harrisson, and William Bolcom, eds. (1986: 216).

Chapter 2

1. Elisabeth Moberly's 1985 study is a good concise presentation of this perspective.

2. Horowitz and Horowitz found in their 1936 study of social attitudes in children that the pronounced intrusion of the "race" category into the social reality can enhance the importance of racial aspects of the child's identity above all others—even more fundamental ones like "sex." Using three separate tests with young southern children, they found "consistent, clear evidence that with the children in these communities race is a more fundamental distinction than sex. [. . .] The general order of importance of attributes appears to be race first, then sex, age and socio-economic status" (1936: 307–8). For a more contemporary consideration of this topic and some striking personal experiences, see Studs Terkel (1992) and Joel Williamson (1984 and 1986). For some contemporary psychological studies on the impact of colour on the development of self-identity, see, for example, Cross (1991); Cross, Pelham, and Helms (1991); Dyson (1993); Gerard (1998); Gordon (1995); Hacker (1992); Helms (1990); Nobles (1997); and Tucker (1994).

3. While it may be downplayed in some contexts, the fundamental racial opposition between black and white persists as an elemental force in the formation of identity (black identity, particularly, perhaps) in the United States today. As psychologists recognise, the development of children's positive self-esteem is usually based on the influences of their families and immediate communities.

[However,] As African American children come under the influence of the larger American society, they are increasingly exposed to manifestations of the white supremacy myth. This threatens to undermine the positive sense of themselves that they attained at home. Therefore, the lessons built into African American folklore, language, religion, and music aid the developing black individual in negotiating these contrasting influences. The challenge attitude ["expecting that there is another, perhaps opposite, meaning to what white authority presents as truth, especially as it pertains to the challenger's self-identity" (Ferdinand Jones, 2001: 133)] guides individuals to disbelieve the destructive white supremacy assumption and to hold on to the positive attributions received from those who are most important in their lives. The challenge instructions are *no less than life-preserving in their psychological necessity* (Ferdinand Jones, 2001: 138) [my emphasis].

While my primary interest in the present study is not what one reader has referred to "the tragic finality of racial lines that have existed for over two hundred years," the reader should not lose sight of the constant and historic presence that this issue of race has for the identity of this community.

4. For a discussion of this development see Iain MacRobert, "The Black Roots of Pentecostalism," in Fulop and Raboteau, eds. 1997: 295–310. First printed in Jan Jongeneel (1992: 73–84).

5. This was, however, not always the case with churches of other denominations, and may be more marked as a phenomenon among African American Baptist congregations.

6. Hans Baer and Merrill Singer attribute what might be described as a somewhat belated celebration of diversity within the black church to a perceived need for black people to unify in the face of outside persecution. "In responding to threat and slander from the dominant society, African-American intellectuals—most of whom until this century have been preachers—have been compelled to stress unity and commonality rather than the celebration of diversity [. . .] a pattern that can be seen in the tendency to equate African-American religion with the 'Black church.' While this concept may have a certain heuristic value, it is misleading in its implication that the religious experience among Blacks has been uniform or monolithic" (1992: xv–xvi).

7. For comments of this nature and descriptions of religious activities conducted by slaves, see, for example, Morgan Godwin (1689), or Charles Colcock Jones (1842). For a more contemporary discussion of these and other sources, see Dena J. Epstein (1977), Lawrence Levine (1977), and Eileen Southern (1971).

8. For discussion of this phenomenon and the rise of African American sacred quartets, see, for example, Kip Lornell (1988) or Ray Allen (1991).

9. While blues was much in evidence around the university campus (the CSSC being a prominent centre for blues research), and in local bars, I attended only a couple of "jook joint" sessions. These were exclusively black affairs, tucked well away from prying eyes in the countryside, with home-brewed alcohol much in evidence. It would have been unacceptable to the Clear Creek M.B.C. community for me to have split my allegiance between these two cultures, and would have jeopardised both my credibility and my fieldwork.

10. A progression, it should be noted, that is also common in gospel music: see Michael Harris (1992).

11. Norms of consonance/dissonance, harmonic structure, meter, and number and treatment of voices are taken from the church's performance of music, and from the norms of the National Baptist Hymnal, i.e., standard Western Christian hymnody.

12. For an elaboration of these ideas see, for example, Michael Harris (1992), Guido van Rijn (1997), and Guthrie Ramsey (2003).

13. Copyright, 1982, by Famous Music Corporation and Ensign Music Corporation. Words by Will Jennings. Music by Buffy Sainte-Marie and Jack Nitzche.

14. MALACO 4392, manufactured and distributed by MALACO, 3023 W. Northside Drive, Jackson, Miss. 39213. For a brief outline of the Jackson Southernaires' career, the interested reader is directed to Sparks (2001: 273–74).

15. It is true, of course, that other gospel singers have released versions of this popular piece that has become almost iconic in the American music sphere. It is even referred to in the unlikely context of black rap artist Tupac Amaru Shakur's (1971–1996) "White Man'z World" which appears on his 1996 album *Makaveli: The Don Killuminati* (Death Row Records/Interscope). Embedded into Tupac's appeal to black youth not to participate in black-on-black crime "Use your brain/It's not them that's killing us/It's us that's killing us," a mis-quotation of the opening lines of "Up Where We Belong" suddenly appears: "Precious boys and girls/Born black in this white man's world/And all I heard was/*Who knows what tomorrow brings/In this world where <u>everyone lies</u>*" (quoted in Ceschi, 2003 [my emphasis]), as opposed to "In a world few hearts survive," in the original.

16. See also Thérèse Smith (1998).

17. For an excellent example of a white performance of "Amazing Grace" in traditional style, the reader is referred to the recordings accompanying *Worlds of Music*, 2nd ed., ed. Jeff Todd Titon (CD 1, track 17), which features a performance by the Fellowship Independent Baptist Church, the congregation which is at the heart of Titon's *Powerhouse for God* (1988). The recording is from a field tape of Titon's made in 1977.

18. As Portia Maultsby put it in 1985, "Soul music may best be described as the secular counterpart of gospel. Many of its performers either are now or were once gospel singers; consequently, they use every vocal device idiomatic to gospel singing and preaching as they continue to find new ways of expressing traditional values, attitudes, and philosophies" (42). Maultsby further elaborated this point in 1990:

> The interrelatedness of soul and gospel music is illustrated through the interchangeability of the genres. For example, many gospel songs have been recorded under the label 'soul' and vice versa. In some instances the text is the only feature that distinguishes one style from another. In others, genre identification may be determined only by the musical identity of the artist who first recorded the song. Performances of soul and gospel music further illustrate that an aesthetic conceptual framework links the secular and sacred traditions to each other (203).

19. For further, more detailed discussion of the interactions between African American sacred and secular musical traditions see, for example, Horace Boyer (1979).

20. This is an issue to which I will return in the discussion of gospel music in chapter 3.

21. I am using the term "rite of passage" as it was posited by Arnold Van Gennep, i.e., "ceremonies accompanying an individual's life crises" (Kimball, Introduction to the translation of Van Gennep [1960: vii]).

22. For Black Baptists in Mississippi, the rite of baptism is an extremely important one. Indeed, as Samuel Hill, Jr., has pointed out, "the American

South is probably the only locus in Christendom to have placed the sacrament or ordinance of Baptism ahead of the Lord's Supper (Holy Communion) in importance" (in Boles, ed., 2001: 14).

23. For a succinct overview of the relationship between Baptists and Evangelicals, which includes examination of central tenets of faith germane to the conversion experience, the reader is referred to Eric H. Ohlmann (1991).

24. See, for example, Boles, ed. (2001); Hill, Jr. (1996): "Everyone knows that this [the Baptist denomination] is much the largest Christian denomination in the region [. . .] numbering at least 25 million" (7); Frank S. Mead and Samuel S. Hill, Jr. (1990); Sparks (2001). Charles Wilson has noted that "in 1957 four fifths of the population [of Mississippi] belonged to churches, and over half of Mississippians joining congregations were Baptist" (1995: 58). Similarly, Patrick Gerster noted in 1989 that "public opinion polls disclose that 9 out of every 10 southerners declare themselves Protestant, with nearly four out of every five of these being Baptist, Methodist, or Presbyterian" (in Wilson and Ferris, eds., 1989: 1122).

25. During revival, the first two pews on the right hand side of the church are reserved for the "mourners," i.e., those who are seeking conversion. At Clear Creek M.B.C., these are usually children between the ages of nine and twelve years old.

26. Rochelle lives with her grandparents in part of what used to be their farm in Springhill. Her grandfather, Robert Thompson, is a deacon at Clear Creek M.B.C., and her grandmother, Ludie Thompson (née Patton) is a mother of the church.

27. For a strikingly similar account of both the conversion experience and baptism, see M. Mitchell, 1994. While I do not agree with Mitchell's assertions of strong African connections in the ritual, the similarities in her description for Black churches in Meridian, Miss., point to a well-established tradition and demonstrate how Clear Creek M.B.C. illustrates that tradition.

28. The interested reader is referred to Walter F. Pitts' 1993 study, wherein the author specifically interprets baptism in the Afro-Baptist tradition as a rite of initiation. While I do not agree with Pitts' sweeping conclusions, his basic interpretation is similar to that suggested here.

29. To some degree, the members' views on the importance of Baptism diverge from what Samuel S. Hill, Jr., has described as the central role of Baptism in the South's religious life.

> In notable ways, the role of the two central rituals of historic Christianity, baptism and the Lord's Supper, reveal the South as a distinctive religious setting. These sacraments, or "ordinances," hold a significant place in regional life and are viewed differently by southerners than by any other Christians in the world. For example, baptism outranks Communion in importance [. . .] on a value scale honored by millions of southern Protestants, especially those most vocal about their positions, baptism has primacy (in Wilson and Ferris, eds., 1989: 1271).

It may be, however, that Hill is not distinguishing discretely between conversion and Baptism, but viewing the whole as a rite of passage. "Baptism understood as a rite of initiation is thus essential. Passage from nominal to genuine practice, from being lost to being saved, from knowing intellectually to experiencing with the heart, becomes a pivotal event" (ibid.: 1271).

30. For further elaboration of this phenomenon, the interested reader is directed to Samuel Hill, Jr. (1994: 16 ff); Frank S. Mead and Samuel S. Hill, Jr. (1990: 34–56).

31. As Baer and Singer remark, "in keeping with Baptist congregationalism [referring in particular to the National Baptist Convention], each church may choose which supra-local bodies it wishes to affiliate with. Similarly, although the national convention publishes its own literature (e.g., hymnals, Sunday school study guides, missionary tracts, training manuals), each congregation has the option of adopting whatever materials it desires. Congregations also hire their own ministers and manage their own fiscal and legal affairs" (1992: 72).

32. When I asked Lee why he referred to the church building as a synagogue, he explained:

A synagogue is a place of gathering. When the Bible speaks of synagogue, it was more like the town square or something, or wherever people gathered to hear the word of God before the temple was erected. To me church too is the same place. Maybe not necessarily, because in a synagogue people was there at all times. And likewise it was in the temple at Jerusalem when it was first constructed. Many peoples was there day after day. Many people went to pray and many people was prayed for day by day. Also I speak of synagogue because it's not only a place of gathering from many, of certain members just members gather, but many people from many different churches come also together (interview, November 17, 1986).

Chapter 3

1. As was the case with spirituals, former slaves from the United States took lined hymnody to Jamaica, Trinidad, and St. Vincent, where it also survives.

2. Alfred Pinkston describes the performance of lined hymns similarly in his study, which analyses their performance amongst "black people in the rural areas of the Southern United States prior to the mid 1960s" (1975: 3).

3. I use the word "audience" for lack of a better one. With African American sacred music especially, the concept of an audience is an uneasy one. Everyone with whom I spoke placed primary importance on "moving" the listeners. Interaction with the listeners is a dynamic process, resulting in the listeners joining in the singing, adding shouts of encouragement and agreement during the course of the performance, tapping feet and clapping hands, crying, laughing, whatever the person is moved to do. But for the audience to sit quietly and passively, as is expected, for example, at a symphony concert, is generally taken as an indication that the performers have failed.

4. Strikingly similar is Pinkston's description of the explanations of the congregations he studied. "During the beginning of the prayer [during the Devotion] the congregation 'moans' the tunes. The worshippers feel that they are communicating with each other and with God, and that the devil can't

understand what they are singing" (1975: 74). In the case of the congregations discussed by Pinkston, moreover, it is the ultimate outsider—the Devil—who is excluded from the communication.

5. For a slightly different rendition by the same congregation, see track 1 on the LP *Moving in the Spirit* (1989).

6. On Dorsey see Michael W. Harris: 1992.

7. It is clear from the quotation of Leroy Thompson in chapter 2, however, that he considers her a blues singer (see p. 44).

8. Copyright 1971 by Colgens EMI Music. The song became hugely popular when it was recorded by James Taylor the following year.

9. As Ray Allen notes:

> Most major cities with sizable black populations boast at least one radio station that is partially or entirely devoted to gospel or inspirational music. Their playlists are dominated by mass choirs, by choir-backed soloists like James Cleveland, Shirley Caesar, and Timothy Wright, by contemporary, smooth sounding artists like Al Green, Andrae Crouch, the Winans, and the Hawkins Family, and by a handful of male quartets and female groups like the Mighty Clouds of Joy, the Jackson Southernaires, and the Clark Sisters (1991: 8).

In the absence of such dedicated radio stations, black congregations in smaller or more rural locations have typically acquired and expanded their Gospel repertoire by listening to similarly dedicated radio programmes. Despite the fact that much Gospel music is composed, copyrighted, and released commercially, most congregations (and many choirs), who are frequently not musically literate, acquire their repertoire through rote teaching.

10. Performance in African American religious music should be understood as the term is used in anthropology, by Bauman, for example. Below is his definition of "performance" in relation to oral narratives:

> I understand performance as a mode of communication, a way of speaking, the essence of which resides in the assumption of responsibility to an audience for a display of communicative skill, highlighting the way in which community is carried out, above and beyond its referential content (1986: 3).

11. For a discussion of the components which form the structural network for song interpretation in Gospel music, see Mellonee Burnim in (1985: 150–65).

12. See Paul Oliver's comments in this regard, quoted in the Introduction, p. 24.

13. When a church has a special programme, of which there are several throughout the year (for example, Harvest Day, Choir Day, Homecoming), the members invite other churches in the area, as well as churches that are farther away but somehow "tied" to the host church, perhaps through kinship ties. Usually at least one person from each of the invited churches will attend in order to "represent" that church.

14. Although Rev. McKinney frequently teases Lee Robinson and uses him as a "bad example" in church, it is a measure of their friendship that

this can be done without causing offence. He reminds the congregation from time to time that he would not dream of saying such things about deacon Robinson, if he for a moment suspected that they were true. If such were the case, he would approach him in private and talk to him about his waywardness.

15. I found many African Americans, especially in the South, to be suspicious of and opposed to any kind of psychological intervention. Deacon Leroy Thompson is one of the few with whom I talked who considered counselling to be a valuable tool. Because there has been so much exploitation of African Americans by psychologists, and so many racist studies proving the inferiority of African American people, it is natural, if unfortunate, that such a distrust should exist.

16. Preacher is what is intended here, as it is clear that the pastor, Rev. Grady McKinney, is also in attendance.

Chapter 4

1. Lee Earl Robinson's description is again strikingly similar to descriptions in Alfred Pinkston's 1975 study, concentrating on the states of Alabama, Georgia, and Florida prior to the mid 1960s.

2. Paternal grandmother is what is intended.

3. Again, characteristically similar for many small southern black communities: as Hans Baer has remarked, "practically all rural black churches in the South [. . .] suffered from the out-migration of people to the urban North as well as the cities of the South" (1985: 7).

4. This community is typical of many African American communities throughout the South. As Charles Reagan Wilson asserts, "[B]etween twenty and twenty-five per cent of all African-American churches are rural (a figure double the size of the black rural population), and churches in the nonmetropolitan South have the highest rates of membership among all African Americans" (1995: 167).

5. One of the salient features of African American spirituals is that they open with the chorus rather than the verse of the song (see Smith, 1983). The songs, therefore, have a chorus-verse strophic structure instead of the more usual verse-chorus structure.

6. This is not true of Main Street Baptist Church in Lexington, Ky., for example, where the membership is so large and the integrating influence of Rev. Baker so strong, that it is virtually impossible to imagine the church without him, despite the presence of five assistant ministers in the congregation. Nonetheless, by the time this book went to press, Rev. Baker had moved to another church.

7. During the 1830s, several treaties were signed with native North American peoples, the Choctaw and Chickasaw nations in this part of Mississippi. They were relocated in Oklahoma. See Dunbar Rowland (1925) and Mary Elizabeth Young (1961). As Rowland notes, "[T]he War Department estimated that about seven hundred and fifty heads of families remained in the State [Mississippi],

more than fifteen thousand Indians of that nation [Choctaw] having migrated westward by 1837. Descendants of these families are still in the State" (1925: 595). See also James Cobb (1992).

8. In contrast to the opinion expressed by Lee Robinson that credit is not extended to black people, Rev. McKinney seems to think that credit is available to everyone.

9. Deacon Thompson grew up about five miles from Oxford. His parents, Rochelle Thompson's grandparents, still live in the same house, although they have virtually stopped farming. When he married, Leroy Thompson moved to his wife's parish in Taylor, Mississippi, which is about six miles on the other side of Oxford. (He and George Price are the members who live furthest from the church.) He still attends Clear Creek M.B.C with his wife, Eulastine Thompson, and their two children, Greg and Pam.

10. As we will see in the following chapter, there is a strong West African basis for this intersection of the spiritual and material worlds.

Chapter 5

1. On the universality of trance, see Erika Bourguignon, 1973.

2. Rouget is here drawing on the work of the great linguistic structuralist, Ferdinand de Saussure (1857–1913), who, in his *Cours de linguistique générale* (Geneva, 1915, reprint, Paris, 1978), analysed a sign as constituted of two components: the concept (*signifiant*) and the acoustic image (*signifié*).

3. Rouget's note: "Or, sometimes, fallaciously. For it can happen not only that the trance is feigned, but also that the extraordinary powers attributed to it are merely illusionist's tricks. [. . .] However, this is merely a marginal and insignificant aspect of trance" (328n34).

4. A good example of possession in an African Diaspora culture is Brazilian *Candomblé*. A possession-devotee of the Yoruba god *Obalyaiye* "becomes" *Obaluaiye*. The possession-devotees of the gods in *Candomblé* dress in the clothes of the god—in the case of *Obaluaiye* an all-raffia crown decorated with cowry shells (*ade iko*), an all-raffia gown (*ewu iko*)—and carry the god's symbolic tool—in the case of *Obaluaiye* a broom (Farris Thompson, 1983: 61–68).

5. On this subject see also Ray Allen (1991: 12–13).

6. Scholars take opposing views on the significance of trance states. Sir Fredric Bartlett posits belief in the spiritual necessity of trance, as a characteristic of highly developed religions. "In a highly developed religion the religious experience may become of the most profound importance, and in the end it may even be the case that without it there is no religion for anybody" (1950: 25). M. Douglas, on the other hand, believes that trance is "symbolic of social dissociation, being the product of loose, permissive social conditions" (1970). While sceptical of hierarchical ranking of religious systems, I am in agreement with Bartlett that trance is certainly not exclusively a product of "loose, permissive social conditions" (Douglas, 1970).

7. There is a Pentecostal minister who attends Clear Creek's services quite regularly, as there are services at his church only every second and fourth Sunday, and at Clear Creek M.B.C. every first and third Sundays. That he has chosen

to attend Clear Creek M.B.C., with so many other churches in the immediate area, says a lot about the spirit in the church, and their relative closeness to Pentecostal/Holiness worship and doctrine.

8. This parallels the belief that Jeff Titon found amongst Primitive Baptists in the Blue Ridge Mountains: "Some false Christians, prophets, and preachers may fool people by appearing to be led by the Spirit; but Satan can animate persons also. Those preachers 'hop up and down and make a lot of noise,' but they are preaching for the devil" (1988: 337).

9. A preacher uses this same phrase ("You're not of yourself") in a dialogue that Alan Lomax collected and presented in *The Folksongs of North America* (1960: 462): "When the ole spirit hit you honey, I'm gonna tell you the truth, you're not of yourself. I've knowed it to trip people, send 'um to the floor." (No date, place, or time is given for the dialogue.)

10. "All power is given unto me in heaven and in earth" (Matthew 28:18).

11. "I will not leave you comfortless" (John 14:8).

"And I will pray the Father and he shall give you another Comforter, that he may abide with you forever" (John 14:16).

12. "But the Comforter, which is the Holy Ghost, whom the Father will send in my name, he shall teach you all things, and bring all things to your remembrance, whatsoever I have said unto you" (John 14:26).

13. "I am the way, the truth, and the life: no man cometh unto the Father but by me" (John 14:6).

14. Mechal Sobel takes up this point in relation to slavery and adds that it was not really that the slaves were worry-free at these meetings, but that the risk-taking itself intensified the experience. Secrecy and illegality in themselves added a very special dimension to black meetings. However, while a certain level of slave religion could have been maintained without secrecy, the slaves would not have been given permission to stay up all night when the following day was a workday, or to engage in what appeared to be African "devil dances." It was only by taking the risk of forbidden meetings that they could freely continue certain quasi-African traditions. The great numbers who took the risk and who were punished for it indicate how important a function these meetings played. The risk-taking itself was important (Reprint, 1988: 170).

15. In his book, *The Negro Church* (1903), W. E. B. du Bois listed a similar range of expression for the shout or the "frenzy," to use his term. "It varied in expression from the silent rapt countenance or the low murmur and moan to the mad abandon of physical fervor—the stamping, shrieking, and shouting, the rushing to and fro, and wild waving of arms, the weeping and laughing, the vision and the trance" (93).

16. This issue of leadership in the black church is, however, beginning to be challenged, both "on the ground" and in the literature. See, for example, Delores Carpenter (1989), Cheryl Townsend Gilkes (1994, 1997), Evelyn Higginbotham (1993, 1995, 1996), Betty Overton (1985), and the collection edited by Judith Weisenfeld and Richard Newman (1996).

17. "Likewise must the deacons be grave, not doubletongued, not given to too much wine, not greedy of filthy lucre, holding the mystery of the faith in a pure conscience. And let these also first be proved; then let them use the office of deacon, being found blameless. Even so must their wives be grave,

not slanderers, sober, faithful in all things. Let the deacons be the husbands of one wife, ruling their children and their own houses well" (1 Timothy 3:8–12).

18. For a more detailed discussion of this issue see Cheryl Gilkes, 1997.

19. Greg is referring to Rev. Kenneth Bonner. Bonner, who now pastors a church in Tennessee, is a dynamic and powerful speaker and was very well received when he preached at the Tallahatchie-Oxford Missionary Baptist convention, August 29, 1982. In 1988 the members still talked about the wonderful spirit that was in the church at the previous year's revival (1987) at which he had preached. Thirteen people were converted.

20. While not wishing to second guess Greg, it strikes me as likely that Rev. Bonner was chanting his prayer as, from the occasions on which I have seen him pray or preach, it is clear that he moves easily and quickly from speech to chant. On further review, it may be that I complicated the issue by using the word "music," as opposed to chanting or singing, for example. "Music" in this community, and indeed in many African American church communities, usually designates instrumental music, or accompaniment.

21. Although a preacher may get "happy in the Spirit," I have never seen one capitulate to the crisis of trance while preaching. It is typically the other members of the church who undergo this crisis. Rev. Benjamin Baker, pastor of Main Street Baptist Church in Lexington, occasionally begins a "dance" around the pulpit towards the end of his sermon. He does not, however, go into trance as Rouget has defined it, as it seems that he never loses consciousness of the congregation or of his situation. He may "move in the Spirit," but it does not, on these occasions, overwhelm him.

22. Prolonged repetition has the apparent psychological effect of "disengaging" the consciousness, allowing one to slip into a deeper level of the subconscious. As I mentioned before, it is a technique commonly used by psychiatrists to move patients into trance. It is also the essence of the ubiquitous swinging pendulum used in popular portrayals of hypnosis. Again the action is a simple and repetitive one.

Chapter 6

1. For some discussion of the historical background to and the differences between the various Baptist denominations, see Walter K. Knight (1993), and James Melvin Washington (1986), in addition to sources outlined in the Introduction.

2. Note that this phrase is picked up the following Sunday by Br. Johnson in the formulation of his prayer as he asks the Lord to unite the church in love (see appendix 2, part III, line 15).

3. See also Gerald L. Davis' book-length study (1985).

4. See appendix 2 for the complete text of this prayer (pp. 214–15).

5. For a complete musical transcription, see appendix 2 (pp. 217–21).

6. See appendix 2 (pp. 213–15) for the texts of two other prayers from this area of Mississippi. The first was delivered by a young deacon, also at the Tallahatchie-Oxford Convention. The second was delivered by an older pastor (he was then in his eighties) of a small rural church five miles outside of Oxford.

7. As Titon remarks, it is impossible to suggest a date of origin for this form.

Chanted and sung preaching is a tradition among black American Protestants, particularly Baptists. Its origins are unknown. Reports of evangelistic preaching during the first Great Awakening called attention to the "holy whine" of such ministers as George Whitefield, and it is possible that Baptist chanted preaching among white Americans today [. . .] derives from this "holy whine." Yet it seems to me that if Whitefield and the others had sung their sermons, observers would have said so. It may be that the sung sermon is the result of black Americans' African-based transformation of the chanted Baptist prayers and exhortations. This would clearly seem to be the case as regards the black Baptist tradition of sung and chanted prayers and sermons (1988: 309).

8. Rev. Bonner's prayer was so successful on one occasion that, when he had finished, the pastor remarked, "We have heard the sermon already." This comment might ordinarily be interpreted as chastisement for overstepping his place. However, as Rev. Bonner himself was to deliver the sermon on this occasion, the remark was most likely intended as a compliment.

Chapter 7

1. The Roper Organization survey of 1986 indicated that 66 percent of American adults got most of their news from TV and another 14 percent from radio. The Simmons Market Research Bureau studies, cited by Lawrence W. Lichty, 1989, 213, challenges this assertion.
2. See the discussion of current scholarship in the Introduction for a more comprehensive overview of this topic.
3. Significantly, Bishop Cleveland is the most fundamentalist of the three preachers who feature in Davis' study.
4. As Jeff Titon remarks:

narratives of the call to preach [. . .] conform to a general pattern. People notice that the future preacher is gifted with words, particularly when he gives testimony. Someone tells him, "I believe God is calling you to preach." Usually he has already realized it himself. He resists the call, sometimes for months or even years, not wanting to give up his way of life; but ultimately he becomes miserable and the burden becomes too great to bear. At that point he gives in and promises God that he will preach the gospel. The parallel with the conversion-narrative pattern is striking. [. . .] The fact that these narratives conform to a pattern suggests the possibility that they are learned. Certainly they are heard and could be learned (1988: 321).

5. This analogy, of course, has biblical foundation. Christ is reported to have said: "Man does not live by bread alone, but by every word that comes from the mouth of God."

6. For a detailed and thoughtful discussion of performance, the interested reader is referred to Titon (1988), particularly pp. 8–14. The following summary is worth excerpting.

> First, a performance is intentional. The people who perform [. . .] intend something by those performances. They intend to move people, and to do so in specific ways. [. . .] Second, a performance is rule-governed. In other words, certain rules or principles operate in any performance to guide exactly how it goes along. [. . .] One performs to affect oneself as well as others. [. . .] Performance is organized, coherent, and purposeful. In order to be that way it must proceed from a set of rules or principles. [. . .] Third, performance is not only intentional and rule-governed; it is also interpreted. Performers interpret their performance as they go along. [. . .] Interpretation involves evaluation—how effective is the performance? Evaluation frequently feeds back into performance: a poor one may be improved or even broken off. [. . .] Last, performance is keyed or marked. People who perform call attention to it as performance. [. . .] Beginnings and endings of performances are marked, and middles, too: extraordinary tones of voice, stylized movements, intent concentration, and so forth. [. . .] Performance is situated within a *community*, what folklorists call a folk group: those people who share affective performance and interpretation. [. . .] [T]he communication is face-to-face [. . .] Because of the shared framework and personal presence, there is a certain informality, and this is missing in encounters with people who are differently attuned. Finally, affective performance in a community is situated in *memory*. [. . .] When memory is made public and shared it can become community history (8–9).

7. Within this context Mary Sanches' definition of religious events is particularly apt. "Perhaps 'religious' events are recognisable by one set of receivers being 'gods,' 'spirits,' 'demons,' or others, where by definition the interpretation of what constitutes a response from them must be determined by other participants in the event" (Sanches and Blount, 1975: 169). This is also what Ray Allen is advocating for interpretation when he states:

> Spiritual experiences should not be reduced to mere physiological, psychological, or social/functional behaviors, as past anthropological studies of religion have tended to do. Rather an experience-centered ethnography of belief seeks to elicit descriptions and explanations of spiritual experience from the actual participants, to understand better that experience from an insider's perspective. Obviously this process demands moving beyond the simple reporting of religious behavior and organization into the realm of interpreting the personal and subjective dimensions of human feelings, expectations, and meanings (1991: 12–13).

8. Compare this statement to what Campbell had said earlier: "if it ain't no shouting, no Spirit in it" (Charles Campbell, interview, November 20, 1986).

9. For an almost opposed view of shouting, i.e., as necessary and beneficial, see the comments of Leroy Thompson in chapter 5.

10. For discussion and analysis of this sermon excerpt (and of an analogous sequence by Rev. Baker), see Thérèse Smith, 1998, especially 64–67.

11. For a slightly different rendition by the same congregation, see track 6 on the LP *Moving in the Spirit* (1989).

12. Very occasionally, the members sing "Amazing Grace" in the Devotion as a Dr. Watts, i.e., they line it out. But as the members almost always sing the song before the sermon, they do not usually sing it somewhere else in the service as well.

13. This was a special programme and, therefore, every speaker and event was introduced by the Master of Ceremonies of the day. This also partially accounts for the elaborate greeting, although Rev. McKinney sometimes uses it at ordinary services.

14. Visiting ministers sit with Rev. McKinney, and are often invited to say "a few words" before the dismissal.

15. For the complete text of this sermon, see appendix 3, pp. 222–28.

16. This is the 6 p.m. service on third Sundays. As I mentioned before, the members in general do not like evening service and do not come in large numbers.

17. For the complete text of this sermon, see appendix 3, pp. 229–33.

18. The issue of "positions" in African American churches is not an insignificant or non-contentious one. As Baer and Singer remark, "[R]egardless of their size and denominational affiliation, African-American congregations tend to exhibit elaborate political-religious structures with a multiplicity of offices and boards, auxiliaries, or committees" (1992: 80).

19. For the complete text of the sermon delivered at the morning service of this same day, see appendix 3, pp. 229–33.

20. For the complete text of this sermon, see appendix 3, pp. 234–42.

21. The interested reader is referred to Aretha Franklin's rendition of "Amazing Grace" with the California Community Choir on the 1972 album of the same name, Atlantic. One particularly effectively instance on this track occurs in the second verse on the line "It was Grace . . .," where Aretha persistently withholds the word "Grace."

22. An ethnodocumentary, *The Performed Word*, produced by Gerald L. Davis (Red Taurus Films, 1981), contains a small amount of footage focused on the visual context of the chanted sermon, concentrating on the visual interaction between preacher and congregation.

23. This belief that preaching is a gift from God directly parallels Paul Ricoeur's designation of preaching as sacramental because it is a "presentation of the holy Being" (Spiegelberg, 1981: 113).

Appendix 1

1. For an analogous and somewhat more detailed account of a service in an urban black Baptist church, see the synopsis in Baer and Singer, 1992: 82–86.

Appendix 3

1. Rev. McKinney lives in Batesville.

2. Rev. McKinney is referring to his conversion at the age of eleven. He was physically present in the church long before then.

3. "Singing in the Heavenly Choir" is a song recorded by the Canton Spiritual Singers. The song relates the story of an old man whom the choir director had not permitted to sing in church. The old man dies and is welcomed into the angelic choir in Heaven, where he can sing to his heart's content. The song was at this time (1986–87) receiving repeated airplay on the church membership's favourite gospel radio programme, *Highway to Heaven*, presented by Nate Russell and broadcast on WKRA, 92.7 FM, out of Holly Springs, Miss.

Bibliography

There are two parts to the bibliography:

1. Interviews
2. Bibliography

1. Interviews

All interviews were conducted by the author.

Baker, Rev. Benjamin S. Lexington, Kentucky. April 15, 1987.
Bonner, Herbert. Springhill, Mississippi. January 24, 1986.
Bonner, Sheila. Springhill, Mississippi. January 26, 1986.
Burt, Lovie. Springhill, Mississippi. November 24, 1987.
Campbell, Charles. Springhill, Mississippi. November 20, 1986.
Fox, Shirley. Springhill, Mississippi. November 10, 1986.
Jones, Sam. Springhill, Mississippi. November 23, 1986.
Jones, Sam. Springhill, Mississippi. November 24, 1987.
McKinney, Rev. Grady. Batesville, Mississippi. November 17, 1986.
Robinson, Lee Earl. Springhill, Mississippi. November 17, 1986.
Robinson, Lee Earl. Springhill, Mississippi. November 22, 1986.
Robinson, Lee Earl. Springhill, Mississippi. November 11, 1987.
Rogers, Marion. Lexington, Kentucky. January 8, 1987.
Smith, Joyce. Lexington, Kentucky. January 10, 1987.
Thompson, Gregory. Taylor, Mississippi. November 22, 1987.
Thompson, Leroy. Taylor, Mississippi. November 22, 1987.
Thompson, Pam. Taylor, Mississippi. November 22, 1987.
Thompson, Rochelle. Springhill, Mississippi. November 23, 1987.

2. Bibliography

Abbington, James, ed. and comp. 2001. *Readings in African American Church Music and Worship.* Chicago: GIA Publications, Inc.
Abingdon. 1981. *Songs of Zion.* Nashville, Tenn.: Parthenon Press.
Abrahams, Roger D. 1970. *Positively Black.* Englewood Cliffs, N.J.: Prentice Hall.
———. 1983. *The Man-of-Words in the West Indies: Performance and the Emergence of Creole Culture.* Baltimore, Md.: The John Hopkins Press.
Ahlstrom, Sydney E. 1972. *A Religious History of the American People.* New Haven, Conn.: Yale University Press.

Akin, Edward Nelson. 1984. "Mississippi." In *Encyclopaedia of Religion in the South*. Edited by Samuel S. Hill, Jr., 481–95. Macon, Ga.: Mercer.

Albert, Ethel M. 1964. "Rhetoric, Logic and Poetics in Burundi: Culture Patterning of Speech Behaviour." *American Anthropologist* 66 (6): 35–54.

Allen, Ray. 1991. *Singing in the Spirit: African-American Sacred Quartets in New York City*. Philadelphia: University of Pennsylvania Press.

Allen, William F., et al. 1867. *Slave Songs of the United States*. Reprint, New York: Peter Smith, 1951.

Allport, Gordon W. 1958. *The Nature of Prejudice*. Garden City, N.Y.: Doubleday Anchor Books, Doubleday and Company.

Ames, Russell. 1960. *The Story of American Folk Song*. New York: Grosset and Dunlap.

Ammerman, Nancy Tatom. 1987. *Bible Believers: Fundamentalists in the Modern World*. New Brunswick, N.J.: Rutgers University Press.

———, ed. 1993. *Southern Baptists Observed: Multiple Perspectives on a Changing Denomination*. Knoxville: University of Tennessee Press.

Anderson, James D. 1988. *The Education of Blacks in the South, 1806–1935*. Chapel Hill: University of North Carolina Press.

Anderson, Victor. 1995. *Beyond Ontological Blackness: An Essay of African American Religious and Cultural Criticism*. New York: Continuum.

Angell, Stephen Ward. 1992. *Bishop Henry McNeal Turner and African-American Religion in the South*. Knoxville: University of Tennessee Press.

Archer, Chalmers, Jr. 1992. *Growing Up Black in Rural Mississippi*. New York: Walker and Company.

Ardener, Edwin, ed. 1971. *Social Anthropology and Language*. London: Tavistock Publications.

Aschoff, Peter R. 2001. "The Poetry of the Blues: Understanding the Blues in Its Cultural Context." In *The Triumph of the Soul: Cultural and Psychological Aspects of African American Music*. Edited by Ferdinand and Arthur C. Jones, 35–68. Westport, Conn., and London: Praeger.

Attali, Jacques. 1985. *Noise: The Political Economy of Music*. Minneapolis: University of Minnesota Press.

Baal, J. Van. 1971. *Symbols for Communication: An Introduction to the Anthropological Study of Religion*. N.V. Assen, The Netherlands: Van Garcum and Company.

Baer, Hans A. 1981. *The Black Spiritual Movement: A Religious Response to Racism*. Knoxville: University of Tennessee Press.

———. 1985. "An Overview of Ritual, Oratory and Music in Southern Black Religion." *The Southern Quarterly: A Journal of the Arts in the South*. Special issue on Black Religion in the American South in the Twentieth Century: 5–14.

Baer, Hans A., and Merrill Singer. 1992. *African-American Religion in the Twentieth Century: Varieties of Protest and Accommodation*. Knoxville: University of Tennessee Press.

Bailey, Ben. 1978. "The Lined-Hymn Tradition in Black Mississippi Churches." *The Black Perspective in Music* 6 (1): 3–11.

Baker, David N. 1973. "A Periodization of Black Music History." In *Reflections on Afro-American Music*. Edited by Dominique René de Lerma, 143–60. Kent, Ohio: Kent State University Press.

Baklanoff, Joy Driskell. 1987. "The Celebration of a Feast: Music, Dance, Possession Trance in the Black Primitive Baptist Footwashing Ritual." *Ethnomusicology* 31: 381–94.

———. 1991. "Traditional Black Musical Events in West Alabama & Northeast Mississippi, 1940–1960: A Classificatory Descriptive Perspective." In *Essays in Honor of Frank J Gillis*. Edited by Nancy Cassell McEntire, 127–50. Bloomington, Ind.: Ethnomusicology Publications Group.

Ballanta-Taylor, Nicholas George Jules. 1925. *Saint Helena Island Spirituals*. New York: G. Schirmer.

Baptist Standard Hymnal. 1961. Nashville, Tenn.: Townsend Press.

Barth, Fredrik. 1969. *Ethnic Groups and Boundaries: The Social Organization of Culture Difference*. Boston: Little, Brown and Company.

Bartlett, Sir Fredric. 1950. *Religion as Experience, Belief, Action*. London: Oxford University Press.

Barz, Gregory F., and Timothy J. Cooley, eds. 1997. *Shadows in the Field: New Perspectives for Fieldwork in Ethnomusicology*. New York and Oxford: Oxford University Press.

Bastide, R. 1971. *African Civilizations in the New World*. Translated by Peter Green. Foreword by Geoffrey Parrinder. New York: Harper and Row.

Bauman, Richard. 1983. *Let Your Words Be Few*. Cambridge: Cambridge University Press.

———. 1986. *Story, Performance and Event: Contextual Studies of Oral Narrative*. Cambridge: Cambridge University Press.

Beattie, John, and John Middleton, eds. 1969. *Spirit Mediumship and Society in Africa*. New York: Africana Publishing Corporation.

Beeman, William O. 1976. "You can take music out of the country, but, . . .: The Dynamics of Change in Iranian Musical Tradition." *Asian Music* 7: 6–19.

Benjamin, Walter. 1969. *Illuminations*. New York: Schocken.

Berger, Peter L. 1967. *The Sacred Canopy: Elements of a Sociological Theory of Religion*. Garden City, N.Y.: Doubleday and Company.

Bergeron, Katherine A., and Philip V. Bohlman, eds. 1991. *Disciplining Music: Musicology and Its Canons*. Chicago: University of Chicago Press.

Berliner, Paul. 1994. *Thinking in Jazz: The Infinite Art of Improvisation*. Chicago: University of Chicago Press.

Berry, Mary Frances, and John W. Blassingame. 1982. *Long Memory: The Black Experience in America*. New York: Oxford University Press.

Bethel, Leonard L., and Frederick A. Johnson, eds. 1998. *Plainfield's African-American: From Northern Slavery to Church Freedom*. Lanham, Md.: University Press of America.

Billingsley, Andrew. 1968. *Black Families in White America*. Englewood Cliffs, N.J.: Prentice Hall, Inc.

Blacking, John. 1969. "The Value of Music in Human Experience." *Yearbook of the IFMC* 1: 33–71.

Blacking, John. 1971. "Deep and Surface Structures in Venda Music." *Yearbook of the IFMC* 3: 91–108.

———. 1973. *How Musical is Man?* Seattle: University of Washington Press.

———. 1977. "Some Problems of Theory and Method in the Study of Musical Change." *Yearbook of the IFMC* 9: 1–26.

———. 1980. "Political and Musical Freedom in the Music of Some Black South African Churches." In *The Structure of Folk Models*. Edited by Ladislav Holy and Milan Stuchlik, 36–62. ASA Monographs, 20. London: Academic Press.

———. 1994. *Music, Culture and Experience: Selected Papers of John Blacking*. Edited by Reginald Byron. Chicago: University of Chicago Press.

Bloom, Allan David. 1987. *The Closing of the American Mind*. New York: Simon and Schuster.

Blu, Karen I. 1980. *The Lumbee Problem: The Making of an American Indian People*. London: Cambridge University Press.

Blum, Stephen, Philip V. Bohlman, and Daniel M. Newman, eds. 1991. *Ethnomusicology and Modern Music History*. Urbana: University of Illinois Press.

Boatner, Edward, arr. 1973. *The Story of the Spirituals: 30 Spirituals and Their Origins*. [New York]: McAfee Music Corp.; exclusively distributed by Lorenz Industries, Dayton, Ohio.

Bodkin, Maud. 1934. *Archetypal Patterns in Poetry: Psychological Studies of Imagination*. New York: Oxford University Press.

Boles, John B. 1972. *The Great Revival, 1787–1805: The Origins of the Southern Evangelical Mind*. Lexington: University Press of Kentucky.

———. 1976. *Religion in Antebellum Kentucky*. Lexington: University of Kentucky Press.

———. 1983. *Black Southerners, 1619–1869*. Lexington: University Press of Kentucky.

———, ed. 1988. *Masters and Slaves in the House of the Lord: Race and Religion in the American South, 1740–1870*. Lexington: University Press of Kentucky.

———, ed. 2001. *Autobiographical Reflections on Southern Religious History*. Athens and London: University of Georgia Press.

Boles, John B., and Evelyn Thomas Nolen, eds. 1987. *Interpreting Southern History: Historiographical Essays in Honor of Sanford W. Higginbotham*. Baton Rouge: Louisiana State University Press.

Bolton, Charles C. 2000. "Mississippi's School Equalization Program, 1945–1954: A Last Gasp to Try to Maintain a Segregated Educational System." *Journal of Southern History* 66 (4): 781–814.

Bourguignon, Erika. 1973. "Introduction: A Framework for the Comparative Study of Altered States of Consciousness." In *Religion, Altered States of Consciousness and Social Change*. Edited by Erika Bourguignon, 3–38. Columbus: Ohio State University Press.

Boyer, Horace. 1973. "An Analysis of Black Church Music with Examples Drawn from Services in Rochester, New York." Ph.D. diss., University of Rochester, Eastman School of Music.

Boyer, Horace. 1979. "Contemporary Gospel: Sacred or Secular?" *The Black Perspective in Music* 7 (1): 5–58.

———. 1983. "Charles Albert Tindley: Progenitor of Black-American Music." *The Black Perspective in Music* 11 (1): 103–32.

———. 1985. "A comparative analysis of traditional and contemporary Gospel music." In *More than Dancing: Essays on Afro-American Music & Musicians*. Edited by Irene Jackson, 127–45. Westport, Conn.: Greenwood Press.

———. 1995. *How Sweet the Sound: The Golden Age of Gospel*. Washington, D.C.: Elliott and Clark Publishing.

Boylan, Anne M. 1988. *Sunday School: The Formation of an American Institution, 1790–1880*. New Haven, Conn.: Yale University Press.

Bril, Jacques. 1977. *Symbolisme et civilisation: Essai sur l'efficacité anthropologique de l'imaginaire*. Paris: Librairie H. Champion.

Brown, William Wells. 1880. *My Southern Home: Of the South and Its People*. Boston: A. G. Brown and Co.

Brundage, W. Fitzhugh, ed. 2000. *Where These Memories Grow: History, Memory, and Southern Identity*. Chapel Hill: University of North Carolina Press.

Burnim, Mellonee V. 1980. "The Black Gospel Tradition: Symbol of Ethnicity." Ph.D. diss., Indiana University.

———. 1985. "The Black Gospel Music Tradition: A Complex of Ideology, Aesthetic, and Behavior." In *More than Dancing: Essays on Afro-American Music & Musicians*. Edited by Irene Jackson, 150–65. Westport, Conn.: Greenwood Press.

———. 1985. "Culture Bearer and Tradition Bearer: An Ethnomusicologist's Research on Gospel Music." *Ethnomusicology* 29 (3): 432–47.

Burt, Jessee and Duane Allen. 1971. *The History of Gospel Music*. Nashville, Tenn.: K and S Press.

Butler, Melvin. 2002. " 'Nou Kwe nan Sentespri' (We Believers in the Holy Spirit): Music, Ecstasy, and Identity in Haitian Pentecostal Worship." *Black Music Research Journal* 22 (1): 85–125.

Caldwell, Erskine. 1995. *Deep South: Memory and Observation*. Athens and London: University of Georgia Press.

Campbell, Joseph, ed. 1970. *Myths, Dreams and Religion*. New York: E. P. Dutton.

Caponi, Gena Dagel. 1999. *Signifyin(g), Sanctifyin' and Slam Dunking: A Reader in African American Expressive Culture*. Amherst: University of Massachusetts Press.

Carpenter, Delores C. 1989. "Black Women in Religious Institutions: A Historical Summary from Slavery to the 1960s." *Journal of Religious Thought* 46 (2): 7–27.

Carpenter, Joel A. 1984. "Evangelical Protestantism." In *Encyclopaedia of Religion in the South*. Edited by Samuel S. Hill, Jr., 239–43. Macon, Ga.: Mercer.

Carr-Hamilton, Jacqueline D. 1996. "Motherwit in Southern Religion: A Womanist Perspective." In *Ain't Gonna Lay My 'ligion Down: African*

American Religion in the South. Edited by Alonzo Johnson and Paul Jersild, 72–86. Columbia: University of South Carolina Press.

Carter, Harold A. 1976. *The Prayer Tradition of Black People.* Valley Forge, Pa.: Judson Press.

Caton, William. 1689. *A Journal of the Life of . . . Will Caton.* London.

Ceschi, Matteo. 2003. "Between 'U.S.': Legacy of the Sixties in the Art of Tupac Shakur." Paper read at "Keeping the Beat: Music, Cultures, Societies," a Milan Group seminar. Milan, Italy, October 29–30, 2003.

Chandos, John. 1971. *In God's Name: Examples of Preaching in England from the Act of Supremacy to the Act of Uniformity, 1534–1662.* London: Hutchinson.

Chapman, Mark L. 1996. *Christianity on Trial: African-American Religious Thought before and after Black Power.* Maryknoll, N.Y.: Orbis Books.

Chase, Gilbert. 1987. *America's Music: From the Pilgrims to the Present.* 3rd edition. Urbana: University of Illinois Press.

Childs, John Brown. 1980. *The Political Black Minister: A Study in Afro-American Politics and Religion.* Boston: G. K. Hall.

Christian, William. 1987. *Doctrines of Religious Communities: A Philosophical Study.* New York: Plenum Press.

Cleage, Albert B., Jr. 1974. "A New Time Religion." In *The Black Experience in Religion.* Edited by C. Eric Lincoln, 168–80. New York: Anchor Press/Doubleday.

Cobb, James C. 1992. *The Most Southern Place on Earth: The Mississippi Delta and the Roots of Regional Identity.* New York: Oxford University Press.

Cohen, Abner, ed. 1974. *Urban Ethnicity.* London: Tavistock.

Cohen, Ronald. 1978. "Ethnicity: Problem and Focus in Anthropology." *Annual Review of Anthropology* 7: 379–403.

Coleman, C. D. 1974. "A New Time Religion." In *The Black Experience in Religion.* Edited by C. Eric Lincoln, 188–95. New York: Anchor Press/Doubleday.

Cone, James H. 1974. "The Sources and Norms of Black Theology." In *The Black Experience in Religion.* Edited by C. Eric Lincoln, 110–27. New York: Anchor Press/Doubleday.

———. 1984. *For My People: Black Theology and the Black Church.* Maryknoll, N.Y.: Orbis.

———. 1995. "Martin and Malcolm: Integrationism and Nationalism in African-American Religious History." In *Religion and American culture.* Edited by David G Hackett, 407–21. New York: Routledge.

Conser, Walter H., Jr. 1993. *God and the Natural World: Religion and Science in Antebellum America.* Columbia: University of South Carolina Press.

Conyers, J. L., Jr. 2001. *African American Jazz and Rap.* Jefferson, N.C., and London: McFarland and Company.

Cook, Philip S., Douglas Gomery, and Lawrence W. Lichty, eds. 1989. *American Media.* Washington, D.C.: The Wilson Center Press.

Cooper-Lewter, Nicholas C., and Henry H. Mitchell, 1986. *Soul Theology: The Heart of American Black Culture.* San Francisco, Calif.: Harper and Row.

Cross, W. E., Jr. 1991. *Shades of Black: Diversity in African-American Identity*. Philadelphia: Temple University Press.

Cross, W. E. Jr., T. A. Parham, and J. E. Helms. 1991. "The Stages of Black Identity Development: Negresence Models." In *Black Psychology*. Edited by Reginald L. Jones, 319–38. Berkeley, Calif.: Cobb & Henry.

Cusic, Don. 1990. *The Sound of Light: A History of Gospel Music*. Bowling Green, Ohio: Bowling Green State University Popular Press.

Daniel, Pete. 1986. *Standing at the Crossroads: Southern Life in the Twentieth Century*. New York: Hill and Wang.

Dargan, William Thomas, and Kathy White Bullock. 1996. "Willie Mae Ford Smith of St. Louis: A Shaping Influence upon Black Gospel Singing Style." In *This Far by Faith: Readings in African-American Women's Religious Biography*. Edited by Judith Weisenfeld and Richard Newman, 32–51. New York: Routledge.

Davis, Angela Y. 1981. *Women, Race and Class*. New York: Vintage Books.

Davis, D. B. 1966. *The Problem of Slavery in Western Culture*. Ithaca, N.Y.: Cornell University Press.

Davis, Gerald L. 1985. *I Got the Word in Me and I Can Sing It, You Know: A Study of the Performed African-American Sermon*. Philadelphia: University of Pennsylvania Press.

Dayton, Donald W., and Robert K. Johnston, eds. 1991. *The Variety of American Evangelicalism*. Knoxville: University of Tennessee Press.

Degler, C. N. 1971. *Neither Black nor White: Slavery and Race Relations in Brazil and the United States*. New York: Macmillan.

de Lerma, Dominique-René. 1970. *Black Music in Our Culture: Curricular Ideas on the Subjects, Materials and Problems*. Kent, Ohio: Kent State University Press.

———. 1973. *Black Music and Musicians in the New Grove Dictionary of American Music and the New Harvard Dictionary of Music*. Chicago: Center for Black Music Research, Columbia College.

———. 1973. *Reflections on Afro-American Music*. Kent, Ohio: Kent State University Press.

Dett, R. Nathaniel. 1959. *Dett Negro Spirituals*. London: Blanford Press.

DjeDje, Jacqueline Cogdell. 1978. *American Black Spiritual and Gospel Songs from Georgia: A Comparative Study*. Los Angeles: Center for Afro-American Studies, University of California, Monograph Series.

———. 1986. "Change and Differentiation: The Adaptation of Black American Gospel Music in the Catholic Church." *Ethnomusicology* 30 (2): 223–52.

DjeDje, Jacqueline Cogdell, and Eddie S. Meadows, eds. 1998. *California Soul: Music of African Americans in the West*. Berkeley and Los Angeles: University of California Press.

Douglas, M. Mary. 1970. *Natural Symbols: Explorations in Cosmology*. London: Barrie & Rockliff, the Cresset Press.

du Bois, W. E. B. 1903. *The Negro Church*. Atlanta: Atlanta Press.

———. 1967. "Of the Sorrow Song." In *The Negro in Music and Art*. Edited by Lindsay Patterson, 9–14. International Library of Negro Life and History. New York: Publishers Company Inc.

Duncan, Curtin Daniel. 1979. *A Historical Survey of the Development of the Black Baptist Church in the United States and a Study of Performance Practices Associated with Dr. Watts Hymn Singing: A Source Book for Teaching*. Ph.D. diss., Washington University.

Durkheim, Emile. 1915. *The Elementary Forms of the Religious Life*. Translated by Joseph Ward Swain. Reprint, New York: Free Press, 1965.

Dvorka, Katherine L. 1991. *An African-American Exodus: The Segregation of the Southern Churches*. Brooklyn, N.Y.: Carlson Publishers.

Dyson, M. E. 1993. *Reflecting Black: African-American Cultural Criticism*. Minneapolis: University of Minnesota Press.

Eighmy, John Lee. 1972. *Churches in Cultural Captivity: A History of the Social Attitudes of Southern Baptists*. Knoxville: University of Tennessee Press.

Ekwueme, Lazarus. 1974. "African-Music Retentions in the New World." *The Black Perspective in Music* 2 (2): 128–44.

Eliade, Mircea. 1959. *Le shamanisme et les techniques archaïques de l'extase*. 2nd edition. Paris: Payot.

———. 1963. *Myth and Reality*. New York: Harper and Row.

Elliott, Emory. 1975. *Power and the Pulpit in Puritan New England*. Princeton, N.J.: Princeton University Press.

Ellison, Mary. 1989. *Lyrical Protest: Black Music's Struggle against Discrimination*. New York: Praeger.

Epstein, Dena. 1977. *Sinful Tunes and Spirituals*. Chicago: University of Chicago Press.

Evans, David. 1977. "Musical Practices in Black Churches of Philadelphia and New York, ca. 1800–1844." *Journal of the American Musicological Society* 30 (2): 296–312.

———. 1978. "Music in the Black Church." *Journal of Church Music* 20: 2–6.

Evans, Rod L., and Irwin M Berent. 1988. *Fundamentalism: Hazards and Heartbreaks*. La Salle, Ill.: Open Court Press.

Feld, Steven. 1982. *Sound and Sentiment: Birds, Weeping and Song in Kaluli Expression*. Philadelphia: University of Pennsylvania Press.

———. 1984. "Sound Structure as Social Structure." *Ethnomusicology* 28 (3): 383–410.

Fenner, Thomas P. 1874. *Cabin and Plantation Songs As Sung by the Hampton Students*. Hampton, Va.: The Institute Press.

Fernandez, Ronald Louis. 1977. "An Assessment of Fredrik Barth's Theory of Ethnicity." In *Symbols: Public and Private*. Edited by Raymond Firth. Ithaca, N.Y.: Cornell University Press.

Firth, Raymond, ed. 1973. *Symbols: Public and Private*. London: George Allen and Unwin.

Fisher, Miles Mark. 1953. *Negro Slave Songs in the United States*. New York: Citadel Press.

Floyd, Samuel A. 1987. *Black Music Biography: An Annotated Bibliography*. White Plains, N.Y.: Kraus International Publications.

Flynt, Wayne. 1981. "One in the Spirit, Many in the Flesh: Southern Evangelicals." In *Varieties of Southern Evangelicalism*. Edited by David Edwin Harrell, Jr., 23–24. Macon, Ga.: Mercer University Press.

Franklin, C. L. 1989. *Give Me this Mountain: Life History and Selected Sermons of C. L. Franklin (1915–1984).* Edited by Jeff T. Titon. Urbana: University of Illinois Press.

Franklin, John Hope, ed. 1968. *Color and Race.* Boston: Beacon Press.

Franklin, Robert Michael. 1989. "Church and City: Black Christianity's Ministry." *The Christian Ministry* 20 (2).

———. 1994. "The Safest Place on Earth: The Culture of Black Congregations." In *American Congregations.* Edited by James P. Wind and James J. Lewis, 2: 257–84. Chicago: University of Chicago Press.

Fraser, Walter J., Jr., R. Frank Saunders, Jr., and John L. Wakelyn, eds. 1985. *The Web of Southern Social Relations: Women, Family and Education.* Athens: University of Georgia Press.

Frazier, E. Franklin. 1939. *The Negro Family in the United States.* Chicago: University of Chicago Press.

———. 1957. *Black Bourgeosie: The Rise of a New Middle Class in the United States.* New York: Collier Books, A Division of Macmillan Publishing Co.

———. 1968. *On Race Relations.* Chicago: University of Chicago Press.

Frederickson, George M. 1971. *The Black Image in the White Mind.* New York: Harper and Row.

———. 1981. *White Supremacy: A Comparative Study in American and South African History.* New York: Oxford University Press.

Frey, Sylvia R., and Betty Wood. 1998. *Come Shouting to Zion: African American Protestantism in the American South and British Caribbean to 1830.* Chapel Hill and London: University of North Carolina Press.

Friedman, Jean E. 1985. *The Enclosed Garden: Women and Community in the Evangelical South, 1830–1900.* Chapel Hill: University of North Carolina Press.

Fulop, Timothy E., and Albert J. Raboteau, eds. 1997. *African-American Religion: Interpretive Essays in History and Culture.* New York: Routledge.

Garcia, William Barnes. 1973. "Church Music by Black Composers." *The Black Perspective in Music* 2 (2): 145–57.

Geertz, Clifford. 1965. "Religion as a Cultural System." In *Reader in Comparative Religion: An Anthropological Approach.* Edited by William A. Lessa and Evon Z. Vogt, 205–15. White Plains, N.Y.: Row, Peterson and Company.

———. 1973. *The Interpretation of Cultures: Selected Essays by Clifford Geertz.* New York: Basic Books, Inc.

Genovese, Eugene D. 1969. *The World the Slaveholders Made.* New York: Pantheon Books.

———. 1972. *Roll, Jordan, Roll: The World the Slaves Made.* New York: Vintage Books.

Gerard, C. 1998. *Jazz in Black and White: Race, Culture and Identity in the Jazz Community.* Westport, Conn.: Praeger.

Gilkes, Cheryl Townsend. 1994. "The Politics of 'Silence': Dual-Sex Political Systems and Women's Traditions of Conflict in African-American Religion." In *African-American Christianity: Essays in History.* Edited by

Paul E. Johnson. 80–110. Berkeley and Los Angeles: University of California Press.

———. 1997. "The Roles of Church and Community Mothers: Ambivalent American Sexism or Fragmented African Familyhood?" In *African-American Religion: Interpretive Essays in History and Culture*. Edited by Timothy E. Fulop and Albert J. Raboteau, 365–88. New York: Routledge.

Gilkey, Langdon. 1994. "The Christian Congregation as a Religious Community." In *American Congregations*. Edited by James P. Wind and James J. Lewis, 2: 100–32. Chicago: University of Chicago Press.

Gillen, Gerard, and Harry White, eds. 1993. *Music and the Church*. Irish Musical Studies, vol. 2. Dublin: Irish Academic Press.

Glazier, Stephen D., ed. 2001. *Encyclopedia of African and African-American Religions*. New York and London: Routledge.

Gluckman, Max, 1961. "Anthropological Problems Arising from the African Industrial Revolution." In *Social Change in Modern Africa*. Edited by A. Southall, 67–82. Oxford: Oxford University Press.

Godwin, Morgan. 1680. *The Negro's and Indian's Advocate, Suing for Their Admission into the Church. . . .* London.

Goodman, Mary Ellen. 1952. *Race Awareness in Young Children*. New York: Collier Books.

Goody, Esther N. 1972. "Greeting, Begging and the Presentation of Respect." In *The Interpretation of Ritual*. Edited by J. S. La Fontaine, 39–71. London: Tavistock.

———, ed. 1978. "Towards a Theory of Questions." In *Questions and Politeness: Strategies in Social Interaction*, 17–43. Cambridge: Cambridge University Press.

Gordon, E. W. 1995. "Putting Them in Their Place." *Readings: A Journal of Reviews and Commentary in Mental Health* 10 (1): 8–14.

Goveia, E. 1966. "Comment on 'Anglicanism, Catholicism, and the Negro Slave.'" *Comparative Studies in Society and History* 8: 328–30.

Grattan, John. 1720. *Journal of the life of . . . John Gratton*. London.

Gratus, J. 1977. *The Great White Lie: Slavery, Emancipation, and Changing Racial Attitudes*. New York: Monthly Review Press.

Gravely, William B. 1995. "The Dialectic of Double-Consciousness in Black American Freedom." In *Religion and American Culture*. Edited by David G. Hackett, 109–26. New York: Routledge.

Grier, William J., M.D., and Price N. Cobbs, M.D. 1928. *Black Rage*. New York: Basic Books Inc.

Groneman, Carol, and Mary Beth Norton, eds. 1987. *'To Toil the Livelong Day': America's Women at Work, 1780–1980*. Ithaca, N.Y.: Cornell University Press.

Grossman, James R. 1989. *Land of Hope: Chicago, Black Southerners, and Great Migration*. Chicago: University of Chicago Press.

Grout, Donald Jay, and Claude Palisca. 1988. *A History of Western Music*. 4th ed. London: J. M. Dent and Sons.

Guthrie, Robert V. 1976. *Even the Rat was White: A Historical View of Psychology*. New York: Harper and Row.

Gutman, Herbert G. 1977. *The Black Family in Slavery and Freedom, 1750–1925*. New York: Vintage Books.

Hacker, Andrew. 1992. *Two Nations Black and White, Separate, Hostile, Unequal*. New York: Charles Scribner's Sons.

Hackett, David G., ed. 1995. *Religion and American Culture*. New York: Routledge.

Hadden, Jeffrey K., and Theodore E. Long, eds. 1983. *Religion and Religiosity in America: Studies in Honor of Joseph H. Fichter*. New York: Crossroad.

Hagedorn, Katherine J. 2001. *Divine Utterances: The Performance of Afro-Cuban Santeria*. Washington and London: Smithsonian Institution Press.

Hall, C. S., and G. Lindzey. 1957. *Theories of Personality*. New York: Wiley.

Hammond, Philip E. 1992. *The Protestant Presence in Twentieth-Century America: Religion and Political Culture*. Albany: State University of New York Press.

Harding, Vincent. 1981. *There Is a River: The Black Struggle for Freedom in America*. New York: Vintage Books.

Harrell, David Edwin, Jr. 1981. "The South: Seedbed of Sectarianism." In *Varieties of Southern Evangelicalism*. Edited by David Edwin Harrell, Jr., 45–57. Macon, Ga.: Mercer University Press.

———, ed. 1981. *Varieties of Southern Evangelicalism*. Macon, Ga.: Mercer University Press.

Harris, Marvin. 1964. *Patterns of Race in the Americas*. New York: Walker.

Harris, Michael W. 1992. *The Rise of Gospel Blues: The Music of Thomas Andrew Dorsey in the Urban Church*. New York: Oxford University Press.

Hayes, Roland. 1948. *My Songs, Aframerican Religious Songs*. Arranged and interpreted by Roland Hayes. Boston: Little, Brown and Company.

Heilbut, Tony. 1971. *The Gospel Sound: Good News and Bad Times*. New York: Simon and Schuster.

Helms, J. E. 1990. *Black and White Racial Identity: Theory, Research, and Practice*. Westport, Conn.: Greenwood Press.

Henri, Florette. 1975. *Black Migration: Movement North, 1900–1920*. Garden City, N.Y.: Anchor Press/Doubleday.

Herskovits, Melville Jean. 1941. *The Myth of the Negro Past*. New York: Harper and Brothers.

Hicks, G., and P. Leis, eds. 1977. *Ethnic Encounters: Identities and Contexts*. North Scituate, Mass.: Duxbury Press.

Higginbotham, A. L. 1978. *In the Matter of Color: Race and the North American Legal Process*. New York: Oxford University Press.

Higginbotham, Evelyn Brooks. 1993. *Righteous Discontent: The Women's Movement in the Black Baptist Church, 1880–1920*. Cambridge, Mass.: Harvard University Press.

———. 1995. "The Feminist Theology of the Black Baptist Church." In *Religion and American Culture*. Edited by David G Hackett, 343–63. New York: Routledge.

———. 1996. "Religion, Politics, and Gender: The Leadership of Nannie Helen Burroughs." In *This Far by Faith: Readings in African-American*

Women's Religious Biography. Edited by Judith Weisenfeld and Richard Newman, 140–57. New York: Routledge.

Hill, Samuel S., Jr. 1966. *Southern Churches in Crisis*. New York: Holt, Reinhart and Winston.

———. 1980. *The South and the North in American Religion*. Athens: University of Georgia Press.

———. 1981. "The Shape and Shapes of Popular Southern Piety." In *Varieties of Southern Evangelicalism*. Edited by David Edwin Harrell, Jr., 89–114. Macon, Ga.: Mercer University Press.

———. 1996. *One Name but Several Faces: Variety in Popular Christian Denominations in Southern History*. Athens: University of Georgia Press.

———. 2001. "Southern Religion and the Southern Religious." In *Autobiographical Reflections on Southern Religious History*. Edited by John B. Boles, 1–16. Athens and London: University of Georgia Press.

Hill, Samuel S., Jr., ed. 1972. *Religion and the Solid South*. Nashville, Tenn.: Abingdon Press.

———, ed. 1984. *Encyclopaedia of Religion in the South*. Macon, Ga.: Mercer.

———, ed. 1988. *Varieties of Southern Religious Experience*. Baton Rouge: Louisiana State University Press.

History of the Tallahatchie-Oxford Missionary Baptist District Association. 1986. Oxford, Miss.

Holloway, Joseph E., ed. 1990. *Africanisms in American Culture*. Bloomington: Indiana University Press.

Holloway, Joseph E., and Winifred K. Vass, eds. 1993. *The African Heritage of American English*. Bloomington: Indiana University Press.

Horowitz, E. L., and R. E. Horowitz. 1936. "Development of Social Attitudes in Children." *Sociometry* 1.

Hubbard, Dolan. 1986. *Preaching the Lord's Word in a Strange Land: The Influence of the Black Preaching Style on Black American Prose Fiction*. Microfilm.

———. 1994. *The Sermon and the African American Literary Imagination*. Columbia: University of Missouri Press.

Hufford, David. 1982. *The Terror That Comes in the Night*. Philadelphia: University of Pennsylvania Press.

Hurston, Zora Neale. 1976. "Spirituals and Neo-Spirituals." In *The Negro in Music and Art*. Edited by Lindsay Patterson, 15–18. New York: Publishers Company Inc.

Hymes, Dell. 1971. "Sociolinguistics and the Ethnography of Speaking." In *Social Anthropology and Language*. Edited by Edwin Ardener, 47–93. London: Tavistock Publications.

Inman, David A. 1968. "The Ontological Anthropology of Paul Tillich." Ph.D. diss., Université Catholique de Louvain, Institut supérieur de philosophie.

Jackson, George Pullen. 1943. *White and Negro Spirituals: Their Lifespan and Kinship*. New York: J. J. Augustin.

Jackson, Irene V., comp. 1979. *Afro-American Religious Music: A Bibliography and a Catalogue of Gospel Music.* Westport, Conn.: Greenwood Press.

———, ed. 1985. *More than Dancing: Essays on Afro-American Music & Musicians.* Westport, Conn.: Greenwood Press.

———, ed. 1985. *More than Drumming: Essays on African and Afro-Latin American Music and Musicians.* [Howard University.] Westport, Conn.: Greenwood Press.

Jackson, Joyce. 1988. "The Performing Black Sacred Quartet: An Expression of Cultural Values and Aesthetics." Ph.D. diss., Indiana University.

Jackson, Michael R. 1984. *Self Esteem and Meaning: A Life-Historical Investigation.* Albany: State University of New York Press.

Jenkins, Adelbert J. 1982. *The Psychology of the Afro-American: A Humanist Approach.* New York: Pergamon Press.

Johnson, Alonzo, and Paul Jersild, eds. 1996. *Ain't Gonna Lay My 'ligion Down: African American Religion in the South.* Columbia: University of South Carolina Press.

Johnson, F. Earnest, ed. 1955. *Religious Symbolism.* New York: Institute for Religious and Social Studies, distributed by Harper.

Johnson, Frank. 1985. "The Western Concept of Self." In *Culture and Self: Asian and Western Perspectives.* Edited by Anthony J. Marsell, George de Vos, and Francis L. H. Hsu, 91–138. New York: Tavistock Publications.

Johnson, Guy, and Howard Odum. 1964. *The Negro and His Songs.* Hatboro, Pa.: Folklore Associates, Inc.

Johnson, James Weldon. 1927. *God's Trombones: Seven Negro Sermons in Verse.* New York: Viking Press.

Johnson, James Weldon, ed. 1925. *The Book of American Negro Spirituals with Musical Arrangements by J. Rosamund Johnson and Additional Numbers by Lawrence Brown.* New York: Viking Press.

———, ed. 1926. *The Second Book of American Negro Spirituals.* New York: Viking Press.

Johnson, Joseph A., Jr. 1971. "Jesus the Liberator." In *The Black Experience in Religion.* Edited by C. Eric Lincoln, 110–27. New York: Anchor Press/Doubleday, 1974.

Johnson, Paul E., ed. 1994. *African-American Christianity: Essays in History.* Berkeley: University of California Press.

Jones, Charles Colcock. 1842. *Religious Instruction of the Negroes in the United States.* Savannah, Ga.: T. Purse.

Jones, Ferdinand. 2001. "Jazz and the Resilience of African Americans." In *The Triumph of the Soul: Cultural and Psychological Aspects of African American Music.* Edited by Ferdinand and Arthur C. Jones, 127–52. Westport, Conn. and London: Praeger.

Jones, Ferdinand, and Arthur C. Jones, eds. 2001. *The Triumph of the Soul: Cultural and Psychological Aspects of African American Music.* Westport, Conn., and London: Praeger.

Jones, Jacqueline, ed. 1985. *Labor of Love, Labor of Sorrow: Black Women, Work, and the Family from Slavery to the Present.* New York: Basic Books.

Jones, Le Roi. 1963. *Blues People.* New York: William Morrow and Co.

Jones, Rhett S. 1975. "Slavery in the Colonial Americas." *Black World* 24 (4): 28–39.

———. 1979. "Structural Isolation and the Genesis of Black Nationalism in Colonial North America." *Colby Library Quarterly* 15 (4): 252–66.

———. 1981. "Identity, Self-Concept, and Shifting Political Allegiances of Blacks in the Colonial Americas: Maroons against Black Shot." *Western Journal of Black Studies* 5 (1): 61–74.

Jones, Reginald L., ed. 1980. *Black Psychology*. New York: Harper and Row.

Jones, William. 1974. "A Question for Black Theology: Is God a White Racist?" In *The Black Experience in Religion*. Edited by C. Eric Lincoln, 139–55. New York: Anchor Press/Doubleday.

Jongeneel, Jan A. B., ed. 1992. *Pentecost, Mission and Ecumenism: Essays on Intercultural Theology*. New York: Peter Lang.

Jordan, Winthrop D. 1968. *White over Black: American Attitudes toward the Negro, 1550–1812*. New York: W. W. Norton and Co.

Joyner, Charles. 1995. "Believer I Know: The Emergence of African-American Christianity." In *Religion and American Culture*. Edited by David G. Hackett, 185–207. New York: Routledge.

Jules-Rosette, Bennetta. 1975. *African Apostles: Ritual and Conversion in the Church of John Mananke*. Ithaca, N.Y.: Cornell University Press.

———. 1985. "Ecstatic Singing: Music and Social Integration in an African Church." In *More than Drumming: Essays on African and Afro-Latin American Music and Musicians*. Edited by Irene V. Jackson, 119–44. [Howard University] Westport, Conn.: Greenwood Press.

Jung, C. G. 1957. *The Undiscovered Self*. Translated by R. F. C. Hull. Reprint, New York: Mentor Books, 1959.

Katz, Phyllis A., ed. 1976. *Towards the Elimination of Racism*. New York: Pergamon Press, Inc.

Katzman, Jamie. 1995. "Religion as an Element of Hope: A Study of Religion within the African-American Experience." Senior thesis, Trinity College (Hartford, Conn.).

Kearl, Michael. 1983. "Time, Identity, and the Spiritual Needs of the Elderly." In *Religion and Religiosity in America: Studies in Honor of Joseph H. Fichter*. Edited by Jeffrey K. Hadden and Theodore E. Long, 157–68. New York: Crossroad.

Keck, George R., and Sherrill V. Martin, eds. 1988. *Feel the Spirit: Studies in Nineteenth-Century Afro-American Music*. Westport, Conn.: Greenwood Press.

Keil, Charles. 1966. *Urban Blues*. Chicago: University of Chicago Press.

Kidwell, Clara Sue. 1995. *Choctaws and Missionaries in Mississippi, 1818–1918*. Norman: University of Oklahoma Press.

Kisliuk, Michelle. 1998. *Seize the Dance: BaAka Musical Life and the Ethnography of Performance*. New York and Oxford: Oxford University Press.

Klein, Herbert S. 1966. "Slavery, Anglicanism, Catholicism, and the Negro Slave." *Comparative Studies in Society and History* 8: 295–327.

———. 1967. *Slavery in the Americas: A Comparative Study of Virginia and Cuba*. Chicago: University of Chicago Press.

Knight, Walter K. 1993. "Race Relations: Changing Patterns and Practices." In *Southern Baptists Observed*. Edited by Nancy Ammerman, 165–81. New Brunswick, N.J.: Rutgers University Press.

Knowles, Louis L., and Kenneth Prewitt, eds. 1969. *Institutional Racism in America*. Englewood Cliffs, N.J.: Prentice Hall, Inc.

Koetting, James T. 1984. "Africa/Ghana." In *Worlds of Music: An Introduction to the Music of the World's Peoples*. Edited by Jeff Titon, 64–104. New York: Schirmer Books.

Labov, William, and Joshua Waletzky. 1966. "Narrative Analysis: Oral Versions of Personal Experience." In *Essays on the Verbal and Visual Arts* (Proceedings of the Annual Spring Meeting of the American Ethnological Society, 1966). Edited by June Helm. Seattle: University of Washington Press.

Landry, Bart. 1987. *The New Black Middle Class*. Berkeley: University of California Press.

Lessa, William A., and Evon Z. Vogt. 1965. *Reader in Comparative Religion: An Anthropological Approach*. White Plains, N.Y.: Row, Peterson and Company.

Levine, Lawrence W. 1993. *The Unpredictable Past: Explorations in American Cultural History*. New York: Oxford University Press.

Lichty, Lawrence W. 1989. "News from Everywhere." In *American Media*. Edited by Philip S. Cook, Douglas Gomery, and Lawrence W. Lichty, 207–16. Washington, D.C.: The Wilson Center Press.

Lincoln, C. Eric, 1974a. *The Black Church since Frazier*. New York: Schocken.

———. 1974b. "The Black Muslims and Black Acceptance." In *The Black Experience in Religion*, 236–53. New York: Anchor Press/Doubleday.

———. 1988. "The Black Church in the Context of American Religion." In *Varieties of Southern Religious Experience*. Edited by Samuel S. Hill, Jr., 52–75. Baton Rouge: Louisiana State University Press.

———. ed. 1974. *The Black Experience in Religion*. New York: Anchor Press/Doubleday.

Lincoln, C. Eric, and Lawrence H. Mamiya, eds. 1990. *The Black Church in the African American Experience*. Durham, N.C.: Duke University Press.

Lippy, Charles H., and Peter W. Williams, eds. 1988. *Encyclopaedia of the American Religious Experience: Studies of Traditions and Movements*. New York: Scribner.

List, George. 1963. "The Boundaries of Speech and Song." *Ethnomusicology* 7 (1): 1–16.

Logan, Wendell. 1984. "The Ostinato Idea in Black Improvised Music: A Preliminary Investigation." *The Black Perspective in Music* 12 (2): 193–216.

Lomax, Alan. 1960. *The Folksongs of North America*. Garden City, N.J.: Doubleday and Co.

———. 1963. *Folk Songs of North America*. London: Cassell.

———. 1970. "The Homogeneity of African-Afro-American Musical style." In *Afro-American Anthropology: Contemporary Perspectives*. Edited by Norman E. Whitten, Jr., and John F. Szwed, 181–201. New York: Free Press.

Long, Charles H. 1986. *Significations: Signs, Symbols and Images in the Interpretation of Religion.* Philadelphia: Fortress Press.

Long, Thomas, G. 1984. "Preaching in the South." In *Encyclopaedia of Religion in the South.* Edited by Samuel S. Hill, Jr., 595–601. Macon, Ga.: Mercer.

Lornell, Kip, 1988. *Happy in the Service of the Lord: Afro-American Gospel Quartets in Memphis.* Urbana: University of Illinois Press.

Lornell, Kip, and Anne K. Rasmussen, eds. 1997. *Musics of Multicultural America: A Study of Twelve Musical Communities.* New York: Schirmer Books.

Lovell, John Jr., 1972. *Black Song: The Forge and the Flame.* New York: Macmillan and Co.

Low, Augustus W., ed. 1981. *Encyclopaedia of Black America.* New York: McGraw-Hill.

Mac Robert, Iain. 1997. "The Black Roots of Pentacostalism." In *African-American Religion: Interpretive Essays in History and Culture.* Edited by Timothy E. Fulop and Albert J. Raboteau, 295–310. New York: Routledge.

Main Street Baptist Church. [n.d.] Chicago: C.P.D. Corporation.

Malone, Bill C. 1984. "Music, Religious, of the Protestant South." In *Encyclopaedia of Religion in the South.* Edited by Samuel S. Hill, Jr., 517–26. Macon, Ga.: Mercer.

Mamiya, Lawrence H. 1994. "A Social History of the Bethel African Methodist Episcopal Church in Baltimore: The House of God and the Struggle for Freedom." In *American Congregations.* Edited by James P. Wind and James J. Lewis, 1: 221–92. Chicago: University of Chicago Press.

Marable, Manning. 1983. *How Capitalism Underdeveloped Black America.* Boston: South End.

Marcus, Geroge E., and Michael M. J. Fischer, eds. 1986. *Anthropology as Cultural Critique: An Experimental Moment in the Human Science.* Chicago: University of Chicago Press.

Marks, Morton. 1974. "Uncovering Ritual Structures in Afro-American Music." In *Religious Movements in Contemporary America.* Edited by Irving I. Zaretsky and Mark P. Leone, 60–134. Princeton, N.J.: Princeton University Press.

Marsden, George M. 1980. *Fundamentalism and American Culture: The Shaping of Twentieth Century Evangelicalism, 1870–1925.* New York: Oxford University Press.

———. 1991. "Fundamentalism and American Evangelicalism." In *The Variety of American Evangelicalism.* Edited by Donald W. Dayton and Robert K. Johnston, 22–35. Knoxville: University of Tennessee Press.

———. 1991. *Understanding Fundamentalism and Evangelicalism.* Grand Rapids, Mich.: W. B. Eerdmans.

Marsden, George M., ed. 1984. *Evangelicalism and Modern America.* Grand Rapids, Mich.: W. B. Eerdmans.

Marsell, Anthony J., George de Vos, and Francis L. H. Hsu, eds. 1985. *Culture and Self: Asian and Western Perspectives.* New York: Tavistock Publications.

Marsh, J. B. T. [1880] 1971. *The Story of the Jubilee Singers with Their Songs.* Reprint, New York: AMS Press.

Marshall, Calvin B., Jr. 1974. "The Black Church: Its Mission Is Liberation." In *The Black Experience in Religion.* Edited by C. Eric Lincoln, 157–67. New York: Anchor Press/Doubleday.

Marty, Martin E. 1981. "Foreword." In *Varieties of Southern Evangelicalism.* Edited by David Edwin Harrell, Jr., i–xiii. Macon, Ga.: Mercer University Press.

———. 1981. "The Revival of Evangelicalism and Southern Religion." In *Varieties of Southern Evangelicalism.* Edited by David Edwin Harrell, Jr., 7–21. Macon, Ga.: Mercer University Press.

Marty, Martin, E., and R. Scott Appelby, eds. 1997. *Religion, Ethnicity, and Self-Identity: Nations in Turmoil.* Hanover, N.H.: University Press of New England.

Mathews, Donald J. 1977. *Religion in the Old South.* Chicago: University of Chicago Press.

———. 1984. "Evangelicalism." In *Encyclopaedia of Religion in the South.* Edited by Samuel S. Hill, Jr., 243–44. Macon, Ga.: Mercer.

———. 2001. "Crucifixion-faith in the Christian South." In *Autobiographical Reflections on Southern Religious History.* Edited by John B. Boles, 17–38. Athens and London: University of Georgia Press.

Maultsby, Portia. 1975. "Music of Northern Black Churches during the Antebellum Period." *Ethnomusicology* 19 (3): 401–12.

———. 1976. "Black Spirituals: Analysis of Textual Forms and Structures." *The Black Perspective in Music* 4: 54–59.

———. 1985. "West African Influences and Retentions in U.S. Black Music: A Sociocultural Study." In *More than Dancing.* Edited by Irene V. Jackson, 25–57. Westport. Conn.: Greenwood Press.

———. 1990. "Africanisms in African-American Music." In *Africanisms in American Culture.* Edited by Joseph E. Holloway, 185–210. Bloomington: Indiana University Press.

———. 1993. "Music in the African American Church." In *Encyclopaedia of African American Religions.* Edited by Larry G. Murphy, J. Gordon Melton, and Gary L. Ward, 520–26. New York: Garland.

Mayer, Philip. 1962. *Ethnic Identity: Strategies of Diversity.* Bloomington: Indiana University Press.

Mays, Benjamin. 1938. *The Negro's God as Reflected in His Literature.* Boston: Chapman and Grimes, Inc.

Mbiti, John S. 1969. *African Religions and Philosophy.* New York: Anchor Books, Doubleday and Company, Inc.

McClain, William B. 1984. *Black People in the Methodist Church: Whither Thou Goest?* Cambridge, Mass.: Schenkman Pub. Co.

———. 1990. *Come Sunday: The Liturgy of Zion.* Nashville, Tenn.: Abingdon Press.

McClary, Susan. 2001. *Conventional Wisdom: The Content of Form.* Berkeley: University of California Press.

McEntire, Nancy Cassell, ed. 1991. *Essays in Honour of Frank J. Gillis.* Bloomington, Ind.: Ethnomusicology Publications Group.

McLin, Lena. 1970. "Black Music in School and Church." In *Black Music in Our Culture*. Edited by Dominique-René de Lerma, 35–41. Kent, Ohio: Kent State University Press.

McLoughlin, William Gerald. 1978. *Revivals, Awakenings, and Reform: An Essay on Religion and Social Change in America, 1607–1977*. Chicago: University of Chicago Press.

McLoughlin, William G., and Robert N. Bellah, eds. 1968. *Religion in America*. Boston: Houghton Miflin.

McManus, E. J. 1973. *Black Bondage in the North*. Syracuse, N.Y.: Syracuse University Press.

McMillen, Neil R. 1989. *Dark Journey: Black Mississippians in the Age of Jim Crow*. Urbana, Ill.: University of Illinois Press.

Mead, Frank S., and Samuel S. Hill, Jr. 1990. *Handbook of Denominations in the United States*. Nashville, Tenn.: Abingdon Press.

Mead, Margaret. 1945. "How Religion Has Fared in the Melting Pot." In *Religion and Our Racial Tensions*. Edited by Dean William L. Sperry, 61–81. Cambridge, Mass.: Harvard University Press.

Mead, Sidney E. 1974. "The Nation with the Soul of a Cchurch." In *American Civil Religion*. Russell E. Richley and Donald G. Jones, eds., 45–75. New York: Harper and Row.

Melton, J. Gordon, ed. 1985. *Encyclopaedia of American Religions*. Supplement [to the] 1st ed. Detroit, Mich.: Gale Research.

———, ed. 1993. *Encyclopaedia of American Religions*. 4th ed. Detroit, Mich.: Gale Research.

Middleton, John, ed. 1967. *Myth and Cosmos*. Garden City, N.Y.: Natural History Press.

Miller, Carol Ann. 1999. *Rituals of Fertility and the Sacrifice of Desire: Nazarite Women's Performance in South Africa*. Chicago and London: University of Chicago Press.

Miller, Terry. 1987. "Lined Hymnody in the British Isles and the Americas: Prologomena on the Variables and Interrelationships." Paper read at the 1987 annual meeting of the Society for Ethnomusicology.

Milner, David. 1975. *Children and Race*. Middlesex, England: Penguin Books.

Mintz, S. W., and R. Price. 1976. *An Anthropological Approach to the Afro-American Past: A Caribbean Perspective*. Philadelphia: Institute for the Study of Human Issues.

Mitchell, Ella Pearson, ed. 1985. *Those Preachin' Women: Sermons by Black Women Preachers*. Valley Forge, Pa.: Judson Press.

Mitchell, Henry J. 1970. *Black Preaching*. New York: J. B. Lippincott Company.

———. 1990. *Black Preaching the Recovery of a Powerful Art*. Nashville, Tenn.: Abingdon Press.

———. 1990. *Celebration and Experience in Preaching*. Nashville, Tenn.: Abingdon Press.

———. 1993. "Preaching and the Preacher in African American Religion." In *Encyclopaedia of African American Religions*. Edited by Larry G. Murphy, J. Gordon Melton, and Gary L. Ward, 606–12. New York: Garland.

Mitchell, J. Clyde. 1956. *The Kalela Dance: Aspects of Social Relationships among Urban Africans in Rhodesia*. Rhodes-Livingstone Papers No. 27.

Rhodes-Livingstone Institute. Manchester: Manchester University Press for the Rhodes-Livingstone Institute.

Mitchell, Mozella G. 1994. *New Africa in America: The Blending of African American Religious and Social Traditions among Black People in Meridian, Mississippi and Surrounding Counties.* New York: Peter Lang Publishing, Inc.

Moberly, Elizabeth R. 1985. *The Psychology of Self and Other.* New York: Tavistock Publications.

Molefi, Kete Asante. 1987. *The Afrocentric Idea.* Philadelphia: Temple University Press.

Montell, William Lynwood. 1991. *Singing the Glory Down: Amateur Gospel Music in South Central Kentucky, 1900–1990.* Lexington: University Press of Kentucky.

Montgomery, William E. 1993. *Under Their Own Vine and Fig Tree: The African-American Church in the South, 1865–1900.* Baton Rouge: Louisiana University Press.

Moore, R. Laurence. 1986. *Religious Outsiders and the Making of Americans.* New York: Oxford University Press.

Morgan, E. S. 1973. *American Slavery American Freedom: The Ordeal of Colonial Virginia.* New York: Monthly Review Press.

Moses, Oral L. 1988. "The Nineteenth-Century Spiritual Text: A Source for Modern Gospel." In *Feel the Spirit: Studies in Nineteenth-Century Afro-American Music.* Edited by George R. Keck and Sherrill V. Martin. 49–59. Westport, Conn.: Greenwood Press.

Moses, Wilson Jeremiah. 1990. *The Wings of Ethiopia: Studies in African-American Life and Letters.* Ames: Iowa State University Press.

Moving in the Spirit. 1989. One 12-inch disc. Production Director (editing, text, and photography): Thérèse Smith. Oxford, Miss.: Southern Culture Records, the University of Mississippi, SC 1705.

Murphy, Larry G. 1993. "Baptists, African American." In *Encyclopaedia of African American Religions.* Edited by Larry G. Murphy, J. Gordon Melton, and Gary L. Ward, 64–66. New York: Garland.

Murphy, Larry G. ed. 2000. *Down by the Riverside: Readings in African American Religion.* New York and London: New York University Press.

Murphy, Larry G., J. Gordon Melton, and Gary L. Ward, eds. 1993. *Encyclopaedia of African American Religions.* New York: Garland.

Nagata, Judith. 1974. "What is a Malay? Situational Selection of Ethnic Identify in a Plural Society." *American Ethnologist* 1: 331–50.

Nash, G. B. 1974. *Red, White, and Black.* Englewood Cliffs, N.J.: Prentice-Hall.

Nelson, Angela M. S. 2001. "Why We Sing: The Role and Meaning of Gospel in African American Popular Culture." In *The Triumph of the Soul: Cultural and Psychological Aspects of African American Music.* Edited by Ferdinand and Arthur C. Jones, 97–126. Westport, Conn., and London: Praeger.

Nettl, Bruno, and Philip V. Bohlman, eds. 1991. *Comparative Musicology and Anthropology of Music: Essays on the History of Ethnomusicology.* Chicago: University of Chicago Press.

Neverdon-Morton, Cynthia. 1989. *Afro-American Women of the South and the Advancement of the Race, 1895–1925*. Knoxville: University of Tennessee Press.

Newsome, Clarence G. 1991. "A Synoptic Survey of the History of African American Baptists." In *Directory of African American Religious Bodies*. Edited by Wardell J. Payne, 20–21. Washington, D.C.: Howard University Press; 2nd edition, 1995.

Nielson, Aldon Lynn. 1997. *Black Chant: Languages of African-American Postmodernism*. Cambridge, New York: Cambridge University Press.

Nielson, David Gordon. 1977. *Black Ethos: Northern Urban Negro Life and Thought, 1890–1930*. Westport, Conn.: Greenwood Press.

Nobles, W. 1976. "Extended Self: Rethinking the So-Called Negro Self-Concept." *Journal of Black Psychology* 2 (2): 15–24.

Ohlmann, Eric H. 1991. "Baptists and Evangelicals." In *The Variety of American Evangelicalism*. Edited by Donald W. Dayton and Robert K. Johnston, 148–60. Knoxville: University of Tennessee Press.

Oliver, Paul. 1984. *Songsters and Saints: Vocal Traditions on Race Records*. Cambridge: Cambridge University Press.

Oliver, Paul, Max Harrisson, and William Bolcom, eds. 1986. *The New Grove Gospel, Blues and Jazz: With Spirituals and Ragtime*. New York: W. W. Norton.

Ó Madagáin, Breandán. 1993. "Song for Emotional Release in the Gaelic Tradition." In *Music and the Church*. Edited by Gerard Gillen and Harry White, 255–75. Irish musical studies, vol. 2. Dublin: Irish Academic Press.

Ong, Walter J. 1967. *In the Human Grain: Further Explorations of Contemporary Culture*. New York: Macmillan.

———. 1967. "The Lady & the Issue." In *In the Human Grain: Further Explorations of Contemporary Culture*, 188–202. New York: Macmillan.

Osofsky, G. 1967. *The Burden of Race: A Documentary History of Negro-White Relations in America*. New York: Harper and Row.

Overacker, Ingrid. 1998. *The African American Church Community in Rochester, New York, 1900–1940*. Rochester, N.Y.: University of Rochester Press.

Overton, Betty J. 1985. "Black Women Preachers: A Literary Overview." *The Southern Quarterly: A Journal of the Arts in the South*. Special issue on Black Religion in the American South in the Twentieth Century 23 (3): 157–66.

Paris, Peter J. 1985. *The Social Teaching of the Black Churches*. Philadelphia: Fortress Press.

Patterson, Beverly Bush. 1995. *The Sound of the Dove: Singing in Applachian Primitive Baptist Churches*. Urbana: University of Illinois Press.

Patterson, Lindsay, ed. 1967. *The Negro in Music and Art*. New York: Publishers Company, Inc.

Payne, Wardell J. 1995. *Directory of African American Religious Bodies*. 2nd edition. Washington, D.C.: Howard University Press.

Peshkin, Alan. 1986. *God's Choice: The Total World of a Fundamentalist Christian School*. Chicago: University of Chicago Press.

Phillips. Romeo. 1982. "Some Perceptions of Gospel Music." *The Black Perspective in Music* 10 (2): 167–78.

Pinkston, Alfred Adolphus. 1975. "Lined Hymns, Spirituals and the Associated Lifestyle of Rural Black People in the United States." Ph.D. diss., University of Miami.

Pitts, Walter F. 1991. "Like a Tree Planted by the Water: The Musical Cycle in the African-American Baptist Ritual." *Journal of American Folklore* 104: 318–40.

———. 1993. *Old Ship of Zion: The Afro-Baptist Ritual in the African Diaspora*. New York: Oxford University Press.

Plessy, Homer Adolph. 1968. *Plessy vs Ferguson Records and Briefs (1893–1895)*. Cambridge: Cambridge University Press.

Polokow-Suransky, Sasha. 2003. "Sins of our Fathers." *The Brown Alumni Magazine* (July/August): 36–42.

Porter, Thomas J. 2001. "The Social Roots of African American Music: 1950–1970." In *African American Jazz and Rap*. Edited by J. L. Conyers Jr., 83–89. Jefferson, N.C., and London: McFarland and Company, Inc.

Pride, T. B. 1971. "Customs and Cases of Verbal Behaviour." In *Social Anthropology and Language*. Edited by Edwin Ardener, 95–117. London: Tavistock Publications.

Proctor, Henry Hugh. 1925. "The Theology of the Songs of the Southern Slave." Chapters 6 and 7 in *Between Black and White*. Boston: Pilgrim Press, 55–87.

Rabinowitz, Howard N. 1978. *Race Relations in the Urban South, 1865–1890*. New York: Oxford University Press.

Raboteau, Albert J. 1978. *Slave Religion: The Invisible Institution in the Antebellum South*. New York: Oxford University Press.

———. 1995a. "African Americans, Exodus, and the American Israel." In *Religion and American Culture*. Edited by David G. Hackett, 73–86. New York: Routledge.

———. 1995b. *A Fire in the Bones: Reflections on African American Religious History*. Boston: Beacon Press.

———. 1997. "The Black Experience in American Evangelicalism: The Meaning of Slavery." In *African-American Religion: Interpretive Essays in History and Culture*. Edited by Timothy E. Fulop and Albert J. Raboteau, 89–106. New York: Routledge.

———. 2001. "A Fire in the Bones." In *Autobiographical Reflections on Southern Religious History*. Edited by John B. Boles, 193–205. Athens and London: University of Georgia Press.

Ramsey, Guthrie P, Jr. 2003. *Race Music: Black Cultures from Bebop to Hip-Hop*. Berkeley and Chicago: University of California Press and Center for Black Music Research.

Rawick, George P. 1972. *From Sundown to Sunup: The Making of the Black Community*. Westport, Conn.: Greenwood Publishing Company.

Reagon, Bernice Johnson. 1993. *We Who Believe in Freedom: Sweet Honey in the Rock—Still on the Journey*. New York: Anchor Books/Doubleday.

———, ed. 1993. *We'll Understand It Better By and By: Pioneering African American Gospel Composers*. Washington, D.C.: Smithsonian Institution Press.

Rice, Timothy. 1994. *May It Fill Your Soul: Experiencing Bulgarian Music*. Chicago: University of Chicago Press.

Rice, Timothy. 2003. "Time, Place and Metaphor in Musical Experience and Ethnography." *Ethnomusicology* 47 (2): 151–79.

Richey, Russell E., and Donald G. Jones, eds. 1974. *American Civil Religion.* New York: Harper and Row.

Ricks, George Robinson. 1977. *Some Aspects of the Religious Music of the United States Negro.* New York: Arno Press.

Ricoeur, Paul. 1981. *Hermeneutics and the Social Sciences.* Edited by John B. Thompson. Paris and Cambridge: Maison des Sciences de l'Homme and Cambridge University Press.

Rijn, Guido van. 1997. *Roosevelt's Blues: African-American Blues and Gospel Songs on FDR.* Jackson: University Press of Mississippi.

Robbins, Thomas, and Dick Anthony, eds. 1990. *In Gods We Trust: New Patterns of Religious Pluralism in America.* New Brunswick, N.J.: Transaction Publishers.

Roberts, John W. 1989. *From Trickster to Badman: The Black Folk Hero in Slavery and Freedom.* Philadelphia: University of Pennsylvania Press.

Roofe, Wade Clark. 1988. "Religious Change in the American South: The Case of the Unchurched." In *Varieties of Southern Religious Experience.* Edited by Samuel S. Hill, Jr., 192–210. Baton Rouge: Louisiana State University Press.

Rosenberg, Bruce A. 1970. *The Art of the American Folk Preacher.* New York: Oxford University Press.

———. 1970. "The Formulaic Quality of Spontaneous Sermons." *Journal of American folklore* 83: 3–20.

———. 1971. "The Genre of the Folk Sermon." *Georgia Review* 25 (4): 424–38.

———. 1991. *Folklore and Literature: Rival Siblings.* Knoxville: University of Tennessee Press.

Rothman, Sheila M. 1978. *Woman's Proper Place: A History of Changing Ideals and Practices, 1870 to the Present.* New York: Basic Books.

Rouget, Gilbert. 1985. *Music and Trance: A Theory of the Relations between Music and Possession.* Translated by Brunhilde Biebuyck. Chicago: University of Chicago Press.

Rowland, Dunbar. 1925. *History of Mississippi, the Heart of the South.* Chicago: the S. J. Clarke Publishing Company.

Royce, Anya Peterson. 1982. *Ethnic Identity: Strategies of Diversity.* Bloomington: Indiana University Press.

Ruchames, Louis. 1969. *Racial Thought in America: From the Puritans to Abraham Lincoln, a Documentary History.* Amherst, Mass.: University of Massachusetts Press.

Rust College. [n.d.] *Dreams Come True at Rust College, Holly Springs, Mississippi.* Holly Springs, Miss.: Office of College Relations, Rust College.

———. *Rust College.* [n.d.] Knoxville, Tenn.: Newman's Creativity Printing.

———. *What You Should Know about Rust College.* [n.d.] Holly Springs, Miss.: Office of College Relations, Rust College.

Ryan, William. 1971. *Blaming the Victim.* New York: Random House.

Sanches, Mary, and Ben G. Blount, eds. 1975. *Sociocultural Dimensions of Language Use.* New York: Academic Press.

Sanders, Cheryl Jeane. 1996. *Saints in Exile: The Holiness-Pentecostal Experience in African American Religion and Culture*. New York: Oxford University Press.

Sankey, Ira D., James McGranahan, George Stebbins, and Philip P. Bliss, eds. 1972. *Gospel Hymns Nos. 1 to 6 Complete*. Vol. 5, *Early American Music*. New York: Da Capo Press.

Sargant, William Walters. 1963. *Battle for the Mind: A Physiology of Conversion and Brainwashing*. Pan Books.

Sarna, Jonathan D., ed. 1998. *Minority Faiths and the American Protestant Mainstream*. Urbana: University of Illinois Press.

Saussure, Ferdinand de. 1915. *Cours de linguistique générale*. Reprint, Paris: Payot, 1978.

Sawyer, Mary R. 1994. *Black Ecumenism*. Harrisburg, Pa.: Trinity Press International.

Schegloff, Emanuel, and Harvey Sacks. 1973a. "Opening Up Closings." *Semiotica* 4: 289–327.

———. 1973b. *Towards an Analysis of Discourse*. London: Oxford University Press.

Schwerin, Jules. 1992. *Got to Tell It: Mahalia Jackson, Queen of Gospel*. New York: Oxford University Press.

Seeger, Charles. 1958. "Prescriptive and Descriptive Music Writing." *Musical Quarterly* 44: 184–95.

Sernett, Milton C. 1975. *Black Religion and American Evangelism*. Metuchen, N.J.: Scarecrow Press.

———. 1991. "Black Religion and the Question of Evangelical Identity." In *The Variety of American Evangelicalism*. Edited by Donald W. Dayton and Robert K. Johnston, 135–47. Knoxville: University of Tennessee Press.

———, ed. 1985. *Afro-American Religious History: A Documentary Witness*. Durham, N.C.: Duke University Press.

Simmons, Henry L. 1986. *The History of Clear Creek Missionary Baptist Church*. Clear Creek, Miss.

Simpson, Robert. 1970. "Black Church: Ecstasy in a World of Trouble." Ph.D. diss. Washington University.

Sinclair, J. McH., and R. M. Coulthard. 1975. *Towards an Analysis of Discourse*. London: Oxford University Press.

Sio, A. A. 1965. "Interpretations of Slavery: The Slave Status in the Americas." *Comparative Studies in Society and History* 7: 289–308.

Skowronsky, JoAnn. 1981. *Black Music in America: A Bibliography*. Metuchen, N.J.: Scarecrow Press.

Small, Christopher. 1998. *Music of the Common Tongue: Survival and Celebration in African American Music*. Hanover, N.H.: University Press of New England.

Smith, Theophus H. 1994. *Conjuring Culture: Biblical Formations of Black Culture*. New York: Oxford University Press.

Smith, Thérèse. 1983. "The Afro-American Spiritual: A Remembrance of Things Past?" Master's thesis, Brown University.

Smith, Thérèse. 1985. "Chanted Prayer in Southern Black Churches." *The Southern Quarterly: A Journal of the Arts in the South*. Special issue on Black Religion in the American South in the Twentieth Century 23 (3): 70–82.

———. 1988. "Moving in the Spirit: Music of Worship in Clear Creek, Mississippi, as an Expression of Worldview." Ph.D. diss., Brown University.

———. 1998. "Lining, Testifying, and 'Blackenizing': The Musical Expression of Black American Families." *Irish Journal of American Studies* 7: 55–78.

Snead, James A. 1984. "Repetition as a Figure in Black Culture." In *Black Literature and Literary Theory*. Edited by Henry Louis Gates, Jr., 59–80. Metuchen, N.J.: Scarecrow Press.

Sobel, Mechal. 1979. *Travelin' On: The Slave Journey to an Afro-Baptist Faith*. Reprint, Princeton, N.J.: Princeton University Press, 1988.

Sosna, Morton. 1997. *In Search of the Silent South: Southern Liberals and the Race Issue*. New York: Columbia University Press.

Southall, Geneva. 1974. "Black Composers and Religious Music." *The Black Perspective in Music* 2 (1): 46–50.

Southern, Eileen. 1971. *The Music of Black Americans*. New York: W. W. Norton.

———. 1989. "Hymnals of the Black Church." *The Black Perspective in Music* 17: 20–46.

Southern, Eileen, ed. 1971. *Readings in Black American Music*. New York: W. W. Norton.

Southern, Eileen, and Josephine Wright, eds. 2000. *Images: Iconography of Music in African-American Culture, 1770–1920s*. New York and London: Garland.

Spain, Rufus B. 1967. *At Ease in Zion: A Social History of Southern Baptists, 1865–1900*. Nashville, Tenn.: Vanderbilt University Press.

Sparks, Randy J. 1994. *On Jordan's stormy banks: Evangelicalism in Mississippi, 1773–1876*. Athens: University of Georgia Press.

———. 2001. *Religion in Mississippi*. Jackson: University Press of Mississippi.

Spencer, Jon Michael. 1987. *Sacred Symphony: The Chanted Sermon of the Black Preacher*. New York: Greenwood Press.

———. 1990. *Protest and Praise: Sacred Music of Black Religion*. Minneapolis, Minn.: Fortress Press.

———. 1993. *Blues and Evil*. Knoxville: University of Tennessee Press.

Spencer, Samuel R., Jr. 1955. *Booker T. Washington and the Negro's Place in American Life*. Edited by Oscar Handlin. Boston: Little, Brown and Company.

Sperry, Dean William L., ed. 1945. *Religion and Our Racial Tensions*. Cambridge, Mass.: Harvard University Press.

Spiegelberg, H. 1965. *The Phenomenological Movement: A Historical Introduction*. 2 vols. The Hague: Martinus Nijhoff.

Stack, Carol B. 1974. *All Our Kin: Strategies for Survival in a Black Community*. New York: Harper and Row.

Stampp, Kenneth M. 1965. *The Peculiar Institution*. New York: Alfred A. Knopf.

Starks, George L., Jr. 2001. "Ethnomusicology and the African American Tradition." In *African American Jazz and Rap*. Edited by J. L. Conyers, Jr., Jefferson, N. C., and London: McFarland and Company, 224–38.

Stewart, John. 1823. *A View of the Past and Present State of the Island of Jamaica*. Edinburgh: Oliver & Boyd.

Stewart, Warren H. 1984. *Interpreting God's Word in Black Preaching*. Valley Forge, Pa.: Judson Press.

Stokes, Martin, ed. 1994. *Ethnicity, Identity, and Music: The Musical Construction of Place*. Oxford, Providence, R.I.: Berg.

Stout, Harry S., and D. G. Hart, eds. 1997. *New Directions in American Religious History*. New York: Oxford University Press.

Stuckey, Sterling. 1987. *Slave Culture: Nationalist Theory and the Foundations of Black America*. New York: Oxford University Press.

Sullivan, Lawrence E., ed. 1997. *Enchanting Powers: Music in the World's Religions*. Cambridge, Mass., Harvard University Center for the Study of World Religions.

Sutton, Brett. 1982. "Shape-Note Tunebooks and Primitive Hymns." *Ethnomusicology* 26 (1): 11–26.

Sydnor, Charles Sackett. 1933. *Slavery in Mississippi*. New York: D. Appleton-Century Company.

Tallmadge, William. 1968. "The Responsorial and Antiphonal Practice in Gospel Song." *Ethnomusicology* 12: 219–38.

———. 1981. "The Black in Jackson's White Spirituals." *The Black Perspective in Music* 9 (2): 139–60.

Tambiah, Stanley Jeyaraja. 1985. *Culture, Thought and Social Action: An Anthropological Perspective*. Cambridge, Mass.: Harvard University Press.

Tannenbaum, Frank. 1947. *Slave and Citizen: The Negro in the Americas*. New York: Alfred A. Knopf.

Tart, Charles T., ed. 1969. *Altered States of Consciousness*. New York: John Wiley and Sons.

Taylor, John E. 1975. "Somethin' on My Mind: A Cultural and Historical Interpretation of Spiritual Texts." *Ethnomusicology* 19 (3): 387–400.

Tedlock, Dennis. 1983. *The Spoken Word and the Work of Interpretation*. Philadelphia: University of Pennsylvania Press.

Temperly, Nicholas. 1981. "The Old Way of Singing: Its Origins and Development." *Journal of the American Musicological Society* 34: 511–44.

Terkel, Studs. 1992. *Race: How Blacks and Whites Think and Feel about the American Obsession*. New York: The New Press.

Terrell, Bob. 1990. *The Music Men: The Story of Professional Gospel Quartet Singing*. Asheville, N.C.: B. Terrell.

The Watch meeting. 1899. *The Southern Workman* 28: 151–54.

Thompson, Robert Farris. 1983. *Flash of the Spirit: African and Afro-American Art and Philosophy*. New York: Random House.

Thompson, Thelma B. 1989. *The Seventeenth-Century English Hymn: A Mode for Sacred and Secular Concerns*. New York: P. Lang.

Thurman, Howard. 1947. *The Negro Spiritual Speaks of Life and Death*. New York: Harper and Brothers.

Tillich, Paul. 1963. *Systematic Theology*, (3 vols.), vol. 3. Chicago: University of Chicago Press.

Tirro, Frank. 1993. *Jazz: A History*. 2nd edition. New York: W. W. Norton.

Titon, Jeff Todd. 1975. "Tonal System in the Chanted Oral Sermons of the Rev. C. L. Franklin." Unpublished paper.

———. 1980. "A Song from the Holy Spirit". *Ethnomusicology* 24 (2): 223–32.

———. 1984. "North America/Black America." In *Worlds of Music: An Introduction to the Music of the World's Peoples*. Edited by Jeff Titon, 105–65. 2nd edition. New York: Schirmer Books.

———. 1988. *Powerhouse for God: Speech, Chant, and Song in the Appalachian Baptist Church*. Austin: University of Texas Press.

Tristano, Richard. 1986. *Black Religion in the Evangelical South*. Athens, Ga: Glenmary Research Center.

Tucker, W. H. 1994. *The Science and Politics of Racial Research*. Champaign: University of Illinois Press.

Tullos, Allen. 1998. "Geography and Justice in the Black Belt: Regionalism Comes with the Territory." In *The New Regionalism*. Edited by Charles Reagan Wilson. Jackson: University Press of Mississippi: 135–47.

Turner, Victor. 1952. *The Lozi Peoples of North-Western Rhodesia*. London: International African Institute.

———. 1967. *The Forest of Symbols: Aspects of Ndembu Ritual*. Ithaca, N.Y.: Cornell University Press.

———. 1968. *The Drums of Affliction: A Study of Religious Processes among the Ndembu of Zambia*. Oxford: Clarendon Press and the International African Institute.

———. 1969. *The Ritual Process: Structure and Anti-Structure*. Chicago: Aldine.

———. 1975. *Revelation and Divination in Ndemnu Ritual*. Ithaca, N.Y.: Cornell University Press.

———. 1982. *From Ritual to Theatre*. New York: Performing Arts Journal Publications.

Tyms, James Daniel. 1979. *The Rise of Religious Education among Negro Baptists*. Washington D.C.: University Press of America.

Tyson, Ruel, Jr., James Peacock, and Daniel Patterson, eds. 1988. *Diversities of Gifts: Field Studies in Southern Religion*. Urbana: University of Illinois Press.

Vandermeer, Philip, ed. 1991. *American Sacred Music*. Boston: G. K. Hall.

Van Carenghem, P. R. 1956. *La notion de Dieu chez les Baluba du Kasai*. Brussels: Académie Royale des Sciences Colonials.

Van Gennep, Arnold. 1960. *The Rites of Passage*. Translated by Monika B. Vizdan and Gabrielle L. Coffee. Chicago: University of Chicago Press.

Vollers, Maryanne. 1995. *Ghosts of Mississippi: The Murder of Megdar Evers, the Trials of Byron de la Beckwith, and the Haunting of the New South*. Boston: Little, Brown and Company.

Wade-Gayles, Gloria. 1995. *My Soul is a Witness: African-American Women's Spirituality*. Boston: Beacon Press.

Walker, Wyatt Tee. 1987. *Spirits that Dwell in Deep Woods: The Prayer and Praise Hymns of the Black Religious Experience.* New York: M. L. King Fellows Press.

Washington, James Melvin. 1986. *Frustrated Fellowship: The Black Baptist Quest for social power.* Macon, Ga.: Mercer.

Washington, Joseph R., Jr. 1964. *Black Religion.* Boston: Beacon Press.

———. 1981. "The Peculiar Peril and Promise of Black Folk Religion." In *Varieties of Southern Evangelicalism.* Edited by David Edwin Harrell, Jr. and David Edwin, Jr., 59–69. Macon, Ga.: Mercer University Press.

Washington, Joseph R., Jr., ed. 1980. *Dilemmas of the New Black Middle Class.* [S.l., s.n.].

Waterman, Chris A. 1991. "Jùjú History: Toward a Theory of Sociomusical Practice." In *Ethnomusicology and Modern Music History.* Edited by Stephen Blum, Philip V. Bohlman, and Daniel M. Newman, 49–67. Urbana: University of Illinois Press.

Waterman, Richard A. 1952. "African Influence on the Music of the Americas." In *Acculturation in the Americas.* Edited by Sol Tax, 207–18. Chicago: University of Chicago Press.

Watson, John Fanning. *Methodist Error: or, Friendly Christian Advice, to Those Methodists Who Indulge in Extravagant Religious Emotions and Bodily Exercise by a Wesleyan Methodist.* Trenton, N.J.: D. and E. Fenton. Reprint, Cincinnati: Philips and Speer, 1819.

Wei-ming, Tu. 1985. "Self and Otherness in Confucian Thought." In *Culture and Self: Asian and Western Perspectives.* Edited by Anthony J. Marsell, George de Vos, and Francis L. H. Hsu. New York: Tavistock Publications.

Weisenfeld, Judith, and Richard Newman, eds. 1996. *This Far by Faith: Readings in African-American Women's Religious Biography.* New York: Routledge.

Whalum, Wendell. 1986. "Music in the Churches of Black Americans: A Critical Statement." *The Black Perspective in Music* 14 (1): 13–20.

Whitten, Norman E., Jr., and John F. Szwed, eds. 1970. *Afro-American Anthropology: Contemporary Perspectives.* New York: Free Press.

Wilder, Amos Niven. 1964. *Early Christian Rhetoric: The Language of the Gospel.* London: SCM Press.

Williams-Jones, Pearl. 1975. "Afro-American Gospel Music: A Crystallization of the Black Aesthetic." *Ethnomusicology* 19 (3): 373–85.

Williamson, Joel. 1984. *A Rage for Order: Black/White Relations in the American South since Emancipation.* New York: Oxford University Press.

———. 1986. *The Crucible of Race: Black/White Relations in the American South since Emancipation.* New York: Oxford University Press.

Wills, David W. 1997. "The Central Themes of American Religious History: Pluralism, Puritanism, and the Encounter of Black and White." In *African-American Religion: Interpretive Essays in History and Culture.* Edited by Timothy E. Fulop and Albert J. Raboteau, 7–20. New York: Routledge.

———. 1998. "Exodus Piety: African American Religion in an Age of Immigration." In *Minority Faiths and the American Protestant Mainstream.* Edited by Jonathan D. Sarna, 136–88. Urbana: University of Illinois Press.

Wilmore, Gayraud S. 1973. *Black religion and Black Radicalism: An Interpretation of the Religious History of Afro-American People.* New York: Maryknoll.

Wilmore, Gayraud S., ed. 1989. *African American Religious Studies: An Interdisciplinary Anthology.* Durham, N.C.: Duke University Press.

Wilmore, Gayraud S., and James H. Cone, eds. 1979. *Black Theology: A Documentary History, 1966–1979.* Maryknoll, N.Y.: Orbis Books.

Wilson, Charles Reagan, 1995. *Judgement and Grace in Dixie: Southern Faith from Faulkner to Elvis.* Athens: University of Georgia Press.

———. 2001. "A Journey to Southern Religious Studies." In *Autobiographical Reflections on Southern Religious History.* Edited by John B. Boles, 206–18. Athens and London: University of Georgia Press.

Wilson, Charles Reagan, ed. 1985. *Religion in the South.* Jackson: University Press of Mississippi.

———, ed. 1998. *The New Regionalism.* Jackson: University Press of Mississippi.

Wilson, Charles Reagan, and William Ferris, eds. 1989. *Encyclopedia of Southern Culture.* Chapel Hill and London: University of North Carolina Press.

Wilson, Olly. 1974. "The Significance of the Relationship between Afro-American Music and West African Music." *The Black perspective in music* 2 (1): 3–22.

———. 1985. "The Association of Movement and Music as Manifestation of a Black Conceptual Approach to Music Making." In *More Than Dancing.* Edited by Irene V. Jackson, 9–24. Westport, Conn.: Greenwood Press.

Wind, James P., and James J. Lewis. 1994. "Introduction." In *American Congregations.* Edited by James P. Wind and James J. Lewis, 1: 1–13. Chicago: University of Chicago Press.

Wind, James P., and James J. Lewis, eds. 1994. *American Congregations.* 2 vols. Chicago: University of Chicago Press.

Wood, P. H. 1974. *Black Majority: Negroes in Colonial South Carolina from 1670 through the Stono Rebellion.* New York: Knopf, Random House.

Woodward, C. Vann. 1961. *The Burden of Southern History.* New York: Random House.

Work, John W., comp. 1940. *American Negro Songs: A Comprehensive Collection of 230 Songs, Religious and Secular.* New York: Howell, Soskin, and Co.

Wuthnow, Robert. 1988. *The Restructuring of American Religion: Society and Faith since World War II.* Princeton, N.J.: Princeton University Press.

Young, Mary Elizabeth. 1961. *Redskins, Ruffled Shirts and Rednecks: Indian Allotments in Alabama and Mississippi, 1830–1869.* Norman: University of Oklahoma Press.

Zaretsky, Irving, and Mark P. Leone, eds. 1974. *Religious Movement in Contemporary America.* Princeton, N.J.: Princeton University Press.

Index

Page numbers in **boldface** indicate illustrations

Abrahams, Roger D., 169–71
Africa, 85; West, 10, 68
African, 9–10, 10–11, 170, 171;
    origins, 33–34, 64; retentions,
    10, 11, 57, 62, 68, 70, 170–71
Albert, Ethel M., 171
Allen, Ray, 3, 7–8, 246n8, 250n9,
    252n5, 256n7
"Amazing Grace," 42, 184, 211,
    257n21; white style of, 247n17
Amazing Grace (LP), 68, 257n21
ambiguity, 5
American Congregations, 2, 206
Anderson, James, 13
antiphony. *See* call-and-response
Ardener, Edwin, 170

backslider, 29, 79, 175, 182, 183
Baer, Hans, 127, 251n3
Baer, Hans, and Merrill Singer, 2, 77,
    101–2, 103, 116, 175, 208,
    244n6, 244nn8–9, 245n10,
    257n1, 257n18; on Baptist
    autonomy, 210, 249n31; on the
    black church, 31, 246n6
Bailey, Ben, 63
Baker, Rev. Benjamin, 57–58, 131,
    143, 147, **159**, 251n6, 254n21;
    prayer by, 157–67
Bakhtin, Michail, 27
Baklanoff, Joy Driskell, 63–64
Baptism, 23, 46–58, 211
Baptismal pool, 52–56, **53**, **54**, **55**
Baptist, 1, 47, 49, 50, 77, 116, 117,
    119, 143, 166, 171, 172, 173,
    175, 183, 184, 234, 254n1,
    255n7; Black, and autonomy,
    210, 245n10, 249n30; and
    male authority, 127, 145;

National organisations, 30,
    142; and racial separation, 31,
    246n5
Baraka, Imiri. *See* Jones, Le Roi
Barth, Fredrik, 32
Bartlett, Frederic, 5, 252n6
Barz, Gregory, and Timothy H.
    Cooley, 12
Bastide, Richard, 10
Bauman, Richard, 173–74, 178, 179,
    250n10
Benjamin, Walter, 178
Berry, Frances, and John Blassingame,
    14–15
Bethel, Leonard L., 31
Bible, 50, 56, 60, 120, 121, 129, 187,
    204, 224, 227, 229, 234
Black Arts Project, 10
Black Power, 10, 110
Black Theology, 101–2, 104, 208
Blacking, John, xx, 190
blues, 9, 33, 40, 44; and gospel,
    36–40. *See also* devil's music
Blues Archive, xviii
Blues People, 10
Boles, John, 12, 13, 248n24
Boles, John, and Evelyn Thomas
    Nolen, 12
Bolton, Charles C., 31
Bonner, Herbert, xx, 70–71, 82, 148,
    211; on blues and gospel,
    37–40; on lined hymns, 66
Bonner, Rev. Kenneth, 148–52, 157,
    159, 164, 172, 173,
    254nn19–20, 255n8
Bonner, Sheila, xx
born again, 32, 50, 79–84, 194–203,
    227–28, 234–42
boundary, 32–33, 35, 50, 58

Bourguignon, Erika, 252n1
Boyer, Horace, 7, 247n19
Brown, William Wells, 125–26
Brundage, William Fitzhugh, 12
Burnim, Mellonee, 7, 71, 250n11

Caldwell, Erskine, 13
Call-and-response, 40, 43, 62, 74, 94
Campbell, Charles, 23; on Baptismal
    pool, 52; on preaching, 172,
    179–80; on race relations, 29,
    108; on shouting, 118, 122,
    172, 179–80, 181, 182
Carpenter, Delores, 127, 128
Carter, Rev., 131, 166, 192
Caton, William, 173–74
Center for the Study of Southern
    Culture (CSSC), xviii, xix, 12,
    246n9
chant, 8, 100, 127, 141–49, 153–68,
    188, 190, 193, 194, 205, 211
Chapman, Mark L., 208
Chickasaw (nation), 15, 251n7
Choctaw (nation), 15, 251n7
Civil Rights Movement, 10
Cleage, Albert B., 101, 104
Clear Creek Missionary Baptist
    Church, **20**, **21**, **22**
Clear Creek Southern Baptist Church,
    20, 29
Cleveland, James, 33, 68, 250n9
Cobb, James, 12, 27, 251n7
Cocker, Joe, 40
colour, 28–29, 31. *See also* race
colourstruck, **28**
community, xviii, xix, xx, 1, 2, 3, 7,
    8–9, 31–32, 36, 223; of Clear
    Creek M.B.C., 13–26, 39, 45,
    55, 87, 206; creation of, 5, 50,
    51, 58, 97
Confederacy, 17
Congdon Street Baptist Church, xviii,
    75, 117, 131, 141, 142, 144,
    146–47, 166, 192, 208; gospel
    choir, 35
congregation, 2, 9, 24–25, 61, 62, 63,
    71, 73, 183, 206, 211; and
    participation, 93, 94, 96,

145–47, 157–66, 167–68, 180,
    181, 185, 190–91, 210, 211
congregational singing, 24, 57–58
conversion, 4, 23, 45, 46–51, 79–84,
    173
conviction. *See* conversion
cotton, 21, 86, 87, **88**, 89, 223
Cross, W. E., Jr., 245n2
Cross, W. E., Jr., et al., 245n2
Crouch, Andrae, 33, 45, 250n9
Cusic, Don, 3, 8, 18–19, 61, 119, 206,
    207; on Christian artists,
    68–69; on gospel and soul, 45;
    on Dr. Isaac Watts, 61

Davis, Gerald L., 3, 8, 172, 173, 180,
    181, 188, 190, 194, 208,
    254n3, 257n22
deacon, 24, 32–33, 48, 55, 62, 75, 145,
    147, 153, 159, 171, 175, 182,
    210, 211, 214, 215, 216, 237
de Lerma, Dominique-René, 7
desegregation, 19, 20, 28, 30, 85,
    107–12. *See also* integration;
    segregation
Devil, 120–21, 227, 249–50n4,
    253n8
devil's music, 33–40, 43–44, 60, 67.
    See also blues
Devotion, xix, 62–63, 75–76, 144,
    154, 210
Djedje, Jacqueline Cogdell, 7
down-home, 105, 118, 142
Dorsey, Thomas, 45, 67, 69
Douglas, M., 252n6
du Bois, W. E. B., 253n15
Durkheim, Emile, 75
Dyson, M. E., 245n2

ecstasy, 25, 116–17, 180, 181
Ekwueme, Lazarus, 10, 57, 170
Eliade, Mircea, 116
emancipation, 12
emotion, 99–106, 122–25, 129–30,
    141, 143, 145, 154, 168,
    179–83. *See also* feeling
Epstein, Dena J., 246n7, 66
ethnomusicology, 4, 9, 11–12, 44, 209

evangelical, 23, 32, 44, 248n23, 49

family, 19, 24, 82
farming, 14, 19, 49, 86–91, 223.
feeling, 3, 24, 35, 39, 42, 123, 180;
    conversion and, 47–48, 83;
    lined hymns and, 66–67, 93, 96
Ferris, William (Bill), xviii, 12
fieldwork, xv–xxi, 12
Fox, Shirley, 73–74, 78, 79
Franklin, Aretha, 44, 45, 68
Franklin, Rev. C. L., 68, 207
Franklin, Robert Michael, 102, 116
Fraser, Walter, et al., 12
Freedmen, 142
Fulop, Timothy E., and Albert J.
    Raboteau, 2, 243n1
fundamentalism, 32, 34, 36, 46, 183,
    209

Gabriel (angel), 133–36, 226
Gates, Rev. J. M., xviii, 207
Geertz, Clifford, xx, 4, 5–6
Gerard, C., 245n2
Gerster, Patrick, 248n24
Gilkes, Cheryl, 170, 253n16, 254n18
Godwin, Morgan, 246n7
Gordon, E. W., 245n2
gospel, 8, 9, 33, 45, 60, 67–74, 85,
    95–96, 100, 166, 168, 200; and
    blues, 36–40; choir, 35; and
    shout, 127; style, choral, 43,
    71, 84, 93–97; style, solo,
    42–43, 70, 71, 91–93, 94,
    96–97, 137
Great Awakening, 47, 255n7
Grossman, James, 13
Grout, Donald J., 60–61
Gutman, Herbert, 15

Hacker, Andrew, 245n2
Hall, C. S., and G. Lindzey, 27, 32
Harris, Michael W., 3, 246n10,
    246n12, 250n6
harvest, 85–97, 134, 138–39, 222–28
Harvest Day, 90–91, 97, 132, 191,
    222–28, 250n13; dinner, 22
Hebrides. *See* Scottish Hebrides

Heilbut, Tony, 7
Helms, J. E., 245n2
hemiola, 39, 57, 71, 148, 149, 167
Herskovits, Melville, 170
heterophony, 63, 64, 67, 74, 94, 96,
    155, 184
Higginbotham, Evelyn Brooks, 2
Highway to Heaven, xviii, 70, 258n3
Hill, Samuel S., Jr., 13, 29, 243n1,
    247–48n22, 248n24, 249n30;
    on baptism, 248–49n29; on
    Baptists, 249n30. *See also*
    Mead and Hill
holistic, 34, 68, 140, 141, 181, 182
Holloway, Joseph E., 10, 17, 170,
    244n3
Holloway, Joseph E., and Winifred K.
    Vass, 10, 170
Holly Springs, xviii, 98, 258n3
Holy Spirit/Ghost, 3, 4, 25, 70, 76, 77,
    83–84, 113–40, 143, 151, 166,
    175, 178–83, 191–92, 193,
    204, 208, 227–28, 233, 240;
    and conversion, 48–51, 80
Horowitz, E. L., and R. E. Horowitz,
    245n2
Hughes, Langston, 100
Hymes, Dell, 169
Hymns, xx, 32, 35, 70, 166, 167, 210;
    Invitation, 82, 103, 177, 191,
    211; lined, 24, 25, 43, 60–67,
    69, 70, 84, 93, 96, 203;
    Meditation, 144; slaves' use of,
    33–34

identity, xxi, 1, 11, 12, 13, 27–58, 59
improvisation, 3, 38, 71, 74, 91–94,
    96, 141, 153, 207
Inman, David, 5
inspiration, 115–27, 130–40, 143,
    151, 166
integration, 31, 64, 106–12. *See also*
    desegregation; segregation
Interpretation of Cultures, The, 5–6

Jackson, Michael R., 27
Jackson Southernaires, 40, 42, 43, 70,
    250n9

James, William, 143
jazz, 35, 44, 45, 179
Jitney Jungle, 18
Job, 188, 224, 230–32
Johnson, James Weldon, 91. *See also* spirituals
Johnson, Paul E., 2
Jones, Charles Colcock, 246n7
Jones, Ferdinand, 245–46n3
Jones, Le Roi, 10
Jones, Sam, 21, 79, 80, 80–81, 111, **146**
Jones, William, 101
Jules-Rosetta, Bennetta, 143, 192
Jung, Carl, 120

Kearl, Michael, 59, 75–76, 77, 84
King Biscuit Blues Festival, 36
Kisliuk, Michelle, 12
Knight, Walter K., 29–30, 254n1
kudzu, 14, **16**

LaBelle, Patti, 44
Levine, Lawrence, 246n7
Lincoln, C. Eric, and Lawrence H. Mamiya, 1
lined hymns *See* hymns; lined
lining out, 61–62
List, George, 141–42, 192
Logan, Wendell, 57
Lomax, Alan, 253n9
Lornell, Kip, 3, 7, 246n8
Lornell, Kip, and Ann Rasmussen, 2

MacRobert, Iain, 246n4
Main Street Baptist Church, 75, 76, 81, 251n6, 174, 177, 208; and baptism, 52–53, **53**, 54, 57–58; gospel choir, 35; and prayer, 144, 147, 157–67, 215–16; and shouting, 126, 131, 254n21
Mamiya, Lawrence H. *See* Lincoln, C. Eric
Marsell, Anthony J., et al., 27
Marshall, Calvin B. Jr., 101
Marty, Martin, 13
Mathews, Donald, 13
Maultsby, Portia, 7, 10, 33–34, 74, 94–95, 170; on gospel, 45,

67–68; on gospel and soul, 247n18
McKinney, Rev. Grady, 22, 23, 26, 79, 83, 96, 99–100, 120, 131, 132, **156**, 180, 210, 211, 212; on backsliding, 79–80; and baptism, 55–56; on blues culture, 36; on being born again, 50, 80; on farming, 87, 88–89; on Holy Ghost, 119, 121–22, 123, 125, 178–79; on positions held, 22; on prayer, 141, 154–57; and preaching, 26, 105, 172–73, 174, 175–77, 182, 184–205, 207; on Sunday, 76
Mead, Frank S., and Samuel S. Hill, Jr., 245n10, 248n24; on Baptists, 249n30
Methodist, 61, 77
Miller, Carol Ann, 12
Miller, Terry, 61
minister, 21, 24, 61, 69, 79, 82, 105, 106, 143, 145, 147, 148, 153, 154, 167, 172, 173, 184, 185, 216, 251n6
ministry, 173, 174, 187, 206; music, 24; music and, 62, 69, 177
Mintz, Sidney, 171
Mitchell, Henry, 182
Mitchell, Mozella, 10–11, 243n2, 248n27, 111, 171
Moberly, Elizabeth, 27
Molefi, Kete, 79, 171
Moses, Oral, 34
mothers of the church, 82–83, 128, 145
Mourners' bench, 248n25, 49, 51–52, 82, 83
Murphy, Larry G., 1
Music and Trance, 113–16
Music ministry. *See* ministry, music
musical sound. *See* sound, musical

Native American, 15, 98
Nettl, Bruno, 11–12
Neverdon-Morton, Cynthia, 13
Newman, Richard. *See* Weisenfeld, Judith

Newsome, Clarence G., 1
Nobles, W., 245n2
Nolen, Evelyn Thomas. *See* Boles and Nolen
Northeast Mississippi Blues and Gospel Festival, 36

Ó Madagáin, Breandán, 154, 186–87, 194
offertory, 143, 154, 211
Ohlmann, Eric H., 1, 248n23, 119
Oliver, Paul, 8, 9, 24
Orange, Jessie, 78, 91, 97
Overacker, Ingrid, 3
Overton, Betty, 253n16
Oxford (Miss.), 17–18

Palisca, Claude, 60–61
pastor, 21, 22, 23, 48, 52, 54, 55, 57, 78–79; authority invested in, 26, 96; part/full-time, 145, 215
Patterson, Beverly, 2
Patton family, 24, 54, 157
Pentecostal, 30, 49, 119, 126, 127, 143, 173, 177, 252–53n7
performance, 6, 7, 9, 24, 40–42, 71, 94–95, 96, 178–79, 229, 250n10; slow, and feeling, 42, 66
phenomenology, 4–7
Pinkston, Alfred, 249n2, 249–50n4, 251n1
Pitts, Walter, 1, 248n28
popular music, 33, 40–42, 68; and gospel, 45–46
positions, 118, 257n18
possession, 115, 143, 193, 209, 252n4
Powdermaker, Hortense, 127
Prayer, xx, 49, 77, 117, 177, 193, 210, 212, 213–21, 224, 233, 234; chanted, 24, 25, 26, 141–68, 171, 180, 186
Preacher, 171–78; guest, 49, 82
preaching, 8, 48, 49, 83, 104–6, 127, 129, 159, 167, 169–205, 207–8, 214, 215, 254n21; preach, call to, 4, 255n4. *See also* sermon

"Precious Lord," 67, 68
Psalter, 60–61

Raboteau, Albert J., 102, 104, 181, 193, 204, 243n1. *See also* Fulop and Raboteau
race, 11, 12, 29–30, 30–31, 142, 188. *See also* colour
Race records, xviii, 9
racism, 109, 209
Ramsey, Guthrie, 9, 40n12; on gospel, 45, 69
Rasmussen, Ann. *See* Lornell, Kip
Rawick, George P., 15
Reagon, Bernice Johnson, 3, 9
religion, head, 29; heart, 29
revival, 49–51, 82–84, 118, 212
rhetoric, 144, 168
Rice, Timothy, 27
Ricoeur, Paul, 3, 4, 6, 257n23
Rijn, Guido van, 246n12
rite of passage, 46, 52, 58
Robinson, Lee Earl, 78, 98, 210, 227, 250–51n14; on baptism, 53; on Baptist autonomy, 57; childhood of, 86–87, 88, 89; on conversion and Holy Spirit, 48, 117, 118–19; on Devotion, 62–63, 76; on gender roles, 128, 128–29; on Holy Spirit, 123, 131; on lined hymns, 63, 64–65; on preachers, 106, 172, 173; on race relations, 108–10; on reliance on God, 78; on sinners, 44–45
Rogers, Marion, 143, 216
Rosenberg, Bruce, 8, 132, 145, 148, 149, 153, 178, 180, 186
Rouget, Gilbert, 113–17, 130, 254n21. *See also Music and Trance*
Rowland, Dunbar, 251–52n7
Ryle, Gilbert, 4

sacred (versus secular), 33–35, 40–46, 67–69
saint (versus sinner), 29, 32–33, 46–53, 189
Sanches, Mary, 256n7

Satan, 183, 230–31
Saussure, Ferdinand de, 252n2
Scottish Hebrides, 153–54, 186
Second Baptist (Oxford, Miss.), 23, 52, 54, 75, 81
Seeger, Charles, 132, 144, 148, 194
segregation, 243n1, 28, 106–7. *See also* desegregation; integregation
selection (choral), 210, 211, 212
sermon, 8, 102–3, 105, 131, 142, 167, 211, 222–42; chanted, 26, 130, 145, 167, 169–205, 255n7; and prayer, 164, 166
Sernett, Milton G.: on communal singing, 50; on racial separation, 30, 101, 145
Shakur, Tupac Amaru, 247n15
sharecropping, 19, 86–87; huts, 18
shout, 51, 70, 105, 106, 122, 123, 132, 142, 175, 179–83, 191, 193, 194, 199–203, 227–28, 232, 233
sin, 46, 51, 78, 81, 83, 182–83, 213, 225, 238
Singer, Merrill. *See* Baer and Singer
"Sinner please don't let this harvest pass," 90–97
slavery, 14, 85, 124, 170, 253n14
slaves, 33–34, 50, 66
Smaw, Rev. Daryl, 145
Smith, Thérèse, 250n5, 251n5, 257n10, 257n11
Snyder, Rev. Henry, 177
Sobel, Mechal, 1, 253n14
Sosna, Morton, 12
soul, 9, 42, 45
sound, musical, 7–9, 10, 29, 43; and amplification, 71–74
Southern, Eileen, 7, 246n7
Sparks, Randy J., 13, 30–31, 31, 110, 248n24; on Jackson Southernaires, 247n14
Spencer, Jon Michael, 8
Spiegelberg, H., 3
spirituals, 8, 35, 249n1, 70, 85, 91–96, 166; as code, 64, 66, 85
Springhill (Miss.), 19, 86, 98
Stokes, Martin, 12

Sullivan, Lawrence, E., 12
synagogue, 249n32
Systematic Theology, 4–5

"Take me to the water," 55–56
Tallahatchie-Oxford Missionary Baptist District Association and Auxiliaries (TOMB), xviii–xix, 23, 24, 91, 127, 134, 148–51, 213, 216
Tallmadge, William, 7, 62
Temperly, Nicholas, 61
Terkel, Studs, 245n2
Thompson, Eulastine, xx, 23
Thompson, Gregory, 70; on blues, 44; on conversion, 47, 51, 82–83; on Holy Ghost, 125, 130; on lined hymns, 66; on music, 51, 58, 130, 131
Thompson, Leroy, 251n15; on blues, 44; on emotional expressivity, 102–4, 105, 106; on gospel, 35; on Holy Spirit, 124, 129; on shouting, 118, 127
Thompson, Pamela: on baptism, 54–55; on conversion, 47; on lined hymns 66
Thompson, Robert Farris, 171
Thompson, Rochelle: on baptism, 54–56; on conversion, 47–48; on farming, 90
Tillich, Paul, 4–5, 5. *See also Systematic Theology*
time, xxi, 1, 43, 59–84, 85
Titon, Jeff, 1–2, 148, 153n7, 154, 173, 177, 187, 247n17, 253n8, 255n6; on Holy Spirit, 25, 145, 178, 179. *See also* "Amazing Grace"
tradition, 1, 49, 52, 69, 76, 85–112
trance, 25, 70, 113–40
transcriptions, xii–xiii, 37, 38, 55, 63, 71, 91, 94, 132–33, 144, 148–49, 154, 157, 194–96
Tucker, W. H., 245n2
Turner, Victor, 6, 127
two versus three. *See* hemiola

University of Mississippi (Ole Miss), xviii, xix, 12, 17, **17**, 23, 81, 88, 107, 110–11
"Up Where We belong," 40–43

Van Gennep, Arnold, 52, 175, 247n21
Vass, Winifred K. *See* Holloway and Vass
Vollers, Maryanne, 244n4

"Wade in the Water," 57–58
Wadlington, Rev. Leroy, 23, 52, 81, 110–11
Warnes, Jennifer, 40
Washington, James, 30, 254n1
Watch Meeting, The, 153
Waterman, Chris, 7
Waterman, Richard, 57
Watson, John Fanning, 34
Watts, Dr. Isaac, 60, 61, 67, 194, 210; style of, 42, 91–93, 155, 184, 211

Weisenfeld, Judith, and Richard Newman, 2, 253n16
West African retention. *See* Africa, West; African retentions
Whalum, Wendell, 69
whooping, 179–80. *See also* shout
William-Jones, Pearl, 7
Williamson, Joel, 12, 245n2
Wills, David, 243n1, 30
Wilson, Charles Reagan, 13, 32, 44, 110–11, 244n7, 248n24, 251n4
Wilson, Charles Reagan, and William Ferris, 13
Wilson, Olly, 10, 57
Wind, James P., and James J. Lewis, 2, 206, 209
worldview, 1, 3, 4, 7, 28, 85, 171, 181, 188, 209

Young, Mary Elizabeth, 251–52n7

"Let the Church Sing!": Music and Worship in a Black Mississippi Community

Religion is a fundamental part of Southern identity, generally, and music is often at its very heart. This is nowhere truer than in the black churches of the Deep South, where communities articulate their view of themselves and the world they live in through the religious songs and hymns that they sing and the highly musical sermons that they hear.

One small, relatively self-contained community in rural Mississippi, Clear Creek, is known in the region, and even beyond, for its intense and imaginative cultivation of music in the context of religious worship. The sermons of their pastor, Rev. Grady McKinney (in common with those of other similar preachers), make resonant use of allusions to daily life as well as to religious principles and Bible stories. Also, the sermons are often delivered in a powerful half-sung manner and underscored by hymn phrases played on the piano. Sometimes the sermons build to a climax that finds its release in a hymn previously hinted at by the preacher and pianist and now sung by the congregation as a whole.

The title of this book, indeed, comes directly from the phrase Rev. McKinney uses to end a service—"Let the Church sing!"—and which cues the congregation, that is, the Clear Creek community, to join their voices in a culminating sung exclamation "Amen!" Thus, "Let the Church sing!" frames the sacred space of formal worship, and facilitates reentry into the more or less secular space of everyday life. In response, a parting song such as "Reach Out and Touch" may be sung, hugs and greetings are exchanged, individuals share news, and gradually the congregation disperses.

"Let the Church Sing!": Music and Worship in a Black Mississippi Community is based on years of fieldwork by an Irish ethnomusicologist, who examines, in more detail than ever before, how various facets of the Clear Creek citizens' worldview find expression through religious ritual and music. Thérèse Smith, though originally very much an outsider, gradually found herself welcomed into Clear Creek by members and officials of the Clear Creek Missionary Baptist Church. She was permitted to record many hours worth of sermons and singing and engaged in community events as a participant-observer. In addition, she conducted plentiful interviews, not just at Clear Creek but, for comparison, at Main St. Baptist Church in Lexington, Kentucky. All of this enables her to analyze in detail how music is interwoven in the worship service, how people feel about the music that they make and hear, and, more generally, how the religious views so vividly expressed help the Church's members think about the relationship between themselves, their community, and the larger world. Music and prayer enable the members and leaders of the Church to bring the realm of the spiritual into intersection with the material world in a particularly active way.

The book is enriched by extensive musical transcriptions and an accompanying CD of recordings from actual church services, and these are examined in detail in the book itself.

Thérèse Smith is in the Music Department, University College Dublin, Dublin 4, Ireland

Praise for *"Let the Church Sing!": Music and Worship in a Black Mississippi Community*:

" '*Let the Church Sing!*' is a careful and fascinating study of a rural black community and its religious center in Northern Mississippi. In it, Thérèse Smith reveals both the profound importance of religious experience and the tragic racial divisions that have existed in Clear Creek."

—William Ferris, Professor of History and Senior Associate Director, Center for the Study of the American South, University of North Carolina (Chapel Hill)

"Thérèse Smith's richly detailed '*Let the Church Sing!*' reveals how tradition, spontaneity, and faith work together in the music making of a black Baptist congregation in northern Mississippi. Through ethnographic skill and self-effacing scholarly expertise she enables church members to offer their own portrait, in word, symbol, and sound, of how they worship, what they believe, and where they fit—on God's earth and in the Christian cosmos."

—Richard Crawford, University of Michigan, and author of *America's Musical Life: A History*

"Thérèse Smith escorts us through the doors of the Clear Creek Missionary Baptist Church and into a sacred space where song, chanted prayer, and sung sermon intertwine in dynamic ritual aimed to stir the soul. Her work makes a convincing argument for the intensive ethnographic study of local African American church culture."

—Ray Allen, Associate Professor of Music, Institute for Studies in American Music, Brooklyn College (CUNY)